IENT PEOPLE

Sarah Wise has an MA in Victorian Studies from Birkbeck College, University of London, and is an Associate of the Raphael Samuel History Centre. Her debut, *The Italian Boy: Murder and Grave Robbery in 1830s London*, was shortlisted for the 2005 Samuel Johnson Prize and won the Crime Writers' Association Gold Dagger for Non-Fiction. Her follow-up, *The Blackest Streets: The Life and Death of a Victorian Slum* (2008), was shortlisted for the Royal Society of Literature's Ondaatje Prize and was a Book of the Year in the *Sunday Telegraph*, *The Economist* and for BBC Radio 4's *Saturday Review* programme. Sarah was a major contributor to Iain Sinclair's compendium *London, City of Disappearances* (2006). She has spoken on BBC Radio 4's *Thinking Allowed*, *All in the Mind*, *Woman's Hour*, the *Today* programme, and Radio 3's *Night Waves*. She regularly lectures to societies and at history events. She lives in central London.

www.sarahwise.co.uk

ALSO BY SARAH WISE

The Italian Boy
The Blackest Streets

SARAH WISE

Inconvenient People

Lunacy, Liberty and the Mad-Doctors
in Victorian England

VINTAGE BOOKS
London

Published by Vintage 2013

2 4 6 8 10 9 7 5 3 1

Copyright © Sarah Wise 2012

First published in Great Britain in 2012 by
The Bodley Head

Vintage
Random House, 20 Vauxhall Bridge Road,
London SW1V 2SA

www.vintage-books.co.uk

Addresses for companies within The Random House Group Limited can be
found at: www.randomhouse.co.uk/offices.htm

The Random House Group Limited Reg. No. 954009

A CIP catalogue record for this book
is available from the British Library

ISBN 9780099541868

The Random House Group Limited supports the Forest Stewardship
Council® (FSC®), the leading international forest-certification organisation.
Our books carrying the FSC label are printed on FSC®-certified paper. FSC is
the only forest-certification scheme supported by the leading environmental
organisations, including Greenpeace. Our paper procurement policy can be
found at www.randomhouse.co.uk/environment

Typeset by Palimpsest Book Production Ltd, Falkirk, Stirlingshire
Printed and bound by CPI Group (UK) Ltd, Croydon, CR0 4YY

This one is for Dad,
Stanley James Wise
(July 1925–June 2004)

Contents

Acknowledgements

I am extremely grateful to David Tuke, great-grandson of Dr Thomas Harrington Tuke (1826–1888), who told me the hearsay evidence of letters between his ancestor and Charles Dickens, regarding the novelist's wife. Many thanks also to Pamela Bater for putting me in contact with Mr Tuke and for alerting me to this previously unrecognised aspect of Boz's life.

Anne Monroe, daughter of Georgina Weldon's biographer Edward Grierson, has generously allowed me to quote from the material he gathered, and to reproduce images from his book, *Storm Bird: The Strange Life of Georgina Weldon*. I am grateful to Dr Helen Nicholson, of Manchester Metropolitan University, for helping me to make contact with Ms Monroe.

Stefan Dickers, archives supremo at the Bishopsgate Institute, has given his time freely in assisting with picture research, and I am indebted to him for many of the images that appear in this book, courtesy of the wonderful Bishopsgate Library, London.

Clare Fleck of Knebworth House Archives allowed me to work through the holdings at the Lyttons' ancestral home. Rod and Celia Fitzhugh kindly offered me the use of their archive pictures of the Agapemone, reproduced in Chapter Four. Paul Lewis, founder of the website www.wilkiecollins.com, was similarly generous in permitting me to use his archive illustrations from *The Woman in White*.

Maisie Brown of the Barnes & Mortlake History Society gave me the co-ordinates of the younger Dr Winslow's last resting place, but I still couldn't penetrate the ivy.

History should consist of a mass of local histories, said someone – I forget who. In this country, we have a multitude of small treasure houses to help us write these tales: Francesca Anyon, of Wirral Archives Service, tracked down the fate of Mary Jane and Charles Turner. Dr Jonathan Oates, of the Ealing Local History Centre, provided background on Lawn House in Hanwell. I would also like to thank: Tudor Allen and Lesley Marshall at Camden Local Studies and Archives Centre; Jane Baxter of Richmond upon Thames Local Studies; Carolynne Cotton of Uxbridge Local Studies and Archives; Valerie Crosby of Haringey Local History Library and Archives; Patricia Fallon, Cecilia Alvick and Alison Kenny at the City of Westminster Archives Centre; Carol Futers and all the staff at Hertfordshire Archives and Local Studies; Carolyn Hammond, Mary Blyth and Janet McNamara of Chiswick Local Studies Library; Isabel Hernandez and Tim Reid of the Local Studies Department at Kensington Central Library; Rhian James of Powys County Archives Office; Kate Jarvis of Wandsworth Heritage Service; Ruth McAuley of the Archives and Local History department at Explore York Library; Kai Michael of Gwent Record Office; Ann Nix of Somerset County Records Office, and Esther Hoyle at the Somerset Heritage Centre; Fiona M. Price of the Lambeth Archives; the staff of Staffordshire Archive Service and the William Salt Library; Janice Sullivan of Sevenoaks Local Studies; Liz Wigmore of the Bury Record Office.

By sad coincidence, of all the local archives that I have consulted the one that is most under threat is the Hammersmith and Fulham Local Studies Library – my own nearest library when I was growing up in West London and where I used to go to get peace and quiet when revising for my A-levels. These days: slashed opening hours, volunteers replacing professional staff, a precarious future. Thanks to Wendy Hawke, LMA senior archivist, and all the rest of the team who battle on in Hammersmith in these less than propitious circumstances.

Thanks also to Dr Lesley A. Hall, Helen Wakely and the staff at the library of the Wellcome Collection; the staff at the British Library and the Newspaper Library in Colindale; the staff of the Westminster Reference Library; the V&A National Art Library, V&A Theatre & Performance Enquiry Service and V&A Prints Department; The National Archives; the London Metropolitan Archives; the British Museum Prints Room; Sally James of Benjamin Franklin House; Colin S. Gale of Bethlem Royal Hospital Archives; Lambeth Palace Library; Peter Hopkins of the Roderic Bowen Library and Archives at the University of Wales Trinity St David; Jacque Roethler of the Archives

Department of the University of Iowa Libraries; Debra Longley, Tamsin Cook and Jonathan Butler of English Heritage; Dr Anne Mouron and the staff at the Bodleian Library; Betty Nixon of the Galton Institute; Professor Malcolm Andrews, editor, and Dr Tony Williams, associate editor, *The Dickensian*, and Elizabeth Velluet of The Dickens Fellowship; and Andrew Roberts for his wonderful Studymore online resource.

Dr Joanna Martin, Georgina Weldon's great-great-niece, is the owner of many of her ancestor's diaries, papers and letters; I am grateful to Dr Martin for the additional information and clarifications that she has kindly supplied, in advance of publication of her own biography of Mrs Weldon.

Thank you Will Sulkin, Jörg Hensgen, Katherine Ailes, Kay Peddle, Anna Cowling, Beth Humphries, Chloe Johnson-Hill and Ruth Waldram at the Bodley Head; Victoria Murray-Browne and Anna Redman at Vintage; and Kate Pool at the Society of Authors.

I have chewed the (Victorian) fat with Dr Michelle Johansen, Lee Jackson, Elizabeth Tames and David Clifford. Thanks especially to Peter, Debbie, Lucia, Caroline and Michael, Tina, Sindy, Diane, Sharon and Matt, Prue, Mandy and Rob, Leigh and Alex, Wanda and Roland, Katie, Lis, Clive, Eve, Sian, Lily, Pauline and Phil; and all the Neishes, big and little.

A Note on Terminology

I use the term 'alienist' throughout, since 'psychiatrist' came into common use only in the final twenty years of the century. 'Mad-doctor' is also used, irreverently – it remained a common insult well into the twentieth century.

Pauper lunatic: unable to pay fees for care, so confined in a lunatic ward of the local workhouse, or in a county asylum, or in a private asylum with fees paid by the parish, out of the 'poor rates'. This was by far the most numerous category of lunatic throughout the century.

Private patient: able to pay fees, or to have fees paid by family, and usually ranging in social class from regularly employed artisan/ tradesman to aristocrat.

Chancery lunatic: a sub-category of 'private patient' – a wealthy private patient who had been found insane by 'inquisition' and whose large estate/income was deemed to be at risk as a result of the patient's incapacity to manage his/her affairs, thereby requiring the protection of the Lord Chancellor. Such cases were dealt with by the Masters in Lunacy and their conditions were inspected by the Lord Chancellor's Visitors.

Criminal lunatic: found not guilty of a crime by reason of insanity and confined in Royal Bethlehem Hospital, or, later, Broadmoor or Rampton hospitals.

Single patient: the term 'single patient' usually implied a wealthy lunatic in non-asylum care, as the 'single house' was the most expensive form of custody. However, poorer communities also boarded their lunatics in private domiciles, and in the following pages, 'single patient' is used regardless of social class.

Provided there was not more than one lunatic boarded, the 'single house', or 'single lodgings', did not need to be licensed by the

Commissioners in Lunacy (when two patients were lodged, this was deemed to be a private asylum, and required licensing and inspection). But all single patients kept for profit were required to have been certified insane by two physicians and their presence notified to the Commissioners in Lunacy.

The exception to this was the insane family member confined at home – kept not for profit but by 'natural obligation' of blood, or marriage, tie. Mrs Rochester in the attic at Thornfield Hall was this type of patient.

Few weeks pass that the papers do not record one or more 'mysterious disappearances'. Who shall say how many of these are simply engulphments in the madhouse oubliette?

Louisa Lowe, *The Bastilles of England*, 1883

The sane people confined in lunatic asylums under the easy facilities of the Lunacy Act are ghosts of newspaper raising. They cannot be brought to the bar as tangible realities.

Dr John Charles Bucknill, *Journal of Mental Science*, October 1858

She has certain impressions with regard to certain persons which are not accurate or true.

Physician's statement on a mid-nineteenth-century certificate of lunacy

It is so easy to prove that an obnoxious relative is insane; it is easier still to aggravate trivial symptoms by persistent bad treatment.

Lloyd's Weekly newspaper editorial, 1 August 1858

The first political lesson instilled into the tender mind of Anglo-Saxon childhood is the doctrine of freedom; and the earliest lispings of infancy are modulated to repeat that our forefathers left us the Habeas Corpus Act as our ample and enduring guarantee against false or arbitrary imprisonment. The young heart has been taught to exult in this legacy as the proudest monument of the inflexible independence of the British race, and as an incontestable mark of our superiority over the abject slaves of foreign despotism. It is a nursery tale which has long gratified our national vanity. It is now our unwelcome task to dissipate a venerable delusion . . . Does this law give adequate protection against illegal restraint inflicted through the agency of the Lunacy Acts?

The Lancet, 24 April 1852

Preface

'Oh yes, all those Victorian husbands getting their wives put away,' said a good friend, when I told her my plans for a book about sane people being declared mad in the nineteenth century. Many others subsequently came out with something similar. But I hadn't got very far into my initial archival dig when the variety of victims of malicious asylum incarceration became apparent; and it appeared that, anecdotally at least, this was slightly more likely to have been a problem for men than for women, certainly in the first sixty years of the century. As for those people who were indisputably mentally disordered, the mysterious lunatic in the attic was as likely to have been Bert as Bertha; the disturbed person in white in the moonlight on the Finchley Road would just as plausibly have been Andrew Catherick as Anne.

The following stories have been selected to highlight the range of people who had to fight for their liberty against the imputation of insanity. Presented roughly chronologically, the tales reveal the various definitions of madness put forward by the physicians, and the suggestions made by campaigners seeking reform of the asylum committal procedure. The stories bring to light, too, the protests that flared up periodically against the mad-doctors and the huge support shown for alleged victims of incarceration conspiracy. What also emerges is a portrait of a bureaucracy – the Commissioners in Lunacy – that was failing to keep pace with both popular feeling and the views of the newspaper opinion-mongers.

Above all, the 'lunacy panics' of the nineteenth century highlighted the fear that the English were sleepwalking into allowing the medical profession to curb individual freedom by labelling unconventional behaviour as a pathological condition, in need of cure or containment. 'No rank in society is now exempt from the fear of being peculiar, the unwillingness to be, or to be thought, in any respect original,' wrote John Stuart Mill, in *On Liberty*, published in 1859 – the year in which a series of notorious cases forced the government to appoint a Select Committee to probe the English lunacy laws.

These disputed insanity cases offer us a way of taking the temperature of the times. Lunacy 'inquisitions' – as with criminal trials and divorce case hearings – brought to the surface the fiercely guarded secrets of the middle and upper classes. Sex and money were thrust to the fore; but we also get a prolonged look at their spiritual lives – at the restlessness of those to whom the traditional forms of worship felt inadequate, and the dangers that could be faced in the search for a more meaningful religious experience.

Although distrust of the mad-doctors was an oddly classless issue, anxiety about being sent to the 'living tomb' (a commonly used metaphor for the asylum) was perhaps felt most intensely by those who had something more than their liberty to lose. Malicious lunacy certification was overwhelmingly a problem for those who had money or property (even if it was just a small estate or income) and for people whose behaviour was deemed to embarrass or to threaten the social standing of another, or others. While individuals from all levels of society feared an accusation of insanity, the poor had better safeguards against this particular social menace. Campaigners did find instances where heavy drinking or the misdiagnosis of a febrile disease had caused a pauper to end up in the lunacy system. And as the huge building programme of public asylums began in the mid-1840s, a corresponding rise was seen in the certification and institutionalisation of 'incurably mentally decayed' elderly people (predominantly women) and of 'naturals' (people with what we today call 'learning difficulties') who had previously lived outside the walls of an asylum. However, no one had much to gain from deliberately mis-certifying the poor, and indeed, many parish Poor Law officials tended not to welcome the expense of institutionalising a pauper. 'For the poor, all are interested in the recovery. For the rich, all may be interested in their retention,' a Gloucestershire magistrate wrote in the 1840s, after a campaign in which he liberated many wrongly certificated private patients.

Perhaps surprisingly, gender was not – to the Victorians – an obvious factor to be borne in mind when pondering the alleged rise in lunacy in England. Most statisticians who undertook detailed work substantiated the belief of the Ancients: lunacy was more likely to strike males than females. For every mad-doctor who cited the female reproductive system and weakly constituted intellect as the cause of female insanity, there was a physician to point out that the far more sophisticated masculine mind was under threat from overwork, business ambition, heavy drinking, the solitary vice, debt, gambling, celibacy or debauchery. High levels of self-control and conformity were demanded of 'respectable' males. There was nothing in law to prevent a wife putting away her husband, or a mother having her son confined, and plenty of women disposed of their menfolk in this way. In a patriarchal society, the biter is often bit.

However, as the century went on, campaigners for the improved property rights of married women, and for greater freedom for all types of woman, seized the lunacy-liberty issue and rolled it into the larger battle. As increasing numbers of women admitted to feeling stifled within the prison of domestic life, the deprivation of civil liberties suffered by a lunatic seemed to mirror the deprivation of legal and economic liberties endured by a married woman: the plight of the alleged lunatic and that of the Victorian wife could appear similar. But what follow are not tales of passivity and victimhood: these accounts demonstrate personal resistance and public protest. And rather than preserving the notion of a unified, confident psychiatric profession, garnering increasing power as the decades passed, we see the Victorian mad-doctors in defensive disarray.

But before the curtain rises, some background. Eighteenth-century concerns about the entirely unregulated madhouse industry (in which no certificates were required before committal to an asylum) had culminated in a devastating article, 'A Case Humbly Offered to the Consideration of Parliament', published in the *Gentleman's Magazine* in January 1763. A Select Committee was immediately convened to consider the threat to individual liberty that the anonymous author had highlighted. But it took a further eleven years for parliament to pass the Act for the Regulation of Private Madhouses, 1774. This, the first legislation to regulate private lunacy care, laid down that madhouse keepers could only accept a paying patient upon the signed certificate of a medical man. No certificate was required if a patient was to be confined in his/her own home; and every madhouse accommodating more than one lunatic henceforth required a licence. Five 'Commissioners in Lunacy', elected by the College of Physicians, were given the power to grant the licences within a seven-mile radius of London and to inspect premises. Beyond that limit, licensing and inspection were to be undertaken by local magistrates.

However, the 1774 Act had serious weaknesses. Paupers sent by their parish to private madhouses (an increasingly common phenomenon) were excluded from the statutory admissions procedures. Furthermore, there was no ban on a doctor certifying a paying patient into an asylum with which he had professional connections. Licences were never revoked, and very few meaningful penalties were ever imposed upon proprietors who were found to have broken the law. Moreover, anyone who called himself an apothecary could sign a lunacy certificate. The following perfectly valid certificate, written by an apothecary in 1809 to commit a man to a private asylum, was presented to a horrified lunacy Select Committee of 1814–15:

> H Broadway A Potcarey of Gillingham Certefy that Mr James Burt Misfortin hapened by a Plow in the Hed which is the Ocaisim of his Ellness & By the Rising and Falling of the Blood And I think A Blister and Bleeding and meddeson Will be A Very Great thing But Mr Jame Burt wold not A Gree to be Don at Home.

The 1814–15 Select Committee was one of four that sat between 1807 and 1827 to hear evidence of poor conditions in asylums and the potential for malicious incarceration. Certain 'arrangements' between medical men and proprietors regarding patient procurement were uncovered; and scandalous mistreatment at York Asylum, Royal Bethlehem Hospital and Warburton's private madhouse empire in East London were revealed. But all attempts to introduce tougher legislation were either thrown out by the House of Lords, or modified beyond recognition. The peers were afraid that state intervention in the care and treatment of lunatics could open up private, domestic lives and distressing personal decisions about insane family members to the scrutiny of bureaucratic strangers. Many peers were also on the governing boards of the nation's larger charitable lunatic institutions, such as Bethlehem and St Luke's Hospital in East London, and tended to see the issue from the point of view of the governors, doctors and proprietors, all of whom opposed any interference from laymen or from any arm of the state.

It is possible (though extraordinarily hard to prove) that the popular revulsion against wrongful incarceration – periodically alluded to in the Select Committees' evidence, and in newspaper reports about lunacy scandals – was exacerbated by the suspension of habeas corpus of 1794 (until 1801) and of 1817 (for several months). The suspensions permitted the authorities to detain anyone indefinitely without a specific charge being brought, during a time of huge social unrest, with the perceived threat of revolution. Habeas corpus, Magna Carta, English liberty – these were the Anglo-Saxon birthrights that radicals repeatedly brandished in the face of governmental authoritarianism, and anti-mad-doctor campaigners, too, did not hesitate to litter their writings with these talismans.

Hack writers kept the issue of wrongful detention in lunatic asylums alive throughout the Regency and into the 1820s, most notably John Mitford, who in 1823 published his *Description of the Crimes and Horrors of Warburton's Madhouse*. When, in 1827, allegations of appalling cruelty and illegal detention at Warburton's were once again brought to the attention of a Select Committee, the legislature at last decided to move. The 1828 Act to Regulate the Care and Treatment of Insane Persons in England (known colloquially as the Madhouse Act) created what the legislators believed was a fail-safe way to protect the sane from incarceration, and the insane from abusive treatment. From now on, two certificates of lunacy were required for private patients, each signed by a different doctor following a separate interview (the interviews to be undertaken within fourteen days of each other); no physician could sign a certificate if he owned, co-owned or was a regular medical attendant at the receiving madhouse. A lunacy order, with an accompanying statement, was to be filled in by the person (usually a relative) who had first alerted the doctors to an alleged lunatic. For pauper patients, only one doctor's certificate was required, with the second being signed by a magistrate, clergyman, schoolteacher, Poor Law officer or other civic figure. A magistrate had no profit motive, and this, it was widely believed, gave the poor greater protection.

The better-staffed Metropolitan Commission in Lunacy replaced the College of Physicians' inspectorate, but local magistrates retained their licensing and inspection powers in the provinces. Notification of admission and discharge of patients in all asylums/licensed houses was to be sent to the Metropolitan Commissioners within seven days. Any patient seeking to sue for false imprisonment had to commence his/her legal action within six months of liberation.

Less than a year after receiving Royal Assent, this radical 1828 Act faced its first test.

I

Being 'Burrowsed'

They burned the effigy on the Thursday night, after a huge public supper at the Castle Inn. This was the fourth successive day of celebration in the Welsh border town of Newtown, Montgomeryshire, and the crowd roared its pleasure as a passable replica of Catherine Bywater went up in flames. The letter telling a local resident of the news from London, that Bywater had failed in her attempt to have her son, Edward Davies, declared a lunatic, was received on the Sunday night; on Monday morning all the bells of the town rang out the general joy. Sheep were roasted in the marketplace and distributed to the poor – the result of a generous response to a subscription set up by Edward's friends and well-wishers in the town. This was a celebration of 'triumph over oppression and cruelty', as local newspapers put it.

Mrs Bywater hadn't been unpopular in Newtown until then. If anything, she was mildly approved of for her rise in the world from servant/cook to being a local small-landowner with a significant stake in a successful business. Her first husband, Mr Davies, had been a warehouse porter and became a publican when they married. He died in 1802, leaving her with two small children, another Catherine and one-year-old Edward. She remarried sixteen years later – to Mr Bywater – but they had only three years together before he, too, died. In 1820 she received a large legacy from a Montgomeryshire relative. Meanwhile, following a move to London, her son Edward had been apprenticed to a grocer and tea dealer in Walbrook, in the City. He had proved so excellent a protégé that, when he came of age, he and his mother used the inheritance to buy an established tea firm, Hodgson of Philpot Lane – the little byway that runs between Eastcheap and Fenchurch Street – which they renamed Hodgson & Davies in 1823.

Mrs Bywater installed herself in the shop area of the building, which, like most City of London merchant premises, also contained living quarters for the family and the domestic servants, as well as warehousing and a counting house. Edward made the major decisions of Hodgson & Davies, most notably in its bulk tea buying, blending and resale. He had developed an exquisite sense of smell and taste, and made brilliant business choices, every one of which he discussed fully with his mother. By the late 1820s, he was known in the City as one of the best dealers in the highly lucrative tea trade, and was employing fifteen staff in the Philpot Lane premises, all of whom respected and felt affection for their unusual boss. He was tall, thin and long-limbed, and prone, since childhood (as his schoolfriends would confirm), to extravagant gesticulation. His face was highly expressive, with an earnest, penetrating gaze, and revealed his tendency to sardonic humour and ironic observations. 'I cannot help being witty, even if I were standing at the mouth of a cannon,' he proclaimed. His voice was expressive too, swooping excitedly when he was discussing a subject of interest to him. While not exactly having a stutter, he would often open his mouth and stare for a short time before the speech came out. All agreed that he was habitually highly strung, quick to take offence, funny, honourable, decent, shy (or at least, wrapped up in himself), whimsical, and that he had a dislike of any conversation he considered improper. He was also a notably submissive son. The Philpot Lane staff observed that this, however, was not enough for Mrs Bywater. She was regularly to be seen with her ear jammed up against doors, trying to listen in on Edward's conversations; senior clerk William Low more than once tripped over her in the gloom as she knelt to gaze through a keyhole.

Low had been a schoolfriend of Edward's and had been recruited to a responsible position in Hodgson & Davies. From his desk in the counting house, he could see most of what went on in the shop, and watched how his friend tolerated behaviour that, Low thought, few grown-up sons would accept. Whenever he wanted spending money, Edward had to ask his mother, who would unlock the till and present him with a pitifully small sum, then follow him upstairs to demand to know what he intended to do with it. If he ventured behind the counter during shop hours, she would shoo him out, in front of customers and staff, sometimes smacking him as though he were a small child. Mrs Bywater also interfered in the running of Philpot Lane. She constantly criticised how the clerks and warehousemen behaved, and she began to sack domestic servants without consulting her son.

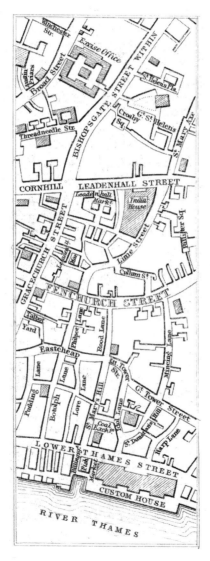

Edward had developed a love of the theatre, but each time he wanted to head to the West End of town to see a play, his mother would allow him to go only if his sister (now married to a Mr Pugh) or another relative or close associate went with him. Strolling back from Astley's Amphitheatre in the Westminster Bridge Road one evening, William Low (whom Mrs Bywater had designated Edward's companion for this night out) listened as Edward told him how unhappy he was. While he had always dreaded doing anything that might make his mother angry, Edward said he had been reduced to stealing from his own funds in order to have some pocket money. Trying to reason with her was like trying to get a river to change its course, he told Low, but he intended to free himself in one way or another.

Catherine Pugh gave birth to a son in 1828, to whom Edward gave £300, settling £1,000 on his sister. Mrs Bywater seemed to dote on the baby, and Edward hoped this diversion of attention might herald greater personal freedom for himself. In the meantime, he seemed unable to stop making money, and colossal profits of £3,000–£4,000 a year were rolling in.* Edward had left school at fourteen to begin his apprenticeship. Now, as his wealth and renown were established, he felt it was time to acquire the learning and leisure pursuits that a gentleman in the late Regency ought to be in possession of. He was the son of a servant and a publican, but only the very spiteful would point out his humble birth; however, he himself felt that it rendered him vulnerable. He saw that his mother's 'coarseness' had been noted by some of his customers, and he worried that this could be detrimental to Hodgson & Davies. So he set about refurbishing himself for his swiftly rising station in life: he applied himself to conquering English literature, and committed to memory vast tracts of poetry; he took up fencing; he bought a horse, a hunting dog and a Newfoundland (angering his mother with this outlay). He pored over the daily newspapers to make himself master of current affairs, and he spotted in one of the journals that the Duc de Chartres was taking boxing lessons from the celebrated Tom Belcher (brother of the even more famous boxer, Jem), and so Edward enrolled too. Belcher bred fancy fowls and rabbits as a sideline, and reading of the popularity among gentlemen of leisure of keeping

* A crude rule-of-thumb way to translate nineteenth-century sums into our own values is to multiply by 65. Edward was making about £200,000–£250,000.

bantams as a hobby, Edward bought some fowls at 10s a bird; Belcher also agreed to sell him the next batch of rabbits that was born.

A gentleman needed to take care of his health, and the naturally cautious Edward began to develop what one of the several physicians he consulted termed 'hypochondriasis'. He turned up at his doctors' premises fearing lumps in his throat, chest and arms; there were none. However, a non-imaginary abscess in his mouth put him in bed for eight days and affected his tea-tasting abilities longer than he cared for.

His success had provoked jealousy in the small world of City tea dealers, and his theatricality, eccentricity, youth and emulation of the ways of gentlefolk made him a very easy target. Rival dealer Mr Delafosse repeatedly called him 'The Lad from the Lane', implying callowness and lack of breeding, and there was general mirth at the dandyish white trousers that Edward now affected. Four times a year huge, fortnight-long auctions of tea took place at East India House in Leadenhall Street, with as much as a million pounds of tea changing hands and vast sums of money being spent by the thirty or so firms who sent their brokers along. The tea sales were well known to be a bear-pit, with between 300 and 400 men in attendance, all joshing, jesting, swapping scandal and making gibes – mostly good-humoured, but not always so. When bidding was fierce, the noise of howling and yelling carried for hundreds of yards outside the building, as though a riotous mob was making its way through the warren of City lanes.

Ahead of these crucial auctions Edward would become even more nervous and on edge, endlessly revising his calculations and his buying strategy and failing to get much sleep. He was, of late, additionally perturbed by the gossip, whispering and sometimes outright insults, and he wondered whether if he became a practised swordsman and pugilist he might feel more confident. But what would really make a man of him, he decided, was a wife. He had two particular ladies in mind, and before going down on one knee to either, in the spring of 1829 he spent £7,000 on a country seat – Oakfield House at Crouch Hill, Crouch End, to the north of London. He announced his intention to marry, his purchase of Oakfield House, and that he was planning to draft his will; and that's when his real trouble began. 'I'll make you repent this before the end of the year!' his mother declared.

Edward Davies's country retreat, Oakfield House,
Crouch Hill, north of London.

The June tea sale at East India House was imminent, and Edward tried to compose his mind. He planned to buy 790 chests of tea, for about £15,000. But he also decided to use the event to expose to the wider world a practice that was bilking the Exchequer of tax revenue. Tea was heavily taxed, and the old East India House custom of selling off the first lots – known traditionally in the trade as 'Directors' Presents' tea – at a deliberately low price was a mechanism for defrauding the Revenue. Edward planned to bid an outrageously high price for the Presents tea and to blow the gaff on the whole operation. Hatching this incendiary plan, together with his annoyance at his rivals' spite towards him and his growing terror of his mother, played on his naturally frayed nerves, as the date of the auction approached.

William Low had noticed that Edward was becoming even more diligent in his attempts not to be overheard in Philpot Lane. Edward had always opened doors to check for an eavesdropper before starting any conversation with Low; now he did this several times during an exchange. He dropped his voice to a whisper, too – though a somewhat melodramatic whisper.

The saleroom at East India House. The roar of the
auctions could be heard streets away.

At least he had Crouch End. He escaped there as often as he could and
his mother deigned to visit only on Sunday mornings. But he became
alarmed by the darkness of the roads north out of the City and near his
new home, in particular Hornsey Lane, where he knew that travellers had
been robbed, and where he believed resurrection men carted their unhal-
lowed loads. Many a North London village churchyard was being ransacked
for corpses at the time, and the trial of Burke and Hare – who had killed
instead of resurrecting – had ended in Edinburgh only five months earlier.
Edward bought two pistols, to make himself feel safer as he travelled back
and forth between Philpot Lane and Crouch End, in case any London-
based 'burkers' should wish to make a fresh specimen of him. But, as he
later admitted, he also sensed that he would feel safer in the tea world if
he had a pistol in his pocket – not to fire, just to know that it was there.

The morning of the start of the June sale found him jumpy. His
trousers were being jeered at as he marched into the East India House
saleroom, approached the auctioneer and announced that he planned
to start his bids for the Directors' Presents tea at 5s per lb (it custom-
arily went for 3s 1d). This was a flouting of House etiquette, and some

men present shouted out, 'Shame! Shame!' Edward retired to the back of the hall where various dealers and brokers saw him striding up and down and looking highly agitated. Two of them, Mr Gibbs and Mr Varnham (who had both been interested in buying into Hodgson & Davies), later claimed to have noticed that even by Edward's standards, his nerviness was out of the ordinary on this day.

After Edward had made his expensive purchases he announced that he planned to tell the Duke of Wellington how he had stepped in to prevent the defrauding of the Treasury; who knows, Edward proclaimed to anyone within earshot, the Duke might reward him with a title and public honours. When he later repeated this to his maternal uncle by marriage, James Brookbank, his uncle laughed 'until his sides shook', knowing that his nephew blended ludicrous pretentiousness with an ironic, oblique sense of humour.

Three weeks after the saleroom drama, on 27 June, the staff and servants at Philpot Lane heard a pistol shot in one of the first-floor rooms, where Edward and his mother were conferring. On entering, they were told that in being pulled from Edward's pocket, the weapon had gone off accidentally. Mrs Bywater didn't seem particularly shaken, and wherever the shot had ended up, it wasn't embedded in her.

Three days later Edward consulted Sir William Lawrence, one of the most eminent and fashionable surgeons of the day, at his home, just off Whitehall. This was another maternally unauthorised expenditure. Edward wanted Lawrence to look at his throat, which felt sore and constricted – he was always worried that his celebrated palate would begin to let him down. Edward explained to Lawrence that he thought he might have damaged his throat during ferocious rows with rivals at the June tea sale, and from there went on to tell Lawrence the whole story – his brave stand against the Customs fraud, the opprobrium of the tea trade, the insults, sneers and grimaces in the street. Lawrence found it hard to keep up as Edward veered from subject to subject, speaking rapidly and with an intensity that the topics did not seem to warrant. There was nothing wrong with Edward's throat, Lawrence decided, but he agreed to call in at Philpot Lane a few days later. When Lawrence turned up, Mrs Bywater nobbled him, before he had the chance to see his patient, and told him her own version of events. When Edward was at last alone with the surgeon, he repeated his complaints and asked Lawrence to listen as he grabbed various books and declaimed page after page of poetry to the bemused surgeon, often interrupting himself to open the door to check if there was anyone there.

Edward was in despair. His mother had decided to take back some of the property in Montgomeryshire that she had signed over to him, comprising a number of buildings in the parish of Kerry, near Newtown. Her solicitor was now asking questions about Hodgson & Davies that Edward found impertinent. He also discovered that his mother had contacted Dr Thomas Blundell, one of the various physicians Edward had previously consulted. She told Dr Blundell she was worried about her son's behaviour, and when Blundell turned up at Philpot Lane, he asked Edward if he had ever been guilty of *** , as the newspapers of the day infuriatingly put it. Later in the Davies case, *** would be used to refer to both sodomy and masturbation, but it is not known which of the two Blundell was alluding to during this encounter. Sodomy was illegal (in fact, it was still on the statute book as a capital offence); and masturbation was severely censured. Edward was shocked and would later say that he thought Blundell 'a dirty filthy fellow'. Blundell told Mrs Bywater her son had 'a screw loose' but later (unconvincingly) protested that in saying this he had not been referring to his head but his thorax, affecting his lungs and throat.

At last, the dam of Edward's fury burst and he shouted at his mother for having arranged the consultation without asking him first. It was probably then that Edward had an inkling of what she had in store for him.

In July he made a series of panicked visits to friends, relatives and professionals in a wild search for advice, assistance and sympathy. He fled to his aunt and uncle Brookbank in Brixton Hill. Edward had previously written to his aunt that he believed himself protected by a supernatural power, which was always hovering at his shoulder and had informed him that he was destined to be a great man. He was very 'boisterous' the night he arrived, his aunt noted, and when he wandered down to the field at the end of her garden, he became alarmed that passers-by returning from the Epsom Races were staring at him. She also claimed that Edward had told her that his mother wanted to murder him. When Mrs Bywater arrived at her sister's house, he fled.

He turned up at the lodgings of his friend, George Griffiths, a bank clerk, in Margaret Street, north of Oxford Street, apologising for not having seen him for some time, but saying that he had been ill. He pointed to his forehead, explaining that it felt hot inside. When the two men subsequently bickered about who had been the more negligent in keeping in touch, Edward declaimed haughtily: 'Sir, it is beneath the dignity of a citizen to visit anyone in furnished apartments.' 'Nonsense, Davies,' said Griffiths, 'how can you talk so silly?' Whereupon Edward drew his pistol and said, 'Nonsense, sir, nonsense? By God, sir, do you see this?' Griffiths later said this had made him afraid, but that Edward had swiftly put the weapon away and they had chatted for a short time more. Much later – suspiciously later, in fact – Griffiths reported the incident to Mrs Bywater, who insisted that he sign an affidavit stating what had transpired on that evening.

On 28 July Edward went to Mayfair, to the Grosvenor Street premises of Dr Peter M. Latham. He brought with him a pamphlet reporting the 1823 Lord Portsmouth lunacy dispute, in the belief that Latham had given evidence at the hearing in favour of Portsmouth's sanity (the medical witness had in fact been Latham's father). The Lord Portsmouth hearing had been notorious for its length (seventeen days) and cost (£25,000), but at the end of it, John Charles Wallop, third Earl of Portsmouth, had been declared of unsound mind and his marriage declared invalid and his sole child illegitimate. Edward took a chair, pulled it close to Latham and, seizing the doctor's arms, trembling and earnest, he said in a whisper (though there was no one else in the room) that he had a tale to relate of the greatest horror. He then flung himself away and searched every corner of the room, asking if it was possible that they could be overheard and begging Latham to lock the door. Standing in the middle of the room, he tore off his cravat and opened his shirt in a theatrical way, striking his forehead with the palm of his hand. Then he returned to the chair and told a story that Latham found difficult to follow. He talked for an hour but never seemed to get round to the 'tale of horror'. Only when Edward was on the point of leaving did he turn around at the door and tell Latham that a few days earlier his mother had revealed that a relative had been insane. Edward insisted that Latham come to Philpot Lane the next day, and as he left, he turned and declaimed: 'If you fail, dread the revenge of a madman, for I carry loaded pistols.' Laughing loudly, he departed. (Later, Edward would claim that he had meant this to be a joke, adding that Latham did indeed turn up the next day, so could not possibly have taken his words seriously.)

In the meantime, William Lawrence had contacted one of the nation's most eminent 'alienists' (lunacy specialists), George Man Burrows, and with Mrs Bywater's consent brought him along to Philpot Lane to examine Edward. Burrows was passed off as just a friend of Lawrence, and Edward had no idea that this consultation about his throat problems was in fact an informal lunacy examination. Burrows, fifty-eight years old in 1829, was tall and had a commanding presence, 'well calculated to inspire respect in the class of patients under his care', his obituarist would note. For six years he had owned the Clapham Retreat asylum in South London. With twenty to thirty patients, of both sexes, the Retreat was considered one of the best-run of London's forty or so private madhouses, in which were detained, in 1829, around 2,000 patients.

At Philpot Lane, Burrows and Lawrence found that Edward's pulse was quick, and the tea dealer complained of headache, dry mouth and poor sleep. Burrows claimed that Edward said to him, 'Come here, I have something to show you,' and pulled out of his pocket a miniature portrait, a small china slipper, some beads and other trinkets. Edward explained that the picture was a portrait of a 'Lady D' to whom he was attached, but Burrows recognised a slightly damaged painting of a naked Danaë with Zeus. Edward said the slipper was an emblem of the lady's foot. When he pulled his pistol out, Burrows insisted that he put it back in his pocket. The alienist subsequently told Mrs Bywater that Edward should on no account be allowed to go around with a loaded gun.

On the evening of Saturday 1 August, Edward strode into the bank of Hankey & Co. in Fenchurch Street and went into the partners' room, where he found his banker, elderly William A. Hankey. He insisted on reading to Hankey from various books he had brought along, to demonstrate to the old man that, despite his defective early education, he was now a man of some attainments. He seemed 'hasty and flurried', Hankey testified later; he had been anxious to shut up the business for the evening. When Edward reappeared at the bank on Monday, he trapped Hankey in his chair by leaning on its arms, gazed into the banker's face and asked him earnestly if he still felt that Edward was a man with whom he could do business. Hankey reassured him that he was. When Edward went out to the counter and tried to cash a cheque for £200 (which he wanted to lend to 'his woman', he said), Hankey nipped round the corner to Philpot Lane and alerted Mrs Bywater. As the pair entered the bank, Edward dashed out. From the bank, he ran round to a dancing academy in Change Alley, where he was spotted pretending to execute complicated steps; then on along Fleet Street, through the Temple Bar, and onwards to a pastry cook's shop in Lincoln's Inn Fields, where he ate a pennyworth of gingerbread; and then to Furnival's Inn Coffee House in Holborn. From here, he sent a note to the attorney with whom he had agreed to make his will, requesting that he come to the coffee house the next morning, to take instruction. He booked himself a bed for the night at the Inn, but at one o'clock in the morning woke the establishment by ringing the handbell in the passageway. When the head waiter arrived, Edward demanded that the house be searched as he had heard pistols going off, and insisted that there must be thieves in the building. When the waiter angrily complained that he had woken the whole house, Edward threw himself on his knees and craved the waiter's forgiveness. Then it happened again at six o'clock in the morning. As the waiter remonstrated with him, Edward made an improper remark about some young women who were passing down the corridor towards the washrooms, along the lines of, 'If they weren't married, I wouldn't mind engaging in certain activities with them.' (The newspapers declined to give more precise wording than this.)

Passersby attempted to rescue Edward Davies when the madhouse keepers grabbed him outside the Furnival's Inn Coffee House.

Henry Cockton's 1840 comic novel *The Life and Adventures of Valentine Vox* shows the seizure by asylum keepers of completely sane Mr Grimwood Goodman, just south of Philpot Lane. Cockton and his illustrator may have been recalling the notorious street abduction of Edward Davies, though the episode here is given a humorous spin. The novel denounces 'a monstrous, barbarous system, which has long been a foul and pernicious blot upon civilisation'.

Edward was up and dressed and awaiting his attorney at around eight o'clock, when a carriage pulled up at Furnival's Inn. The other coffee house customers watched as two men strode in, seized Edward and marched him out of the building and towards the carriage. Some left their breakfast and followed them out, and on the pavement a small crowd instantly gathered, barracking the two men and attempting to grab Edward. Attempts at crowd 'rescue' were common in London at the time; when an individual's liberty of movement appeared to be threatened by any authority figure, it was often contested by bystanders. Parish constables and (from September 1829, the month after Edward was seized at Furnival's Inn) the Metropolitan Police frequently found themselves outnumbered and surrounded when trying to question or apprehend a beggar, pauper or child. The mob violence that had characterised city life throughout the eighteenth century and first few years of the nineteenth was fading into memory, but as late as 1820, genuine political mass protests had been used as a shelter for gangs of street robbers, who came along not to demonstrate but to steal and terrify. What remained in the generally better-behaved 1820s was a hair-trigger anti-authoritarianism of people who took being policed as an imposition, not a public service. When the crowd outside Furnival's Inn demanded to know on what authority the young man was being removed, the two men brandished a piece of paper, on which was written: '10 Montague Street, The bearers are two of my attendants, authorised by the family of Mr Edward Davies, who is insane, and also by me, to take charge of him, and convey him to his house at Hornsey. George Man Burrows MD.' One of the crowd shouted out that this was not a certificate of lunacy, to which one of Burrows's men replied that Davies was not being taken to an asylum, only to his own home, so this informal note did not indicate forcible confinement. This seemed to satisfy the people on the street, and the protest melted away.

Burrows's men drove Edward to Oakfield House, where a succession of doctors now came to talk to him, sometimes singly, sometimes in battalions. One of the physicians, Benjamin Hands, found Edward in his four-poster bed at noon, with his arm around his hunting dog, describing the mastiff as his most faithful friend. He spoke in an excited whisper, insisting that the four-poster curtains be closed. Hands thought that in Edward's situation, he too might have felt his dog to be his best friend. The doctor also disapproved of the fact that keepers Mr Mitten and Mr Sherrey – 'Mr Burrows's satellites', as Hands called them – had made themselves thoroughly at home and spent a great deal of time at Edward's billiard table.

On the second day of Edward's house arrest, Burrows himself drove up to Crouch End, and on entering Oakfield House at about three in the afternoon, he heard an almighty crash. When he came into the drawing room he found Edward covered in blood and brawling with the keepers, who were being pulled at by Edward's servants while the two hounds barked at them all. Spotting Burrows's carriage approaching, Edward had tried to escape through the window, fearing that he would be driven away to a lunatic asylum. When the keepers had grabbed him, his arm had smashed a windowpane. Edward's loyal servants shouted at Burrows and tried to force him from the room and at this point the doctor warned that he would use a 'strait waistcoat' on Edward if he would not calm down. The use of such an implement on even a raving lunatic had become hugely controversial by 1829, and the very threat of its use on a gentleman within his own home would prove to be a black mark against Burrows. Edward swiftly calmed down, and Burrows told him that he was simply paying him a routine visit.

The next day, two of the Philpot Lane staff called on Edward at Crouch End and subsequently reported to Mrs Bywater that he seemed 'as well as usual'. She was furious to hear such news, for she had wasted no time in petitioning the Lord Chancellor to hold a commission *de lunatico inquirendo* – the 'lunacy inquisition' process that dated back to 1324. 'Inquisition' was an unfortunate antique term allowing those so minded to elide the horrors of the Spanish Tribunal of the Holy Office with the seemingly mysterious and sinister probing of an English mind for oddity and eccentricity, with a view to a lifetime of incarceration for failure to conform. Inquisitions were held on individuals who had money or property which, if they were indeed of unsound mind, could be squandered or stolen as a result of mental incapacity to manage their affairs. This was intended to be a protective move, placing the assets ultimately under the jurisdiction of the Lord Chancellor. However, in reality the task of managing a lunatic's affairs was handed to two committees – one, a committee 'of the estate', and the other 'of the person' – which were entitled to a percentage of the patient's wealth that they were administering. Their activities were unaudited and they could potentially levy huge 'expenses' claims for their time spent in dealing with the lunatic's estate. It was the make-up of these committees, and their interest in the assets, that roused suspicion in many quarters whenever a lunacy inquisition was instigated. *Cui bono*? The alleged lunatic, or those who sought to become committee members, in charge of the purse strings? This was how Mrs Bywater's petition for an inquisition on her son would be interpreted: for many, it was simply a grab for control of the lucrative business, the running of which would naturally pass to her once Edward was deemed legally incapable of overseeing it.

In most instances, however, people suspected of being lunatics did not face an inquisition. After the passing of the 1828 Madhouse Act, the normal process was for two doctors separately to interview an alleged lunatic. Each would then sign a lunacy certificate, upon which he stated his reasons for believing the patient to be insane.* In 1829, there were an estimated 14,500–16,000 people in England and Wales who had been officially identified as insane, but only a small percentage of these had been wealthy enough to have required the inquisition process. In the 1820s, a total of 373 inquisitions took place, with over two-thirds of the subjects being male – a figure that suggests strongly the comparative wealth of males (who were the main inheritors of family money and who, when they married, obtained a wife's entire property); and suggests less strongly, the high bar set for males to prove their impeccably rational and seemly behaviour, if they wished to retain full control of that wealth.

The Agrippina of Philpot Lane had quickly set about securing affidavits regarding Edward's instability in order to support her petition to the Lord Chancellor. Her own main argument was that she had felt her life to be in danger since he had fired the pistol on 27 June. She persuaded banker Hankey to open a new account in her name and she transferred funds across from Hodgson & Davies. She was shelling out, apart from anything, for eight doctors to interview Edward with a view to swearing to the Lord Chancellor that he was mad. Not one of them knew him of old, and all believed that his fear of his mother was 'morbid' and 'unnatural', and that his claim that he was widely disliked in the tea trade was 'delusional'. But as they were in the pay of Mrs Bywater, it is not surprising that these were their conclusions.

Mistakenly believing that William Lawrence thought him sane – unaware that Lawrence had been co-opted by his mother – Edward continued to confide in him. Lawrence soothed him and persuaded him to agree to go to 'a lovely house on Regent's Park', where he could collect himself and spend some time in quietness. So on

---

* See p. 387 for a brief summary of the Acts concerning certification.

A rare depiction of a lunacy inquisition, from R. S. Surtees's 1843 comic novel
Handley Cross, illustrated by sometime Dickens illustrator John Leech.
Lawyer Martin Moonface (above) presents the case against the sanity of
the novel's hero, John Jorrocks.

On the stand, Jorrocks's manservant testifies to his master's sanity. The
fictional inquisition is set at the Gray's Inn Coffee House, where many
inquisitions were held, including that of Edward Davies.

14 August, after ten days' confinement at home, Edward was driven to Mrs Mary Wardell's at 14 Portland Terrace, on the north-west edge of the park. Mrs Wardell ran a small licensed house for the care of the insane, and as Edward still had not been certificated as a lunatic, this was highly irregular. He and Mrs Wardell took an instant dislike to each other, and she later recalled him as 'very wild' at first, wandering about the passageways with a candle, gesticulating, and asking her if she knew who he was. Wasn't his nose a fine nose? he asked. Didn't she know he was a snuff-maker to Jupiter and that he was going to be a greater man than Peel or Wellington? He rose at five in the morning the next day and shouted 'Murder! Murder!' out of the window. Mrs Wardell was even less pleased when a young attorney turned up, demanding to see Edward and reassuring him that he would assemble plenty of affidavits to vouch for his sanity at the forthcoming inquisition. Francis Hobler, who was on his way to becoming a minor London legal celebrity, said he intended to sue for a writ of habeas corpus, to force the delivery of Edward to a court of law to investigate his detention. Mrs Wardell overheard the conversation and had Hobler thrown out, but on successive hot summer nights he stood beneath Edward's window and the two men discussed Hobler's progress long into the small hours.

Edward realised that he had been betrayed by William Lawrence. 'Oh God! I am now nearly overpowered by my feelings,' he wrote to him. 'Instead of the benefits which you expected, or pretended to expect . . . from the change of air, change of scene, and such hypocritical cant, what do I experience? Falsehood, increased restrictions, confined rooms . . .' On the night of the 17th, Mrs Wardell overheard Francis Hobler beneath Edward's window proposing a rescue attempt. She informed Mrs Bywater of this and at half past eight on the morning of the 19th, Dr Burrows's carriage arrived to take Edward away. It would have been illegal for Burrows to have signed a patient into his own madhouse, but William Lawrence and Thomas Blundell now signed certificates of lunacy for Edward's admission to Burrows's Clapham Retreat. Mrs Bywater had filled out the lunacy order. Edward put up no fight.

The tea merchant had his own bedroom and sitting-room suite at the Retreat, and shared the asylum with eighteen male and four female patients; the males included four clerks, two army officers, a surgeon, a silversmith, a tobacconist, a bricklayer and a wine merchant. He was allowed as many as twenty visitors a day, and the staff from Philpot Lane trooped along regularly. In fact, Edward carried on running the business from the madhouse, demonstrating that he still knew a hawk from a handsaw in commercial matters. More than one visiting doctor noted the detailed instructions Edward gave to his staff. However, because the doctors hired by Mrs Bywater intended to claim that he was suffering from 'monomania' – a partial insanity that could leave most of the intellect undamaged – this acumen in business matters did not prove that Edward was of sound mind.

On 26 August, Mrs Bywater told clerk William Low that 'in a few days' the entire property would be hers. But she was overestimating the speed at which the Lord Chancellor moved, and weeks passed as the petition for the lunacy inquisition was pondered. Mrs Bywater then sacked Low and placed her son-in-law, Cornelius Pugh, in charge of the clerks; she went on to dismiss more of the staff at Philpot Lane and instructed them not to swear to Edward's sanity at the forthcoming hearing.

At the Retreat, Edward had lost weight and he was described as looking skeletal. Dr Burrows refused Francis Hobler the right to visit his client (visits to an asylum inmate were at the discretion of the proprietor and the signatory of the lunacy order) so the attorney complained directly to the Lord Chancellor, who advised Burrows, on 15 September, that he must allow Edward to start preparing his case for the inquisition. Edward told Hobler that the male attendants at the Retreat persistently made accusation, by gesture and imitation, that he was 'addicted to unnatural offences'. They would also lift up the back flaps of his coat as he passed them, indicating that they thought him a sodomite. He was often unable to stop crying. Two of the doctors hired by Mrs Bywater, John Haslam and George Tuthill, reported that he wept because he had still not had sight of his baby rabbits, born at Tom Belcher's; on another occasion he cried when he recalled the sweetness of the gingerbread he had eaten at the Lincoln's Inn pastry cook's shop on his last night as a free man. 'The British public are interested in the success of my cause,' Edward told Haslam, who noted it down as evidence that Edward's grandiosity was pathological. But it was Edward, not Haslam, who would be proved correct, and the doctor was to discover

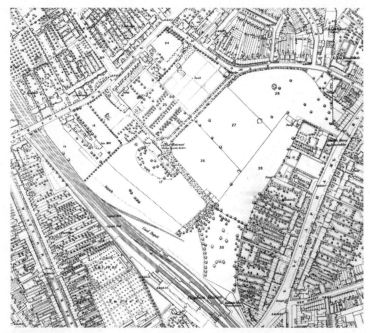

The Clapham Retreat was demolished not long after this map of 1870 was
drawn. No image of the building has survived.

that the public furore about wrongful asylum incarceration was
growing.

In November, Dr Burrows's keepers caused outrage again. They had
been apprehended by a group of angry Lambeth locals who attempted
to rescue Freeman Anderdon. Anderdon was an elderly eccentric bachelor,
who, despite having a fortune of thousands of pounds, chose to live in
a run-down cottage in impoverished York Street, Lambeth Marsh. In the
summer of 1829, he had begun to spend large sums on paintings, and his
hovel was filling up with artworks, to the horror of his brothers, who
were hoping that when he died his money would come their way. He
was well liked in the neighbourhood as an amiable old man who preferred
to wear ancient clothes, ragged footwear and a battered, huge-brimmed
straw hat. On the night of 1 November he was seized near his front-garden
wicket gate by Burrows's men. A policeman of the new Metropolitan
force noticed the ensuing street melee and recognising that Burrows's
standard note ('The bearers are two of my attendants, authorised by the

family . . .') was not a certificate of lunacy, took the attendants into custody and kept them overnight in the local watch-house; in the bag they carried the policeman found rope and manacles. Anderdon decided to prosecute Burrows for assault, and although the legal case would not 'come on' until the following April, the notion of Burrows being no better than a kidnapper or a 'burker' was firmly in the public mind as the Edward Davies inquisition approached. Being 'Burrowsed' entered London slang, and after dark, citizens had one more sinister phenomenon to be wary of if a carriage and two strangers appeared to be lurking.

The Lord Chancellor had urged the Davies–Bywater–Pugh family to try to reach a compromise before the expensive public proceedings began. He wished they would make a 'private arrangement, on account of the extraordinary delicacy of the investigation', but neither Edward nor his mother would call off the hearing. Mrs Bywater wanted the business, and Edward – according to his counsel – wanted 'to emancipate himself from the thraldom of his mother'. Francis Hobler had collected fifty-one affidavits in support of Edward's sanity – many of them from old friends who testified to his eccentric, melodramatic nature and clumsy attempts at humour, and who placed his seeming bizarreness into the context of a lifetime. Hobler claimed that he could deliver the Lord Chancellor three times the fifty-one sworn statements, but that he did not want to overwhelm His Lordship.

More bad news for Mrs Bywater was that one of the doctors sent along by the Lord Chancellor himself had strongly disagreed with the majority of medical men. Dr William MacMichael reported that, following several interviews, he had concluded that Edward had a theatrical manner, an over-polite way of conversing, a high opinion of himself, yet while 'diffuse' in conversation, he was coherent if he was patiently listened to. He seemed easily roused to anger, but he was not delusional. Dr MacMichael said that the seclusion at the Retreat had probably been good for him, and that if he were allowed to return to his Crouch End house he would fully recover his equilibrium. Since the cause of his 'irritation' was still *in situ* at Philpot Lane, it was not a good idea for him to return while his mother was there, wrote the doctor.

Forty medical witnesses turned up at the Gray's Inn Coffee House on Monday 14 December, the first day of the inquisition. This was a record number: not even Lord Portsmouth's dilemma, six years earlier, had brought out such a crowd of physicians. Coroners' inquests and lunacy inquisitions regularly took place in the largest 'public' building an area possessed, and very often these were inns and taverns. Competition for seats was keen, and the newspaper reporters noted the high proportion of beautifully dressed ladies of fashion who crammed themselves into the coffee house. The case would feature certain huge stars of the Bar, the brightest of whom was Henry Brougham, former Whig leader of the House who within a year would become Lord Chancellor himself; and with the likely chance that intimate and sexual matters not normally in the public realm would be discussed during the proceedings, this was the must-see show in town. (Four years earlier, Brougham's closing address at a lunacy inquisition at the Gray's Inn Coffee House had been accompanied by the sound of workmen hammering beneath him in an attempt to shore up the floor, which was straining under the weight of the multitude who had crowded into the room.)

Like coroners' inquests, inquisitions were heard before a 'special jury' which could vary in number between twelve and twenty-four, at the discretion of the Lord Chancellor. In an era when only male householders of property over a certain rateable value were permitted to serve as jurors, an additional limitation placed on the pool of lunacy jurymen was the ability to understand the medical as well as the legal arguments of a *de lunatico inquirendo*. Magistrates predominated on the special juries, and many of the same men turned up again and again as inquisition jurors.

Proceedings in the Davies case were overseen by Commissioner William Phillimore, who told the jury they would need to be certain that Edward was unable to take care of himself and of his property. 'Unsoundness of mind' was the term that had been used since a landmark judgment of 1802 and was tantamount to 'a declaration of lunacy', he explained. 'Unsoundness of mind, as when the mind had been worn out by cares, grief, old age or disease', came under the legal sense of lunacy; additionally, 'weak-mindedness', 'imbecility' and 'idiocy' could all render one unable to manage one's affairs – intellectual derangement was just one of the conditions recognised as 'unsoundness'. The jury need not worry about fine distinctions, Phillimore told them, but were solely to examine Mr Davies's ability to manage his property and himself. The Commissioner also expressed the wish that there would be no personal attacks upon Mrs Bywater during the hearing; clearer evidence of popular ill feeling against her has not survived, but Phillimore's request indicates that strong support for Edward had come to his notice. Various newspapers and journals had alluded to the 'excitement in the popular mind' and 'public dissatisfaction' since the seizure of Davies and the attempted seizure of Freeman Anderdon but had declined to go into detail, perhaps to avoid being accused of taking sides before the Davies hearing opened.

The doctors who had been hired by Mrs Bywater presented the various incidents already described as clear proof that Edward was of unsound mind and unable to run a business. But William Low and others loyal to the tea dealer recast each incident of apparent insanity to reveal the 'slant' that was being given to Edward's behaviour.

Mrs Martha Ings, to whom Edward was planning to lend the £200 he had wanted to cash at Hankey's, was the owner of a small brewhouse at Mount Pleasant, Holborn. The doctors produced her in court to tell the tale of the July morning on which Edward had called upon her to settle up for the horse he had recently bought from her. He had appeared 'extremely excited . . . [with] a wild and extravagant manner'. He had torn off his neckcloth, untied his shoes and begun jumping up and down on the sofa, she told the inquisition. But Henry Brougham drew from her the admission that, put another way, all he had done was to walk to her house on a very hot day in July, arrived sweating, taken off his neckcloth and shoes to cool down, and rather than jumping up and down on her sofa, had flung his long limbs across it as he felt comfortable in her company – so much so, in fact, that he proposed to lend her a vast sum of money. Brougham similarly befuddled Aunt Brookbank, who became flustered when the lawyer challenged her account of how Edward had behaved at Brixton Hill: 'Don't be excited, Ma'am,' he told her, 'don't be "wild", "boisterous", "irritated". It's rather dangerous, you know – you see the consequences.' The spectators were by now laughing openly and loudly at Edward's accusers. Commissioner Phillimore was surprisingly lenient in his attempts to rein in the rowdy and partisan crowd. Despite outbreaks of foot-stamping or hissing when a doctor said something particularly detrimental about Edward's sanity, Phillimore only occasionally threatened to adjourn proceedings if better behaviour was not shown.

He instructed all the ladies to withdraw when *** was to be discussed, and they made it very clear that they objected to this eviction. Eventually they complied, but not before each woman had reserved her place by putting her gloves or shawl on her seat. Later, when the subject of abortion came up, they simply refused to shift from the room; the Commissioner told them that he was no longer prepared to make any effort to spare their 'feelings', therefore they could stay if they insisted. So they were present when during a spat between the two medics, Dr Haslam accused Dr Blundell of 'making slips for married men', a term that had to be explained in court as procuring an abortion for a woman who had been made pregnant by an adulterer. As abortion was still on the statutes as a hangable offence, Dr Blundell was allowed to take time to clear himself of the charge.

The superintendent of the Clapham Retreat, William Pollard, could hardly make himself heard above the jeering laughter that erupted throughout his testimony. Similar hilarity greeted much of Burrows's evidence. He must have sensed which way the tide was running, as the doctor now claimed that he wanted rid of Edward from the Retreat, and that the certification had been intended only as a short-term measure until the inquisition got under way. Loud applause broke out when Burrows declared that he would relinquish care of Edward regardless of the decision of the jury. Brougham ascertained from Burrows that the doctor had had few personal interviews with Edward, as he visited his own asylum just twice a week, for a couple of hours. Yes, said Burrows, it was perfectly in order to take a family's version of events as the basis of certification, as these were the very people best placed to spot a change in behaviour and to note down examples of oddness. Mrs Bywater had probably saved her own life, he said, by her prompt calling in of the doctors, and if the jury were to find Edward of sound mind, it might lie heavy on their conscience if Mrs Bywater were subsequently murdered by her pistol-carrying son. This statement elicited visual signs of disapproval and disgust on the faces of the jurymen. In a final flourish, Burrows declared that Edward was clearly insane because he had been following the daily reports of his case in the newspapers and had told him that the doctors – 'men of character and honour', as Burrows called them – were telling falsehoods about him at the inquisition. Only a madman would come to such a conclusion.

A doctor from the London Hospital stated that Edward had a 'delu-sion of manner about him' – a form of words abruptly described as 'Nonsense!' by Edward's counsel. Hissing and jeering broke out in the room when Dr Algernon Frampton said that the reason he had concluded that Edward was insane on 7 December was the patient's refusal to admit that he had been insane on 8 August. Commissioner Phillimore threatened to clear the room if the spectators would not cease their abuse of the witnesses.

Other witnesses came forward to say that the danger on the Hornsey roads was a perfectly good reason for Edward to have bought pistols; that £7,000 had been the correct market price for Oakfield House; and that tea dealers Gibbs's and Varnham's testimony might be coloured by their known desire to become partners in Hodgson & Davies.

Dr John Haslam was asked by Brougham if he had read through all the affidavits collected by Edward's accusers before holding his own interview with the patient, and he said that yes, he had. This mode of proceeding – reading up on the alleged delusions first, and then trying to confirm their existence – was jeered at by both Brougham and the spectators, because of its lack of methodological rigour.

On the tenth day of the inquisition, Christmas Eve, the jury went to see Edward for themselves at the Retreat; although alleged lunatics could attend their own hearings, many (including Edward) chose to spare themselves the ordeal. They were back at the coffee house again at eleven o'clock on Boxing Day morning, and the foreman of the jury told Commissioner Phillimore that there was no need for the case to continue – the jurymen were unanimously decided and they believed they knew what was being attempted against Edward Davies, and why. This was a highly unusual development in a lunacy hearing, and the Commissioner informed the jury that the family had the right to continue to put its case, but it is clear from the tittering that punctuated the remaining testimony how the entire room was minded. The ongoing laughter 'was difficult to suppress', the *Morning Chronicle* reporter stated.

Mrs Bywater's counsel plodded on – for four hours – telling the jury that 'Mr Davies had not only thought himself a Pitt in finance, a Fox in eloquence, a Byron in poetry, but an Apollo in beauty'. He accused Edward's legal team of treating the mad-doctors 'not as men of science, but as a kind of resurrection men – medical poachers, laying springs [traps] for His Majesty's subjects'.

Nevertheless, cheering and loud applause greeted the jury's unanimous verdict that Edward was of 'perfectly sound mind', and experienced reporters wrote that they had never seen such 'warm' reaction to a jury's decision.

The verdict that freed Edward destroyed Burrows's career. About 250 people demonstrated outside the Retreat, and the doctor received nearly forty threatening letters, including one that read, 'Dr Burrows is cautioned to take care of himself. His consummate villainy will be expiated by BLOOD only.' Four months later, at the end of April 1830, when Freeman Anderdon won £500 from Burrows in his successful lawsuit for assault and false imprisonment, the wreck was complete. 'The effervescence of popular prejudice' and the 'painful animadversions on my character', as the doctor put it, effectively meant that Burrows could no longer be taken seriously as a lunacy specialist. The newspapers had had to hold fire while the Davies case was in progress, but as soon as the verdict was announced, opprobrium rained down on Burrows and the mad-doctors. *The Times* editorial stated that the commission against Edward had looked very much like 'persecution'. Failing to be cheered by the Davies verdict, *The Times* insisted that, 'The melancholy fact is that your thorough-going mad-doctor takes for granted that hardly anyone is sane . . . It is the law of England that any one of us may be seized by a pair of ruffians, under the warrant of a mad-doctor . . . and plunged for life into that hopeless prison, which is calculated to unsettle the steadiest intellect.' The influential *Quarterly Review* described

the extraordinary case of Mr Davies [as] by far the most important lunatic cause which has been tried in our time: it brings into broad daylight the important question, whether great eccentricities of character, or, to take wider ground still, the minor degrees of mental unsoundness, make a man fit subject for confinement in a madhouse . . . It ought to be made punishable, by a heavy fine and imprisonment, to deprive a man of his liberty for any cause excepting mischievousness to others and to himself, and the parties who commit such outrages ought to be prosecuted at the public expense.

Like Edward Davies himself, Dr Burrows had had no family connections or influential friends to help him start out in life; his widowed
mother had had him apprenticed, at the age of sixteen, to a surgeon.
He had been an outstanding and naturally gifted boy who had made
his own way in the world, founding one of the first medical journals
in England, and in 1815 he had played an important role in improving
the professional standing of physicians by insisting on standardised
qualifications. In 1828, Burrows published his *Commentaries on the
Causes, Forms, Symptoms and Treatment, Moral and Medical, of Insanity*,
one of the major early-nineteenth-century compendia of thinking
about insanity.

Like most (but not all) alienists of the time, Burrows believed that
insanity was a hereditary disease; and he thought that Edward had
been in need of urgent treatment. The earlier the intervention, the
greater the chance of cure, was the cry of the alienists. 'This perverse
concealment has often a very baneful effect,' Burrows wrote regarding
families who failed to come forward to report the mental disturbance
of a relative, fearing the shame that such a disclosure could bring.
Burrows's long experience of treating lunacy had, he claimed, led him
to spot instantly, within the tales told to him by the family, the
undoubted signs that mental affliction was setting in. It had been clear
from what Mrs Bywater had told Burrows that her son's 'malady
appeared to be progressive'. There was every reason to be hopeful
that an eventual cure for Edward would be achieved, Burrows had
believed, so long as he was in a place of custody where appropriate
treatment could be administered.

It was a mark of optimism that 'cure' and 'treatment' were on the
alienists' agenda at all: up to the end of the previous century, containment and restraint had been the main responses to the onset of
insanity. But this 'progress' had gone hand in hand with what, to many,
seemed to be the pathologising of perfectly ordinary human weirdness. Burrows himself had written in his *Commentaries*:

Eccentricity itself is a link in the catenation of the phenomena of a
morbid mind. Individuals are often distinguished by a singularity either
of ideas or of pursuits; or by an equipage or dress unlike that of
anybody else. There must be some obliquity in the perception and
judgment of such persons, for they certainly do not perceive the

difference between themselves and the commonalty. Many of these
eccentricities or singularities, however, if unnoticed and unchecked,
grow stronger with time, and ripen into perfect insanity.

There could scarcely be a passage more likely to inflame the average
Briton. Except perhaps this, 190 pages later: Dr Burrows believed that
all lunatics gave off a smell that he could compare only to henbane,
a toxic plant also called 'stinking nightshade' (with rather pretty
yellow flowers). 'I consider the maniacal odour a pathognomonic
symptom so unerring, that if I detected it in any person, I should
not hesitate to pronounce him insane, even though I had no other
proof of it.' This was a view sincerely held by Burrows, though a
renowned alienist would later insist that all he was smelling was the
stink of the asylum and the hard-to-shift miasma caused by the doubly
incontinent.

Burrows appeared to have no idea of how diagnosis by sniffing was

Dr George Man Burrows (1771–1846), pioneering alienist
and private asylum proprietor.

likely to be viewed by non-physicians. For all his belief in mad-folk's 'obliquity in perception and judgment', he seems to have been a man curiously short on self-awareness. *The Lancet* drew the comparison of Burrows with Witchfinder-General Matthew Hopkins's smelling out of witches in seventeenth-century East Anglia – a cruel undermining of the thrusting empiricism Burrows had set store by.

Yet it is slightly unfair to mock such notions as the smell of a madman; because, in fact, the texts of many nineteenth-century alienists reveal not so much bumptious over-confidence as an agonised consciousness that they were still in a state of ignorance of the anatomical or psychological causes of mental problems. 'The current state of our imperfect knowledge' was a typical expression they used; in fact, Burrows himself had written that 'we are in the infancy of our knowledge'. Many alienists knew that they were still advancing guesswork. What is less easy to forgive, though, is the flawed, or even specious, reasoning used by certain doctors; and the mocking laughter that punctuated the Davies inquisition showed that the public, as speedily as the lawyers, had spotted the methodological errors of the men who tried to prove Edward's insanity. They had approached Edward believing him to be insane, and then set about tracking down any evidence that would bolster that opinion. The *London Medical Gazette* despairingly noted: 'As to the evidence of the medical witnesses, it was, with a few exceptions, wretchedly bad. In some instances, it was absolutely imbecile; in others, pompous, vulgar and absurd . . . There is nothing of which the public are more jealous than any measure interfering with personal liberty emanating from a private source, and it is right they should be so.' The doctors did not appear to have considered that Edward's 'paroxysms' could have been the actions of a sane man enduring extraordinary levels of stress. The *Gazette* stated that Edward did appear at one point to be 'suffering from functional disorder of the nervous system, with anxiety, restlessness, vigilance and exaltation bordering upon delirium', and that – of the doctors chosen by Mrs Bywater – only Dr Peter Latham had appeared to wonder how this behaviour might fit in with Edward's usual demeanour.

The *Quarterly Review* quoted John Haslam's 1809 book, *Observations on Madness and Melancholy*, as an example of alienists' flawed diagnostic procedure. 'The physician's own mind must be the criterion by which he infers the insanity of any other person,' Haslam had written. In this way, the *Review* pointed out, doctors had elected themselves arbiters of normality; and so when they came up against an extra-ordinary but sane person, such as Edward Davies, they categorised him as mad. If the doctors hired by Mrs Bywater had broadened their inquiry and properly investigated the odd manner that Edward had displayed throughout his life, there would have been no need for an inquisition costing £5,000.

Of the medical men of his day, Dr Burrows was perhaps the most adamant on the subject of the irrelevance of a layperson's opinion. He had dedicated his early working life to the professionalisation of medicine, identifying and excluding charlatans and the unqualified. Burrows believed that anatomical and observational work by medical men alone would one day reveal the causes of insanity, and thereby enable its cure. He knew that brain dissection had so far failed to do this, and was minded to take more seriously French hypotheses that the seat of insanity might lie in the guts or the respiratory system. However, in his *Commentaries*, Burrows did not go along with the notion of the uterus having special bearing on female psychological states, quoting with approval French alienist Étienne-Jean Georget, who stated that the female reproductive system scarcely ever disturbs the cerebral functions. 'The majority of the insane are men,' wrote Burrows, presenting as evidence figures for lunatics in private asylums in England for the years 1812 to 1824, which put the male total at 4,461 and the female at 3,443. Burrows felt that fear of financial failure, and the resort to drink to alleviate such anxieties, were the factors that made male sanity more fragile; these outweighed the challenges to female sanity caused by the physical and emotional strains of preg-nancy, childbirth and menstruation, although he thought that women's traditional lack of education might make them prey to superstition and religious fanaticism. As a hereditarian, Burrows also believed that the very wealthy were disproportionately prone to insanity because of intermarriage within noble families, a habit he wished they would begin to check.

With regard to his procedure of 'arresting' an alleged lunatic by means of a note wielded by his attendants, Dr Burrows had chosen to interpret the lunacy law as permitting him to order a patient to be detained within his or her own home without a formal lunacy certifi-cate, filling out the paperwork only when the patient was to be placed in a for-profit institution. The legal grey area respecting the home-based family lunatic does just about make this defence plausible, and as Chapter Six will show, the failure of the legislature to protect sufficiently the rights of non-asylum-based lunatics had permitted Burrows to attempt to override habeas corpus. It was necessary, Burrows claimed, to get the alleged lunatic into a safe place where diagnosis could take place, but often 'the mob' would attempt to thwart this: 'It frequently happens, in removing a lunatic from one place to another, that he is very violent, or endeavours, by making artful appeals to those near him, to attract their attention, and raise a feeling to rescue him. In such a case, the populace are almost always sure to side with the lunatic and sometimes liberate him.' In Edward Davies's case, 'the coach was stopped as he was being conducted from Furnival's Inn to his own house, and he was prevented being released by the production of it [the note].' Burrows complained of the huge contrast between the stance of the London crowd and the capital's newspaper editors, and foreign attitudes to doctors and scientific progress: 'What a revolution! While a British public heap with obloquy those medical practitioners who devote themselves to the improvement of the means of a cure, and amelioration of the condition of the insane . . . France, Germany, Italy, and all the most civilised parts of Europe, nay, even Russia, vie with each other in encouraging them.' Science was not at home in England so long as lunacy specialists found themselves under attack while going about their work.

After insisting that his mother leave Philpot Lane, Edward again took up the reins of Hodgson & Davies. At first, all went well, but his self-consciousness and prickliness meant that he resented being the object of stares and mutterings in the locality. A false report that he had suffered a relapse was placed in the *Standard* newspaper, in the very week that the Anderdon trial was about to begin, which seems to suggest some kind of muck-raking by a supporter of Burrows or an enemy of Henry Brougham, who was prosecuting the doctor in the Anderdon case. Eventually, a deal was thrashed out between mother and son, whereby he yielded to her and his brother-in-law the tea business in Philpot Lane, in return for all the land and property near Newtown. And so in the mid-1830s, Edward became a Welsh gentleman farmer, with 154 acres, although he remained a sleeping partner of Hodgson & Davies until the final dissolution of the firm in 1843, four years after his mother's death.

So it was a happy ending for Edward. He married a local woman, Mary, in 1838, had four children and died in his seventies, having built the now-listed Snowfield mansion for himself.

George Man Burrows continued to run the Clapham Retreat until 1843, but was no longer a wealthy man. He died three years later, aged seventy-six.

The Edward Davies case had been the first big test of the 1828 Madhouse Act, and the legislation had been found wanting. A doctor of Burrows's eminence had believed the Act had given him the right to kidnap from the street a highly strung man, at the behest of a family member with everything to gain from his declaration as a lunatic. How else was he to undertake a diagnosis? he had asked. Edward had then been held against his will in his own home, before being tricked into custodial care – at Mrs Wardell's – and then misdiagnosed by the two doctors who signed his lunacy certificate, nineteen days after his initial detention. The furore that erupted when Edward's inquisition had belatedly got under way – four months after his abduction at Furnival's Inn – reminded the doctors, lawyers and parliamentarians that the public were still prepared to express their anger at curbs to individual liberty through direct action and misbehaviour at public lunacy hearings. If oddness was to become medicalised, there was going to be a battle.

2

The Attorney-General of all Her Majesty's Madmen

At first glance, it looked like any other very smart parlour in a country house – fine furniture, good-quality (if rather featureless) decoration and a view out across well-tended garden grounds to picturesque countryside beyond. But as the eye adjusted, certain oddities made themselves known: the venetian blinds were made of iron, the furniture was securely attached to the floor, and in the huge bay window at the far end of the room, twelve gentlemen sat strapped on to wooden seats, each in a separate niche. Each strait-waistcoated man was fastened in with a wide length of leather across the belly, attached to a padlock and to a ring in the wall, and his feet were secured by lower-leg manacles ('socklets'), also made of leather, to a ring in the floor. Most were quiet, one or two wept, one had his head slumped on his chest, one may have fouled himself, and John Perceval will have been attempting to asphyxiate himself by pressing his neck against a small wooden projection on the wall of his niche, or to snap his neck by extreme jerks of the head.

Occasionally, Mr Perceval was unchained and allowed to walk to the fireplace, or to the large table in the middle of the room. Sometimes the iron fire grate had a hideous face moulded into it, grimacing out at him, but on other occasions, someone had cleverly refashioned the detail in the metal into an ornamental basket of flowers. Mr Perceval would, from time to time, decide to waltz around the parlour table, and once, as he spun round, he caught sight of a wild-looking creature in the mantel looking-glass and was horrified to realise that it was himself: the whiskers he had worn all his adult life had been removed, and his hair was close-cropped on the crown but flowing down at the back. On these journeys around the room, the spirits would usually order him to wrestle with an attendant or servant, and these attempts at sport would lead to him being swiftly strait-waistcoated and returned to his niche. After the evening meal, Mr Perceval would be taken upstairs to his smart but bleak bedroom, and upon his bed would be secured to the wall by one foot and one arm. He would sleep badly, unlike his attendant, who spent the night on a bed on the other side of the room, its door locked and bolted and the iron venetians fastened.

Twice a day, the gentlemen were unstrapped and taken for walks through the glorious landscape, a greatcoat being placed over the strait-waistcoat so as not to arouse curiosity in passers-by. The route was often across a steep wooded bank alongside a river to 'the battery' – a precipice with a parapet, a terrace and a summerhouse, with views across Somerset and into Wales: an obvious suicide spot, Mr Perceval would later note. On these walks, he would 'halloo!' and sing and cry out to passing carriages, 'I am the lost hope of a noble family – I am ruined! I am ruined! I am lost! I am undone! But I am the redeemed of the Lord!' He would recognise Jesus in a farm labourer and fall to his knees before him; and to serve the Lord, he would throw himself headfirst over every stile and gate they came to, for which he was caned each time by his attendant. The injuries from the caning, stile-leaping and his own assaults upon his neck while strapped in soon mounted up. On bad-weather days, when there were no walks, Mr Perceval sat in his niche singing and noting a mucousy, painful sensation in his upper palate and throat; he sang all the louder in the parlour to try to relieve the pressure in his throat and mouth.

The other men in the niches included a young Devonshire clergyman, a sea captain, a Quaker banker, a noisy, red-faced solicitor who jabbered passages from Virgil, and an elderly Bristol merchant, whose mind and body deteriorated over the months that Mr Perceval spent in the parlour. Some of the men would be untied to play silent games of whist together or with the servants. If a particularly gifted bowls or billiards player was found among the inmates of the second-class or third-class male accommodation, such a man would be permitted to come among the gentlemen to enliven the sport.

Once a day, Dr Edward Long Fox, the aged Quaker who had established the house, would come into the parlour and address a few words to them. Short, grey-haired, wearing his blue frock coat, broad-brimmed hat and carrying a walking cane, Dr Fox would totter in with his mad-doctor sons, Francis Ker, Charles Joseph and Henry. The Foxes would have a smoke with the gentlemen, and occasionally a game of cards too. Mr Perceval would ask the senior Fox to wrestle with him, but the doctor always declined.

Mr Perceval suspected that many epochs had passed since he had first been placed in his niche. God was punishing him by allowing him glimpses of the newspapers for 1831 only – left on the parlour table each morning, alongside the huge bible – so that Mr Perceval would remain in ignorance of the centuries that were rushing by. He often felt that he was in two or three places at the very same time – inhabiting separate planes all at once. Mr Perceval would skim the newspaper when he was allowed out of his niche. When he had read a sentence he looked away but when he looked again, the words had shifted themselves around. Faces and features changed too, as he peered at his fellow inmates, attendants and servants. Almost everyone around him had multiple personas, with various names and predominant attributes.

The most important person in his life was his attendant, Herminet Herbert (who was also 'Zachary Gibbs', 'Jesus' and 'Samuel Hobbs' – by which name the rest of the world knew him). Herminet Herbert was a divinity, and during supervised, strait-waistcoated visits to the privy, Mr Perceval would propel himself off the WC, through the unlocked closet door in order to fall upon his face and chest at Herminet Herbert's feet, in worship. Herminet Herbert would then throw Mr Perceval back on the WC and rain blows down on his head and stomach.

Herminet Herbert would often attempt to humour Mr Perceval with childish or coarse jokes, or by jingling spoons in his face, but this levity swiftly turned to violence whenever Herminet Herbert had become bored with it or if Mr Perceval had not laughed sufficiently, or just whenever the attendant felt like it. One of Mr Perceval's many terrors was that he would be dissected, since the Foxes were doctors and therefore interested in anatomy, and Herminet Herbert's favourite threat was, 'I'll cut your guts out!'

Bath-time happened once a week, but was also kept in reserve as a punishment for refractory patients. The large pool used for this was in a gloomy, freezing, top-lit outbuilding. Although Mr Perceval never resisted, Herminet Herbert and another attendant would always take the opportunity to throw him into the freezing water backwards, and his head would be forced under with an iron bar pressed on his neck. He would shake with cold for half an hour afterwards and experience toothache and headache. An alternative to the pool was the shower-bath, and for this he would be walked naked across a courtyard to a small outhouse. There, he would be seated, chained in and the attendant would stand astride him and pour two or three pails of cold water on to him, bringing on convulsive jerkings and more tooth and head pain.

Despite being chained all night, Mr Perceval only once wet his bed. For this, he was placed in an outhouse at the bottom of the first-class male airing-court, hard up against Dr Fox's kitchen garden wall. There were three or four cells in this part of the complex, of bare stone and top-lit. A straw mattress and straw pillow that smelt of cows were placed on a wooden bed-frame, and Mr Perceval was strapped down and manacled to the wall. But he felt happier here; he was alone, for one thing, and in seclusion he was able to sing and 'halloo!' as often as the spirits directed him. He spent a fortnight in his cell.*

The beatings by Herminet Herbert, together with the regular self-inflicted head and neck injuries, caused a large swelling on the left side of his head near the ear. He believed the lump was filled with the tears of blood that he had not been able to shed. A surgeon came to bleed the left temporal artery, and Mr Perceval later said that this operation had caused permanent damage to his hearing.

Mr Perceval felt surprisingly little of the physical pain he endured. His agony was 'the agony of mind occasioned by the incomprehensible commands, injunctions, insinuations, threats, taunts, insults, sarcasms, and pathetic appeals of the voices round me'. The voices 'flocked' about him 'like bees', issuing contradictory orders. When Herminet

* Mr Perceval's experience of the cold-bath and shower treatment, and his seclusion in the bare cell, are very similar to complaints that had been made in 1822 by Trophimus Fulljames (1779–1864), who had been placed in Dr Fox's asylum by his brother. Fulljames's letters to Robert Peel, then Home Secretary, and to other parliamentarians contained three illustrations to back up his claims of 'unauthorised human misery' and 'unparalleled cruelties' at the asylum. These are reproduced on pp. 38–9. The local visiting magistrates were directed to investigate and they cleared Dr Fox of the charges.

Herbert brought him his breakfast of a basin of tea and small squares of bread and butter, one spirit would say, 'Eat a piece for my sake'; another would say, 'Refuse it for my sake'; and yet another would demand, 'Don't eat that piece, eat that one, for my sake.' His hesitation as he tried, in anguish, to work out which spirit to appease would look to Herminet Herbert like rebelliousness and he would often be struck.

It felt to Mr Perceval as though the voices were mostly speaking inside his own skull, but sometimes they would sound as though they were emanating from another part of the room, or just hovering somewhere in the air. He counted over fourteen of them. Every voice was different and each was 'beautiful, and, generally, speaking or singing in a different tone or measure, and resembling those of relations or friends', as he put it. The voices of 'contrition' inhabited his left temple and forehead; those of 'joy and honour' were coming from the right. Over his eyebrows were two who were quicker and more 'flaunty' than the others: over the right eyebrow was the spirit of Mr Perceval's eldest sister, and over the left, the spirit of Herminet Herbert.

Voices would sometimes address him in verse; once, a hurdy-gurdy appeared to circle his bed, playing a tune that made him weep to know that he had lost a father's love. The music conjured up visions of him living in Portugal as a child and then as a young monk, who repaid the kindness shown to him by robbing the church and partaking of 'unnatural' lusts with other young monks; he then killed a pig for sheer enjoyment, plunging it alive into boiling water. During this episode the spirits told him that all his problems arose from an act of ingratitude in his childhood. Another voice told him that he was responsible for the drowning of an old woman on the City side of Blackfriars Bridge. Faces appeared on walls or furnishing fabrics – those of God, his family and his father, who began to weep: Mr Perceval felt the tears drop on to his own skin. 'Thus my delusions, or the meshes in which my reasoning faculties were entangled, became perfected; and it was next to impossible thoroughly to remove them,' he later wrote. Despite his confusion about time and place, Mr Perceval knew that he had a mother as well as brothers and sisters. His eldest brother came to visit him six months after he had been admitted, and stayed two days. He examined the niches in the parlour, saw the isolation cell, heard about the cold-water treatments, and on the second night, he shook Mr Perceval's hand and simply left. Just before leaving, he asked Mr Perceval why he insisted on talking with his mouth shut. When Mr Perceval raised his hand to his mouth as he spoke in reply, he was horrified to realise that this was so.

One day, when the buttercups and daisies were blowing in the meadows outside, something peculiar happened as Mr Perceval sat in his niche. When a command was being issued to him by one of the voices, he hesitated to obey it, suddenly realising that it was a 'ridiculous' request. In fact, it occurred to him that much of what the spirits were saying was quite 'absurd'. From this point, he thought very deeply about every command he was given and began to compare what the voices said with what he heard and saw going on around him. He realised, for example, that other people would speak of Herminet Herbert as 'Samuel Hobbs', and so Mr Perceval deduced that this was probably his real name. He began to understand that he was in a madhouse – that it was in England, that it was near Bristol, that it was, in fact, Brislington House Asylum. It was June, and the

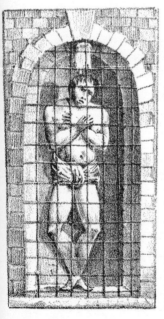 

newspapers had not been a divine deceit: it really was 1831, and so Mr Perceval must be twenty-eight years old; and he had been deposited here by his eldest brother, who was called Spencer, some seven months earlier, when the snow was deep, as he remembered. Spencer hadn't said goodbye when he had driven off in the snowdrifts.

Mr Perceval asked for a pocketbook, so that he could begin to keep the date and to write memoranda. On paper, he found, he could collect, arrange and rearrange his ideas. He began regularly to disobey his spirit commands, and found that no punishment resulted from this; therefore, he *reasoned*, they had no real power at all. His quieter, more pensive demeanour meant that Mr Perceval was released from his niche for much of the day now; he was allowed to sit alone in a parlour upstairs in a wicker chair and to take walks out in the yard without Samuel Hobbs. In the doorway to the yard he passed the surgeon who had operated on his damaged ear and he told the doctor, 'Oh! sir, I have been in a dream, a fearful dream, but it is gone now.'

One day, Dr Francis Ker Fox also met him going into the yard

These three drawings were sent to the Home Office by Trophimus Fulljames. On the left Fulljames depicts the Brislington shower-bath, and in the centre is his experience of the isolation cell. The image on the right illustrates an incident that Fulljames was told of by another patient – a cruel prank played by attendants, when a coffin had been delivered to the asylum for a deceased patient. Fulljames, a surveyor, has adapted the image to show that the patient was shut into the coffin for the amusement of the keepers.

and asked him, 'Pray, was it *your* father who was shot in the House of Commons?' It was a heartless question, but it was a reminder of an actual biographical fact, and not one that the spirit voices were likely to have come up with. The insensitive question also prompted another train of renewed rational thought: that the Foxes were unable to understand that their patients had the full range of emotions and might be acutely sensitive to such a subject being brought up. Prime Minister Spencer Perceval had been shot dead by an embittered failed businessman, John Bellingham, on 11 May 1812 in the Commons lobby, and John Perceval, after recovering from his illness, would write, 'I fear the death of my poor father was at the root of all my misfortunes . . . I do not YET understand his loss . . . a cruel blow [that] deprived my mother of a husband, and her family of a father.' He began to piece together the order of events that had led to his brother Spencer, with their mother's agreement, leaving him at Fox's asylum one evening in the previous winter.

A fanciful depiction of the assassination of Prime Minister Spencer Perceval, on 11 May 1812. 'I fear the death of my poor father was at the root of all my misfortunes,' John Perceval would later write.

Spencer Perceval the elder and Jane Wilson, John's parents, painted shortly
after their marriage, which took place in 1790.

Their father, in private life at least, had been by all accounts a good-
hearted man who strove to live by his Evangelical Anglican principles,
and his death had shattered the family. He had not been wealthy, and
his widow and twelve surviving children had been rescued from the
threat of shabby gentility by a generous government grant. Mrs
Perceval remarried in 1815, becoming Lady Jane Carr, but lost her
second husband in 1821. Spencer the younger became an MP, 'winning'
three rotten borough seats in succession, from 1818, and becoming an
under-secretary at the Home Office.

John had been educated at Harrow and then joined the 1st Regiment
of Foot Guards, The Grenadiers, with which he saw active service in
Portugal in 1827. There, he had felt scared and bored in equal measure,
greatly missing the studious life and the company of women. He was
a withdrawn, bookish, analytical young man, much exercised by
Evangelical questions, and had always found women more congenial
than men. He was contemptuous of the heavy drinking, gambling
and debauchery of his fellow Guardsmen. They in turn ribbed him
about his piety, seriousness and love of solitude.

His Portuguese adventure taught him a dislike of parliamentary politics. In Mr Perceval's view, the Duke of Wellington had sold the

Portuguese into the hands of a despot, King Dom Miguel I, for selfish, tactical reasons: 'I felt . . . that we had been made fools and tools of . . . the blind instrument of power. My last attachment to the Tory party, and to the pride of being an Englishman, were then severed. I had thought my country upright, noble and generous, and that party honest and honourable. I now despised the one, and began to hate and fear the other.' Such experiences forged within him an odd combination of radical and conservative: an acutely snobbish lover of the oppressed; a generous friend to the outcast who expressed contempt for those without aristocratic breeding; a very kind and exquisitely sensitive autocrat.

From Portugal, his regiment was sent to Dublin, and while his colleagues carried on roystering and rogering, Mr Perceval set up a Scripture study class. He found both Dublin society and the Irish poor far more interested in and respectful of religion than the English of all classes; and when he returned to his mother country to begin studies at Oxford, he worried that the irreligious attitudes he saw everywhere would tempt him into wickedness. He wanted a wife, but met few eligible women during his studies; in his spare time, he mingled only with other serious young men and they would pore over the Bible together. He often fasted, and now began to wake himself at intervals during the night in order to pray – to 'watch'. Sometimes on these nights, he would have visions, and he noticed that they were often prophetic, but that the events foretold by the visions would feature certain discrepancies when they did come to pass. He began to believe that it was some disobedience within him which had led to his prophetic visions containing inaccuracies. 'You do not understand this, my reader – nor do I,' he would later write. 'Suffice it to say, I was expecting the fulfilment of the divine prophecies concerning the end of the world, or the coming of the Lord.' He could see no reason for the non-fulfilment, except that his soul was lacking faith.

His brother Spencer, and their good friend, Henry Drummond – banker, politician, economist and historian – had also been seeking a more satisfying religious experience and had become involved with the Irvingites, who had one of their bases at the Clydeside town of Row. The 'Row Heresy', or the 'Row Miracles', as their activities were variously called, of the late 1820s had involved healing, prophecy, automatic writing and 'speaking in tongues', and when John travelled to Row, he, too, fell in with the sect. One afternoon, at luncheon at the house of a believer, one of the 'inspired ladies' left the table and called John out of the room. She led him into the drawing room, and with her arm raised and moving rhythmically, she exclaimed, 'Hola mi hastos, Hola mi hastos, disca capita crustos bustos.' John asked her what it meant and she said she didn't know because the Holy Spirit was addressing him directly through her. 'I could not help being awed,' John wrote: 'the sounds, the tone, the action were most impressive . . . I thought I recognized the marvellous work of the Almighty.' (It turned out that it meant 'Tarry ye not in Jerusalem'.) Before long, he too was channelling the Holy Spirit, and 'opening my mouth, sang in beautiful tones words of purity, kindness and consolation . . . the words, the ideas even, were wholly unthought of by me, or at least, I was unconscious of thinking of them . . . The voice was given me, but I was not the master of it.' He would throw his head back, and hear the beautiful sounds sailing up out of his throat. 'I now attribute this sensation in a great measure to extreme nervous excitement,' he would write later, 'but at that time it led to the destruction of my new-formed peace and ultimately to my ruin.'

Back in Oxford, he assumed that the Holy Spirit would now keep him safe from sin and the 'whirlpool of dissipation' around him. As he returned to his college after dinner with friends one evening, he was accosted by a woman of the town, to whose solicitation he replied by quoting Scripture. Five minutes later, another such woman walked towards him. This time, she 'led me away to my destruction'.

Terrified that he might have contracted venereal disease during the encounter, he dosed himself with mercury. To cleanse himself, he would scrub his entire body with cold water in his draughty room. Still fasting, waking in the night to pray and to scrutinise his soul, by the third week of November 1830 he was unable to speak even on trivial subjects without 'internal rebuke and misgivings' and was 'exhausted, weary and broken-hearted'.

He fled to Dublin in December, to its more devout atmosphere and the company of old friends. But his disintegration continued:

Until now, I had retained a kind of restraining power over my thoughts and belief. I now had none . . . I became like one awake yet dreaming, present to the world in body, in spirit at the bar of heaven's judgment

seat; or in hell, enduring terrors unutterable, by the preternatural
menaces of everlasting and shocking torments; inexpressible anguish
and remorse, from exaggerated accusations of my ingratitude, and a
degrading and self-loathing sense of moral turpitude from accusations
of crimes I had never committed. I had often conceived it probable
that insanity was occasioned by a loss of honour; I had not suspected
that an imagined loss of honour could also effect such a ruin.

His friends became so alarmed by his behaviour that they summoned
a local physician, Dr Piel, to visit him in his room. Mr Perceval was
tied to the bed by his hands and feet for a fortnight, as his brain and
his body became the battleground for good and evil.

He imagined the Almighty was examining him with a view to
casting him into the third degree of hell, with worms, bats and moles.
He was to be eternally damned, alone, in multiplied bodies and in
infinite solitude and darkness. It was made known to him that the
Almighty in His three persons had descended upon earth, had entered
London and had revealed all these things to the King, who was also
preparing on earth the most cruel torments for Mr Perceval. A spirit
came on to the pillow by his right ear and made him raise himself
up on his feet and the back of his neck and, thus arched, to swing
and rock from side to side. Voices that appeared to be both outside
and inside his head were becoming louder, along with the sound of
a bellows fanning flames and the clanking of iron. Only by obeying
Jesus and maintaining the arched-back position would Mr Perceval
avoid waking in hell in the morning. When dawn came, he realised
he was saved, but then discovered that because Jesus had descended
to help him fight the fires of hell, any sin of his would now be doubly
heinous. A voice obliged him on pain of dreadful torments to admit
his ingratitude; but when he did so, he was rebuked for doing this all
wrong. When he pleaded that he did not know what to do, he was
rebuked for looking for a way of not obeying the commands.

Dr Piel and John's friends had sent for Spencer, and in the meantime
engaged the help of a Dublin lunacy specialist; together they attempted
to feed, medicate and calm the patient. Mr Perceval would later point
out that such enforced idleness only gave the delusions greater power,
as his mind was unoccupied and the lack of exercise further debilitated
his physical self. At the same time, however, he noted and remembered

the mundanities of the fortnight: his belief that Dr Piel, as a Unitarian, would not be able to understand Mr Perceval's spiritual torments; the fact that the broth they fed him was not sufficient nourishment; that the medicine tasted of iron; and that giving him an enema was an indecent, indelicate action upon the body of a gentleman. He was mad and sane at the same time, he later wrote: '[I had] so much sense and reflection left to me . . . [but] no one who has not been deranged can understand how dreadfully true a lunatic's insane imagination appears to him, how slight his sane doubts.'

When Spencer arrived, the spirits instructed John to say, 'I am desired to tell you that you are a hypocrite.' Spencer and the doctors dressed him and took him by hackney coach to the quayside where they boarded a steam packet for Bristol. John had thought he was being taken home, but the carriage in England took him instead to Brislington.

Spencer had been appointed a Metropolitan Commissioner in Lunacy in 1830 – an entirely coincidental appointment, but in keeping with the Perceval sense of Evangelical civic duty. He had proved the most diligent and thorough Commissioner, and took his huge workload very seriously. Yet you would know none of this from John's writings: Spencer's commitment to asylum regulation and the implementation of national standards of care do not rate one mention by his younger brother. Spencer himself had been called 'mad' in the House of Commons, no less, because of the piety of his speeches there. Others would jeeringly call him 'Saint Perceval', for he twice called on the government to back a national day of fasting and 'humiliation' as a response to the cholera epidemic of 1831–32. And it was Spencer, as the senior male blood relative, who had signed John's lunacy order.

At the end of the previous century Edward Long Fox had run a small asylum at Downend, near Bristol, in an ordinary private house. In 1799 he purchased part of the recently enclosed Brislington Common for £4,000 and constructed his large new asylum, which opened in 1806. The building may have been the first purpose-built large private asylum in England, and was designed to segregate patients by gender and according to social class. Two identical wings housed the two sexes, with a dividing wall that ran right through the middle of the complex. On each side of the house, further partition ensured that the aristocracy did not have to come across the tradesman class, and

BRISLINGTON HOUSE—BACK VIEW, 1836.

The entire complex was divided up by walls so that the social classes and genders did not mix and the 'excitable' were kept apart from the non-violent.

that neither would be forced to mix with those of still shallower pocket. Within each social class, the violent and the non-violent were segregated: the parlour with the niches where Mr Perceval spent most of his days was set aside for the violent, or potentially violent, first-class gentlemen; the cold cells with straw bedding were for the most refractory or for the 'dirty' patients, who were either doubly or singly incontinent. Mr Perceval noted the building's cold, hard, echoing surfaces: Dr Fox Snr had insisted on iron and stone, rather than wood, in order to minimise the risk from fire. No hooks or nails were allowed in the walls, in case anyone should attempt to hang themselves; fire utensils were chained to grates so they could not become weapons. A number of small villas in the grounds housed the super-exclusive patients who did not need to enter the main building and could bring their own domestic staff, horses and vehicles. According to the prospectus that the Fox sons published five years after Mr Perceval had fetched up at Brislington, the establishment was 'A hospital for the curable, and a comfortable retreat for the incurable.' Set in a wooded estate nine miles from Bath and three from Bristol, Brislington was secluded enough to protect patients from the curious, and to cause minimal anxiety to its neighbours.

Charging its first-class patients £300 per annum, Brislington was the joint most expensive and prestigious asylum in the country and, along with Ticehurst in Sussex and Laverstock House near Salisbury in Wiltshire, was the venue selected by those of the aristocracy who chose not to care for their insane family members either at home or lodged at someone else's home as a 'single patient'. Families could feel relieved to know that their troubled relative was in luxurious surroundings, and in the care of one of the most renowned and well-liked lunatic doctors in England. Spencer had witnessed day after day the privations and poor conditions in some of London's private and pauper asylums, and is likely to have viewed Brislington's cold baths, stone cells and bay-window imprisonment in a very different light to John. Even at its worst, Brislington was better than the majority of institutions in which an agitated person could be deposited.

It wasn't only Spencer who failed to see anything the matter at Brislington; the visiting magistrates, too, could discern no problems. Outside the London area, local JPs had the duty of asylum inspection and licensing. Mr Perceval encountered them on three occasions but thought them 'absurd-looking old gentlemen' and burst out laughing when they entered the parlour. He said they spent just ten minutes in a room that was filled with lunatics, most of whom probably took the magistrates to be creatures from another world. Patients' grievances were expected to be aired in front of the Foxes. One of the visitors looked kind, and was the only official Mr Perceval came across who appeared able to sympathise with a lunatic, to any degree. However, his promise to help Mr Perceval came to nothing.

Dr Fox admonished Mr Perceval when he complained of Samuel Hobbs's coarseness: 'I must own that it not a little surprised me that you, as a humble follower of Christ, would think of him or any other as your inferior. Do we not know that God is no respecter of persons?' Yet as Mr Perceval observed, 'I never saw Mr Hobbs sitting at Dr Fox's dinner table.' The hypocrisy went far deeper: the great levelling philosophy of the Quakers did not prevent Dr Fox making a very good living from running an asylum that stratified humanity according to accident of birth or level of wealth. The Quakers had been a major force behind the English revolution in lunacy care, with the opening in 1792 of the York Retreat by Quaker tea and coffee merchant William Tuke, in which humane, therapeutic 'moral [i.e. psychological] treatment' would replace physical and mechanical restraint and such barbarities as bleeding, purging and narcotics. Edward Long Fox no

Edward Long Fox (1761–1835) founded Brislington House in 1806.

doubt took advantage of the famous Quaker humanitarianism of the York Retreat: the wealthy would have less anxiety in handing over their relatives to a place where restraint had been abolished. So how to explain the niches, the manacles and socklets, the cold-water treatment, the stone cells at the end of the yard, and the beatings? The last of these was a sackable offence, according to the Foxes; but the doctor and his sons would, of course, need to be made aware of a violent incident in order for an attendant to be dismissed. And who was going to believe a lunatic's tale? As for the restraints and cold water, they were regrettable extreme measures imposed only during episodes of unmanageable physical excitability. The kind and clever doctors said so, and that was good enough for most observers. In fact, the kind and clever Foxes indulged in the very type of casual attitude towards incarceration that the 1828 Madhouse Act had sought to stamp out, by touting for patients and making certification appear to be a fast, simple, straightforward procedure. Their 1836 prospectus contains an invitation to obtain blank lunacy certificates from Brislington – giving the impression that taking away a person's liberty was little different to writing out a prescription for gout.

The Foxes claimed that the quickest and longest-lasting cures came about by the removal of the patient from the family home. Associating with strangers and being cared for by skilled staff in the beautiful countryside offered a far better chance of recovering one's wits. Or, for those who were never going to get well, the best environment in which to remain mad. Well-intentioned relatives, according to the Fox ethos, unwittingly worsened the patient's condition; and the excitements of the town could make maniacal paroxysms more likely. But this approach to patient care brought havoc to the Perceval clan, as John mistakenly believed that he had been abandoned by his family, in an isolated spot, so that he would not embarrass them. Dr Fox retained many letters written by Mr Perceval, which he considered likely to distress Lady Carr, and he later told Mr Perceval that he should have been grateful for this, as they had been written when he had been in 'a degraded condition of mind'. Mr Perceval's early letters also contained complaints about his treatment at Brislington, but when Lady Carr eventually received one of them, she found it so full of confusion that she assumed the allegations were groundless. She did not reply, because Dr Fox had advised that this would be bad for the patient. Terrified of making her son more ill, Lady Carr communicated instead with the Foxes.

In a vacuum, with no information from his family, Mr Perceval began to concoct his own explanations for why he had been dumped among strangers instead of being cared for at home. When Spencer did at last visit, he told John that one of the many good things about Brislington was that when he recovered, he could be certain that nobody he knew would ever have seen him in this distressing state. John thought, rather, that it was the shame of the Percevals that was being spared. Lady Carr still had several offspring to marry off and may have feared that, if madness in the family were suspected, important blood alliances would be threatened. Very few of the family's letters and private papers have survived, and so we don't know why it was that only two of the six Perceval daughters married, particularly as they would have been regarded as highly eligible. It may be that they themselves made the decision not to marry because of the fear of hereditary insanity. Nevertheless, if there were fears about passing on a mental illness, such notions only went so far. Half of Chancery lunatics were discovered, in the 1830s, to have relations who were employed by government, often at very senior level. People continued to marry, mingle and employ regardless of any ancestral or parental insanity. John Perceval himself would later state that the notion of insanity passing down through families was seen by the 1830s as a mere 'vulgar error'. While a folk belief in inherited insanity may have fluttered around the minds of many laypeople in these years, and various alienists would hold fast to the hereditarian theory, there was no sense of biological inevitability, yet.

Although we do not have Lady Carr or Spencer's account of John's asylum stay, there is nothing in the letters and documents that have survived to suggest that they were motivated by anything other than the wish for John to recover as quickly and fully as possible. The Percevals had been a notedly loving family, and Lady Carr, now sixty-three, was living happily with her four unmarried daughters. In their distress and terror in the face of John's breakdown, the family had sought out the most highly reputed professional advice on how he could be recovered to himself. Lady Carr had also, it turned out, investigated whether John could be cared for as a single patient in a doctor's house but had been informed that his violent language made him an unsuitable person to be placed in a private residence. John would never forgive his family for bringing between him and themselves a layer of outsiders who had financial and professional motives for keeping him in seclusion. His mother, he wrote, had always been of such a nervous and sensitive condition that she couldn't even bear the sound of a newspaper being opened near to her. But she had willingly overridden her natural maternal feelings in favour of 'this besotted and worse than papist trust' in doctors. 'Shallow-hearted swindlers' and 'ignorant empirics' were just two of his epithets for alienists and asylum proprietors; they were men of 'low origin' and 'little education', unfit to mix with 'a race of the highest antiquity' (that is, the Percevals). 'The revolutionary and infidel liberal principles of the present day,' wrote John, 'mock at high birth, and insolently sneer at long descent as a mere accident, a matter of chance endowing men with no distinction.' It was to these liberals that lunatics had been handed over:

Gentlemen of England . . . that race of presuming upstarts who in various guises admitted by your condescension to terms of familiarity, sit at your tables, hiding their conceit in a false humility and in silky smiles; whilst they ape your manners and dupe your generosity. Be assured, whoever ye are, who have to deal with children or lunatics, if you are not looking after them yourselves you are not respecting them. The doctors know that, and take advantage of it.

When Dr Fox did at last permit correspondence, Lady Carr and other family members kept their messages bland and brief, in the hope that they would not upset John. But he interpreted this as evasion. His mother's short, kind and commonplace letters – on the musk-scented writing paper that reminded him of his childhood – were seen by John as a failure to engage with the issues that concerned him. John's childhood had been full of love, but now he pored over the past and wondered if the whole tribe of Perceval had been dissembling during all those years. When he became ill, his family 'showed me no real desire to inquire, no delicacy, no beauty of feeling'. How could they not wish to understand a 'mystery like that of insanity . . . most grand and most terrible, most important and most instructive'? We must do what the doctors say, was Lady Carr's response to his complaints.

As Mr Perceval calmed still more, in the late summer and autumn of 1831, old Dr Fox would ask him to dine in his family quarters along with 'young Dr Fox and his pretty little wife'. Henry Fox asked Mr Perceval to read Virgil with him, while Charles Joseph Fox suggested he take up woodwork. All the Foxes had a kindness of expression, Mr Perceval noted, which perplexed him all the more in his attempt to understand how they could permit such a coercive regime as Brislington's. The old Bristol merchant opposite him in the bay window had seemed rational and calm in conversation, yet by the summer had been reduced to a creature who messed himself, gobbled at his food, and whose head was sunk on his chest for the rest of the time. 'If I understand the system of Dr Fox's house,' thought Mr Perceval, 'we are allowed to go on as pigs till we come to a right state of mind.'

Other members of the vast, extended Perceval family now also began to send him dull, pointless letters. When Mr Perceval complained to one of his sisters that he had been sat for months in a gloomy room with twelve others 'of no rank, no birth, little education, no

manners, and thoroughly dead to all gentlemanly and moral feelings',
she replied that the first class at Brislington was never going to include
solely the noble families but would contain lesser gentry too; and as
in ordinary life, John would be expected to mix with those of less
gentility and refinement than himself. Mr Perceval did not like this
answer and felt that his family failed to understand the class antagon-
isms at Brislington. On 31 October 1831, the night the Bristol Riots got
under way, Mr Perceval heard the servants and keepers speaking 'very
licentiously and seditiously' of what ought to be done with the gentry
and he became anxious about what revenge might be taken upon
himself and the other captive first-class gents. Two attendants came
into his bedroom since it offered the best spot in the house from
which to view the flames as the city's palace, custom house, gaols and
hundreds of private houses went up. The next day, while botanising
in the shrubbery, Mr Perceval heard two servants predicting a mass
popular uprising, and he rushed into the thicket, crying out, 'Oh! my
country, oh! my country!' Spontaneous riotous celebration had erupted
in a number of towns when his father's assassination was announced,
and the Bristol Riots may well have felt to Mr Perceval like the resumption of an attack upon his father.

Mr Perceval thought that low pay led to the employment of such
ruffians as Samuel Hobbs. In fact, Brislington was paying the going
rate for attendants, and the staff-to-patient ratio was high. Low levels
of staffing were often behind the use of mechanical restraint and
attempts at chemical sedation in the nation's asylums – as cheaper,
easier options than one-on-one surveillance by an attendant – but this
was not the case at Brislington. Mr Perceval believed that the use of
force against a lunatic was wicked and preposterous, and should be
applied only in extreme cases. Indeed, he thought, attendants at
asylums should be recruited solely from the ranks of women, children
and elderly men, whose gentle natures and inability to use force would
assist in the recovery of the mentally troubled. It was kindness that
had gone missing – from family life, lunacy care and from poor old
England in general. As this barbarous century continued, the social
pact was being shattered – the hierarchy, where each had a place and
each had responsibilities as well as dues. Spencer the younger was
doing his best in parliament to hold back the tide of Reform, but the
country was becoming a place where sensibility, generosity, honour

MAIN ENTRANCE LODGE, 1836.

The gateposts and porter's lodge of Brislington House. Mr Perceval left the
asylum on 9 February 1832 after fourteen months of detention.

and civility had no role. Lunatics – like children, like women, like the
honest poor – were being crushed by the profane new age: stamped
on, exploited, overruled. The England of his father and his noble
uncles had been taken over by the smugly ignorant (Dr Fox) and the
brutal (Samuel Hobbs). All winter 1831–32 Mr Perceval turned these
things over in his mind.

Early in the new year his family told him they were willing to give
in to his demands that he leave Brislington. Spencer and one of his
other brothers arrived on 9 February 1832 to remove John. On the
asylum front steps, Mr Perceval bowed to each of the Foxes and shook
hands with Henry and Charles Joseph, who had shown him kindness.
However, Francis Ker's final words were, 'Goodbye Mr Perceval, I
wish I could give you hopes of your recovery.'

If John had expected to return to the Perceval family home, he was
disappointed. The brothers made a two-day journey by carriage to Sussex,
to the equally exclusive Ticehurst Asylum. So furious was John at this
continuance of his incarceration, he refused to shake hands with his
brothers upon their departure. He was relieved, though, at what he found
at Ticehurst. He had his own ground-floor parlour, with a bedroom above,

containing furniture that was not bolted to the floor. The rooms, to him, seemed cosy and cheerful, with a sofa, a mahogany table, a well-stocked bookcase, a lockable desk where he could keep his own papers, and an open fire roaring beneath a marble mantelpiece (the fire tongs were wooden, though, in case of assault). Later, Spencer and his mother sent him a piano. He was also allowed his own toilet items, but he was angry to see that his razor and other sharp implements had been removed from the set. Ticehurst prided itself on its views and ornamental grounds, though alas, Mr Perceval's (barred) windows looked across to the asylum's pigsty and cow yard, barely screened by a small fir plantation.

Although he had begun to recover mentally, Mr Perceval was in poor physical condition when he arrived from Brislington. His teeth had been neglected and were causing him pain, and his toenails had never been cut in his whole fourteen months with the Foxes. His hair still had the peculiar style applied to it by Samuel Hobbs – cropped on top and rats' tails at the back. His nerves were so bad that even the ticking of a watch was painful to him. His new captor, Dr Charles Newington, however, was far easier to get on with – initially at least – and free of the religious cant of the Foxes. Mr Perceval's recovery speeded up as his physical strength returned, in the comparative homeliness of his Ticehurst suite. By May 1832, as far as he was concerned, he was fully sane again.

And this presented his next problem. How could he possibly demonstrate his recovery and win back his freedom? He realised there was no ladder back up into the world from the pit of the asylum, so how was a sane person to clamber into the sunlight? He was to learn that such apparatus as did exist was rickety and treacherous. Mr Perceval came to believe that it might as well not exist at all. The 1828 Madhouse Act stated that before a patient in a provincial asylum could be discharged as sane on the orders of a visiting magistrate, three separate visits would have to be made, each twenty-one days apart. Given that JPs were not obliged to visit an asylum more than four times a year, this could in theory mean delays of at least four months before the discharge of a sane patient. In any case, such discharge could take place only if a magistrate were willing to go against the word of a proprietor and that of the signatory of the patient's lunacy order. Former Brislington patient Trophimus Fulljames, for his part, had alleged cosiness between the magistrates and the Foxes. In fact, the Metropolitan Commissioners in Lunacy had alerted the Home Office to the ongoing laxity in provincial asylum visiting and the inadequacy of returns and other documentation, stating that furthermore, there were no funds set aside to prosecute provincial proprietors who evaded the lunacy laws. Everything depended on the honesty of the local magistrates, and the Metropolitan Commissioners requested that Whitehall send out a circular to the provincial visitors reminding them of their statutory duty to inspect and compile reports. Yet not until 1858 would the Home Office compile a comprehensive list of the provincial visitors – in response to a parliamentary question highlighting how very loose was the government hold on lunacy law implementation outside London. The great Benthamite project of inspection, improvement, efficiency, appeared to be – in lunacy care at least – a phantom: old networks, patronage and corruption clung on in the 1830s asylum world.

Ticehurst proprietor Charles Newington, son of the asylum's founder and fifty years old when Mr Perceval arrived, denied him his wish to travel to London – firstly to consult his lawyer about suing the Foxes; secondly to have two surgeons who had known him since childhood examine him with a view to making affidavits on his physical and mental state; and thirdly to consult a dentist, to help with his decaying mouth. Dr Newington offered the use of his own lawyer instead, which Mr Perceval declined, sensing a trap; Newington recommended a dentist in nearby Tunbridge Wells; and he would hear no talk of London surgeons deciding upon the state of Mr Perceval's mind. But Mr Perceval realised that if he did not swiftly allow a third party to see the physical and nervous trauma caused by the Foxes, his chance of mounting a successful lawsuit would be lost. As each day passed at Ticehurst, Mr Perceval was becoming stronger and calmer, and it was crucial that his lawyer and doctors interviewed him while he still exhibited the damage. As it was, it took many months before Mr Perceval could speak about Brislington without stuttering in broken sentences – a phenomenon that would be used as proof of his continuing unsoundness of mind.

Dr Newington informed him that he was 'a nervous patient', as distinct from a lunatic, and that his confinement would continue no longer than was necessary. To release a patient who was still in the stages of recuperation would be a terrible mistake, the doctor told him: nervous patients must be kept away from anything that would excite them. But Mr Perceval had by now discovered that the exact opposite was true: that it was strange new situations and encounters with other points of view that had revealed his errors of thinking and strengthened his reason. Quiet and seclusion was simply not the answer. Here, thought Mr Perceval – pondering the sophistry of Dr Newington – was yet another man of 'infallible dogmas'. And so a battle of wills began.

Ticehurst Asylum in Sussex. Proprietor Charles Newington (1781–1852) spent a great deal of money creating picturesque and 'therapeutic' scenery in the 60 acres of grounds.

Those family members who replied to John's increasingly furious letters stated that they were unwilling to go against Dr Newington's expert medical advice. Thus, the rift between John and his family grew ever deeper. 'You have all of you shown little sympathy with, and compassion for, my melancholy and, as I thought, desperate situation,' he wrote. 'I would not have left a dog in such circumstances.' But this fury itself became another of Dr Newington's excuses for continuing to recommend Mr Perceval's detention at Ticehurst. For this, Newington was receiving possibly the highest fee for care of a lunatic in the whole country – six and a half guineas a week (half a guinea more than Brislington's highest fee). What is more, the prestige of caring for a member of the Perceval clan added to the renown of the asylum; other wealthy families would want to place their relatives in an institution that was good enough for the son of a prime minister. However, it is also true that Charles Newington used a significant proportion of his profits to reduce the fees of his poorer patients; until 1825 Ticehurst had accommodated a number of pauper patients from the parish, for whose care he had either remitted or reduced payments, as he continued to do for the one-third of his paying patients who were not middle or upper class. Much of his money was also ploughed back into the fabric of the place, in particular the ongoing programme of creating picturesque, therapeutic grounds.

The angrier Mr Perceval became, and the more details he accumulated with which to argue the injustice of his situation, the tighter the net he found himself in. In his diary, he wondered whether his mother was keeping him confined to suppress his involvement in the 'Row Heresy'; but in fact, Spencer resigned his parliamentary seat and his role as a Metropolitan Commissioner in Lunacy in 1832, in order to become an Irvingite 'Apostle', and so John's suspicion had no basis. The Irvingites, for their part, had repudiated John Perceval, saying that his 'speaking in tongues' had been inspired by the Devil, not the Almighty – no doubt fearing a link being made between their practices and lunacy.

John also wondered whether his mother feared that he would return to London to live a life of sensual excess; or that he might harm himself or others. On balance, he decided that it must be the latter: 'My family have not much originality of idea, or independence of mind. They thought, with the world, that lunacy was an impenetrable mystery.' When Lady Carr failed to back him in his plan to sue the Foxes, he ceased writing to her. 'God blast their souls. God damn their eyes. God confound their judgments for ever and ever,' he wrote in his diary. He realised that what was being demanded of him was hypocrisy. Paradoxically, doctors were more likely to view as becoming sane a patient who gave up his or her individuality and autonomy. The patient was required to become a simpleton, with childlike affections, without anger or analytical powers: manhood was replaced by childishness and a slavish adherence to common expectations of social and emotional normality. Mr Perceval said he was brutalised into concealing his true feelings – and that there was thus something profoundly immoral about 'moral treatment'. 'The glory of the old system was coercion by violence; the glory of the modern system is repression by mildness and coaxing, and by solitary confinement', and now the patient 'must learn to kiss the fists that had brutally and unnecessarily cudgelled him'. Quietness in the expensive houses had to be achieved at any cost, Mr Perceval deduced, in order to show that the doctors were in full control.

It was at Ticehurst that the tears came at last. He missed his friends, the company of women and having his own belongings about him; he grieved for a lost childhood and lost family love. He wrote eighty-nine letters at Ticehurst, but, except for those addressed to his siblings, Dr Newington forwarded them all straight to Spencer. Unaware of this, John could not understand why no one – old friends, beloved aunts, uncles and cousins – would reply to him. He was dejected and scared that his confinement would never end. Pity for others had always come upon Mr Perceval. Leaving Brislington, he had promised to write to Captain W——, a seaman with a cork leg, withered arm, dark, expressive eyes and glossy dark hair, who stood all day gazing out of the parlour window, saying nothing except 'Bruim!' occasionally, or insulting the Duke of York. (It is to be feared that Captain W— did not receive the letters, as both Drs Newington and Fox dealt so tightly with patient correspondence.) The plight of some of the men at Ticehurst moved Mr Perceval, too, and it was through this concern for others that a sense of purpose began to take root in him. 'Who shall speak for these if I do not?' as he would later ask. 'Who shall plead for them if I remain silent? How can I betray them and myself too by subscribing to the subtle villainy, cruelty and tyranny of the doctors?' Later still, he would declare himself 'the attorney-general of all Her Majesty's madmen', fighting for those who could not defend themselves. There was Charles Nunn, a wealthy old man who spent the final nine years of his life quietly in his rooms at Ticehurst; a huge proportion of his money had gone into the Newington pocket when all he wanted was to be lodged with a sympathetic carer as a single patient. Then there was Mr B—— who believed that he was to be boiled alive at the Brunswick Theatre; when he was walking in the Ticehurst grounds, voices would call to him, 'Look here, Harry!' from the bushes, but when he went to look, there was never anybody there. His derangement was said to have been brought on by heavy drinking. Alexander Goldsmid was an elderly Jewish man who had converted to Christianity; stout, short, with white hair and a merry face, he spoke several languages and was developing new techniques in bridge construction. He and Mr

Perceval became good companions and John thought that his friend was probably not mad – or at least not mad enough to be in an asylum. During their long therapeutic walks in Ticehurst's gardens together, Mr Perceval noted Goldsmid's habit of saying funny things seriously and serious things as though they were a joke. All he missed about the outside world were his children, he admitted. Mr Goldsmid would often come in and play Mr Perceval's piano at breakfast time, and could sometimes be seen crying over the Bible.

Such friendships helped to make up for what Mr Perceval saw as the shortcomings of his Ticehurst attendants. Hervey the butler infuriated Mr Perceval by pouring out his medicine one day with the words, 'Pretty colour, isn't it, sir?', as though he was a child. After getting rid of two local lads in succession, for insubordination, Mr Perceval ended up with young Tom Rolfe as his servant, who quickly disappointed him by never having heard of the House of Lords and claiming that he only washed himself once a year. After Mr Perceval made a run for it one day, while out walking with Rolfe, he was condemned to have the servant sit with him all day, and to be manacled at night, with Rolfe and another male servant sleeping in his room. He was no longer allowed to be alone.

Ticehurst's position on a hilltop was not appreciated by Mr Perceval, who noted angrily in his diary every time a cold northerly blew, and he would spend hours by the fire with his feet on the fender. Now that the spirit voices had departed, a thousand indignities intruded themselves upon his thoughts. He disliked the fact that he could be watched by so many people – the staff and patients, both indoors and in the grounds. He felt exposed and under surveillance. He was not able to lock anyone out, but the doors of his suite could be bolted from the outside and had a peephole. He was not even allowed a lock on his own privy, and many a time a servant would pull open the door and see him at stool. His excrement was to be left in the pan and not removed until a physician had been to examine it, as a marker of physical health.

Privacy and dignity were thus persistently denied to those shattered souls who probably had greatest need of them. In the corridors outside his rooms, the high jinks of the servants, attendants and patients – running, whistling, singing, fluting, fiddling, jig-dancing and wrestling – made him ever more irritable. Much more enraging, though, were his interactions with the local magistracy and the asylum's visiting

physician, Dr Thomas Mayo. Three Sussex justices of the peace were
the parties who were supposed to comprise the safeguard against the
incarceration of the sane, or the prolonged detention in an asylum
of a patient who had recovered. Mr Perceval was lying on his sofa
one rainy Monday morning with his waistcoat unbuttoned, reading
Henry IV Part 2, when his own Justices Silence and Shallow burst in,
accompanied by Dr Newington and Dr Mayo. Asked if he had any
complaints, Mr Perceval told them that it was clear that he was recovered and should be allowed to leave; his detention here was solely to
allow Dr Newington to earn even more in fees and in repute. He
complained that he was never allowed one moment alone, but he was
interrupted and told that he was imagining these things; it became
apparent to Mr Perceval that the JPs were not going to listen to him
and try to understand his concerns. 'The magistrates are little better
than the mere executors of the laws that confine the liberty of the
subject,' Mr Perceval decided. For his part, Dr Mayo commented that
his complaints were frivolous and that Lady Carr was doing her utmost
to help her son. Couldn't he see that? Mayo spent the rest of the
interview gazing out of the window at the pigsty.

When the visitors had left, Mr Perceval realised that in his haste to
fasten up his waistcoat, he had wrongly buttoned it and he feared that
this dishevelment had undermined his claim that he was of sound
mind. How unfair it was, he thought, that doctors and magistrates
could expect an individual who had been through his terrible ordeal
instantly to regain the demeanour and tone of voice of someone
unscathed by mental torment. Mr Perceval began to keep a small
looking-glass in his pocket, and after any interaction with another
person he would whip it out to check whether his facial expressions
might appear to be those of a madman.

Dr Newington seemed to find ever new grounds to prove that Mr
Perceval was still not fit to be at large. Why, the very fact of his arguing
that he was sane was proof that he was not; plus his hostility to his
family; plus being so finicky about Tom Rolfe and the high jinks in the
corridor. And then there was his appearance. After the ludicrous haircut
he had been given at Brislington, and the removal of the whiskers he
had cultivated since adolescence, Mr Perceval was determined to reas-
sert his individuality by growing his hair and beard long; his hair he
arranged in ringlets, partly to hide the disfigurement to his left ear and

temple. This was a more 'natural' and manly look, he believed. But one of his sisters wrote to him to say that the doctors had told the family that the wildness of his hair was proof of his ongoing mental infirmity.

So his hair grew, the months passed, and Mr Perceval wrote his thoughts down in his peevish diary, the stupidities of Rolfe and the shifting direction of the gales blowing up the hill and into Ticehurst both featuring large. He busied himself in teaching one of the attendants to read and write, and in practising the piano (badly). Then, surprisingly, ten months after his arrival at Ticehurst, his family did yield to his requests. It was announced to him that he was to be released into the private care of Dr Robert Stedman of Sevenoaks in Kent, with whom he was to live, so that his readiness to be discharged from his lunacy certificates could be monitored. This was how the Metropolitan Commissioners in Lunacy liked to proceed with patients who were becoming calmer and quieter – gradually to reintroduce them into outside life, with no sudden shock upon re-entry to society, which could trigger a relapse.

Mr Perceval wrote very little about his time as a single patient. He was finally discharged from his certificates in October 1833, when, as Dr Stedman would later write, 'Lady Carr thought proper to allow him to have his liberty, altho' he could not then be said to be perfectly sane, and the family physician, Dr Tattersall of Ealing, stated to Lady Carr that if she did let him have his liberty he would very soon do some foolish act that she would repent of.' The 'foolish act', in Stedman's view, was Mr Perceval's marriage, in March 1834, to Anna Gardiner, the daughter of a Sevenoaks cheesemonger, which Dr Stedman declared was a match 'quite out of his station in life'. The marriage was to be a long and happy one, and once again reveals that odd clash within Mr Perceval of aristocratic hauteur and a genuine love for individuals whatever their social background.

Dr Stedman was additionally infuriated by Mr Perceval's zealous campaigning on behalf of the labouring classes. The Poor Law Amendment Act ('New Poor Law') was passed in 1834 but Mr Perceval had led a vigorous campaign in Kent against the introduction of the new workhouse system and its buildings – the 'bastilles' in which families would be split up, wife torn from husband and children from parents. The romantic High Toryism of his father and eldest brother reveals itself in the series of pamphlets and handbills that John wrote, printed and distributed around Kent and Sussex and which Dr Stedman bundled up and posted to Whitehall, informing the Home Secretary that they were 'calculated to inflame the lower orders'. ('Please do not let on I have written this,' the craven doctor added at the end of his letter.) The enclosed literature comprised cogent attacks on the New Poor Law, the appalling conditions prevailing in workhouses and the assault upon a working man's self-respect by this brutal new regime. The link between these 'modern' attitudes to the poor and the treatment of lunatics was clear in Mr Perceval's mind: 'The author feels assured that some lunatic doctor, or some patron or intimate ally of lunatic doctors, has devised and concocted the New Poor Law and its machinery,' he wrote. Once again, 'the infidel spirit of modern "liberality"' was wreaking social havoc.

Mr and Mrs Perceval headed for Paris in 1835, and here the first two of their four daughters were born. Here, Mr Perceval set about the painful task of recalling and writing down in detail all that had happened to him. *A Narrative of the Treatment Experienced by a Gentleman during a State of Mental Derangement; Designed to Explain the Causes and the Nature of Insanity and to Expose the Injudicious Conduct Pursued towards many Unfortunate Sufferers under that Calamity* is an extraordinarily insightful account of mental disintegration, but also shows how a mind can return itself to health. In its indictment of the prevailing medical attitudes to mental illness, and the sheer cruelty practised at Brislington, the book foreshadowed by 130 years arguments that would be put forward by the anti-psychiatry movement. Its recommendations and analyses proved remarkably prescient. Mr Perceval believed that patients were best placed to inform their carers of the nature of their problem, and instead of ridiculing the seeming nonsense of the patient's speech, what was required was a sympathetic attempt to unravel the source of distress. This task was best undertaken by those who knew the patient well – family, old friends or general physicians of long acquaintance. It was no task to be given to a money-minded, vainglorious stranger. A lunatic was an individual, with an individual cause of his or her illness, and required an individually tailored attempt at cure. 'Many persons confined as lunatics are only so because they are not understood, and continue so because they do not understand themselves,' Mr Perceval wrote. Instead, lunatics had to surrender their bodies and minds to the doctors, who were permitted to work their mischief or test their misguided and unproven theories upon them.

The mad-doctors made the mistake of thinking that lunatics had no feeling; but in fact it was the flight from their extreme sensitivity that could lead patients to behave with either boisterousness and impudence or the very opposite, apathy and passivity. That is not an absence of feeling, but the inability to cope with strong emotion. More metaphysically, Mr Perceval believed that the phenomena of lunacy were common to all humankind, which was evident in such things as a slip of the tongue or a misread sentence. In both lunacy and these 'sane slips', 'the phenomenon is the same – the organs of speech are made use of without the volition, or rather intention, of the person speaking'. The 1840s were a time when theorising about what we now call the subconscious was making significant advances, and Mr Perceval stated that he thought the mind always ran in terms of opposites, which he believed proved the residence within the brain 'of two distinct powers, or agents, or wills'.

Mr Perceval's reflections were pearls before swine. The first (anonymous) volume of *A Narrative* was largely ignored in 1838; and when Mr Perceval published an enlarged second volume under his own name two years later, the influential *Examiner* was sniffy: 'The chief branch of his complaint, urged through some hundreds of most vituperative pages, is that sufficient distinction was not made between himself and lunatics of inferior rank. He does not seem to think even that dreadful disease a leveller in the least.' But the reviewer admitted that while 'much regretting the publication of this book, we should by no means despair of its redeeming many evil tendencies by some good if the grievances to which it refers in such a melancholy spirit of exaggeration attract the attention of some moderate or well-informed person'. The *Dublin University Magazine*'s brief mention of the work praised Mr Perceval's courage in revealing himself to have been a madman, as well the acuteness of his criticism: 'Details such as he has given are rarely communicated to the public.'

But far more significant than any reviews of his book was something he spotted in the autumn of 1838, by which time he was living with his wife and baby daughters in Notting Hill Square, West London. On 8 October, 'by a singular and providential occurrence', he picked up a copy of *The Times*, and saw this:

MR. PATERNOSTER.

TO THE EDITOR OF THE TIMES.

Sir,—It is due to Mr. Richard Paternoster, whose seizure and confinement as an insane person have excited so much interest, that the public should be informed, that after a full investigation of the circumstances by the Metropolitan Commissioners in Lunacy (set on foot immediately upon their being made acquainted with the fact), and after a detention of six weeks in Mr. Finch's Lunatic Asylum, at Kensington, he has been released. We are, Sir, your most obedient servants,   LAKE AND CURTIS

Solicitors to Mr. Richard Paternoster

11 Basinghall-street, October 5, 1838

3

The Alleged Lunatics' Friend Society

Richard Paternoster had been certified into Kensington House Asylum in London by his father, surgeon John Paternoster, following a row about money. Thirty-five-year-old Richard had been found a position as a clerk to the East India Company by his father and had worked in Madras before ill health forced his return to England after just three years. The Company had agreed a pension of £150 per annum, which it paid to Paternoster's father, on the understanding that it would be disbursed to Richard. This failed to happen, and Richard found himself living from hand to mouth, finding sporadic employment as a freelance journalist in London, contributing articles to various Radical publications. He wrote his father a series of increasingly threatening-sounding letters (he had intended them to be satirical and scornful, he later said; 'very saucy' was his term for the language he had used).

At around eight o'clock on the morning of Friday 24 August 1838 Richard was getting dressed at his lodgings at 49 Haymarket when two men burst in and attempted to pinion him. A long and violent struggle followed, and his landlady, Mrs Scott, called in a policeman from the street, who established that the assailants, Launcelot Sharpe and George Hillier, were asylum attendants, who had an order for the apprehension of Paternoster. The policeman had no idea how to proceed and insisted that all three men come with him to Marlborough Street magistrates' court. Here, a number of newspaper reporters were milling around, waiting to hear if any of the night charges would turn out to be interesting snippets for the news columns, and this is how Richard Paternoster's plight drew immediate press interest. He was of 'very gentlemanly' appearance and had clearly been badly beaten, yet was putting up an articulate verbal struggle. He certainly didn't seem mad. Despite this, Magistrate Dyer refused to offer Paternoster any protection, after having read through the two lunacy certificates and the lunacy order – signed by Richard's father – testifying to his insanity. The reporters heard Paternoster arguing every point incisively with Dyer, and the *Times* representative reported the next day: 'The answers to the questions put to Mr Paternoster indicated quite as large a portion of rationality, and infinitely more cleverness, than possessed by the querist [Dyer].' It is also tempting to conclude that the gentlemen of the press had spotted one of their own in a dreadful situation, and that this contributed to their desire to champion him. Nevertheless, when the asylum owner, William Finch, arrived, Paternoster was thrust into a hackney coach and carried west, to Kensington House.

Richard Paternoster got himself officially discharged from confinement and certification in a record forty-one days and had no hesitation in attributing this not to those alleged safeguards of liberty, the Metropolitan Commissioners in Lunacy, but 'to the blessings of a free press'. His trusty landlady had kept the news-papers fed with the background to the story. 'You have behaved like a mother to me,' wrote Paternoster to Mrs Scott in a letter dated 27 August, in which he gave her detailed instructions on which bills of his would soon fall due and whom she should contact about this. 'I sink rapidly with pining,' he continued, and went on to tell of filth, degradation and violent assaults made upon some of the patients. The female nurse made repeated, aggressive sexual approaches to him. There had even been a murder, he claimed – the man in the next room, John Milroy, was beaten to death by the attendant, three weeks after Paternoster's arrival. Mrs Scott copied the 27 August letter for each of the national newspapers, and thus Paternoster's case achieved in a matter of hours the type of furore that John Perceval's *Narrative* had failed to bring about in the same year. A London magistrate who had for many months regularly witnessed and co-signed financial and legal paperwork for Paternoster visited him at Kensington House, found him as sane as he had ever been, and personally agitated for the Metropolitan Commissioners to visit and investigate the case in full. The Commissioners spent an unprecedented three days of five-hour sittings deciding the Paternoster case, with the chairman declaring (without substantiation):

> A more heartless ruffian, one more low in mind and coarse in language, though a man of talent and education, never entered the walls of a prison or a madhouse. The opposite party, however, could not prove against him one single act of personal violence; his words, his manner, his feelings, were awfully wicked; but had never as yet broken out into action. In fact, a decision on our part, that he was rightfully detained, would have authorised the incarceration in a Bedlam of seven-tenths of the human race who have ever been excited to violence of speech and gesture.

Reluctantly – and with a majority verdict of six to four – the Commissioners declared Paternoster sane and free to leave Kensington House.

Kensington House Asylum, demolished in 1872, stood on the south side of Kensington Road, and Kensington Palace is visible in the left background. The wall in the asylum garden divided the genders.

During his forty-one days in the asylum, Paternoster had used his journalistic and clerical talents to attempt a survey of his thirty-seven male fellow inmates (there were twenty-five female patients, too, but the sexes were segregated and so he had little chance to speak to any of the women). He believed that many of the males were perfectly sane, and stated that he had found not one case of what could be termed 'mania', while others were merely 'imbecile', or 'weak-minded', or elderly and confused. Every one of these men would have benefited from being in a non-custodial environment, Paternoster believed, and after asking them how they came to be at Kensington House, he concluded that many had been 'put away' in order that their property and money could be controlled. Of the thirty-three male patients that Paternoster did get to speak to, eighteen knew who had put them into the asylum: eight had been confined by a wife; four by a mother; three by a father; one by a sister; one by a brother; and one by a son. Paternoster recognised that only the press interest – which had come about purely by the lucky coincidence that the newsmen were at Marlborough Street as his plight was being heard – had saved him from becoming just like these men, enduring a lifetime in unlawful imprisonment.

In early October 1838 he instructed his solicitors to write to *The Times* that he was now free; and Mr Perceval, reading the letter, and fascinated to hear that Paternoster had succeeded in being freed by the Commissioners, got in touch right away.

So did William Bailey, an inventor and businessman in his late forties, who had managed to lose a substantial amount of money in a speculation in the early 1830s. His wife then had him committed into Hoxton House Asylum in East London, in October 1835, assisted by Mr Bailey's brothers, who also wanted to put a stop to his 'extravagant' behaviour. He spent fifteen months at Hoxton House until the Metropolitan Commissioners freed him. The following year, he spotted Paternoster's solicitor's letter in *The Times*; in responding to it he also met Mr Perceval, and he told both men – who had by now formed a friendship – of his plight. They promised to help him fight in the courts for redress for this wrongdoing; but Mrs Bailey and the brothers were on the march again, and with the help of a pliable pair of doctors, they had Bailey re-committed. At each madhouse he was taken to, the proprietors expressed reluctance to detain Bailey longer than a few days, as there appeared to be nothing even eccentric about him. And so the family moved him from the lunatics' ward of the Tothill Fields bridewell in Westminster, to Warburton's in Bethnal Green, to Kensington House, to Tow's madhouse just behind the church at Battersea. Here, Messrs Paternoster and Perceval would hang about beneath Mr Bailey's window at dusk, and Mr Bailey was able to throw down to them documents that included written permission for Mr Perceval to act for him in his battle to be declared sane. But then Mr Bailey was moved again, this time to Fairford House Asylum in Gloucestershire. The Metropolitan Commissioners informed Messrs Paternoster and Perceval that they were considering Mr Bailey's case, but that each time they wished to interview him, he would be whisked off to a new asylum on the orders of Mrs Bailey, which they were reluctant to countermand; their much-preferred mode of proceeding was to persuade the person who had signed the lunacy order to accept that the patient had regained his or her sanity and to permit the liberation. This approach often worked, but whenever a signatory refused to compromise, the Commissioners were shown to be nervous and ineffectual about using the powers they possessed to free a patient. Richard Paternoster claimed that the Metropolitan Commissioners had never revoked a private madhouse licence, and had only ever mounted one prosecution of a lunacy doctor.

The packages tossed from the window of Tow's allowed Perceval and Paternoster to compile a petition which they hoped to present to both the House of Commons and the House of Lords. Using his family's extensive social and political connections, Mr Perceval requested Sir Henry Hardinge, the War Secretary, to present Mr Bailey's case to the Commons, and the Duke of Wellington to present it to the Lords. He received an evasive answer from the former and 'a cold, forbidding reply' from the latter, which disgusted Mr Perceval, who wrote of 'these High, but not high-minded, Tories, despising the prisoner's prayer and being unwilling to mix up their reputation with that of one under the cloud of the imputation of lunacy'. Captain George Brooke-Pechell, the Radical Liberal MP for Brighton, agreed to present the Bailey petition, but the Commons took no notice of it.

Mr Bailey was eventually freed by the Gloucestershire magistrates in September 1842. He intended to fight a common-law case against his conspirators but found – as had so many released alleged lunatics – that he had neither the money nor the mental energy for the battle, which had to be started within six months of liberation. What's more, all his personal papers and other chattels had been confiscated by his wife and brothers during his incarceration, something that had also happened to Richard Paternoster during his time at Kensington House. The loss of documentation had the potential to undermine any legal case the men might wish to bring. Mr Bailey had also suffered the loss of his potentially lucrative drawings of concepts for improving the design of mail coaches and for the widening and lowering of Blackfriars Bridge. Mr Bailey and Mr Paternoster never got their belongings back.

This 1840 illustration, by Dickens's illustrator Hablot Knight Browne ('Phiz'), is a comic take on the popular anxiety that a sane person could be mistaken for a lunatic. The man on the left is, in fact, insane but has persuaded an asylum keeper that the sane man is a lunatic, and the greedy and ignorant keeper duly hauls away the wrong man.

And then there were four: Lewis Phillips was a manufacturer of glass-wares and lamps who ran his profit-making Regent-Street-based firm in partnership with his brothers, Samuel and Ralph. On 18 March 1838 he was seized by keepers from Thomas Warburton's madhouse and taken in a hackney coach to one of his notoriously ill-managed and brutally run asylums. Six months later, when Phillips felt that if he could not get free he would indeed become insane, he finally agreed to sign a document that his brothers had repeatedly put in front of him – relinquishing all his interest and rights in the firm. He signed on 8 September and, as part of the deal, was immediately taken to St Katharine Docks and put on board the *Antwerpen*, bound for the Belgian city. Here, recovering his equilibrium, he regretted the bargain, returned to England, arranged to visit his mother in the Edgware Road but fell into the trap that she had sprung: Mrs Phillips was in on the plot and had alerted Samuel and Ralph, who arrived with Warburton's keepers. Lewis Phillips made a run for it and managed to remain free. He was utterly ruined but was determined to obtain any redress that Messrs Perceval and Paternoster could suggest.

The small band was growing: Captain Richard Saumarez, RN, had for years been concerned about Chancery lunatics and the vulnerability of their fortunes to unauthorised and unaudited charges – and sometimes even outright theft. An Act to improve their situation had been passed in 1833, increasing official visitation and laying down new rules for those who administered their estates, but in Captain Saumarez's view the Act had failed significantly to improve the lot of the Chancery patient. The captain had two brothers who had been confined by their father (not incorrectly, in the captain's view, though he believed single-patient care would have been more appropriate): Frederick Saumarez had been in Brooke House, Clapton, since 1823, and Paul, a vicar, in Cowper House, Chelsea, since 1834. As a teenage midshipman aboard the *Spartan* during the Napoleonic Wars, Captain Saumarez had helped pulverise several castles on the Adriatic coast; now he was laying siege to the lunacy laws.

The group was joined by surgeon John Parkin, a much-published epidemiologist. He was pondering whether there was a connection between malaria and volcanic eruptions, and whether cholera was linked to tropical hurricanes, when he suffered a breakdown; he then spent time in an asylum and became concerned at madhouse conditions. Even more muscle came a little later, with the arrival in their circle of Luke James Hansard, of the parliamentary-printer firm, whose family had two female members in asylum care; and solicitor Gilbert Bolden, who was filled with alarm that a sane English citizen could be 'disappeared' if a sufficiently malevolent person should wish to exploit the lunacy law loopholes.

Buoyed by the financial and moral support of the Perceval–Paternoster group, some of the asylum survivors managed to mount their own legal cases, in default of any statutory right to a hearing and compensation. Richard Paternoster himself sued his father and the other conspirators and won; while Lewis Phillips won £170 from his family and Thomas Warburton when he sued them for conspiracy.

The group had no formal identity yet, and each man was happy to tackle one particular aspect of the cause or to join with another in a campaign of letter-writing, pamphleteering and the lobbying of MPs and government departments with demands for change. They sought a total overhaul of asylum admission procedures, including the right to a jury hearing for anyone accused of being of unsound mind: the jury system, they believed, was 'the privilege which belongs to every Englishman, of knowing his accusers, the charges brought against him, and of being present at every examination relating to his case, in person, or by attorney'. They also wanted an appeals system that would rescue from confinement anyone who had recovered their wits after certification. Additionally, a magistrate should examine all certificates, whether of pauper or private patients, before any asylum admission, and should be satisfied that asylum care was the best course of action for that individual. The Scottish lunacy certification system interposed the figure of the local sheriff, and many wished that English legislators would use the magistracy in this way, to make asylum admission a civic, not purely medical, matter – removing the final say from physicians.

The men felt that there was an urgent need, too, for coroners' hearings to be held whenever a patient died in care; and for an invigorated new inspection system to stamp out the appalling treatment and poor conditions each man had witnessed for himself. To defeat the greedy, they advised that, the moment any patient was certificated, his or her property be placed in government hands and invested in safe government bonds and gilts, so that the full sum could be returned to the patient upon recovery. 'By such a provision, the public would completely defeat the ends and manoeuvres of the evil-designing,' declared the group, in its first annual report. 'No immediate member of the family, or other relation, or base deceiving friend, could then have any pecuniary interest in irritating such will, upon base motives, from its quiescent daily rule of home duties, or from its social peace.' Most urgently, the men demanded a Select Committee to inquire into the entire lunacy system of England and Wales.

In this battle, they faced one obstacle even more enormous than apathy and lack of parliamentary time. Anthony Ashley Cooper was the ultra-Evangelical Tory peer whose efforts on behalf of the downtrodden were conferring on him a saint-like status. (Cooper was known as Lord Ashley until 1851, when he became the seventh Earl of Shaftesbury; for convenience, he will be referred to here as Shaftesbury.) He would die in 1885 immensely proud that he still had the same outlook and opinions he had formulated in early adolescence. To many, this was very unfortunate, since he positioned himself at, or close to, the heart of most social questions between the late 1820s and mid-1880s. John Perceval wrote that 'it is known how much weakness and futility is combined in him, with much nobleness and generosity'. Others were much harsher: Thomas Mulock, a journalist who campaigned to improve the lunacy laws, believed that Shaftesbury was 'void of the honest manliness which openly retracts error . . . wriggling himself into notice with fresh schemes of sham benevolence'; while a later opponent simply called him 'a Jesuitical old humbug'.

His early fame came with his agitation for the protection of child industrial labourers – particularly the infant mine-workers – which then broadened into moves to provide education for pauper children (on a charitable basis) and to improve the housing of the working classes. The poor were not to be empowered to improve their own lot, or to increase their own rights: Shaftesbury deplored trades unionism and the concept of universal suffrage. Instead, it was for gentlemen to reach down and offer the hand of kindness and charity. Unfortunately for the Perceval–Paternoster circle of agitators, Shaftesbury next directed his benevolence towards the nation's lunatics, and in 1834 became chairman of the Metropolitan Commissioners. The immense respect he had won appeared to allow Shaftesbury the final word on all matters concerning madness. As his diary entries reveal, the important public role of chairman had been filled by a gentleman-amateur who felt evangelically obliged to take on these tasks as part of his portfolio of worldly burdens:

[I] Did not wish for such an employment, but duty made it imperative. Walked after dinner to Kensington and studied a little astronomy . . . Saw the planet Saturn and his ring; it is a spectacle worthy of God alone . . . There is nothing poetical in this duty; but every sigh prevented and every pang subdued, is a song of harmony to the heart.

Anthony Ashley Cooper, the seventh Lord Shaftesbury (1801–1885), was appointed chairman of the lunacy commissioners in 1834, a position he held until death.

Here was a man straight from the social, political and religious world of John Perceval, and they had been near-contemporaries at Harrow; but their mature views diverged widely. While Shaftesbury took pride in his unchanging opinions, Mr Perceval's breakdown had brought him the freedom to examine an issue from many viewpoints and had hugely enlarged his range of sympathies. And Mr Perceval would come to change his mind on important aspects of the lunacy question: on the role of the local magistracy he would move from despairing disapproval of the provincial JPs to a keen advocacy of localism; and he would shift from an appreciation that private asylums could offer a discreet alternative to the county asylum system, to viewing all private madhouse proprietorship as inherently corrupt. His detractors saw these changes of heart as evidence of ongoing intellectual infirmity; rather, they show an analytical mind that constantly turned over each subtle point, attempting, across three decades, to reach what Mr Perceval felt were the correct conclusions.

Mr Perceval wrote of Shaftesbury that he could 'scarcely believe that he is the man that was educated with us at Harrow – that gentlemanly and public-spirited school'. Both men wondered in the 1830s what should be done to offset the worst social and cultural effects of industrialism–mercantilism. As High Tories, they would have preferred that the pastoral landlord–tenant nexus had never ended, but it had – so was it for the state or for certain spiritually enlightened individuals to counter the ill effects of the new age? Mr Perceval eventually (and reluctantly) came to the conclusion that only state intervention would have had the power, when he was asylum-bound, to free him and to do so publicly, as a warning to others. However, he could not let go of the notion that small, less visible, private pressures should be brought to bear in policing the nation's asylums. A point of conflict with Captain Saumarez was Mr Perceval's insistence that men of God should be appointed at every level of lunacy care – as inspectors, magistrates and asylum staff. He appeared, in his campaigning, to be seeking a Benthamite big-state, but with individual churchmen operating at the blunt end. Bringing God into everything irritated some of his fellow campaigners but it is something that Shaftesbury did too, which made the two men odd opponents, when they agreed on so many first principles.

The campaigners got nowhere with their demands for a lunacy Select Committee. However, there was immense behind-the-scenes activity in the early 1840s. An Act of 1842 expanded the staff of the Metropolitan Commissioners by two barristers and two doctors and allowed them a trial period of three years to extend their remit beyond the metropolis to include inspection of all types of institution where lunatics might be kept throughout the nation (including charitable hospitals, the lunatic wards of workhouses, prisons housing the criminally insane, and military and naval hospitals). One of the fruits of this expansion beyond London was the report of the Commission in 1844 to the Lord Chancellor, which recounted many of the poor conditions and patient abuses that Mr

Perceval and others had been publicising for years. It may well be the case that the torrent of eyewitness accounts and criticism coming from Mr Perceval and his associates had percolated into official minds – so that while being officially shunned, the campaigners were instead succeeding slowly by the 'transmission of ideas', as one historian has noted.

With regard to wrongful incarceration, worries were expressed in the 1844 report regarding a small number of individuals confined in public asylums and charitable hospitals; but no private licensed house was cited in connection with doubtful certification or prolonged detention. The individuals concerned were, according to the Metropolitan Commissioners, 'persons who are termed morally insane, about the propriety of whose detention there are frequently great doubts'. However, they stated that: 'We have rarely found any patient confined in a lunatic asylum who, as far as we could judge, had been sent there whilst in a decidedly sane state.' Rather, they believed, there had been a strong social or moral, rather than medical, case for incarceration: habitual drunkards who either assaulted their wives and families or threatened to do so; 'imbeciles' and 'idiots' who exposed themselves or otherwise behaved indecently in public; a wife who had repeatedly threatened to poison her husband; a 'quarrelsome idiot' who had threatened to stab someone. Instead of malicious certification, the Commissioners concluded, the larger problem was the difficulty in deciding when recovery had occurred and at what point liberation should take place – John Perceval's very own problem of 1832, in fact.

This validation of the status quo within the private asylum system was no help at all to Mr Perceval and his fellow campaigners. Nor were a series of infamous murders in 1843. On Saturday 22 April, thirty-seven-year-old William Ferry escaped from Mr Kent's Asylum at Sheriff Hill in Gateshead, near Newcastle, and returned to his family home on the quayside at Monkwearmouth. Here, his wife, Hannah, and his father-in-law deliberately baffled the keepers' attempts at recapture, claiming they did not know Ferry's whereabouts. On the Monday morning, Mrs Ferry went to the local Poor Law officer, admitted that she was sheltering her husband and implored that he be allowed to stay at home with her and their children, since the insanity for which he had been incarcerated for two years had been cured. The official noted how rational Mr Ferry appeared, and how much in need of a male wage the family was, and so agreed to this, writing to Mr Kent that he would not return his patient. That night, Ferry battered to death his wife and adolescent daughter. At his trial at Durham Assizes three months later, the jury found him not guilty by reason of insanity, and Ferry spent the rest of his life confined as a criminal lunatic.

Also in 1843, delusional Glasgow woodturner turned actor Daniel M'Naughten fired a pistol into the back of Prime Minister Robert Peel's private secretary, Edward Drummond, believing Drummond to be Peel himself. Drummond died from the infection in the wound. Twenty-seven-year-old M'Naughten had been haunting Whitehall for days in search of his quarry, believing that he was under surveillance by the Tory party at all hours of the day: 'They follow and persecute me wherever I go, and have destroyed my peace of mind . . . In fact, they wish to murder me,' he claimed. M'Naughten went on to make English legal history: the 'M'Naughten Rules' laid down for over a century the parameters of what could and could not constitute insanity in a legal defence at a murder trial. M'Naughten spent the rest of his life as a criminal lunatic, dying in Broadmoor Hospital in 1865.

Then there was the case of artist Richard Dadd, who had become insane and dispatched his father with a knife and razor in Cobham Park, Kent, in August 1843, and then attempted to kill a passenger as he fled by boat to France. He was committed to Royal Bethlehem Hospital the following year, before being transferred to Broadmoor.

These cases of 1843 provided extremely stony ground in which Mr Perceval tried to plant his proposals to minimise custodial care for the unsound of mind. The madman who did not appear to be mad had reappeared in the English public mind, in his most bloody mode. Ferry, M'Naughten and Dadd were full-blown delusionals who had walked the streets with no obvious markers of insanity about them. Who now cared if a few eccentrics were taken out of circulation if this was the price of protecting public safety? Reports of lunatics and 'idiots' being killed in asylums or single-patient care did shock the nation but failed to match the terror that mad-folk evoked in the public – and legislative – imagination. No matter how much genuine sympathy Mr Perceval and his friends were able to drum up, fear of lunatics triumphed every time.

But then in the spring of 1845, the campaigners got wind of Shaftesbury's plans for an overhaul of English lunacy legislation, and realised that it was time to consolidate their separate and slightly diffuse efforts. They decided to become the Alleged Lunatics' Friend Society – an unwieldy name that mockers would reformulate as 'The Lunatics' Society'. The apostrophe would wander around from time to time in their own publications, and sometimes an 's' would be added to 'Friend', all of which reinforced the impression of a quaint and rather unworldly set of naïfs, all at sea in a world of parliamentarians, Lord Chancellors, doctors, lawyers and asylum keepers. The Society announced their arrival by taking out newspaper advertisements such as the one opposite.

Luke James Hansard complained about 'the railway speed and confusing commotion of this legislative proceeding'; writing that these 'lunatic bills' were 'steaming hot-headedly on their course', while what was required was the calm consideration that a Select Committee would bring. However, members of parliament and other influential men did begin to lend an ear to the evidence that the Alleged Lunatics' Friend Society had collected. Around eight Liberal MPs and an equal number of Tories gave their backing to the Society, both sets of parliamentarians being opposed for their different reasons to the monolithic, centralised Poor-Law-style lunacy administration that was being hatched. Though the Society would never number more than sixty full members, and received little funding from any source other than its membership's own pockets, it attracted some heavyweight backing. Most prominent among its supporters were Thomas Wakley, Radical Liberal MP, founder (in 1823) of *The Lancet* and coroner for Middlesex; and Thomas Slingsby Duncombe, also a Radical Liberal MP, champion of Chartism, religious liberty and prisoners' rights. New cases were continually making contact and calling at the Society's offices, which were originally in Coleman Street, near the Bank of England, and subsequently at Gilbert Bolden's place of residence, 44 Craven Street, Charing Cross.

*   *   *

ALLEGED LUNATICS' FRIEND SOCIETY,

founded July, 1845.—At a MEETING of several Gentlemen feeling deeply interested in behalf of their fellow-creatures, subjected to confinement as lunatic patients,

It was unanimously resolved :—

That a Society be now formed, to be entitled "The Lunatics' Friend Society," and it has subsequently been agreed to name the same "The Alleged Lunatics' Friend Society."

That this Society is formed for the protection of the British subject from unjust confinement, on the grounds of mental derangement, and for the redress of persons so confined; also for the protection of all persons confined as lunatic patients from cruel and improper treatment.

That this Society will receive applications from persons complaining of being unjustly treated, or from their friends, aid them in obtaining legal advice, and otherwise assist and afford them all proper protection.

That the Society will endeavour to procure a reform in the laws and treatment affecting the arrest, detention, and release of persons treated as of unsound mind.

VICE-PRESIDENTS.

Lord Viscount Lake	Hon. W. N. Ridley Colborne, M.P.
James Ackers, Esq., M.P.	T. Slingsby Duncombe, Esq., M.P.
W. Bagge, Esq., M.P.	Major-Gen. W. A. Johnson, M.P.
Sir H. Winston Barron, Bart., M.P.	Sir John W. Lubbock, Bart.
Peter Borthwick, Esq., M.P.	S. C. H. Ogle, Esq., M.P.
Col. Henry Bruen, M.P.	John Patrick Somers, Esq., M.P.
R. A. Christopher, Esq., M.P.	Edmund Turner, Esq., M.P.
W. Sharman Crawford, Esq., M.P.	The Hon. C. Pelham Villiers, M.P.

Trustees—Sir John Wm. Lubbock, Bart. ; Luke James Hansard, Esq. ; John T. Perceval, Esq.

Treasurer—Luke James Hansard, Esq.

Honorary Solicitor—Henry F. Richardson, Esq.

Bankers—Messrs. Hoare, Fleet-street

Subscriptions and donations of any amount will be thankfully received at the office, 36, Coleman-street ; by the Directors ; Luke James Hansard, Esq., the Treasurer, 7 Southampton-street, Bloomsbury ; John Thomas Perceval, Esq., the Honorary Secretary, Campden Cottage, Notting-hill-square ; or by Mr. John Taylor, the Secretary, at the office of the Society ; and by the following bankers—Messrs. Hoare, Fleet-street ; the London Joint Stock Bank ; the London and County Bank ; the London and Westminster Bank ; Messrs. Praed & Co., Fleet-street.

Cases of great interest are now under the consideration of the Board, and every information can be obtained at the offices, where attendance is given daily, and the Committee will be happy to give attention to any case which may fairly come within its rules and regulations.

JOHN T. PERCEVAL, Hon. Sec.

JOHN TAYLOR, Secretary.

36, Coleman-street, London, March, 1846

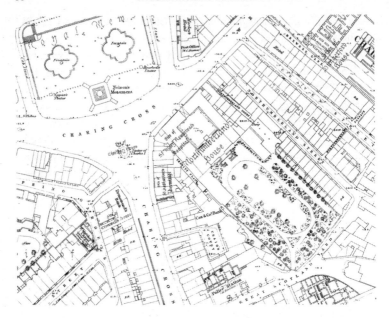

The Alleged Lunatics' Friend Society moved to Craven Street, Charing
Cross, at around the same time that the Lunacy Commission shifted its
headquarters to Spring Gardens at the top of Whitehall; Scotland Yard lay
between the two.

The fabric of the new legislation was woven by two men who would
go on to become oblique influences on some classics of Victorian
literature. Lawyer Bryan Waller Procter, credited with devising many
of the clauses, was also 'Barry Cornwall', a minor poet of the
Romantic school. Procter would have *Vanity Fair* 'affectionately dedicated' to him by Thackeray in 1847–8. Procter was also suspected of
being 'Currer Bell', author of *Jane Eyre*, until Charlotte Brontë broke
cover in 1848; no doubt his expertise on lunacy matters contributed
to the notion that he was the creator of poor Bertha Mason. Later,
in 1860, Procter would be the dedicatee of Wilkie Collins's *The
Woman in White* (perhaps Procter fed the author tales of asylum
escapes). Lawyer Robert Wilfred Skeffington Lutwidge, meanwhile,
whose input into the new laws was significant, was Lewis Carroll/
Charles Dodgson's favourite uncle, 'Uncle Skeffington'. Certainly,
many of the exchanges between patients, doctors and inquisitors

have a *Wonderland / Through the Looking-Glass* feel to them. Carroll
was known to have had in his immense personal library many books
and pamphlets on lunacy matters, and it is tempting to wonder
whether Uncle Skeffington discussed official business with his
nephew. Carroll's notoriously obscure 1876 poem *The Hunting of the
Snark* has recently been decoded as a parable of the Lunacy
Commissioners, with 'The Bellman' representing Shaftesbury. The
Snark was published three years after Uncle Skeffington was murdered
during his inspection of Fisherton House Asylum in Salisbury, by a
patient who hammered a rusty nail into his skull as he was leaning
over to read a ledger.

Bryan Waller Procter, Lunacy Commissioner from 1832. Thomas Carlyle
described him as 'A decidedly rather pretty little fellow. . . bodily and spiritually; manners prepossessing, slightly London-elegant. . . a sound honourable
morality, and airy friendly ways. . . something curiously dreamy in the eyes of
him.' Procter wrote poetry under the name 'Barry Cornwall' and was well
liked in literary circles – Wilkie Collins and Thackeray both considered him a
friend. Along with Lewis Carroll's uncle, Robert Wilfred Skeffington
Lutwidge, Procter drafted the 1845 lunacy legislation.

In the August of 1845, two major Procter- and Lutwidge-constructed pieces of lunacy legislation were shunted through and given Royal Assent. The first obliged every county in England and Wales to provide asylum accommodation on the rates for its pauper insane. (By 1847, thirty-six of England and Wales's fifty-two counties had built their own asylums, and the programme would be pretty much complete by the end of the 1850s.) The second, the Act for the Regulation of the Care and Treatment of Lunatics, amended the 1828 Madhouse Act, but in Mr Perceval's view perpetuated all the 'odious defects' of the existing legislation. Despite an excellent performance in the Commons by Thomas Slingsby Duncombe, only a few of the Society's recommendations were incorporated into the 1845 legislation. From now on, the two certificates required to commit a paying, private patient to custodial care had to state in full the reasons the doctor had for believing there was unsoundness of mind – a simple assertion was no longer enough. The proprietor of any new asylum would now have to live on the premises. And the time limit within which an individual was permitted to mount a legal action for false imprisonment following release from an asylum was extended from six months to twelve.

Duncombe failed to achieve the legal right of the patient to be told who had instigated the committal, to know the evidence given as proof of insanity, to be present at meetings relating to his/her case, or even to be represented at such a hearing. This, stated the Society, remained 'a blot upon our legislature'. Their demand for a coroner's hearing into every lunatic patient's death was excluded, too, although it was conceded that the registrar now had to be notified of such a death within forty-eight hours. The new Act also offered no greater protection to patients' property; and no notice at all was taken of the foresighted suggestions by the Society for halfway houses to be set up, in which voluntary patients could place themselves for observation before any formal certificates of lunacy were signed.

To the Society's horror, the Metropolitan Commissioners were not done away with and replaced by a jury and appeals system: instead, they were augmented. The new Board of Commissioners in Lunacy employed six full-time Commissioners (three lawyers and three doctors), assisted by up to five lay members, with power to inspect all 949 national institutions in which certified lunatics could be found. They were in charge of licensing asylums within the metropolitan area, with the provincial JPs retaining their power of local licensing. Lord Shaftesbury stayed on as chairman of the Commission (and would remain so until his death).

With the creation of the Commissioners in Lunacy, a centralised inspectorate came into being one hundred years before the National Health Service, and far in advance of any comparable body to oversee other vulnerable groups in society. Lunacy was furnished with a very un-Victorian publicly funded administrative machinery, prompted in equal measure by humanitarian concern for the insane and the urge to control those who suffered the distressing condition.

The new Commissioners intended to continue their predecessors' preference for persuasion – in cases of doubtful incarceration – to make the signatory of the lunacy order agree to remove the patient. As *The Lancet* pointed out, this turned liberation into a 'favour' to be granted, rather than a civil right. The Commissioners planned to act only in cases where the confiner could not be persuaded despite either overwhelming evidence of the sanity of the patient or unambiguous proof that malice had been behind the certification. One new ruse within the 1845 legislation that facilitated this non-confrontational approach was the provision for the Commissioners to remove an asylum patient temporarily 'for reasons of health'. This could prove a valuable way of avoiding making scandalous accusations of malice against the signatory of the lunacy order or charges of improper admission and detention on the part of the proprietor.

Remaining outside the scope of the new Lunacy Commission were all Chancery patients, who continued to be overseen by the Lord Chancellor and his Masters in Lunacy; also, controversially, Royal Bethlehem Hospital, which was permitted largely to continue its self-regulation.

The Alleged Lunatics' Friend Society composed and presented to parliament, via Mr Duncombe, a whole new Bill in 1847, but it failed to get past the first reading. Further unsuccessful attempts were made in 1848, 1851 and 1853. But in the meantime, the Society continued a range of practical activities, with the intention of becoming 'the alter ego to the Lunacy Commission'. In fact, the battle to expose physical abuse and foul conditions in private care, county asylums and single-patient confinement would turn out to occupy most of the Society's energy and time. But there were also vigorous attempts to publicise cases of wrongful incarceration,* including some hands-on attempts at 'rescue', as Captain Saumarez called it – some of it very hands-on indeed. He had been for a time the mayor of Bath, and became Admiral Saumarez in 1853, despite (rather than because of) some swashbuckling on the part of an alleged lunatic. On 4 January 1856, Admiral Saumarez entered the garden of Effra Hall Asylum in Brixton, South London, and stole away Anne Tottenham, a young Chancery patient who had spent eight months at the asylum because her mother had wanted to control her finances. Miss Tottenham had not been able to get any sense out of Lunacy Commissioners Procter, Hume and Gaskell (the writer Elizabeth Gaskell's brother-in-law), but had, via her loyal brother, Algernon, been able to smuggle out an account of her ordeal to the Alleged Lunatics' Friends. The admiral lodged her for a year with alienist Dr Forbes Benignus Winslow and one year later they were able to get the Chancery 'of unsound mind' verdict overturned, with the legal assistance of Gilbert Bolden. The expense of the battle cost Miss Tottenham half of her fortune, which added to the admiral's fury about the expense of Chancery cases.

For his part, Mr Perceval was told by the owner of Manor House Asylum in Chiswick, West London, 'I would rather see the Devil in my asylum than you.' Thanks to the Society's intervention to free a sane man, the proprietor had lost the £300 a year paid for the patient's keep.

In the West Country, the Society teamed up with formidable local magistrate Purnell B. Purnell, who instigated a thorough probe of

---

* See Appendix 3 on p. 395 for brief sketches of individuals who the Society believed had been wrongfully certified as lunatics or had been kept in confinement long after they had become well.

Effra Hall (near the Church) Brixton London
A Home for Ladies Nervously or Mentally afflicted

Effra Hall Asylum stood in Effra Road, Brixton, South London, and was a small private asylum for women.

Purnell Bransby Purnell (1792–1866) was a campaigning Gloucestershire magistrate who discovered numerous miscertificated patients in that county's private and public institutions in the late 1840s. Grateful locals raised a large subscription to express their thanks.

Gloucestershire's private and county asylums, with devastating conclusions that grabbed national headlines in 1849. One asylum was shut down and two proprietors had their licence renewals refused. Many lunacy certificates were found to be invalid, some downright untruthful, and some patients had clearly become sane but had been unable to obtain their discharge. (Incidentally, Mr Perceval's violent attendant, Samuel Hobbs, was discovered among the staff at exclusive Ridgeway House, near Bristol.) The intention of Purnell and the Friends was not just to root out bad practice and malevolent incarceration, but to demonstrate to the Commissioners in Lunacy and to magistrates in other parts of the country just what could be achieved if only there were sufficient zeal. Purnell became a huge local hero, and a subscription raised in Gloucestershire to thank him for his help in liberating the wrongfully incarcerated and improving the conditions in asylums raised thousands of pounds; this was spent on the gift of an ebony and rosewood table with silver inlay. It was displayed at the Great Exhibition and to this day remains the V&A Museum's grandest example of nineteenth-century presentation silver.

The Friends sometimes rushed in too hastily to offer assistance where it was not wanted, and this tended to undermine the support they had gathered. In 1848, one Mr Pulverstoft, detained at Northampton Hospital, and a Mr Dixon, at Northwoods Asylum near Bristol, were infuriated to learn that the Society had raised their cases with the Lord Chancellor and the Commissioners in Lunacy, respectively. They had not been seeking intervention, but Gilbert Bolden had taken up the cudgels on their behalf anyway. Bolden also had to make an embarrassing volte face in the case of Captain Jonathan Childe, whom he had believed to be sane, until Childe repeatedly insisted – from his room at Hayes Park Asylum, Middlesex – that Queen Victoria was deeply in love with him. The *Medical Times* remarked: 'The members of this Society are apt to see things through a hazy and distorted medium . . . They have wandered about the country, prepared to lend a willing ear to the idle story of every lunatic they could meet with; they have pestered the Home Secretary, and ever and anon obtruded their opinions and schemes upon such members of the Upper and Lower House as would listen to them.' The public simply did not want these matters forced upon its attention, continued the editorial:

'The hand of humanity will always draw a veil over such a domestic calamity.'

One of the governors of Northampton Hospital wrote of John Perceval: 'His sympathies with the insane are of a very morbid character and his judgment to the last, feeble and weak.' Mr Perceval admitted that he had suffered relapses in his mental condition, with which he had periodically had to battle, and that this had depleted his energies in the battle for England's lunatics. For this he blamed the Brislington House operation on his temporal artery, holding to the concept that lunacy might be brought about by poor circulation of the blood in the vessels of the brain. But these vicious attacks on him and the Society took no account of how reasonable and lucid the Friends mostly were. In a letter to the Home Office, Mr Perceval took particular exception to the accusation that his plan was to liberate all madmen:

I have heard from two or three quarters that I have been misrepresented by parties who have been interested in defeating me, and who do not like their antiquated privileges to do what they please in the matter to be meddled with . . . Through the long continued obstinate and perverse or indolent neglect of this subject by the government, harmless and inoffensive patients and even persons of unsound mind are confined as insane, whilst madmen – that is, persons who are deranged and with direct evidence of furious and malevolent intentions – are allowed to go at large, to which circumstance I attribute the melancholy death of my father and of my friend, the late Mr [Edward] Drummond.

This letter was written in the midst of the biggest coup that Mr Perceval was to pull off – freeing a man after fourteen years of false imprisonment and in the process overturning five centuries of self-inspection at Bethlehem Hospital. While inspecting the conditions there, Mr Perceval came across Professor Edward Peithman, who had been certificated following a clumsy attempt to interest fellow Saxon Prince Albert in his schemes for educational reform. Failing to understand that England did not offer the same open-access approach to royalty as the German states, the professor believed that he could simply wander into Buckingham Palace and await an appointment with the German prince. The police were called to the palace on 29

June 1840 and Professor Peithman was escorted to the Whitehall office of the Home Secretary, the Marquess of Normanby. The professor had in advance of his palace visit sent the eleven volumes of his collected works, as well as his testimonials and diplomas, to Prince Albert. The Home Secretary concluded that this constituted serious harassment of His Royal Highness. Moreover, the professor's intrusion into Buckingham Palace had occurred just nineteen days after the Queen had had a pistol brandished at her by one Edward Oxford, who was later to be found not guilty at his trial, by virtue of insanity. The Home Secretary (rather than the Commissioners in Lunacy) retained responsibility for all criminal and dangerous lunatics, and could himself recommend the incarceration of an individual deemed to be dangerous. As Peithman was treated as a pauper because of his lack of funds, only one medical certificate of lunacy was required, the other to be signed by a magistrate. A London magistrate and a doctor, informed by the Home Secretary himself that Peithman's action had seemed that of a dangerous man, duly signed the papers during a hearing that was held behind closed doors, committing the professor to Bethlehem. And there he stayed for years, until Mr Perceval happened to drop by.

Bethlehem was at this time situated in St George's Field, Southwark. The building was poorly maintained, and Professor Peithman's cell, in which he spent twelve hours a day, was just eight feet square, gloomy and airless; he had little access to drinking water or washing facilities. Fluent in five languages, able to read Latin and Greek and knowledgeable in all the sciences, the professor was considered by the Bedlam officials to be harmless and tranquil, although his case notes do also show that he was described as 'uncouth', 'untidy' and with occasional 'indecent propensities'; three of his keepers later testified that they considered him quite sane. But his many petitions to the Home Secretary were taken as proof of the professor's ongoing unsoundness of mind. Meanwhile, attempts upon the life of Queen Victoria continued throughout the 1840s, creating a climate in which Peithman's bid for freedom was unlikely to succeed. The Commissioners of the Metropolitan Police complained to the Home Secretary that their manpower and budget were being put under strain by the unpopularity of the royal couple. In 1848 Scotland Yard devoted many man-hours to keeping under surveillance one Lieutenant Mundell, who stalked the streets with a loaded pistol, openly intent on revenge upon the Queen as he believed her to be instrumental in blocking his promotion. Unlike Peithman, Mundell *was* dangerous, but the police and the Commissioners in Lunacy had failed to persuade the Home Office to take action against him; one of the loopholes in the 1845 legislation was the lack of a clause empowering the police to detain a 'wandering lunatic' who was not a pauper and who did not belong to the raving variety of madman. Eventually, a relative of Mundell's was persuaded to sign a lunacy order consigning him to private care. This was a shambolic situation, but one that did not surprise Mr Perceval: in his view, pistol-packing querulants such as Lieutenant Mundell, Daniel M'Naughten and John Bellingham could roam Whitehall for weeks, seething with grudges against royalty and government ministers, while a harmless eccentric like Professor Peithman had been instantly thrown into Bedlam.

Mr Perceval had only accidentally come across Peithman, during an 1850 pastoral visit to Bedlam patient Arthur Legent Pearce, who had been confined ten years earlier following a violent assault upon his wife. After obtaining an interview with the professor, Mr Perceval decided to campaign to release Peithman as well as Pearce. 'My heart bled at the confinement of a man of so elegant a mind,' he wrote of Peithman. An old friend of the professor's had written to Perceval stating that those who did not know him might see 'a certain eccentricity or abruptness of manner . . . but geniuses are proverbially eccentric'. Perceval believed Peithman was 'a harmless innocent' and had been incarcerated because in the mid-1830s he had offended an illustrious Dublin family. Peithman was educating the sons of the second Lord Cloncurry (Valentine Lawless) at their home at Lyons Castle, Country Kildare. Peithman had been found the position by the Marquess of Normanby, Lord Lieutenant in Ireland at the time. When a maid in the household had become pregnant by the eldest son, Peithman had refused to take the family's side and to lie to a magistrate after the maid threatened to make public her dismissal. The Marquess of Normanby went on to become the very Home Secretary who spirited Peithman into Bedlam. Many who came to know of the Peithman case smelt an enormous rat.

Mr Perceval's agitations at last bore fruit, though the correspondence, held at The National Archives, reveals the contempt in which he was held by certain Whitehall men: 'No answer, he is half crazy himself', scribbled Lord Palmerston on the back of one plea from Mr Perceval. In February 1854 the Commissioners released Peithman on a three-month probationary trial, and he went to stay near Mr Perceval and his family in their out-of-London home in Herne Bay, Kent. Unfortunately, the professor wasted no time in writing to Albert and Victoria, explaining what had happened to him. And when he received a reply from Prince Albert expressing sympathy but stating that he had no powers to effect any compensation, Peithman one day walked into the chapel of Buckingham Palace during Sunday service to talk to the Prince. He then found himself back in custodial care, this time in the Middlesex County Asylum at Hanwell.

The nation took the side of the professor in the ensuing kerfuffle, and John Perceval explained that in the German states, royalty, ministers and all authority figures welcomed deputations into their presence – you could even thrust a petition into an important person's carriage, or buttonhole them at their place of worship, he argued. Professor Peithman simply could not understand that in England, the land of liberty, power was not quite so approachable. Mr Perceval said that many English people believed that there was a growing isolation and arrogance on the part of the powerful, and indeed, *Punch* ran a piece about the professor, entitled 'What on Earth Has He Done?' The article stated that 'several of what the authorities might call "very impertinent questions" crowd upon us. Firstly, What has Dr Peithman done? Secondly, Why send him to a lunatic asylum? And thirdly, If it was proper to send him there, why take him out again?' Moreover, the fact that the Home Secretary had retained exclusive powers to order asylum detention for a suspected violent lunatic in a modern quasi-democracy was a horrible thought to Tory and Liberal Lunatic Friend alike. For many, it raised the spectre of the infamous *lettre de cachet* system of the French *ancien régime*, whereby without trial or tribunal a person deemed an enemy of the state could be confined to prison (and, less commonly, an asylum) by the simple order contained in a private letter from a minister.

Testimonials to Peithman's sanity poured into the Home Office, and the Middlesex magistrates themselves insisted that he be liberated.

In late August 1854, Peithman was released from Hanwell, on the condition that he leave the country immediately in the company of Mr Perceval, who would ensure that he had everything he needed on his journey and that he would be reunited with his family, who were now settled in the Rhineland town of Elberfield.

The requirement that a harmless and extremely unworldly man should be forced to leave the country caused greater furore in the press. It meant sweeping under the carpet a dreadful miscarriage of justice, as the chief Middlesex magistrate, Reverend Dr J. A. Emerton, wrote to the Home Secretary:

> His simplicity of character has apparently led him to trust in certain ideal promises, which, if made, he ought to be aware were never intended to be kept . . . If he be banished from the country at present, no one who knows the whole circumstances will believe that English justice has been awarded him; whereas, by giving him a trial you will have the satisfaction of knowing that, in your regard for the wishes of the powerful, you have not forgotten the claims of justice and humanity, and that, in endeavouring to save the Prince from annoyance, you have not sacrificed that liberty of individual action which it is the glory of England to maintain.

The Germans were furious too, and great indignation was expressed that a Prussian subject should have been so treated, and denied redress. Englishmen who had come to official harm in the German states were recompensed and their grievances looked into. Albion must explain herself, Oberbürgermeister Jochman told the Prussian Upper Chamber. But Albion didn't. On these matters Albion didn't even explain herself to her own citizens. Professor Peithman received neither apology nor compensation.

During his time in Germany with Professor Peithman, Mr Perceval forged some important links on the Continent and fed the Alleged Lunatics' Friend Society details on systems such as the Prussian full judicial inquiry before lunacy certification; and the French and Belgian *conseil de famille* system, where relatives and the alleged lunatic put their cases before an independent tribunal. But in England Shaftesbury would not countenance any system that had been devised by a Continental autocracy. For his part, Mr Perceval believed the English lunacy system was out of keeping with Magna Carta and that the Commissioners in Lunacy were a 'hideous "Holy Office" . . . restoring us to the cruelty of the Inquisition . . . that monstrous tribunal'. The secretive nature of the Commissioners' modus operandi was likely to increase 'the general servility of mind which exists in the country where it is admitted of'. How could England have ended up with such an illiberal system – more appropriate to nations in which the Church demanded total abasement from its populace, he wondered? This was not entirely fair, though, as it was the Commissioners who, once roused, had set about freeing the professor from Bedlam. And it did not occur to Mr Perceval, in his anti-Papist passion, that the countries whose lunacy procedures he was hoping could be emulated were Catholic, while Protestant England was persisting with its occult and mysterious system of incarceration.

These inconsistencies notwithstanding, the Peithman case reflected well on Mr Perceval and his Friends and raised the Society's profile, encouraging more 'victims' to come forward. The Society's surviving paperwork strongly suggests that it was mainly males who presented themselves, or were being winkled out as subjects of wrongful incarceration: the documents show a ratio of twenty-two males to five females in the known cases of people helped by the Society to fight malicious certification or prolonged detention. It is difficult to know how far this gender imbalance reflects an unwillingness among mid-nineteenth-century women to come forward with their complaints, especially to a Society that had no females on its executive; or how far sane males were disproportionately likely to find themselves landed in a private asylum as a result of family disputes about cash, property and inheritance. John Perceval was clear that wrongful confinement was not just a man's problem, informing the Home Secretary, in 1840, that daughters were as likely as sons to be the victims of parents who wished to prevent an unsuitable marriage, that women were just as likely to adopt unorthodox religious opinions, and to fail to curb their behaviour to suit 'the sobriety and severity of the age in which they live . . . Husbands also have incarcerated their wives to enjoy their property in the arms of an adulteress; sons have sworn away the liberty of their mother and have deprived them of their possessions. We cannot therefore hesitate to give females every protection.'

Nine years after Mr Perceval wrote this, the legislation of 1845 and the new Commissioners faced the first celebrated female case of abduction and highly questionable asylum incarceration. Mr Perceval found the woman's dilemma 'a perfect illustration of the dangerous defects and abuses of our present laws'. He made sure he had a ring-side seat.

4

'Oh Hail, Holy Love!'

Louisa Jane Nottidge lived in a mansion close to the village of Wixoe, Suffolk, with her mother, Emily, her father, Josias, and four sisters. A fifth sister had married London merchant Frederick Ripley, and there were also two brothers: one had gone into the Church, the other into business. Josias, a retired wool merchant in his early eighties, was very comfortably off, and in 1842 he settled £6,000 upon each of his unwed daughters, who ranged in age from twenty-four to forty (Louisa). In his will he granted Mr Ripley power of attorney over their financial affairs for as long as they remained spinsters. Upon marriage, each daughter's property would come under the full control of her husband, as per the law of the land.

Louisa and three of her unmarried sisters were more devout than respectability required and attended the parish church of St John the Baptist at Stoke by Clare, near Wixoe. In 1843, a new incumbent arrived at Stoke. Reverend Henry James Prince had come to Suffolk after being dismissed by the Bishop of Bath and Wells from a curacy in Charlinch, Somerset, where his zealous revivalist preaching had caused offence to many a wealthy farmer – Prince had declared certain of them to be 'unsaved' – and his doctrinal eccentricities had led almost to riot on occasion. The Charlinch faithful had also been unsettled by the allure that Prince held for women and girls. Prince had brought to Stoke his brother-in-law, Reverend Samuel Starky, also out of favour with the Bishop of Bath and Wells. Starky and Prince shared a house at Stoke, where they would soon receive daily visits from Louisa and her sisters Harriet, thirty-seven, and Agnes, twenty-four. Their parents strongly disapproved of these unchaperoned meetings; Josias had no respect for Prince and Starky's religious views, and Mrs Nottidge would not have them inside Rose Hill, the family home. Stoke soon proved to be as incendiary as Charlinch, and the Bishop of Ely dismissed the pair.

The clergymen had been members of the 'Lampeter Brethren', students who had proved to be particularly argumentative and provocative during their time at St David's theological college, Lampeter. Graduating in 1839, Prince and Starky and certain other Brethren founded a mission called the Agapemone – from the Greek, meaning 'abode of love' – with branches in Brighton, Weymouth, Swansea and Charlinch. When Prince set up the Adullam Chapel in Windsor Street, Brighton, Louisa, Harriet and Agnes, now joined by their sisters Clara, thirty-two, and Cornelia, twenty-nine, rented a house nearby to be able to hear him preach. His seashore sermons were said to be especially affecting. The Nottidge sisters would also travel with him, unchaperoned, to Weymouth, Wales and the West Country, putting up in hotels and lodging houses – behaviour that called their social standing and appreciation of decorum into question. They paid Prince's travel and hotel bills as well as their own.

Their parents were aghast, but their requests that the sisters return to Rose Hill were ignored. Even in the spring of 1844, when Josias's health failed, they were reluctant to leave their little god and come home to Suffolk. As Mrs Nottidge would later state: 'I sent for them from Brighton when he was dying; and when they came, they told me they should not have done so but for "the will of God".'

Josias died in May, and when the Nottidge daughters went back to Brighton, Emily decided to go with them in an attempt to salvage some propriety for her girls. She would not allow Prince into the house she had rented for herself and her daughters, and on one occasion, Emily would testify, he had forced his way into the lodgings and she had had to lock herself in the bedroom to prevent him intruding upon her.

It got worse. In June 1845 Louisa, Harriet, Agnes, Clara and Cornelia went to Somerset to attend the opening of the Trinity Free Church at Four Forks, near the hamlet of Spaxton in the parish of Charlinch. This chapel, which Prince, Starky and their supporters had built, would provide a more permanent home for the Agapemone, which had continued to recruit new followers. The Agapemonites attracted adulation and hostility in pretty much equal measure. Itinerant preaching, with ecstatic shouting and bellowing, and stress placed on the most unlikely syllables in a sentence, had caused annoyance in various southern and western counties and led to complaints to the magistracy. A Somerset newspaper, the *Bridgwater Times*, noted that young girls in particular appeared to be attracted to the open-air ranting and singing. Colonel Howard, a Weymouth magistrate, complained to the Home Secretary, Sir George Grey, about the disturbances that Prince and his followers were causing; Howard had recently committed three young women to the county lunatic asylum at Forston, for religious delusions that had been whipped up by Prince. He alleged that women wishing to join the Agapemonites had to present themselves naked, and if they refused to do so they were told that they were damned for eternity. Howard wanted the Home Secretary to send an investigator, such as an officer from Bow Street, to Weymouth with a view to finding legal means of clamping down on the sect's activities. The Home Secretary wrote to the mayor of Weymouth, asking for more detail, which was duly presented, but no further action was taken by Whitehall.

Criticism of the Agapemone was growing in Brighton too, and when one of the Lampeter Brethren defected and began to explain to the town's citizens the heretical nature of some of Prince's doctrines, attendances at the Adullam Chapel fell. For Prince had declared that the Sabbath was not sacred, that prayer was pointless, that blood relationships and friendships were meaningless, that the Day of Grace had passed and the Day of Judgement had arrived, and that only his own followers would be saved. When Prince shortly afterwards abandoned Brighton for Wales and the West Country, he damned it by composing a new hymn:

> Woe, Woe, Woe to Brighton
> Because she hath loved and believed a lie
> Woe, Woe, Woe!

Only Louisa returned to her mother's Brighton accommodation following the opening of the chapel at Four Forks, and Emily berated her for the impropriety of travelling by herself, in a carriage, on the Sabbath. Louisa replied that Prince had written a prayer which revealed that it was 'the will of God' that she should do so. Louisa burst into tears as she told Emily the shocking news of what had happened at the Giles Castle Hotel in Taunton, where the Nottidge daughters had been staying. Prince, with Starky by his side, had commanded Harriet to marry one of his most loyal disciples, twenty-five-year-old Reverend Lewis Price. Next, Agnes was told that she was to marry 'Brother' George Thomas. And two days later Clara was ordered to marry William Cobbe, a relatively new convert to the Agapemone. Each of these men was younger than his Nottidge bride-to-be (in Harriet's case, by fifteen years). Prince, himself thirty-four, was the widower of a woman who had been significantly older than him, although his second wife, Julia Starky, was of similar age to her husband. Agnes had caused some annoyance to Prince when she had appeared reluctant to be betrothed to order; she had also asked her intended if some of her £6,000 could be set aside in trust for her, and Brother Thomas had agreed to this. But he then changed his mind, telling Agnes that he had discovered that God forbade such a settlement. Trust settlements, under the law of equity, were a way of allowing married women to own and control a proportion of their own property, and helped to get round some of the legal and financial disabilities imposed upon wives by common law. But the considerable cost of drawing up and implementing such an arrangement meant that only an estimated one in ten of all English marriages in these years featured separate property settlements.

Prince had told the three women that these marriages were the will of God; and that it was also the will of God that they should be spiritual unions only. He said that because the Day of Judgement had arrived, and the Agapemonites were the only redeemed among humanity – had been reborn as pure Spirit, casting off all matters of the flesh – no further children were to be brought into the world. So Agnes was silenced when she asked why she would not be allowed to become a mother. For the same reason Prince declared that all previous ties of affection – to family and friends – were nullified. Harriet, Agnes and Clara were therefore forbidden to tell their mother about their impending marriages.

Louisa had been permitted to travel to inform Emily of the weddings and also that Brother Thomas was coming to Brighton that night, and that he would be staying at Emily's rented home. Emily protested that this was 'very improper', but Louisa told her that it was the will of God. It must have been, because at ten o'clock Brother Thomas arrived and installed himself **upstairs** in the house. Emily fled to a friend's home. When it became **clear the** next morning that he would stay another night, Emily packed her things and returned to Rose Hill.

Prince now reluctantly allowed two of the fiancées to go to Rose Hill to pick up clothing and personal belongings; but he advised them to read the Book of Jonah beforehand and to ponder the implications of disobedience to God's commands. During this rushed visit, Emily failed to change her daughters' minds. She was not present at the service, at St Mary's, Swansea, on 9 July 1845, where Reverend Starky gave away each of the three spiritual brides, who wore black, with white hats and black veils. Some £18,000 now passed directly to the control of the Agapemone.

Clara's spiritual husband, William Cobbe, twenty-nine, had been a senior engineer of the Bristol & Exeter Railway Company and now spent his considerable wealth on developing the Spaxton Agapemone. He had donated his own land at Four Forks as well as some existing cottages and outbuildings and would go on to create a fantastic Abode of Love behind high walls, comprising a main house with over twenty bedrooms, a chapel, terraced pleasure grounds, a shrubbery, glasshouses (in which orchids were grown), stables and a granary. Over the chapel flew a flag with Prince's freshly invented insignia, depicting a lion and a lamb, and his motto, 'Oh hail, holy love!' In addition, four farms in the locality were bought with the Agapemone's rapidly increasing funds, so that the community of the saved could be self-sufficient and would not be starved out, should local tradesmen decide to impose boycotts.

The Abode of Love took a long time to complete, and the sect was still peripatetic. While the Nottidge cash provided a big boost to building work, many other moneyed professionals and people of independent means were continuing to respond to Prince's charisma. The Agapemone was their true family, he declared, and as in all families, resources must be pooled for the common good. Prince had an idiosyncratic way of soliciting funds from the faithful: 'The Lord hath need of £50,' one letter read, 'to be used for a special purpose unto His glory. The Spirit would have this made known to you. Amen.'

As well as new arrivals, there had been defections. Some of his original Lampeter associates felt that Prince was presenting a new article of faith when he declared that the Holy Spirit had found fleshly lodgings within him. Was Prince claiming to be the Messiah? That would be blasphemy. Prince's convoluted language – the declarations that endlessly circled back on themselves, ridden with qualifiers and hedging and contradiction – made it difficult to ascertain (before the late 1860s at least, when he became a lot clearer on the matter) whether he was or was not revealing himself as Christ's successor. His latest pronouncement was that those friends and relations of his followers who did not see that the Holy Spirit dwelt within Prince were, in fact, damned. This brand-new ultimatum, this attack on natural harmonious relationships (the gauntlet it threw down to domesticity and familial happiness), appeared to some to be reason enough to desert Prince.

Emily Nottidge – in her mid-seventies in 1845, and having lost three of her daughters, with their financial settlements, to a religious sect – was by now living back in Suffolk with Louisa and Cornelia. Cornelia had abandoned the Agapemone, disgusted by many aspects of doctrine as well as everyday life under Prince, and had settled back into life with her mother. But Louisa was becoming restless; she especially missed Harriet, the sister to whom she had been closest. But Agnes wrote letters to Louisa warning her against Prince, his growing dominance within the Agapemone 'family', and the control he had assumed over the marital lives of those living at the Abode; she strongly urged Louisa to stay away. When she was composing such a letter in the drawing room at the Weymouth house one afternoon in November 1845, Agnes had not been aware that Brother Thomas Williams had stalked silently up behind her high-backed armchair and read the entire draft over her shoulder. He grabbed it and took it to Prince, who then shouted abuse at Agnes. From this point on, she was shunned by the whole household.

Then, in December, Reverend Starky and another Agapemonite appeared on Emily's doorstep and declaimed that it was the will of God that Louisa come with them to the Abode. They gave her two hours to pack and during that time Emily pleaded with Louisa to stay. Louisa told her mother that 'it is tearing the flesh from my bones to leave you, but it is the will of God that I do so'. Starky and his colleague rolled up in a carriage and took her away.

For weeks Emily looked for Louisa in Agapemonite haunts, fearing she might be living in 'the greatest sin and iniquity'. Then one day, Agnes suddenly returned to Rose Hill. Despite having been instructed that her marriage was of the spirit only, she had become pregnant. On learning of this, Prince had said of Agnes, 'This comes of sin. She is faithless, she is fallen, she must be cast away.' When Agnes had tried to persuade her husband to leave the Agapemone with her and their unborn child, Prince had clenched his fist and shouted at Agnes, 'If you dare attempt to influence your husband again, in acting contrary to my commands, God will crush you out of the way.' Brother George Thomas banned his wife from their bedroom, telling her, 'You are lost . . . you enter here no more. There is an empty room, go and find such rest as you deserve, you who have crossed the Servant of the Lord.'

Agnes fled, and on 4 June 1846 gave birth to a son; she was very ill after the birth. She wrote to Brother Thomas, asking him if there were any name he would like to give the baby, and requesting money to help with the child's subsistence. Her letter was returned with a note renouncing her for ever. Prince, too, posted her abusive letters.

Harriet had also fallen pregnant but managed to reconcile herself to Prince, despite his furious scorn at her condition. Harriet's child did not live long after being born, and Agnes would later claim that its death had been highly suspicious; Harriet insisted that the sickly baby had died in her arms, and that plenty of witnesses would attest to this.

Emily was delighted to have Agnes back, with her new grandson, George Nottidge Thomas, but she was nevertheless distraught about the loss of Louisa and the likelihood that Louisa's £6,000 would go the way of the other Nottidge thousands. There was also the grim prospect that upon Emily's death, the three brides plus Louisa would bring to the sect a further £12,000, which had been settled upon his daughters by their late father. She continued to search for Louisa for months, even offering a financial reward for news of her whereabouts. 'I was in such a wretched state of mind about her,' Emily later said. Although Clara and Harriet refused to give Emily any information on her likely whereabouts, news suddenly came that Louisa was at Four Forks, as the Agapemone complex was reaching completion. On hearing this, Emily made a drastic – and disastrous – move.

On 10 November 1846, Louisa was getting ready for bed upstairs at the cottage of labourer George Waterman, which backed on to the Agapemone site. Waterman had been putting up Prince (who was absent that night), Mrs Julia Prince and Louisa for the past three weeks. That night, he had deliberately left his back door ajar when the household went up to bed, as two well-dressed gentlemen from London had requested of him. Hearing noises downstairs, Louisa assumed that Prince was returning to the cottage, but moments later her bedroom door burst open and there stood her brother Edmund and her brother-in-law Frederick Ripley. You must come with us now, they said, your mother is dangerously ill. Be quick or it might be too late. When Louisa refused to believe this, the two men grabbed her, carried her out of the cottage and into a waiting carriage, as she fought and screamed. She had not been allowed time to dress herself: she had no bonnet, no shawl, and was wearing slippers. She continued to scream as the carriage drove off through the deep and remote country lanes.

We do not know where that night was spent, but wherever it was, Louisa tried and failed to escape through a window. The following day, she was presented to her mother at the Ripley home in Woburn Place, Bloomsbury. There was no fond reunion, as Louisa well knew that Emily had commissioned the abduction. Ripley, Edmund and Uncle John (Emily's bank director brother) asked why she was so determined to throw her lot in with a charlatan such as Prince. According to Emily, her daughter replied: 'I know no such person. God now dwells only at Charlinch in the flesh of Him I once knew as Mr Prince. God who made me, and all the world, is now manifest in Him whom I once called Mr Prince. He has entered His tabernacle of flesh among men, and I have seen God face to face. He will deliver me, wherever I am taken.' Louisa added that she had now become immortal. Prince taught that all at the Agapemone had conquered the flesh, and because they were saved, they could not die; any follower of his who did die had consequently not been among the saved. Uncle John later said of Louisa, 'In my opinion, her mind was under a strong delusion.' He thought Louisa might do herself some injury and that she should not be left alone. No matter what question he put to her, Louisa would reply that it was the Lord's will that she should return to Charlinch. After two hours of this, Uncle John called in the medical men.

Dr Thomas Morton was a Woburn Place neighbour of Frederick Ripley; he was surgeon to University College London and to the Queen's Bench prison. The Ripley family's GP, Dr Silas Stedman, recommended Dr Richard Rowland for a second opinion; he too lived in Woburn Place. Each man spoke to Louisa separately and alone, as required by law. At first she would not answer their questions, but then she repeated her assertions about Prince and about her immortality. The doctors now filled in their certificates, and the order for Louisa's committal was signed by Emily. Upon his certificate Dr Rowland stated: 'I found that she had of late estranged herself from her mother's house, where she had previously resided, to follow a person of the name of Prince, whom she believed to be Almighty God, and herself immortal.'

The asylum, Moorcroft House in Hillingdon, Middlesex, was chosen because Louisa's brother Edmund had spent spells there recovering his own wits during bouts of psychological problems. Emily hoped that Louisa would soon be able to return to Rose Hill, to live with her and be cared for with the help of a hired nurse, or attendant. Emily had been desperate not to attract publicity to the shameful behaviour and opinions of her daughter; she believed that Louisa, just like Edmund, was experiencing a temporary bout of unsoundness of mind. For these two reasons, Emily did not seek a lunacy inquisition. It would turn out to be an unwise decision.

Moorcroft House Asylum near Hillingdon in Middlesex, which is still standing today.

Louisa was driven to Moorcroft House, where thirty-two-year-old Dr Arthur Stillwell had taken over the running of this family madhouse, in 1839. (His own mother, Ann, had become a patient there after developing some kind of mental affliction in her seventies.) Dr Stillwell was Dr Silas Stedman's brother-in-law, a propinquity that would later cause anti-incarceration campaigners to suspect a profit-related motive; but Emily and Uncle John had full trust in Stillwell. A Commissioner in Lunacy described Moorcroft House as one of the best-run asylums in the nation, 'most agreeably situated' and 'only intended for persons moving in the higher ranks of society, and such as could afford to pay high terms for their board and attendance'. There were twice as many males as females at the asylum and by the time Louisa arrived there it was filling up with barristers, architects, army officers and medical men. Moorcroft had ornamental grounds, orchards, meadow-land, gravel walks, a shrubbery and pleasure gardens – not unlike the Agapemone itself, and it is tempting to fancy that Louisa was merely exchanging one luxurious madhouse for another.

The Stillwell family placed adverts, such as the one below, which were highly contentious, as they could be construed as touting for patients. The Commissioners in Lunacy monitored such advertising but it is unclear whether proprietors faced any serious censure.

We strongly recommend Mr. Stilwell's Lunatic Asylum, at Hillingdon, near Uxbridge, to all who may have friends or relations afflicted with mental derangement. We have seen every part of this excellent establishment, which is conducted without keepers, and without coercion. The health, comfort, and amusements to be completely studied, and the patients with whom we conversed, expressed their gratitude for the care and attentions of Mr. and Mrs. Stilwell, and for the prompt and humane assistance which they invariably received from the medical attendants.

For the first few days, Dr Stillwell found Louisa uncommunicative. He allowed her full use of his private library and after a while she began to open up to him. She explained that Prince was God made flesh; that the Day of Grace was past and the Day of Judgement had arrived; that she was immortal and should not therefore be buried in a coffin as she would be taken up to heaven 'in the twinkling of an eye'. She had ceased to pray and now only sang praises to God. 'She attempted to explain to me, but it was such a mass of confusion that

I could not make anything of the explanation,' recalled Dr Stillwell. And of her songs, the doctor said that she 'never used any intelligible words'.

Louisa, Dr Stillwell noted, refused to wear a bonnet and took little interest in how she dressed. She also manifested 'loss of all feeling for her family'. Emily visited her twice at Moorcroft House, but Louisa declared that she had no mother, and would not communicate with her. She would later swear in an affidavit that Emily, Frederick Ripley and her sister Maria Ripley had all attempted to shake her sanity when she was in the asylum by putting to her foul and disgusting assertions about what was going on behind the walls of the Agapemone. Clara, still very happily living at the heart of the Abode of Love, for her part claimed that Emily had forbidden her to visit Louisa and was deciding who was allowed to visit or write to her daughter. This was, in fact, Emily's legal right – the controversial power that was granted under the English lunacy laws to whoever had signed the patient's lunacy order. Ripley, meanwhile, still enjoyed full control over Louisa's finances and paid Stillwell's bills, of three guineas a week, out of Louisa's money.

Ripley also visited the Commissioners in Lunacy, and as a result of his agitation, Lord Shaftesbury sent a memorandum to the Home Secretary, who in turn contacted Metropolitan Police Commissioner Richard Mayne, who sent a 'confidential person' down to Spaxton to investigate the activities and beliefs of the Abode of Love. The secret agent read his notes to the Commissioners in Lunacy on his return; these have not survived, but whatever was in them failed to cause alarm, since no further action was taken. The Commissioners in Lunacy wrote to Ripley apologising that they had no powers to interfere any further in the matter but assuring him that Prince and his sect were under 'the consideration of the government'. Again, no paperwork survives to tell us any more about this surveillance and assessment.

In the meantime, Thomas Cobbe, the brother of Clara's husband William, had also travelled from London to snoop around the Abode of Love in an attempt to gather evidence that could be used to have the wealthy William put into an asylum – or at least to find a legal means of preventing the sect from getting any more of his money. The doctors Thomas consulted on his return to London advised that

William appeared to be suffering from 'monomania', his partial insanity limited to religious matters, but urged caution in attempting to have him certified, and Thomas proceeded no further. However, he too called in on the Commissioners in Lunacy to ask their advice. Their response is not known, but it is noteworthy that both Ripley and Cobbe felt able to make face-to-face contact with a Whitehall body in order to discuss intimate family matters; the urgency and distress of the issue of insanity seems to have broken down the traditional gulf between governmental departments and officials and members of the public.

Dr Arthur Stillwell, meanwhile, was determined to 're-cover' Louisa, to return her alienated self – the person she had been before meeting Prince in 1843. After the first few months Louisa was permitted to go out on her own in the immediate locality of the asylum; such outings allowed Dr Stillwell to gauge the extent to which patients had recovered their wits and to see whether they could 'conduct themselves in the world', as he put it. He also asked the Commissioners in Lunacy to come to Moorcroft House to interview Louisa. They spoke to her at length but were concerned that they were unable to 'open up' her mind on the nature of her religious beliefs. All she would reply was, 'I believe in the same God as you do.' They were additionally alarmed at the bitterness she expressed about Emily and about her non-Agapemonite family members. She stated no other delusional opinions except those regarding Prince and the Agapemone; but – as the Edward Davies case also shows – many alienists insisted in these years that monomania was characterised by insanity in one area only, with the rest of the mind seemingly unaffected. The Commissioners decided not to order her release.

Keeping a keen eye on the Nottidge case were John Perceval and the Alleged Lunatics' Friends. Sympathising entirely with Louisa's stubbornness about her religious beliefs, Mr Perceval wrote that she had every reason not to want to open up to the Commissioners, who, she had rightly guessed, would be unable to enter into any meaningful discussion of doctrinal matters. Louisa had described Prince to the Commissioners as 'the tabernacle in which the spirit of God dwelt', and in this she had been correct, wrote Mr Perceval to a national newspaper: St Paul had stated that each Christian must regard other Christians as a tabernacle of God. She had said that she was immortal – well, that too was entirely in accordance with

Scripture, and anyone holding such a view ought not to be condemned to a madhouse. Mr Perceval had himself, after all, seen close up the intolerance shown to the Irvingite sect, of which his brother, Spencer, was now a senior member.

Eight more interviews with the Commissioners in Lunacy would take place over the coming months; all resulted in the declaration that Louisa was of unsound mind.

Louisa appears to have been infuriated and terrified in equal measure, but she was convinced that another life awaited her, with her true family, at the Agapemone. Now in her mid-forties, she had been controlled by her parents all her life; even her finances were still being administered by her brother-in-law. As an ageing spinster, she was considered to be little more than the refuse of a society that worshipped domesticity, motherhood, moneyed leisure, physical beauty and fecundity. Prince and the enclosed little world he had created presented another way of life – a rival set of values that could allow her to be treasured, not scorned. It had given her a vigorous new sense of purpose and usefulness: Prince had encouraged her to go out proselytising and collecting funds, at Weymouth and Brighton, and she had proved very capable in this role. Her spiritual family at Four Forks (the community now numbered about sixty converts) passionately wanted her to be among them; even more importantly, Louisa could not bear separation from her beloved, favourite sister, Harriet. Most significantly, perhaps, the charismatic Prince seems to have excited emotions within her she could not recall ever having had before. And the money she wanted to hand over to him would be placed into communal funds, from which all the Agapemonites would draw whatever they needed, and even whatever, within reason, they desired. Her mother seemed keen that her father's bequest should be eaten away slowly, paying for long years of unjust, lonely, shameful incarceration at Moorcroft House; she herself was footing the bill for the iniquity that had been practised upon her. Her mother was now revealed to be chief among those 'enemies of God' of whom Prince had warned her so often.

Emily knew that she had used extreme measures to bring her beloved child to heel – but what choice did she have when she had seen her corrupted and exploited by diabolical people? Having lost

Clara and Harriet and, for a while, Agnes and Cornelia, to the sect, Emily was determined to use modern medical advances to cure Louisa of her religious delusion. And she was determined that Louisa's £6,000 should not go to Prince. In the meantime, Emily had to try to keep the Nottidge name out of the newspapers. If her daughters' association with improper heretics should become known, Emily would end her days in disgrace and ostracism and her family would bear the shame and damage to their reputation for generations.

On 6 January 1848, after fourteen months of detention, Louisa asked Dr Stillwell if she could have use of a carriage to visit the doctor's wife, who lived at Laurel Lodge, not far from the asylum. Her request was granted, but Louisa instead made her way to a small family hotel in Cavendish Square, central London. She then notified Clara's husband, William Cobbe, that he was to come and collect her and bring her back to the Agapemone. When Cobbe arrived at the hotel they spoke for many hours. No one at Spaxton had known of her fate, following her disappearance from Waterman's cottage, so Louisa told Cobbe about life at Moorcroft House, that she believed her kinsmen only wanted her money, and that as soon as she was free, she would give it all to the Agapemone. But it was not to be. When the pair arrived at Paddington station to start their journey to Somerset, Louisa noticed one of Moorcroft House's attendants walking towards them on the platform. Someone must have notified Dr Stillwell of Louisa's arrival in London and the doctor may have guessed that she would plan to travel to Somerset by train. Louisa was returned to Moorcroft House, distressed but not putting up a struggle.

When Cobbe returned to the Agapemone and told the brethren of her incarceration, senior members of the sect began to agitate for her formal discharge. Cobbe and Harriet's husband, Reverend Lewis Price, insisted that Louisa be re-examined, and on 9 May 1848 two more Commissioners came to Moorcroft. Their verdict was that although she had spoken 'in a very rational manner', she was nevertheless 'of unsound mind'. Louisa had refused to talk to them about religious matters. Indeed, she later explained that she knew that so long as she gave honest answers about her beliefs, she would remain in the asylum. Not wanting to be dishonest, she kept quiet.

Emily implored the Commissioners not to allow Louisa's release, because 'she worships a false god'. Agnes told them, 'If my sister were discharged, she would return to Mr Prince and would do anything he told her. He is far from a moral man . . . I believe that when I was one of Mr Prince's followers I was not in my right mind.' Edmund Nottidge, meanwhile, not in the best of emotional health himself, swore that around Somerset 'Mr Prince is generally reputed to be and believed to be insane'.

Dr Stillwell thought that Louisa was 'as mad on 9 May when the Commissioners saw her as she had been at other times. Persons labouring under religious delusions usually become gloomy and of low spirits, and are the more likely to commit an injury upon themselves by suicide.' He could, though, see that Louisa's physical health was declining as a result of her detention – she was significantly thinner and more wan-looking than upon her arrival eighteen months earlier. The only delusion she had ever expressed was on religious matters, and this monomania did not appear to prevent her from being competent to manage her own affairs; therefore, he now said, he agreed with the Commissioners (with one objector among their number), who strongly recommended, on 15 May 1848, Louisa's 'temporary' removal from confinement for reasons of health. The Act of 1845 had allowed such a discretionary discharge for non-violent or non-disruptive patients. But Louisa's case was filled with contradiction: she was declared to be delusional yet able to cope with everyday matters and to be rational most of the time. This was the bind that a diagnosis of monomania often created. So should monomaniacs be incarcerated, or left to live within the community? Adding to the confusion, Louisa had been found to have suicidal thoughts but was set at liberty in case she harmed herself if she were forced to stay in the asylum. Muddying the waters even further, Bryan Waller Procter, a Commissioner with seventeen years' experience, declared that the reason no formal lunacy inquisition had been mounted in the Nottidge case was that Louisa's illness had been deemed 'temporary' in nature; but this contradicted his colleagues' findings that her persistent religious delusion was unchanging and unchangeable. Louisa's case had brought to the surface the highly unsatisfactory elements of the monomania theory of insanity.

Not surprisingly, upon release Louisa abandoned for ever 'the enemies of God' and fled to the Agapemone, where on 29 May she transferred all her stock holdings to Henry James Prince – £5,728 7s 7d worth of Three

Per Cent government consols – without consulting Frederick Ripley, her trustee. He did not contest this, perhaps unwilling to insist upon his custodial role in her finances in such controversial circumstances.

The Abode of Love that she installed herself in, for the final ten years of her life, was now a complete little world in itself. Its relations with its neighbours had deteriorated: the walls were heightened, and blood-hounds were kept on the premises, to deter intruders. A siege mentality was developing. As Reverend Starky explained: 'We have no business with the world, nor has the world anything more to do with us. We have no saints. We simply give ourselves to God, of whom this mansion is the seat. At yonder gates we leave the world behind; its words, its laws, its passions, all of which we hold to be the devil's kingdom.'

It is not easy to winnow fact from rumour in the story of the Abode of Love. The paucity of babies and children at Four Forks gave rise to wild tales of infanticide and burial beneath the complex's spectacular lawns; or, less wildly, it was attributed to the forcible separation of man and wife that was demanded by Prince. The *Bridgwater Times* (always hostile to the sect) would speculate on 29 January 1852 that the Agapemonites 'must be cursed with barrenness, or the where-abouts of their progeny shrouded in mystery'. The practice of burying deceased members in the garden was perfectly legal but added to the sense that something awful was going on behind the walls. Indeed, the death of one female Agapemonite in 1851 was not reported to the authorities for a full month, and such refusal to deal with the outside world intensified suspicion about the secretive community.

More prosaically, the Agapemone was resented for its lack of chari-table activity. Even on the Sabbath, Prince would lead his followers in a cavalcade around the narrow lanes of Charlinch, in the coach and four he had bought from the estate of the late dowager Queen Adelaide (a presumptuously materialistic purchase for such a spiritual man); but the Agapemonites failed to fulfil their expected role in the local economy of providing cash donations to the local poor, or at least coal, food, clothing or nursing assistance. Prince was said to have been attacked by a mob in his carriage and could have been killed had not the farmers who had instigated the assault called off the attackers.

Louisa enjoyed sailing through the countryside in the coach, accompanied by various Agapemonites astride beautifully kempt horses (Prince's own mount was called Glory) and a pack of fine

The devil rides out? Reverend Henry James Prince sweeps out of the
Agapemone in the coach he bought from the estate of the late Queen
Adelaide. These parades around the lanes of Somerset caused resentment
among the locals.

dogs. But, as the eldest member of the Four Forks community, she
took no part in the scandalous games of hockey that took place in
the grounds, in which both men and women participated. The yokels
who stood up on ladders and branches to peer over the wall saw
this activity as unnatural; it could not be right that mature, moneyed
men and women should wield large sticks in pursuit of a small ball
– running, shouting, sweating, laughing. They even did it on Sundays.
(Though people had been hitting a ball, and each other, with curved
sticks for centuries, what we recognise today as field hockey was
relatively new to Britain in the mid-nineteenth century: the first
official club was formed in London in 1849. Throughout the Nottidge
case, hockey would have to be explained to witnesses, and one had
it described to him as 'a game something like football'.) On the

evening of 5 May 1849 – one year after Louisa had returned to the Abode of Love – labourer Isaac Thomas and his friends clambered into positions that gave a clear view over the wall and saw forty men and women playing hockey. One of Isaac Thomas's cronies, or Thomas himself, threw a stone, which hit, but did not injure, Prince. Twenty male Agapemonites then rushed out of the Abode's gate (hockey sticks in hand), and three of them beat Isaac Thomas so badly that his skull was visible to the surgeon who later attended him. In their defence at the ensuing trial, the Agapemonites said that for many months they had endured the stoning of their chapel windows, stones being lobbed over the wall into the gardens, and the persistent shouting of obscenities; they believed that Isaac Thomas was the ringleader. The court's verdict was that the Agapemonites should have requested the aid of the law and not taken their own defensive action. Damages of £11 were imposed upon them, but since Isaac Thomas had been seeking £20, it seems the court had some sympathy with the Agapemone's predicament.

The following month, Louisa brought a lawsuit in the Court of Exchequer against Ripley and Edmund on the grounds of assault and false imprisonment. The judge was the Right Hon. Sir Frederick Pollock, Lord Chief Baron of the Court of Exchequer. To Emily's horror, the national newspaper reporters were in attendance when the hearing began in Westminster Hall on Saturday 23 June 1849. Despite appalling physical conditions, the place 'was crowded to suffocation throughout the day', reported *The Times*. The judge complained of the stench in the court – the ventilation system of the new Houses of Parliament and the Hall had been an expensive disaster – and as the temperature rose steadily it was found that the windows could not be opened. A cholera epidemic was killing 14,000 Londoners at the time, and the miasmatic theory held that 'bad air' caused the deadly disease; but this didn't seem to have deterred anyone from coming along to witness the latest legal case concerning false incarceration.

In his opening statement, Louisa's counsel stated that his client wanted not just to erase the stigma of insanity from herself, but to show the world that Frederick Ripley and her brother had connived with her mother to falsely imprison her in a lunatic asylum. Moreover,

Yᵉ AGAPEMONE · WITH · A · PROSPECTE OF ᵡ BROTHERS AND · SISTERS · A PLAYINGE AT HOCKEY. – ALSO ᵡ BROTHER Svᵐ MISTER · PRINCE bᵞˢ 4 IN HANDE .

Punch magazine satirised the hockey-playing at the Agapemone.

they had made her pay for this injustice from her own pocket. Louisa believed that her certification had been undertaken for pecuniary greed.

Three questions would dominate the three-day hearing. On what grounds was it asserted that Louisa had been of unsound mind? Was the Agapemone an heretical sect? Why did they play hockey?

Witness after witness from the Abode described Louisa as 'ladylike' and 'gentle'. John Williams, a gentleman and a former farmer, testified that she had never been a 'serious' woman, but that since 'she had glimpsed the spirit of God' she had become 'joyous'. Life in the Agapemone was about mirth, pleasure, music, gardens, games, reading, riding – it was 'life made easy'. But if Williams had thought this lotus-eating revelation would recommend the Abode of Love to the court, he had misjudged the mood.

All the Agapemone witnesses denied that Prince was, or had ever claimed to be, the Messiah. William Cobbe told the court: 'Mr Prince is not the head of us, but God is. God has the care of us. We look up to Mr Prince with respect, but not with veneration, nor with reverence, but we look up to God in that way. I should say it would be a gross delusion to look up to Prince as God.' Mrs Julia Prince confirmed that her husband's teachings were identical to that of the Church of England, except that prayer was no longer of any use, since the Day of Grace was past and the Day of Judgement had arrived.

Reverend Lewis Price admitted under pressure that hockey was 'a manifestation of goodness for God', which caused hilarity among the onlookers. He denied that Prince habitually signed his letters 'Amen' and that he requested local tradesmen to address their bills to him in the form, 'My Lord, The Agapemone, Four Forks, Spaxton'. Lewis Price insisted that the Agapemone was not a sect but 'a private family'. As well as the incomprehensibility of holy hockey, the spectators were baffled by the Agapemonite assertion that blood family could be broken down and wholly replaced by a 'family' of fellow feeling and shared spiritual certainties. This was a social heresy.

The law teams included some of the stars that glistened brightest in the Victorian legal world. Future Lord Chancellor Sir Frederick Thesiger, defending Ripley, stated that it was nobody's right to interfere with the sincerely held beliefs of an adult. But in a speech that met with huge applause from the stifling and stewing onlookers, Thesiger said he would reveal that the Agapemonites 'creep into families, and there spread dismay and desolation'; he hoped to show that Louisa had not been 'a free agent, and had been . . . drawn into a low, degrading and disgusting association'. It had been her blood family's high moral duty to rescue her, and he asked the jurymen whether, if they had had daughter after daughter seized away for £6,000 each by these mercenary people, they would not have tried all available means to win her back.

But now rose the brilliant Alexander Cockburn, a future Lord Chief Justice of England. He said that Louisa had endured many months of odious confinement simply for seeking to worship the Almighty in the way that had seemed sincere and correct to her, even though this may have seemed to others to have been the worship of 'a most presumptuous sect'. And even if she was mistaken, the Almighty would look with compassion upon such errors and 'pardon the mistaken energy of his creatures', he claimed. Cockburn realised that there was no need to whiten the image of the Abode of Love: his appeal was to English liberty, which must be extended to 'half-wits' (*The Times*'s devastating description of all the Nottidge daughters) and even to charlatans themselves, since their beliefs were errors, not madness.

The judge, Baron Pollock, closely questioned the Commissioners in Lunacy about their reasons for believing Louisa to be insane. Commissioner Mylne admitted that Louisa constituted no danger to herself or to others. Then why detain her? the judge demanded. Pollock tripped up Dr Stillwell, too, when the latter revealed that Louisa had been allowed out on her own. Surely, the judge argued, the fact of being allowed out of an asylum alone was sufficient proof that the patient was not insane.

Baron Pollock's summing up was a blow to the alienist profession:

> It is my opinion that you ought to liberate every person who is not dangerous to himself or to others. If the notion has got abroad that any person may be confined in a lunatic asylum or a madhouse who has absurd or even mad opinion upon any religious subject, and is safe and harmless upon every other topic, I altogether and entirely differ with such an opinion; and I desire to impress that opinion with as much force as I can in the hearing of one of the Commissioners.

So long as such strange religious opinions were not 'forced offensively, or contrary to law, upon the public notice, or against public morals' they should be tolerated – although Pollock understood 'the horror and disgust' the public felt for the 'strange fancies' that had been adopted by certain religious movements in recent years.

The Agapemonites could have done more to avoid being viewed as fortune hunters, the judge continued. Had the three Nottidge daughters drawn up marriage settlements, this would have thrown off all suspicion of mercenary motives in three men marrying older women. (Agnes, as already stated, had of course asked for just such an arrangement.)

Pollock told the jury that the defendants had acted on Mrs Emily Nottidge's assertions alone. They had seized Louisa and had her certificated without an inquisition. 'They should have had the sanction of the law for such a step,' he said of the defendants, and this rendered them liable to whatever punishment the jury thought fit to apply.

The jury was out for an hour. They came back in with a majority verdict in favour of Louisa, but imposed damages of just £50 (she had been seeking £1,000), stating that they did not think Ripley and Edmund had acted for financial gain or any other 'unworthy' motive.

Pollock's opinion that only those dangerous to themselves or to others should be incarcerated was applauded by all the national newspapers, who saw the judge as reasserting English liberty in the face of an intrusive alienist profession. Not surprisingly, with a few exceptions alienist reaction to Pollock was indignant. The most thorough rebuttal came from Dr John Conolly, who in July 1849 published his response as an open letter, 'A Remonstrance with The Lord Chief Baron Touching the Case Nottidge versus Ripley'. Conolly, risking a libel action from Louisa, asserted that there was no room for doubt as to the actual insanity of Louisa Nottidge. He argued that danger was far from the sole criterion to be taken account of when asylum committal was under consideration. His letter placed great faith in what mad-doctors were capable of, in terms of both curative measures and improving society. Conolly's position on the role of asylum care was social and civic-minded, and in opposition to the libertarian defence of the individual put forward by Pollock. Conolly believed that families and society in general needed freedom from the anxiety, shame and moral contamination to which the behaviour of the mentally unsound subjected them.

His point of view was based on a blend of humanitarianism and something altogether more worldly. Conolly wanted sufferers of delusions (those prone to 'suggestions made by voices in the air, or words written in the sky') to receive the best possible care and chance of cure. But additionally, he knew that dynastic prestige and wealth were at risk if only dangerous family members were to be committed: the asylum had a broader role in dealing with those individuals whose disturbed behaviour interfered with the social system. Conolly believed that the following were sufficient grounds for incarceration:

If the liberty of an insane person is inconsistent with the safety of his property or the property of others; or with his preservation from disgraceful scenes and exposures; or with the tranquility of his family, or his neighbours, or society; if his sensuality, his disregard of cleanliness and decency, make him offensive in private and public, dishonouring and injuring his children and his name; if his excessive eccentricity or extreme feebleness of mind subject him to continual imposition, and to ridicule, abuse, and persecution in the streets, and to frequent accidents at home and abroad; his protection and that of society demands that he should be kept in a quiet and secluded residence, guarded by watchful attendants, and not exposed to the public.

It was morally right, argued Conolly, that society should be helped to become more pleasant and more decent by the removal of its upsetting and disgusting elements and those who did not know right from wrong. He recommended medical intervention for the many sorts of waywardness found in youth (both boys and girls), as this would check the progression to full-blown insanity, which was inevitable if adolescent introversion, promiscuity, narcissism, drunkenness, hilarity and financial recklessness went untreated. The best-run asylums, Conolly claimed, diverted thoughts, calmed morbid excitement, roused the apathetic and restored control of reason.

Conolly's letter was even-handed in attributing bad moral habits, mental delusion and weakness of intellect to both males and females. But when he moves on to discuss the Nottidge case, a gendering of misbehaviour becomes apparent. In a passage entirely based on hearsay, Conolly described Louisa as a 'weak-minded lady', who shunned her mother and experienced 'insane delusional worship of a mere man'. He quoted Emily, who had apparently told him of 'a tendency to mental disorder [that] existed in some of her children'. According to Emily, the Nottidge daughters all had 'weak understanding' and Louisa was 'the least intellectual'. However, although Edmund had spent time at Moorcroft House, there is no evidence to corroborate this hereditarian opinion of a devastated mother who had lost four of her children to the Abode of Love.

Placing Louisa in Moorcroft House had therefore been the correct course of action, Conolly asserted. Louisa had needed protection because she had been unable to take care of herself or her property. But it is hard to understand why Louisa's lack of wisdom and judgement, in handing over her whole estate to Prince, should be regarded as proof of insanity. She had had the choice

This plate appeared in a psychological textbook by Sir Alexander Morison, purporting to show the facial features of a woman suffering from 'religious monomania' or 'theomania'. The caption confidently asserts, 'She conceives herself to be more than mortal, and is full of self-complacency and benevolence to those about her; she is, however, thrown into a state of fury and agitation if her divinity be questioned.'

of having her money administered for her by Ripley, or by Prince, and she simply chose one form of control over another. As she would later claim, 'I enjoyed more the benefit of it [her money] than I ever did before.'

Religious fanaticism was the most frequent cause of insanity in women of all degrees of intellect, Conolly went on. Such afflicted women, 'at once gloomy and presumptuous . . . are easily induced to believe that God speaks to them more directly than to others; they soon learn to despise their parents; they denounce their relatives and friends; write foolish or abusive letters to persons in their neighbourhood; interfere in every family; and put their whole trust only in the vilest flatterers of their folly, to whom their property is willingly confided.' *Nottidge* v. *Ripley* had shown, he claimed, 'the peculiar danger of leaving imbecile, visionary, and fanatical women at large, particularly if possessed of property'. Unable to resist citing the rumours of sexual impropriety at the Abode of Love, Conolly wrote that it was immoral in a Christian country to have released Louisa to 'legalized robbery' and to 'the possibility of legalized prostitution'; this 'mock religion' destroyed 'all sense of modesty'.

If Conolly's proposals had been adopted, they would have made alienists key to the proper functioning of English bourgeois life. Yet Conolly had himself previously written at length of the inadvisability of asylum incarceration for anyone except the dangerous. His *Inquiry Concerning the Indications of Insanity*, published in 1830, had suggested that incarceration usually had a bad effect on patients and should be reserved for the utterly raving or the idiotic. As one present-day commentator has written, 'Conolly's changing views appear to mark an almost perverse shift, from enlightenment to error.' The prospect of financial gain may have been the reason for this change of mind. By the late 1840s, the habitually spendthrift Conolly was the proprietor of three private asylums as well as a consultant at Moorcroft, where he received a percentage of patient fees – a fact that, as we will see in a later chapter, would cause huge damage to his reputation.

The implications of Pollock's judgment were felt immediately by the Commissioners in Lunacy. In August 1849 they were informed by the Poor Law officials of Wem in Shropshire that all non-dangerous pauper patients in the Salop County Asylum were to be transferred to cheaper forms of care, such as the workhouse lunatic wards or boarding-out as single patients. The Commissioners by way of reply sent them a copy of Conolly's letter and urged them to reconsider.

Dr Forbes Benignus Winslow, another successful and well-known alienist (who ran two madhouses of his own), in favourably reviewing Conolly's letter despaired at the anger of an ignorant public, obsessed with wrongful detention and the alleged cruelty within asylums. It was threatening the progress of the profession in England, Winslow wrote (this had been Dr George Man Burrows's lament twenty years earlier): 'The public mind seems drunk, if we may so express it, with humanity upon this matter . . . If this feeling were allowed to dominate unreproved, the humanity-mongers would soon degrade the treatment of insanity into a branch of quackery, for none would be held fit to treat the insane but those willing to bow to the prejudices of ignorance and jealousy.' Those who supported the liberation of uncured lunatics were, in effect, 'accessories before the fact to many of the murders and suicides which, from time to time, shock society to its core.

'We have all experienced the dread of kidnapping in early child-hood,' Winslow declared. 'The public, made up of "children of larger growth", has taken up the notion that medical men are kidnappers, or the instruments of kidnapping, and that lunatic establishments are the receptacles of their victims.' In any case, he pointed out, malicious incarceration would involve the complicit co-operation of two doctors, an asylum proprietor, the visiting inspectorate or at least two Commissioners in Lunacy: how likely was that?

Emily's family had by now become a focus of national interest. The very privacy and discretion that Conolly believed a properly func-tioning asylum system offered were not to be available to Mrs Nottidge. Worse still, she found that two of her daughters had become her dedicated enemies. Eight months after the successful damages claim, the Agapemonites Clara and Harriet were found lurking in the shrub-bery at Rose Hill; they had travelled up from Somerset to assist Brother Thomas in his attempt to seize his son, George, now aged four, from his mother, Agnes. On 1 March 1850, Brother Thomas walked into the yard, addressed the little boy and then attempted to lead him away to a carriage, but was prevented from doing so when a stable hand intervened. Agnes and Cornelia then wrestled the child away, bolted the door and sent for the police. Officers came to guard the house as the Agapemonites made repeated attempts to intrude at Rose Hill.

Two months later, the Lord Chancellor was petitioned by Agnes and Ripley to make George a ward of court. The petition requested that Brother Thomas be restrained from bringing a writ of habeas corpus to obtain the boy, and from any future interference in George's life. In the meantime, Louisa, Clara and Harriet had concocted a joint affidavit, blaming Agnes's 'rebellious' temper for the failure of her spiritual marriage and vigorously refuting any criticism of the Agapemone. Lord Justice Knight Bruce, hearing the petition, pointed out that Brother Thomas had repudiated Agnes with 'coarse, harsh and unmanly treatment', and had for four years shown no interest in his own son. He believed that Brother Thomas had brought nothing to the marriage in terms of money, property or prospects. Of Thomas's ostracism of the pregnant Agnes, the Lord Justice declared: 'One is driven with shame and indignation to hope that there may not be a second human being capable of such extravagant indecency.'

Happily married sex was the right and natural thing, as Agnes's pregnancy had illustrated. The perversity of repudiating a woman who had become pregnant as a result of her marriage, and demanding that the union remain unconsummated, was evidence of the upside-down world of the Agapemonites. In the Abode of Love, a child – the intended consequence of marital sexuality – was seen as unnatural; and sexlessness within the wedded state was something to be striven towards. And so now, for the second time, a Nottidge family lawsuit led to a significant legal judgment that went against the grain: the court awarded Agnes full power over George's upbringing and education. Previously, despite the landmark 1839 Infant Custody Act – which for the first time permitted English mothers of proven 'good character' to bring a case for custody of a child under seven following a separation – there had been immense legal difficulty for any mother seeking sole care of her infant when she had deserted the marriage, when the father contested custody and he had no previous conviction for violence within the home. If Agnes were not granted custody of George, the boy would fall under the spell of 'a fanatic, or pseudo-fanatic, preacher', as Prince was described in the judgment of Knight Bruce, who continued, 'As lief would I have on my conscience the consigning [of] this boy to a camp of gypsies.'

Agnes had always downplayed the informality of relationships at the Agapemone, possibly to exonerate her sisters: 'I do not believe the reports which have been circulated on the subject of promiscuous intercourse as respects my sisters,' she swore in an affidavit. 'There were no secret or immoral proceedings in the acts of worship when I was with Mr Prince [but] I am certain that Mr Prince and Mrs Starky live in adultery, having seen her come out of his bedroom.' However, it was sex that would dominate public discussion of the Agapemone for the rest of its existence. In the 1850s Prince's behaviour became increasingly outlandish and dictatorial. Local newspapers reported that he would pick a fresh bride each week from the spouses of his followers. The women would sit on a revolving stage which the husbands spun, and when it stopped, whichever woman was sitting opposite Prince became his wife, spiritual or otherwise, for the week.

Prince's ostentatious, narcissistic display was in evidence in 1851, when he astonished visitors to the Great Exhibition by driving around

Hyde Park in Queen Adelaide's carriage with an immaculately caparisoned team of four horses. Dressed in ermine-trimmed scarlet robes, he was announced by a team of outriders: 'Blessed is he who cometh in the name of the Lord!'

To slough off the apathetic, to sniff out doubters and to haul in a new set of converts, Prince frequently changed Agapemone doctrine and shifted his ground on house rules. This capricious shuffling of the pack of his followers intensified as the decade went on – he had become a very moody Messiah. Locals told the press that they believed there had been as many as nineteen defections from the Agapemone in the mid-1850s. Lawyer James Rouse, an Agapemonite from the late 1840s, dressed up as a shepherd to make his escape at night over the Agapemone wall, since vigilance inside the compound had been stepped up. He and his brother-in-law later abducted Mrs Rouse when she was out riding in the carriage late one night. In some cases, those who had left the Abode were harangued and manhandled in order to get them to return. Clara Nottidge tracked down Hanna Styles, a thirty-two-year-old widow and grocery shop owner, in Dorchester, shouting, 'I am God, I am God, I am God!' as she tried to drag the apostate out of her bed and into a waiting carriage to return her to the Abode of Love.

Then the suicides began. John Williams hanged himself from a tree near the Agapemone farm at Higher Aisholt, using a luggage strap, in September 1854. Thomas Wilshire, a tax collector and overseer of the poor, cut his throat in May 1856. A female Agapemonite killed herself at Weymouth. A farmer called Scutt attempted suicide in the summer of 1856 but failed, and was subsequently sent to an asylum. All except Wilshire had signed over their money and property to Prince.

A wealthy Swansea family, comprising Arthur Maber, his son and four daughters, had become Agapemonites in 1848. In April 1851 one of the daughters, Charlotte, died; the coroner would later state that she had died of 'disease of the brain', and not tuberculosis, as the Agapemonites had claimed. Her sister, Mary, was fifty-six years old in June 1856, when she appeared to have fallen into 'a despairing state', according to Starky, who saw her walking alone in the Agapemone gardens one evening. The next morning, the house door and the gate into the lane were found ajar. On top of Mary's sewing box her sister Fanny found a note that read: 'This is the day of judgement to me, and fearful perplexity. When I go, self will go from the Abode. If my wretched heart were not stone and unbelieving, what Beloved [Prince] said would have relieved me.' Later that morning, Mary's body was found in a trench used for sheep-washing, two miles away and close to the Agapemone-owned Blaxhold Farm, at Enmore. There were no signs of injury, and the coroner's jury's verdict was death from asphyxia by drowning, caused by suicide during a bout of 'temporary insanity'. Mary's much-loved six-year-old niece, Phoebe, had been seriously ill and would die soon afterwards; her sister Charlotte had died five years earlier. Did this mean that Phoebe and Charlotte were among the damned? Had Prince not declared that those who proved themselves mortal (by dying) were not to partake of Grace? Such doubts are likely to have been a powerful factor in Mary's disastrous loss of faith in Christ, and, more importantly, in Prince.

The inquest gave the coroner, W. W. Munckton, the opportunity to air the latest allegations about life behind the high walls. He asked the Agapemonite witnesses if Mary's unhappiness could have been caused by the turning upside-down of traditional social hierarchy by Prince. The coroner had heard that maidservants – the young and pretty ones, at least – were now mistresses of the Agapemone, and that this had led to a feeling of 'de-gradation' for the ladies at the Abode of Love. He understood that certain privileged individuals ate the best food, had the use of the best-furnished rooms, and now formed an inner sanctum around Prince, while other members of the sect had to accept a lowering of their living standards to fund increasing opulence for Prince and his favourites. Coroner Munckton had been told that any complaints voiced about this state of affairs were said to emanate from the Devil. Witness Starky denied all such stories, declaring that 'We are all one in Christ'. (But even the loyal Starky had felt Prince's displeasure and had for a while been demoted to bootblack/stable hand.) On the subject of money, Starky admitted that Mary Maber had transferred £1,700 to Prince at the time of her sister Charlotte's death, and that in her will, Mary left everything to the Agapemone.

Coroner Munckton had intended to write to the Home Secretary about the Agapemone and to ask Whitehall to send someone down to observe the inquest, in the interests of the public. Munckton had also been planning to institute his own inquiry because he believed the number of recent suicides gave 'prima facie grounds for supposing there was something wrong in the establishment'. We don't know why Munckton then changed his mind: in the end, the Home Secretary was never alerted, although another female member of the sect attempted suicide three months later.

It is tempting to believe that the emotional and spiritual traumas which led to the wave of suicides and suicide attempts were the result of 'the Great Manifestation'. That shocking event cannot be safely dated, though it is likely to have taken place in the first half of 1856. The location, at least, is known. After the completion of the complex, the Agapemone chapel had become a sumptuous drawing room. Just as prayers and Sundays had no special status now that the Day of Judgement had arrived, no one place was particularly holy for the Agapemonites. The deconsecrated chapel/mystical drawing room had stained-glass lancet windows, a large crimson sofa, a red Persian carpet, a roof of oak, scarlet curtains, a green baize billiards table, oak and brass church furniture and fixtures, a large plaster statue of Prince's symbols (the lion and the lamb), flanked by billiard cues, a harp, a mechanical organ called a euterpean and cases of books, most of which looked unread.

Prince, now forty-five, had decided upon a new doctrine. This was his decree: a virgin was required, to purge man of sin, to receive man into grace and to fuse with the Holy One for ever. Out of a mystic moment of union a series of beautiful phenomena would flow. Flesh would be liberated from sin and made perfect. Whoever was chosen would not be entitled to refuse. Many Agapemonites would have expected her to be one of the Patterson girls – Anne and Sarah Patterson were the daughters of a widow who had joined the Agapemone. The humbly born Pattersons had been among the domestic staff at the Abode, but Prince's favour saw them enter his inner circle, and one of the girls, probably Anne, was said to have been given the title 'Queen of the Terrace' and was to be addressed as 'Milady'. It was to this inversion of social norms that Coroner Munckton had alluded during his inquiry and such a situation may have left Mary Maber and other female sect members with feelings of deracination and alienation.

The chapel of the Agapemone, after it had been returned to its original, devotional use. During its time as a drawing-room, it was the site of The Great Manifestation.

There was great excitement in the Abode on the day of the Great Manifestation: everyone knew that something important was about to happen. One female Agapemonite would later say, 'I have never felt so strange a joy and wonder as I felt in that hour.' In the chapel/ drawing room twelve Agapemonite men dressed in black, and twelve of the women, dressed in white, sang:

> All Hail, thou King of Glory, now
> Thy love their homage brings
> Now waits until the nations bow
> But crowns thee King of Kings.

Prince entered, dressed in red velvet, and sat upon an elevated seat that was doing duty as a throne. A large 'altar' (possibly the billiard table) had been draped in scarlet. The chosen virgin entered wearing a white Honiton lace dress with a train. Within this get-up was either Anne or Sarah Patterson – a fact never established for the outside world. The most lurid accounts of what happened next state that Prince and the maiden had intercourse on the altar while the Agapemonites watched. Others report that some kind of marriage ceremony took place (as Julia, the legal Mrs Prince, looked on in approval) and that the pair consummated their union later. (It is possible that consummation had already taken place, and so this public 'marriage' was required to cover up the fact.) Among the twenty-four watchers it is likely there stood Louisa Nottidge.

Whatever the case, nine months later, or thereabouts, the chosen one gave birth to a baby girl. Prince was astonished that a child should materialise from a union of the flesh. He now declared that the Great Manifestation had been a trick played upon him by the Devil. The child was Satan's, he said. But the rejected little girl grew up to be Eva Willett Patterson, who would be a revered member of the Agapemone later in the century. The chosen Patterson girl attempted suicide in September 1856 – after Coroner Munckton had concluded his inquiry into the death of Mary Maber. The attempt failed, and she returned to the Agapemone, where she stayed for the rest of her life.

The Great Manifestation and the denunciation of the baby as Satan's may have played a role in the suicides of Maber, Thomas Wilshire and the female sect member at Weymouth and in the attempted suicide of Farmer Scutt. It certainly brought a rush for the exit by certain Agapemonites, who were now having serious doubts about the meaning of the term 'spiritual love'. The most senior defection was that of Harriet Nottidge's husband, Reverend Lewis Price – a co-founder, with Prince, of the Lampeter Brethren in the 1830s. Those who stayed loyal to Prince, however, were rewarded with grandiose new titles. Arthur Maber was now the 'Angel of the Last Trumpet'; while William Priest, Samuel Trickey, Cornelius Voss, William Gulliford, John Brown, Josias Croad and William Puddy became the 'Seven Witnesses'. Agnes's husband, Brother Thomas, was henceforth to be referred to as 'The First of the Two Anointed Ones' and 'Keeper of the Seven Stars and the Seven Golden Candlesticks' – windy names that were inspired by the Book of Revelations.

Harriet, now in her early fifties, did not leave with her husband, preferring to stay with her beloved sister Louisa, who had gone through so much to be at the Abode. And so Lewis Price returned one night with a mob to demand that she come to live with him. His gang, which included a bailiff and a local newspaper reporter, searched the

Agapemone complex. When they crowbarred down the door of the Abode's main building, they found themselves facing the sect, who were barricaded behind furniture and brandishing firearms. The invaders did not find Harriet. Later she admitted that she had been secreted in a water cistern within the house.

So, for the third time, the Nottidge family became notable in a court of law, when in 1860 Reverend Lewis Price sued for a writ of habeas corpus for Harriet. He failed; but when Prince subsequently attempted his own habeas corpus for Harriet, the judge found for Lewis Price, stating that if a husband believes that his wife 'intends to leave him to reside in an improper place, he has a right to restrain her. She must, therefore, return to her husband.' Harriet was forced to live with her husband for the rest of her life, as the law demanded of an English spouse unless persistent or extreme physical cruelty could be proved.

During the habeas corpus hearings, Lewis Price explained that Prince's word was law at the Abode and that he had put words in people's mouths when it came to affidavits; he had pressured Lewis Price to give false testimony during Louisa's 1849 suit for false imprisonment in the asylum.

Louisa died at the Abode in July 1858 and her 'distressing' death, Lewis Price said, was a large factor in his decision to quit Prince and

The lawns of the Abode of Love complex were also used as a graveyard for the departed Agapemonites.

his through-the-looking-glass world. Prince had little sympathy for Louisa and her sufferings, reiterating that those Agapemonites who had died, 'have erred and they are gone. The Lord has done His will upon them.'

The *Bridgwater Times* of 4 August 1858 reported that Louisa had died insane, but since that newspaper had always detested the Agapemone and was aware of the Moorcroft House incarceration case, this claim must be viewed with scepticism; there is no evidence to corroborate it. Frederick and Maria Ripley and Louisa's other brother Ralph (Edmund had died in 1853) saw that she was buried in the graveyard of Spaxton parish church. She was on no account to go under the lawn of the Agapemone with the rest of the 'unsaved'.

The Nottidge family rallied and in a fourth noteworthy legal tussle, in the summer of 1860 – three years before Emily's own death – Ripley and Ralph challenged the gift of her entire property that Louisa had made back in 1848. They claimed that 'undue influence' and 'religious delusion' had prompted Louisa to transfer her £6,000 in Three Per Cent consols to Prince as soon as she had got out of Moorcroft House. Prince for his part stressed that all contributions made to him and the Agapemone were purely voluntary; he also denied tales that he had repeatedly visited Louisa on her sickbed in an attempt to dictate her last will and testament. Louisa had in fact died intestate.

The court found that the £6,000 had been 'improperly obtained' and must be handed to the Nottidge family, with costs.

Things began to quieten down for the Agapemone from the mid-1860s, though they would never be liked by their neighbours. The loss of the Nottidge money was not, in the event, a significant blow. Life continued in comfort for those deemed most loyal.

The only interview ever granted by Prince took place in 1867, when the preacher was fifty-six. Author and journalist William Hepworth Dixon described him as spare of build, of medium height, pale, and with 'the traces of much pain and weariness in his wan cheek. His face is very sweet, his manner very smooth. He has about him something of a woman's grace and charm. His smile is very soft; and the key of his voice is low. He has the look of one who

The only known picture of Prince; front row, third from the left.

has never yet been vexed into rage and strife. In his eyes . . . [you see] a light from some other sphere.' Dixon was unnerved by the oddly paranoid nature of the Abode of Love: 'Each Saint appears to keep watch and ward upon his fellow. Prince may dwell apart and hold himself accountable to none. But the rest of his people lie under bonds and only act and speak in each other's presence. They move in pairs, and trines, and septetts.' Of the women, only one appeared to be in perfect health; they all had a 'hush about them', Dixon noted, and had waiting eyes and silent lips. What perplexed him most, though, was that whatever horror had taken place during the Great Manifestation was accepted by these otherwise thoroughly respectable folks as perfectly normal.

Most of the Agapemonites whom Dixon met in 1867 were already well over the hill; in the next two decades they proved themselves all too mortal, and the lawns began to fill up with their bodies. Clara, the only remaining Nottidge woman left at the compound after 1860, and her husband William Cobbe made it into their late eighties, and Prince lived on and on, spending most of his time on a chaise longue, ministered to by fresh recruits. Having abandoned his once strong opposition to alcohol, he now drank with lunch and dinner from an expensively stocked cellar. He had chosen as his successor Reverend John Hugh Smyth-Pigott, who had become an Agapemonite in 1887;

Prince seems to have become aware that his own immortality had been an erroneous belief.

Prince nearly made it into the twentieth century and did not go under the garden until 1899, aged eighty-eight. Smyth-Pigott had his work cut out to convince the sect that this physical death had not called into question Prince's claim that Agapemonites were immortal. He somehow managed it, and the Abode's rackety life continued. A senior elderly member would be tarred and feathered in the Edwardian years, sustaining injuries that led to his early death; the attackers had believed that they were attacking Smyth-Pigott. Shock at this violence, together with the increasing charitable role the Abode had adopted, made the sect more tolerated in the neighbourhood. Yet as late as the 1960s, Spaxton residents would from time to time be doorstepped by reporters seeking tales of geriatric wife-swapping involving an altar and a revolving stage.

The money ran out at last, and the complex was sold in 1962 and converted into private housing, the Agapemone bodies having been exhumed and re-interred at the parish church. The chapel was used as a film studio for a while, and between 1966 and 1969 the BBC's *Watch With Mother* children's shows *Camberwick Green* and *Trumpton* were filmed in a room in which events more suited to the *oeuvre* of Roger Corman or Hammer films had taken place over a century before.

5

'If I had been poor, they would have left me alone'

Metropolitan Police constables James Richards and Arthur Parsons were patrolling their beat on the St John's Wood–Maida Vale border in the early hours of Friday 1 February 1851, when they heard screams of 'Murder!' coming from a house in Howley Place. Rushing towards the source of the cries they discovered an elderly woman with her head thrust out of a first-floor window, shouting that her servant was about to murder her. When the PCs gained entry to Herbert Villa, servant Mary Rainey explained that her mistress, Mrs Catherine Cumming, was insane. The officers rushed upstairs and PC Richards knocked at Mrs Cumming's bedroom door.

'Who's there?'

'Police.'

'What do you want?'

'I am come up to interfere respecting your servant who is going to kill you. Will you give the servant in charge?'

'Oh yes, take her away.'

'I must see you personally before I take the charge.'

'I cannot, I am undressed, and you can tell from my voice that I am in bed.'

PC Richards asked Mrs Cumming to dress and open the door, but she refused. When her coachman, Charles Crane, and the officers failed to break the door in, PC Richards climbed out of the landing window and edged round on top of the conservatory roof to the bedroom window. Once he had reached it, he smashed a pane, raised the sash and tumbled headfirst into the room, making Mrs Cumming scream again. When she rushed to throw herself from the same window, she spotted PC Arthur Parsons on the villa's driveway.

'Who is that?' she shouted down.

'I'm a policeman.'

'You are an infernal liar, you are not a policeman but a keeper from the madhouse in disguise, come to take me away.'

PC Richards noted a short, stout, evidently physically infirm lady, who still bore traces of having been extremely handsome in her youth; she was wearing a nightcap but a day dress. A large fire blazed in the grate, and the room smelt awful. Mrs Cumming told the officers that her servant had attempted to tie her to her chair with a white shawl and intended, when she had thus straitjacketed her mistress, to have her conveyed to a lunatic asylum. Gradually, the officers and the coachman calmed the seventy-two-year-old, who said that she wouldn't be pressing charges against Mary Rainey. Charles Crane agreed to spend the night at the villa to protect Mrs Cumming, and the officers left the bizarre scene. As they were on their way out, Rainey explained that Mrs Cumming had threatened to cut her own throat – committing suicide in order to 'put an end to "all this"'.

The next day, Mrs Cumming sent a request that her former servants George and Elizabeth Clarke would come and stay with her at Herbert Villa. Because of several painful physical conditions Mrs Cumming did not often leave her room, and she was very frightened of Rainey, who, she said, was of a passionate temper, used foul language on her, and had installed herself as 'Queen of the Lower House'. Mrs Cumming also believed that after dark her servant admitted others into the ground-floor quarters of Herbert Villa – she claimed she could hear male voices downstairs talking long into the night.

The Clarkes had worked for Mrs Cumming between March 1849 and April 1850, when they had left service to set up a greengrocer's shop; they had remained on friendly terms with their former employer and would visit her from time to time. They now discovered that Mary Rainey had indeed admitted guests: the Hickey family had frequently stayed the night, and sometimes friends of the Hickeys too. When George Clarke challenged her about using Herbert Villa as a doss-house, Rainey flew into a rage. Mrs Cumming ordered her dismissal and made up her final pay packet. Rainey screamed to Clarke that Mrs Cumming's children were coming for her, to take her to a madhouse. Then she flounced out of the house, for good.

The Clarkes had been instructed by Mrs Cumming to screen all visitors to Herbert Villa, demanding their names and taking a physical description. A number of gentlemen and ladies asking for admittance were refused – none of them gave names that Mrs Cumming recognised. Clarke warned off one man attempting to clamber over the garden wall, who was later seen conferring on the pavement with two well-dressed women. Carriages would lurk outside Herbert Villa, with the passengers peering out at the house. On 9 February, Mrs Cumming fled, and two days later sent for her furniture to follow her.

This flight from Maida Vale was in keeping with the course of her life for the past four years. Since December 1846 she had had to be taken in by friends and well-wishers each time she believed that her family were close to seizing her and confining her in a madhouse. This peripatetic life – in search of 'quietude', as she put it – was all the more remarkable since she was often in great pain. Mrs Cumming suffered from paralysis of the bladder and bowel problems, conditions that rendered her doubly incontinent and about which she was very embarrassed and apologetic to the servants who looked after her; in addition, she had recurrent ophthalmia, rheumatism and had endured a bout of pleurisy, an epileptic fit and bronchitis. Her physical suffering was more than matched by the intense pain of the hatred that had grown up between herself and her two daughters, Thomasine and Catherine. And the catastrophic breakdown of her family life had, to her horror, become national tittle-tattle.

Mrs Cumming was born Catherine Pritchard, the only child of a landlord of estates in Monmouthshire. Her parents intended to bequeath her everything. In 1808 she married – against her parents' wishes – Captain Charles Cumming, quartermaster of His Majesty's West Gloucester Regiment of Local Militia. Captain Cumming had represented himself as a man of property, but after the wedding it became clear he was no such thing; in fact, he had come to the altar burdened with gambling debts. Catherine's father immediately changed the nature of his bequest to her to a 'life interest', which meant that Catherine had to pass the properties on to any children she might have; she became, in effect, a trustee for her descendants.

Mr Pritchard was keen to keep as much of the inheritance out of the hands of the captain as possible.

The Cummings' marriage was a very unhappy one. The captain fathered at least two illegitimate children, and some of Mrs Cumming's income was used to contribute to their upkeep. He repeatedly ran up gambling debts and worked his way through a good deal of his wife's money to pay them off. Some of Mrs Cumming's furniture was seized by bailiffs, including heirlooms and items of sentimental value, and the Cummings had to move home three times and live under assumed names to dodge the captain's creditors. Throughout all, Mrs Cumming remained an astute businesswoman who appeared to enjoy the running of the Welsh estates, control of which had passed to her upon her father's death in 1811. Some of her Welsh properties would eventually fall into disrepair, however, for she was unable to look after them without making the Cummings' whereabouts known to the creditors.

Captain Cumming was declared bankrupt in 1839, when he was eighty-two years old; he subsequently spent two and a half years in the Queen's Bench prison. Her lawyer advised Mrs Cumming to seek a judicial separation from her husband, as this would offer some protection against his wasting of her money, but she refused, stating, 'I have hitherto done my duty to him and I will still continue to do so.' She often visited him in the debtors' prison, taking him spending money and his favourite delicacies: mock-turtle soup, beef tea and jellies.

Mrs Cumming had maintained a cheerful facade throughout the 1820s and most of the 1830s. She was highly sociable, with a lively but astringent wit. Even those who liked her would describe her as 'irritable', 'imperfectly educated' (i.e. badly brought up), 'of rather a violent temper' and 'obstinate and self-willed'. She had found great solace in her daughters, Thomasine and Catherine; she doted on the latter, her youngest. But then in 1836, Thomasine, at the age of twenty-two, became engaged to a man of whom Mrs Cumming violently disapproved. Perhaps he was too strong a reminder of the captain when he had wooed her. Benjamin Bailey Hooper, aged thirty, had played the French horn in various London theatres before joining the army as a bandsman, and later worked as a clerk for the Excise Office at Custom House. When Thomasine announced her engagement, Mrs Cumming forbade her to marry 'the trumpeter', or 'the bandsman' (as she habitually referred to Hooper). However, with the connivance of her sister Catherine (who had become the wife of surgeon-apothecary John Ince in 1833), Thomasine did marry Hooper. Mrs Cumming's relationship with both her daughters now cooled considerably, since she viewed Catherine and John Ince's behaviour as treacherous; but in 1839, after the birth of the Hoopers' second child, a tepid reconciliation took place. Hooper used the thaw to ask his mother-in-law for a loan, to which she agreed. She also assisted him in obtaining credit, and gave in to his request to be allowed to collect in the rents from the Welsh properties, but three months later she ended this agreement.

Then, in about 1840, so her daughters would claim, their mother's conduct and habits changed dramatically: from being ladylike and civil, she became 'strange'. Once gregarious and vain about her appearance and her dresses, she began to shun her friends and grew dishevelled. Always a very strong-minded individual ('When I am angry, I generally make people aware of it,' as she put it), she now habitually expressed herself in the strongest language, thought the worst of anyone, and would become enraged at the smallest provocation. When at a family dinner one evening Thomasine noticed her pocket handkerchief was missing, Mrs Cumming blurted out that she would always take the word of a servant over her daughter's if she were to claim that the handkerchief had been stolen by a servant. The Hoopers left the house immediately and did not communicate with Mrs Cumming for some time. On another occasion, when Catherine turned up ten minutes late for a dinner at her mother's house, she was refused entry. Mrs Cumming would complain bitterly about each daughter to the other; and when one of the Inces' young children died, Mrs Cumming made some extraordinarily insensitive remarks at the deathbed. Much would later be made of this incident.

By the early 1840s, Mrs Cumming's furniture and belongings had become widely travelled as a result of the efforts to prevent them being seized by her husband's creditors. She also had to sell off a Pritchard heirloom – a small basket made of silver – to raise cash. She had immediately regretted this and had given her son-in-law John Ince a large sum of money so that he could buy it back and return it to her. For many years Mrs Cumming claimed that Ince had given her neither the basket nor the money back. She also believed that Benjamin Bailey Hooper had taken and pawned the captain's gold watch, as 'the trumpeter' was proving unable to control his own spending.

After the captain's release from prison in 1842, the aged couple's life together at 1 Belgrave Terrace, Pimlico, was distressing and pitiful. Captain Cumming, in his mid-eighties, had disease of the prostate gland and suffered leg ulcers and poor hearing. Despite this, according to some of Mrs Cumming's servants and her solicitor, the captain 'endeavoured to take improper liberties' with many female servants and hired nurses, putting his hands down their dresses and making indecent suggestions. In addition, Mrs Cumming (using one of those euphemisms that can make aspects of nineteenth-century life seem so opaque) spoke of 'certain indelicacies that he was addicted to that she did not like to specify'. He could be violent too, and once seized a stick to beat a servant, missed, and split a wooden table instead. Mrs Cumming told her solicitor that the captain had pawned her watch and seized her rings from her fingers, drawing blood. In March 1846, a police constable was called in from the street when the captain locked his wife and her servant out of the parlour, barricading himself in with furniture stacked against the door. Mrs Cumming was crying and she pleaded with PC John Green not to harm her husband. When the constable broke into the room he was faced by the captain wielding a hot poker and a knife. PC Green was chased around the room by the octogenarian, who stabbed the constable in the hand (resulting in four days' sick leave) before the officer could overcome him. PC Green later stated, 'He had been using the poker about Mrs Cumming, by all accounts.' When asked why he hadn't fought back, Green said, 'The police authorities do not allow us to do that . . . He was considered as a madman. I believe the police had had interference since then and before.'

Rows at Belgrave Terrace were usually less violent, but raised voices and foul language were often heard by most of the servants and intimate friends; theirs was a 'cat-and-dog life', according to servant Martha Bowen. Both were drinking heavily, brandy and water being their drink of choice.

On the night of 11 May 1846, so John Ince later claimed, Captain Cumming fled the house in fear of his life because of one of his wife's rages. Mrs Cumming would state that the captain had been persuaded by the Inces to take with him in a hackney coach his entire writing bureau and all the paperwork it contained. It is possible that reading through the documents within the bureau, the Inces may have discovered something that set in train the following events. Or perhaps the events had been planned for quite some time.

Although Mrs Cumming had become cantankerous in the extreme, she nevertheless remained very fond of children and animals. She had become particularly attached to fourteen-year-old Elizabeth Buck, the daughter of one of her servants. On 12 May, the day after the captain had headed for the Inces' house, Mrs Cumming was teaching Elizabeth to write. They were seated in the parlour, poring over the girl's copybook, when two female strangers and two policemen entered the room, threw a straitjacket over Mrs Cumming, who began screaming 'Murder!', and bundled her out of the house, into a waiting carriage. A shawl was wrapped around her head to stifle her screams and she was forced down into the footwell of the vehicle. Elizabeth Buck also saw Mrs Cumming's servants attempting to keep out of the house two more policemen and John Ince himself; Ince forced open the parlour window to gain entry and, as the girl noted, rummaged throughout the house before leaving with several items.

York House in Battersea, South London, was used as a female asylum between 1844 and 1857, with a maximum of twenty-three patients.

Mrs Cumming was driven across the river to York House Asylum, near the Thames at Battersea, where she was questioned by Pimlico-based surgeon Thomas Wilmot, who spoke with her for an hour before heading off to talk to the captain, now back at Belgrave Terrace. After having seen the state of the house, Wilmot signed a certificate of lunacy for Mrs Cumming. The other certifying medical man was George Cornelius Johnson, Ince's business partner of thirty-four years – a fact that enhanced the sense of conspiracy. Questioned later, Johnson said of his decision to sign the certificate, 'Mrs Cumming appeared to labour under a perversion of all natural feeling towards her children.' Although it was Captain Cumming's signature on the lunacy order, Mrs Cumming and those servants who had remained loyal to her (the majority of the household, though by a slender margin) were in no doubt that the incarceration had been cooked up by Thomasine, Catherine and their husbands.

The celebrated alienist Sir Alexander Morison himself came along to York House on 18 and 19 May to speak to Mrs Cumming; a few weeks earlier, he had accompanied John Ince to Belgrave Terrace, when the son-in-law had sought his informal opinion on Mrs Cumming's sanity. On that occasion, Mrs Cumming had refused to allow the men into the house. Of his York House session with her, Morison stated that while Mrs Cumming was shrewd in business matters, she could nevertheless have been tutored by well-wishers to suppress the appearances of mental confusion; and that, said Morison, would account for how she could demonstrate business acumen while being of unsound mind. Morison quizzed her closely about the contents of her will and asked to whom she had chosen to leave bequests. During their talk, Mrs Cumming repeated to Morison her assertion that her husband had immoral relations with his nurses; she stated that a solicitor – John Dangerfield – had robbed her and that John Ince had been instrumental in the death of one of Thomasine's children (the Hoopers lost at least two of their children in infancy, and possibly more. The Inces suffered the death of at least three children in infancy). Morison concluded that Mrs Cumming was suffering from monomania, and this was also the conclusion of Dr John Gideon Millingen, co-proprietor of York House Asylum. In his casebook Millingen noted that Mrs Cumming was suffering from a single derangement, relating to her family's behaviour. Her delusions, he wrote, were that her daughters were prostitutes and their children illegitimate, and that her husband was 'a libertine'.

Millingen's paperwork was notoriously sloppy: only three months before Mrs Cumming's admission he had been reprimanded by the Commissioners in Lunacy for his lax patient casebooks and record-keeping and 'irregular' medical certificates and was warned that legal action would be taken if this negligence continued. A rather eccentric and rackety character, Millingen was also a playwright, writing such stage farces as *Ladies at Home; or Gentlemen, We Can Do Without You* (1819) and *Who'll Lend Me a Wife?* (1834). William Makepeace Thackeray consulted him for the Waterloo scenes in *Vanity Fair* (1847–8), because Millingen had had a long career as an army surgeon; and it has been claimed that Dickens used the doctor's researches on spontaneous human combustion for Krook's demise in *Bleak House* (1853). Millingen had also published respected works on 'the passions' and was a member of the Society for the Protection of the Insane – the informal forum for private asylum proprietors set up by Sir Alexander Morison. Totally against the spirit of the lunacy laws, members exchanged 'single patients' between them, and met regularly at Morison's home for social occasions. It is quite possible that Morison's patronage and professional friendship shielded Millingen from harsh treatment by the Commissioners; certainly, less well connected proprietors faced stronger censure and threats to their licences for such persistent case-book misdemeanours and breezy lack of concern. In 1839 Millingen had been sacked from the huge Middlesex County Asylum when local magistrates found restraint and other punitive measures still in force; it was felt that Millingen's military background was not suited to the more humane regime that was being demanded of county asylum superintendents.

In the same week as Morison's visit, two Commissioners in Lunacy came to see Mrs Cumming and concluded that she was 'full of delusions, most absurd in her conversation and certainly of unsound mind'. Commissioners William Campbell and James Cowles Prichard reported that she made no complaint to them about being confined in York House. They requested that the Inces, the Hoopers and certifying doctor Johnson come to the Commission's headquarters to discuss the case; when they did so, the Commissioners unanimously sided with the family.

Dr John Gideon Millingen (1782–1862) won an illustrious reputation for his work on the battlefields of Europe and subsequently for his writings on 'the passions'; but he later came under fire for his cavalier attitude towards certification and the physical wellbeing of his patients.

Campbell and Prichard had been shocked by Mrs Cumming's allegations against her family and by the filthiness of her home, which they had visited after seeing her in York House. It is worth noting that the keys to 1 Belgrave Terrace from the time of Mrs Cumming's removal to the asylum were held by the Hoopers and the Inces, and this would have given them plenty of occasion to dirty the premises and make up any story they liked about its state. Perhaps the start of this activity is what young Elizabeth Buck witnessed when she noted Ince rummaging around in the upper rooms on 12 May.

Like many private asylums, York House had beautiful grounds. The house and estate dated back to the late fifteenth century and there was a locally held belief (probably erroneous) that Anne Boleyn and Henry VIII had conducted part of their courtship here; more certainly, George IV and Mrs Fitzherbert had canoodled within the Georgian rebuild. But Mrs Cumming preferred not to walk in the grounds. Pointing out of the window at two female patients strolling in the gardens, she objected that, 'I have been associated with *those* people', and she refused all social mixing with other inmates. However, she also felt that the solitude and seclusion of this 'dull and gloomy' place was having a bad effect on her, as she was 'accustomed to society'. Mrs Cumming was therefore requested to dine in the private quarters of Mr and Miss Parkin, the brother and sister co-proprietors of York House, who oversaw the day-to-day management of the asylum. This Mr Parkin is the surgeon, and former asylum patient, who had joined the Alleged Lunatics' Friend Society, and it remains a mystery why we now find him on the other side of the fence (or wall). The Parkins grew to like Mrs Cumming and introduced her to their friends. Nurse Elizabeth Davis also became fond of her: 'I think she was of stronger mind than I am myself,' she said later. 'Considering her years, she was of very sound understanding . . . She lamented her daughters' cruel treatment of her in tears many times.' But Davis's opinion of Mrs Cumming's state of mind was never sought by anyone; she later claimed that nurses and attendants had 'no control' over matters if they ever believed that a sane person had been confined.

Before long the Parkins allowed Mrs Cumming to leave York House for carriage rides, with attendants. The Parkins were becoming worried that 'the cries of the lunatics' in the asylum might push Mrs Cumming into full-blown mania; but the presence of attendants on her drives, with the implication that she was not to be trusted, annoyed her. Mrs Cumming also complained that her friends were being denied access to her. Catherine called upon her mother just once, to supply her with some of her clothes, but the old lady did not wish to see her. Thomasine did not call at all. Mrs Cumming's agent for one of the Welsh properties was not allowed to consult her, and the Inces and Hoopers would tell him nothing of what had happened to her when he called on them to inquire. So it was Dr Millingen who in August had the task of telling Mrs Cumming, as gently as he could, that the captain had died in mid-July. Mrs Cumming's first response was anger, reported Millingen: 'They have done for him, and now they want to do for me,' she told the doctor.

The Inces and Hoopers revealed that they wished Mrs Cumming to agree to have an official receiver appointed by the Commissioners in Lunacy, for her rental income and the administration of her estates. This was communicated to her by solicitor John Dangerfield, who Mrs Cumming had already concluded was a robber. Since her incarceration, Dangerfield had been collecting the Welsh rents but Mrs Cumming never received any written accounts of these transactions; Dangerfield later claimed that he had rendered her verbal reports of her business affairs. At York House, Dangerfield (wrongly) told Mrs Cumming that by having a receiver appointed by the Commissioners, she could manage to avoid the expense and embarrassment of a lunacy inquisition. But the Commissioners soon advised Dangerfield that they could not undertake such a move, because the 1845 Lunatics Act severely limited the size of the estate to which such an avoidance applied. Put simply, Mrs Cumming was too rich to avoid an inquisition. Despite her husband's profligacy, she was still believed to be worth £30,000 – and so on trial she would have to go. And in a pub. Catherine Cumming would have her psyche scrutinised before the press, spectators and drinkers at the Horns Tavern near Kennington Common.

The inquisition opened on Saturday 29 August 1846. Mrs Cumming was without legal representation, because access to her at York House had been controlled by John Ince, who permitted only John Dangerfield to visit her. By contrast, her accusers had hired three lawyers and four doctors. Commissioner Francis Barlow was in the chair, and his jury numbered sixteen.

The allegations flew at Mrs Cumming from many directions on that first day. Harriet Quin, a servant at 2 Belgrave Terrace, claimed Mrs Cumming had once threatened to dash Quin's brains out against the wall. It was alleged that Mrs Cumming had placed an advertisement in a newspaper for a small girl whom she could adopt as her own, but when one Sarah Boswood had been put forward as a potential new daughter, Mrs Cumming had so mistreated the child that Sarah was removed. It was claimed that Mrs Cumming had sought out orphaned or abandoned girls in order to upset Thomasine and Catherine. Mrs Cumming did not deny that she had regularly described one such child companion, Cecilia Bartolini, as 'her daughter'. This lack of affection for her own children and the attempt to supplant them was offered as evidence of Mrs Cumming's unnatural state of mind.

Thomasine had cried off attending the inquisition, due to 'delicate health', but Benjamin Bailey Hooper was there, claiming that the captain had twice run away to the Hoopers. When Hooper had brought him back to Belgrave Terrace, Mrs Cumming had told him, 'I would rather see my husband brought back dead than brought home by such a scoundrel as you.'

Dr George Vernon Driver, who had worked at John Ince's medical practice for seven years, stated that during one social call Mrs Cumming had taken him into the garden of Belgrave Terrace to show him the birds she kept, and 'in my presence she made water, without offering any remark'.

John Ince alleged that his mother-in-law had always been prone to fits of outrageous temper and for years had made dreadful allegations of immorality against her husband, whom Ince described as 'the mildest of elderly gentlemen'. He recalled that after the captain had got out of prison, Mrs Cumming would regularly lock him in his room and that because she had kept such a filthy house, the captain's health had rapidly declined. Ince reported that in July, two months after Mrs Cumming's incarceration, 1 Belgrave Terrace had been searched and up to forty parcels of sugar were found scattered about a dusty lumber room, alongside banknotes tossed around with old papers, firewood and rubbish. (This would not have been news to Ince, as he had had the run of the house since mid-May.) His mother-in-law had borrowed money from him, Ince claimed, yet for years had accused her family, servants and lawyers of robbing her.

Catherine Ince confirmed everything her husband had said and emphasised the 'unnatural' hatred her mother had for her children and grandchildren. She claimed that, although her grandchildren were very young, Mrs Cumming would fall to her knees and call out for God to curse them. Catherine also testified that Mrs Cumming had accused John Ince of killing one of the Hoopers' children for financial gain.

The jury was told that Mrs Cumming had stated that she had three additional daughters – one in France; one called Lady Dillon; and one in India, called Sarah. This may have been Mrs Cumming's rather generous attempt to include the captain's illegitimate offspring within the family circle; or perhaps she used the word 'daughter' in a figurative way, to speak of young women friends to whom she felt close. Mrs Cumming's often oblique humour and allusive use of language were to play a significant role in the misfortunes of her old age.

Extraordinary emphasis was placed in these hearings on Mrs Cumming's relationship with her five cats – Vic, Viz, Mrs Thomas, Kitty and Tommy. Those servants who testified against her sanity claimed that the creatures were never allowed out of her bedroom and so 'performed all the offices of nature there'; as a result, the room stank and the house became 'offensive'. The cats were said to have had 2lb of top-quality meat prepared for them each day by Mrs Cumming herself, who would place a clean white cloth, the best china bowls, a silver plate and napkins on the floor, so that the cats would dine in style.

Allegations about the filth at Belgrave Terrace, Mrs Cumming's vile temper and bad language, her neglect of her husband, her accusations of his 'gallantries' with his female attendants, and her love of brandy were made by six servants and two of the captain's former nurses. Elizabeth Browne, an elderly nurse, testified that during her nine weeks at Belgrave Terrace, at the start of 1846, Mrs Cumming had been cruel to the captain, that she kept her paper cash in her boots and slept with her boots on. Browne said she had been accused by her employer of impropriety with the captain. But when Commissioner Barlow asked Mrs Cumming if she had made such an allegation, Mrs Cumming replied, to the public's great amusement, 'Oh no, gentlemen, look at her face – it is not likely.'

Watching as this torrent of calumny flowed at Kennington was West End solicitor Robert Haynes. When he learned that Mrs Cumming was legally unrepresented, he made himself known to her at the close of the first day's proceedings, offering her his services.

On Tuesday, 1 September the jury went to see the state of 1 Belgrave Terrace for themselves. It was indeed filthy and full of strewn rubbish, and Mrs Cumming's own rooms had been filled with brandy bottles. The jury was horrified by the second-storey room that Mrs Cumming had used as a loft for her pet birds. Later that day, the Commissioner announced that there would be one week's adjournment, so that Mrs Cumming could belatedly instruct counsel. She had been impressed by solicitor Haynes's approach, and when proceedings began again on Tuesday the 8th, she began to take a more active role in the inquiry,

although anxiety had prevented her from sleeping during the adjournment and she was now eating very little.

Dr Millingen came to the tavern to repeat his assertion that Mrs
Cumming was suffering from monomania. 'I found her delusions
unbending,' he told the inquiry, running through all of Mrs Cumming's
angry accusations about her family, lawyers, the captain's nurses and
certain servants. When Millingen had told her at York House that an
inquisition was to be held, she said of her family, 'Here is another
piece of villainy.' Millingen told the jury – and this tale would be
repeated many times against Mrs Cumming – that on viewing the
laid-out corpse of the Inces' dead young son she had accused John
Ince of having murdered the boy and then painted and varnished the
face, to disguise the true nature of his death. Mrs Cumming would
later claim that what she had actually remarked out loud was that the
dead child had been made up to look like a Regent Street tailor's shop
mannequin, waxen and doll-like – she had called it 'a very handsome
corpse'. John Ince may have added his own varnish to the tale.

Mrs Cumming was then questioned by her own counsel, Robert
Haynes, and all the newspaper reporters present at the Horns hearings
noted the lucidity of her answers and her impressive composure in
such a mortifying environment. She spoke for an hour and a half,
during which she was able to give a detailed account of her properties
in Wales; repeated that she considered Ince, Hooper and Dangerfield
to be dishonest; and claimed that she had always retained affection
for her favourite child, Catherine. Yes, she had used far too strong
language in her condemnations of Thomasine, but her eldest daughter
and the trumpeter had behaved very badly towards her. And yes,
unhappily, her late husband had been faithless throughout their
marriage, had always kept low company and acted licentiously; the
hired nurses themselves had complained to her of his behaviour when
they came to her to give notice of their resignation. As for her pigeons
and fowls, they were simply her hobby, and, along with the cats,
produced no noxious smells in the house.

A succession of friends, business associates, servants and one of the
captain's nurses next spoke in Mrs Cumming's defence, contradicting
in detail the allegations of violence, rudeness, filth and eccentricity.
The jury, press and public were told of a wife who showed great
restraint in the face of her husband's abusive and lewd behaviour; they

heard that he had regularly shouted 'Bitch!' and 'Whore!' at her and had claimed that Thomasine was not his child. The witnesses reported Mrs Cumming's constant attempts to keep the house clean in spite of her husband's love of squalor; the captain's pawning of her personal effects in order to obtain cash for drink; her attempts to ensure that he ate regularly and well; and her touching love of animals, which were pampered but did not cause mess at Belgrave Terrace.

There is only one explanation for these two utterly contrasting sets of evidence: bribery. There can be no reconciling of the oppositions in the Cumming case unless we assume that certain witnesses had been induced to tailor their evidence either to suit the Ince–Hooper axis, or to ensure Mrs Cumming's liberty. The Hoopers and the Inces had £30,000 to gain from depriving their mother of control of her estate, while Mrs Cumming had a deep pocket with which to tempt witnesses to refute her family's allegations. Immersion in the surviving written accounts suggests that the case against Mrs Cumming was got-up. A sense of orchestration rises off the page – the pat-ness of the anti-Cumming camp and the mysterious visits paid to the Inces and Hoopers by certain servants point to a conspiracy. An unloved mother could have her uncontrollable mouth, extreme moodiness and periods of confusion – caused by an unhappy marriage, illness and old age – turned against her for financial gain. All that was needed were medical men happy to pathologise Mrs Cumming's eccentricities and strong opinions. And fortunately for the Hoopers and Inces, Drs Millingen, Morison, Wilmot, Johnson and Driver, together with Commissioners Campbell and Prichard, testified that Mrs Cumming's intense dislike of her family was so unnatural as to be a symptom of insanity.

James Cowles Prichard was a scientist of extraordinary intellectual gifts, being an early, pre-Darwinian evolutionary thinker, and in his alienist work developing, from the mid-1830s, the concept of 'moral insanity' – what we would today describe in terms of 'personality disorder', or any psychological or behavioural disorder that leaves rationality intact. The concept of moral insanity had deep roots in both philosophical and medical thinking, and in France at the turn of the century, Philippe Pinel and his student, Jean-Etienne Esquirol, had made huge advances in exploring 'non-intellectual insanity', or *manie sans délire* – mania without delusion. But Prichard explored the idea, and theorised it, through clinical observation. In his *Treatise on Insanity and Other Disorders Affecting the Mind* (1835), he described moral insanity as:

> a morbid perversion of the natural feelings, affections, inclinations, temper, habits, moral dispositions, and natural impulses, without any remarkable disorder or defect of the intellect or knowing and reasoning faculties, and particularly without any insane delusion or hallucination . . . The subject is found to be incapable, not of talking or of reasoning upon any subject proposed to him, for this he will often do with great shrewdness and volubility, but of conducting himself with decency and propriety in the business of life.

Prichard's ideas framed much of the discussion of Mrs Cumming's mental state.

Others believed that any deviation from maternal affection was a strong indicator of moral insanity. To a lesser extent, lack of familial warmth in a male could also be made into a case of unsoundness of mind, as Edward Davies had found to his cost. Prichard admitted that the borderline between 'normal' and 'abnormal' was a perilous one to try to define with exactitude; he was responding to those who worried that the concept of moral insanity could bring within its remit all kinds of unorthodox behaviour. Other critics of his theory stated that there could be no emotional disturbance without some degree of intellectual disturbance. Still others wondered whether moral insanity was a transient condition; or whether it was the prelude to what would inevitably become full-blown intellectual collapse.

With regard to Mrs Cumming, there was a more mundane refutation of Prichard's view: that there was nothing unnatural or morbid about her dislike of her children because they had behaved so very badly towards her. And unfortunately for the Goneril and Regan of this case, Robert Haynes had drummed up no fewer than five doctors, who examined Mrs Cumming at York House and were willing to go on record that they found her to be of unusually sound mind for an aged lady who had suffered so much anxiety and ill health.

The newspaper reporters soon came over to Mrs Cumming's side; she was sparky and witty and highly quotable. Could it have been this Fleet Street change of heart, together with Mrs Cumming's perfectly reasonable demeanour as a witness, that ensured the hearing would not go as the Hoopers and Inces wished? Or was it the announcement by Mrs Cumming's counsel that an important new witness was on his or her way from France to testify? On 22 September, after an adjournment of a fortnight, Mrs Cumming entered the room at the Horns 'gay and smiling and evidently in high spirits', according to one newspaper reporter. Both sets of counsel announced that the inquisition was being abandoned, and that 'an arrangement' between the interested parties had been agreed. This was unprecedented. Commissioner Barlow, confessing himself flummoxed as to how to proceed, said he needed to have a word with the Lord Chancellor. Mrs Cumming's counsel declared that, pending a final decision, Mrs Cumming could no longer be detained at York House. On the announcement of the restoration of her liberty, Mrs Cumming was immediately surrounded by a crowd of cheering friends and well-wishers, who bore her away to a carriage.

The inquisition had cost her over £5,000 (the cost of Edward Davies' lunacy hearing), but had still not cleared her of the allegation that she was of unsound mind and unfit to manage her affairs. The deal that had been worked out by the rival lawyers – which would stop the ongoing expense of the inquiry and (in the touchingly naive view of the Lord Chancellor and the Lunacy Commissioners) help to repair the fractured family – was to place Mrs Cumming's property under the care of three trustees. One trustee would be appointed by Benjamin Hooper and John Ince; another by Commissioner Barlow; and the third by Mrs Cumming's friend of twenty years' standing, Stephen Hutchinson, a civil engineer. Mrs Cumming was to have sole use of her money during her lifetime, but after her death, one-third was to pass to Catherine, one-third to Thomasine and one-third to whoever Mrs Cumming wished; if the latter failed to be nominated, this third would automatically pass to her two daughters. It was stipulated that neither son-in-law was to have any control of the funds left to their wives.

The *Sun* newspaper editorialised that the Cumming compromise was an extremely worrying new feature of lunacy procedure:

If Mrs Cumming, being sane, has been (in conformity with law) incarcerated as a lunatic, gross injustice has been done to that lady. If Mrs

Cumming, being lunatic, has been liberated as sane, gross injustice has been done to the public, the safety of every individual composing which is jeopardised by the liberation from all restraint of an insane person. In either case, the law is unjust, as both the incarceration and the liberation are according to . . . the iniquitous lunacy laws which at present disgrace our statute book.

The Lancet was more terse: 'A compromise with a lunatic!' By being asked to sign a legal agreement, Mrs Cumming was being deemed to be of sound mind, yet the agreement itself did not declare her to be sane and therefore competent to sign.

Why had she been smiling so much that last day at the Horns? Had she realised that this legally shambolic outcome could be used to her advantage at a later date? Or was she looking forward to never again having to set eyes on the Hoopers and the Inces? Mrs Cumming went straight from Kennington to stay with Stephen Hutchinson and his wife Sarah at Vauxhall, and remained with them for some months. During this time she made an astonishing discovery: she found out that the revised settlement of 1809 that her father had made following her disastrous marriage was invalid; his original bequest, giving her 'absolute' – rather than solely 'life' – interest in her property, was therefore still in force. This made her position considerably more powerful: it gave her the right to dispose of her property as she saw fit, and to bequeath it to whomever she liked. Instantly she repudiated the Horns agreement, and, newly invigorated by this good news, set about making large-scale changes in Monmouthshire – selling properties and land, making repairs and re-drafting tenancies. She had to take the trumpeter to court to get back the deeds of the Welsh holdings. Much of her paperwork had been seized by the Hoopers and the Inces during her stay at York House and Hooper told her that he would return the deeds only if she settled half of her estate upon her grandchildren. Mrs Cumming refused, sued him to obtain the documents – and won. When the Hoopers counter-sued a few months later, the court decreed that she must settle the fairly paltry sum of £50 a year upon Hooper. In both these legal actions Mrs Cumming was treated by the law as a sane person.

By October 1847 Mrs Cumming was living at Gothic Villa, 59 Queen's

Road (today Queen's Grove), St John's Wood, a house she had bought from her solicitor Robert Haynes. She believed that her family had not traced her to this address, and indeed St John's Wood was a wise choice for anyone who wished to lie low or lead a surreptitious life. Behind the high walls of a St John's Wood villa, many a wealthy Victorian man housed his mistress, and the roofed-over pathways from garden gate to front door that were a feature of some of the houses gave nosy parkers at first-floor windows only the briefest glimpse of who was coming and going. The area's moneyed seediness was expressed physically, in lush shrubberies and bushes, the lilac and laburnum trees that whispered, curtains of Virginia creeper, high garden walls and doorways with peepholes. But the seclusion offered by its architecture meant that St John's Wood could protect other secrets, too. Poor mad Mary Lamb (sister of Charles, and murderess of their mother) lived out her last years in the 1840s at number 41 of the now disappeared Alpha Road. Next door at number 42, another elderly single patient, Mrs Parker, signed into his own care by the illustrious Dr Alexander Sutherland, was being abused by her nurse, as the Commissioners in Lunacy would discover. In fact, Sutherland housed most of his 185 patients under single care in St John's Wood and Maida Vale. Not for nothing did Wilkie Collins route Walter Hartright's night-time walk with the Woman in White along Avenue Road, past the end of Queen's Road; while the novel's villain, Count Fosco, lived at the fictional 5 Forest Road, St John's Wood.

Anne Catherick meets Walter Hartright in *The Woman in White*. On their walk through St John's Wood, they pass the end of the road where Mrs Cumming was in hiding from her family, who wished to incarcerate her. St John's Wood was one of the most popular districts for the discreet placement of lunatic single patients.

In the first week of October, three of Mrs Cumming's fowls were found dead in their bird-house in the garden of Gothic Villa. Two days after this, she poured milk from a jug for the cats, but the creatures would not drink after sniffing it. In a state of high suspicion, Mrs Cumming had the milk jug and the remaining bird-meal sent to Dr Robert Barnes of Gloucester Terrace, Hyde Park, for analysis. Dr Barnes found that the scrapings from the bird-house contained acetate of lead, a poisonous substance used in dyeing and varnishing, while the dregs of milk contained Epsom Salts. As he later recalled, 'Mrs Cumming was very much agitated and very much annoyed at the occurrence . . . She at first was inclined to think that her family had been the means of having it placed there to kill the fowls and for the purposes of annoying her.' In fact, Dr Barnes said he was not confident that she understood that the unpleasant milk the cats had rejected was not poisonous, and that it had no connection with the poisoning of the fowls – which may well have been accidental, if, say, a workman had left odd-job-related acetate of lead in the garden or near the bird-house. Mrs Cumming remained perplexed and suspicious.

She now moved from Gothic Villa to Herbert Villa, Howley Place, when she discovered that the Hoopers and Inces had approached the Lord Chancellor and the Commissioners in Lunacy with a fresh request that she be sent to an asylum. They stated that her 'unnatural' wish to have no family life, alongside her erratic relationships with lawyers and agents, was proof that the Horns inquisition should have concluded with a verdict of insanity. Unwilling to be dragged back into the distressing private family tragedy, the Commissioners and Lord Chancellor declined to interfere.

It was at this point, on 1 February 1851, that the police broke into Mrs Cumming's bedroom in Herbert Villa.

The following months Mrs Cumming spent shifting between Blackfriars, Edgware Road, Kennington, Bromley and St Leonards-on-Sea, taking her cats wherever she went. Her health declined, and an increasing weakness in both legs meant that she could walk only with difficulty.

She had appointed a new local agent, Ebenezer Jones, to help collect the rents for the Welsh properties, but Mrs Cumming quickly became suspicious of Jones and sacked him. And rightly so: Jones was a spy for the Hoopers and Inces. Now a new round of persecution began. Put up to it by her family, Jones intended to prosecute Mrs Cumming for perjury in connection with an affidavit of hers drawn up during the suit with Hooper. Her family hoped that a judge would find Mrs Cumming not guilty of the charge by reason of insanity – a far quicker, and cheaper, route of getting her into an asylum and thereby achieving control of her money. But the perjury charge was instantly dismissed by a magistrate.

A simultaneous tactic was to malign Mrs Cumming not just to business associates but to local shopkeepers and suppliers, whenever her latest address was discovered. Her Welsh tenants were instructed by the Hoopers and Inces not to pay her any rent, and potential buyers were warned off making purchases of her land and houses. Although wealthy, Mrs Cumming's cash flow was now drying up, and she became increasingly reliant for liquidity on a series of lawyers, whom she hired and fired with all the capriciousness and foul temper that she had shown in her dealings with servants over the years.

Looking down from her window at number 6 Edgware Road, at the Marble Arch end, where she had been given shelter by the family of James Oldfield, one of the Hutchinsons' employees, she would see her daughters gazing up from the pavement. They would pace up and down outside the house, stopping passers-by and talking with them; once they gathered some policemen around them and pointed up at the window. Sarah Hutchinson saw them too. The servants at number 6 had been instructed not to allow Mrs Ince or Mrs Hooper inside, and Catherine Ince began a campaign of constant hammering on the door. Then, one day, she managed to rush past the servant who opened the door, dash up a flight of stairs, and, pushing another servant out of the way, burst into Mrs Cumming's room. Exclaiming, 'Mama!', she threw her arms around the old lady's neck. Mrs Cumming, ill and immobilised in her chair, believed she was being attacked. When Mrs Oldfield and the servants rushed in they heard her shouting, 'Oh, I think she's come to strangle me!' However, of the frightening embrace, Mrs Cumming later insisted, 'I reflected, on recovering from my momentary fear, and dismissed the impression that my daughter was about to strangle me.'

Mrs Ince refused to leave, despite being asked to by her mother and by Mrs Oldfield, and continued to attempt – incongruously in such a hostile, charged environment – to make small talk with the mother she had not seen for four and a half years. Mrs Cumming and Sarah Hutchinson noted that her eyes appeared to range around the room and linger on every object within it. When Mrs Cumming protested to her daughter that she had put her in York House Asylum knowing her not to be mad, Mrs Ince cried out, 'Mr Haynes put you there, Mama, and we got you out!' – a ludicrous allegation, as Haynes did not meet Mrs Cumming until three months after her incarceration. After an hour or so, Mrs Ince agreed to leave, but the next day she returned with Thomasine and a small group of strangers and repeatedly knocked at the door.

Mrs Cumming fled again, first to the Middlesex village of Southall, where she engaged a new servant, Mrs Albina Watson; then to Worthing on the south coast, and then to 5 Bloomsbury Place, near the seafront at Brighton. She was also accompanied by Sarah Hutchinson and received regular visits from Robert Haynes, Dr Barnes, yet another new physician Dr Henry Caldwell, and a local doctor, Dr Robert Hale. Her legs were now described as 'semi-paralysed', but each day, to get fresh air, she would ride out in her carriage, taking the cats with her.

But her freedom was coming to an end. Although her family had failed to obtain a new inquisition, the Lord Chancellor did give in to their requests that she should undergo an informal medical examination into the soundness of her mind. Sir Alexander Morison and a Brighton doctor, William King, were granted the authority to do this.

Mrs Cumming had been tracked down to Brighton by John Turner, the Inces' and Hoopers' latest solicitor – a talented snooper, who found her in the seaside town after she had been there just a month. On Monday 27 October 1851 Drs Morison and King, Mr Turner, Mrs Ince and the keeper and nurse of a London madhouse, gained entry to 5 Bloomsbury Place and hammered on Mrs Cumming's bedroom door. 'Who's there?' cried the old lady. 'It's me, your daughter,' Mrs Ince replied. 'I have no daughter now.' 'Yes you do, Mama!' When at last they gained entry, the interrogation began: Morison and King questioned her for two and a half hours – about her fondness for cats, her aversion to her daughters, the properties she owned, why she kept moving house. Did she claim that her late husband had had 'connexion' with his nurses? Did she believe that Mrs Ince had tried to strangle her in the Edgware Road? Did she think that her daughters had tried to poison her cats and birds? Mrs Cumming strongly denied the last two suggestions, and refused to speak ill of the dead; she would also not answer impudent questions about her finances. But she made a very unwise attempt at sarcasm, stating that 'Oh I have dozens and dozens of cats, and not only do I take them with me on carriage rides, I've even appointed one as my coachman and another as my postillion'. Alas, Morison and King took this straight.

Three days later, in spite of a certificate issued by Dr Hale, stating that Mrs Cumming was too physically infirm to endure any more harassment and must on no account be moved, Morison, King, Turner, the madhouse proprietor and the nurse went again to 5 Bloomsbury Place. This time they were accompanied by Superintendent Chase, the aptly named head of Brighton police. Albina Watson, Sarah Hutchinson, Robert Haynes and Mrs Cumming locked themselves in the old lady's bedroom but Chase broke the door down with such force that part of the frame came off. Mrs Cumming, seated in a chair near the bed, was unable to move and cried out in terror as her friends tried to comfort her. Robert Haynes grappled with the chief of police and threatened to throw him down the stairs. The madhouse owner, Cyrus Alexander Elliott, informed Mrs Cumming that he had come to remove her to Effra Hall Asylum, in Brixton, South London. A certificate for her removal, signed by Morison and King, was waved about.

Mrs Cumming cried out in pain as she was bundled downstairs, and it was only with difficulty that she could be got into the vehicle waiting outside, with Dr King shouting, 'Don't you know how to get someone into a carriage?!' and giving her a massive, indelicate shove from behind. Not only was Mrs Cumming in physical agony, she had – since their creation – had a terror of the railways, so great that she had never ridden the iron horse, and was still using her carriage and four, like the Regency lady she had remained in this barbarous new age. She was in great distress at the prospect of experiencing the high speed, deafening noise, filth, commotion and enforced proximity to strangers that rail travel involved. (The extra alarm that railways could cause to patients had already been noted by the Commissioners in Lunacy, who in 1847 had issued a circular entitled 'The Conveyance of Lunatics by Railway'.)

At Brighton station, the Effra Hall staff dragged her along the platform by her elbows; she was unable to walk but this was interpreted as resistance. Mrs Hutchinson called out, 'She is a lady, and she must travel like a lady!' but was ignored. Her friends were not allowed to be in the same railway carriage as Mrs Cumming. The savagery continued at the other end, and the old lady was seen yelping in pain and fear when they arrived at London Bridge.

Effra Hall Asylum employed Dr William Vesalius Pettigrew as medical superintendent. He knew the Inces very well: in fact, two years earlier, Catherine had asked Pettigrew if he would come and observe her mother and give an opinion on her sanity. Pettigrew lived just around the corner from the Inces, and worked alongside John at the Pimlico Dispensary; he had treated Mrs Ince for bilious attacks. His closeness to the family was not noted by anyone at the time, not even the ever-vigilant Mrs Cumming herself. Pettigrew would be the only doctor to maintain that Mrs Cumming had no grounds whatsoever to believe she could be poisoned or strangled. He would also claim that the old lady's peculiarities of gesture and the vehemence of her speech were typical of the insane.

Mrs Cumming spent most of her month-long stay at Effra Hall wrapped up warm, seated by a fire or propped up in bed. She wasn't impressed by Effra Hall's victuals, pushing away her roast beef and complaining, 'I can get nothing else for dinner in this place but this bone.'

The Chancery appeal court had selected Dr Forbes Benignus Winslow to visit Mrs Cumming at Effra Hall, but when the doctor turned up at the madhouse on 30 October he was denied entry. Solicitors for the Hoopers and Inces, on the other hand, had been given full access to the patient. Six days later, Dr Winslow was visited in his Albemarle Street home by John Ince, who put to the doctor his own views of his mother-in-law's state of mind. Winslow listened and then went on to study all the available documentation on the case. He needed to address in particular the three reasons for confinement that were given on Mrs Cumming's lunacy certificate: her dislike of her children; her claim that they had attempted to poison her cats and birds; and her belief that Mrs Ince had tried to strangle her at Edgware Road. Winslow concluded that her dislike of her children was entirely understandable; and that for this reason it was not a delusion when she feared a poisoning attempt. He also noted that Mrs

Cumming had quickly admitted that she had been too rash in accusing Mrs Ince of strangulation. Dr Winslow was allowed into Effra Hall one week after his initial attempt, and during one of many interviews, Mrs Cumming asked the doctor, 'How can I love my children when I recollect how they have treated their mother? But they wanted my money. If I had been poor, they would have left me alone.'

On 3 December, Dr Winslow gave his diagnosis in a carefully phrased letter to the Chancery appeal court:

> Mrs Cumming's family have, on different occasion, influenced, it may be, by the most humane, but perhaps mistaken, motives, endeavoured to guard Mrs Cumming against the operation of extraneous influences by throwing about her person and property the protection of the law . . . [but] I cannot bring my mind to the conclusion that the aversion Mrs Cumming manifests towards her children is a result either of delusive impressions or the consequence of the perverted affections of a disordered mind.

Mrs Cumming told Dr Winslow that the anxiety she was experiencing meant she got little sleep at Effra Hall, and that she wished now to be left to die. But fate wanted to play with her for a little longer, and on 7 January 1852 her second pub-based lunacy inquisition began – this time at the Eyre Arms, a large tavern and assembly rooms situated near the end of Queen's Road, St John's Wood. The Lord Chancellor had assented to Dr Winslow's request that Mrs Cumming be released from the asylum to live at Gothic Villa, Queen's Road, because of her failing health. She was able to take with her a doctor's widow, Mary Moore, with whom she had struck up a friendship, and whose companionship the Lord Chancellor himself had approved.

Commissioner Barlow was in the chair once again, and he told the jury that they must decide whether Mrs Cumming was of sound or unsound mind. If she were sound, that was the end of the matter; if they found her unsound, they must decide at what point she had become so, and whether she would still be able to take care of herself and her property. Mrs Cumming was to be examined in person, but Barlow believed she was in such frail health that he and the jury would probably have to go to Gothic Villa for the interview.

But Mrs Cumming did make it to the Eyre Arms for the first day, looking 'a confirmed invalid' and observing the proceedings with an air of 'bewilderment'. She sat and listened to the very similar pattern of testimonies to that presented at the Horns Tavern, five and a half years earlier. The inquisition began with three servants alleging filth and disorder at Gothic and Herbert Villas, as well as extreme eccentricity, wild mood changes and a love of liquor. Yet, as before, those testifying on behalf of Mrs Cumming would soon contradict these allegations. Mary Rainey and the Hickeys, in particular, did not make a good impression, Rainey failing to dispel the idea that she had been an abusive and occasionally violent employee, and admitting that she had regularly allowed the Hickeys into Herbert Villa to stay the night. Mrs Hickey told the unlikely tale that she had tracked down John and Catherine Ince's address using the trade directory so that she could tell them of her worries about Mrs Cumming; Mrs Cumming's counsel suggested that Hickey had been in the Inces' pay in the first place.

Counsel for the Hoopers and the Inces alleged that solicitor Robert Haynes had been the evil genius behind the 1846 compromise deal, so that he could gain sway over Mrs Cumming and over her money. The incident of a will that she wrote but never signed, bequeathing Haynes and his wife large sums of money, was brought up to support this argument, and so was an allegation that Haynes had sold Gothic Villa and another house in Queen's Road to Mrs Cumming at inflated prices. (This latter point was disproved by two independent house agents.)

When one witness claimed that she had revoked one of her wills, Mrs Cumming staggered to her feet and shouted, 'That is a gross falsity! It is a vile conspiracy!' When the same witness claimed that she had often been under the influence 'of something she had been partaking of' (i.e. drink), she called out: 'It is very unmanly in a man saying that, when he is, perhaps, in the habit of doing it himself!'

Alienated from her children, Mrs Cumming had developed monomaniac fears about her personal safety, suggested the Hooper–Ince lawyer, and she had persisted in saying that an attempt had been made to strangle her and to introduce poison into her home. The counsel told the jury that 'there were persons studiously active in cherishing these delusions operating upon that subject in the mind of the lady'. He meant Robert Haynes. Mrs Moore, said the counsel, was a plant in Mrs Cumming's life, placed there by Haynes. Moore had 'huge mesmeric power' over the old lady and 'telegraphed' signals to tell her how to answer any questions from doctors that might have betrayed Mrs Cumming's madness. The contemporary mesmerism, or hypnotism, furore led some to fear that one human being's consciousness could be controlled by another individual; the allegation of mesmeric telegraphing implied that Mrs Moore wielded occult power over Mrs Cumming and added a new uneasy, paranoiac element to the case.

John Ince was unable to attend, suffering from 'nervous depression', giddiness, numbness, the partial paralysis of one hand and a loss of vision in one of his eyes, and so it was Catherine Ince who had to come to the Eyre Arms to explain that their poor mother had fallen into the power of an unscrupulous lawyer who intended to deepen the hostilities between them in order to gain the entire estate when Mrs Cumming died.

Surgeon Thomas Wilmot, who had signed her lunacy certificate of 1846, was asked what insanity was. He replied that he had never seen a decent explanation of it. Then how could he have certified Mrs Cumming as mad? 'I considered she was labouring under delusions.' How did he know that they were delusions? Wilmot cited the filthy state of her house; and said that the swollen condition of the captain's prostate gland meant that it was agony for him to pass so much as a teaspoonful of water, and so he could not have been capable of 'inconstancy'. He might have had the desire, said the surgeon, but not the means to act upon it.

When told that Mrs Cumming insisted on cutting up her pets' food with a clean silver knife and fork, the jury thought she had given the cats their own cutlery to eat with, and they asked for clarification on this point. And her sarcasm caught her out again: a hostile witness claimed that she had once accused one of the landlords at whose property she had lodged of weighing every single feather in the bed that she was to sleep in. This had been her mordant way of pointing out how parsimonious the landlord was, yet it was quoted as evidence of bizarre, delusional thoughts.

Nineteen doctors came to the second inquisition; ten claimed that Mrs Cumming was of unsound mind, nine that she could take care of herself and her affairs. Dr Winslow was one of four star turns, along with John Conolly, Sir Alexander Morison and Dr Edward Thomas Monro. These were the huge authorities: Monro was a veteran of 400 such hearings, and in only two cases had the jury ever returned a verdict that was at odds with his evidence.

Dr Winslow stated that he had examined few individuals as evidently sane as Mrs Cumming, and he refused to budge from this position under ferocious questioning. Being mistaken was not the same thing as being delusional, he said, regarding her fears about her family's behaviour. Dr Winslow was ridiculed by one of the Hooper–Ince lawyers for the latitude of his approach to madness, and he read back to the doctor a passage from his 1843 work, *The Plea of Insanity in Criminal Cases*: 'Insanity does not admit of being defined . . . The malady assumes so many forms, and exhibits itself in such Protean shapes, that it is out of our power to give anything the semblance of a correct or safe definition as could be referred to as a standard in doubtful cases of derangement of the mind.' Dr Winslow stated that the past nine years had done nothing to shift his position, but a significant point was scored when counsel extracted from him the admission that old age, rather than insanity, could affect an individual's ability to manage his or her affairs. Forgetfulness and wilfulness came under the umbrella of 'unsoundness' of mind, and proving full-blown mania was not the sole purpose of a lunacy commission, he was reminded. Commissioner Barlow told Dr Winslow of the case of an elderly man who thought that one of his legs was his own but that the other belonged to celebrated actress and singer Madame Vestris, and that when asked to walk, the man said he could not do so without checking with the lady for permission. Dr Winslow agreed that 'so absurd a notion' would indeed be an indication of an unsound mind. Quite how it connected to Mrs Cumming was anybody's guess.

Dr Robert Barnes was another staunch (paid) defender of Mrs Cumming's sanity, echoing Dr Winslow in his belief that the seemingly outrageous claims of poisoning and strangulation were not delusional because of the complex background to the case; and anyway, Dr Barnes pointed out, he had often taken note that Mrs Cumming regularly checked over her own accusations and questioned the correctness of her conclusions, but mad people never attempted to probe and rationalise their beliefs. Furthermore, Barnes – a heredi-tarian – reported that he had done as much ancestral research as was possible, and had concluded that there was no lunacy among Mrs Cumming's antecedents and relatives. Like Dr Winslow, he had a very broad notion of what constituted madness, stating, 'We are all under some delusion or other . . . I think there is in every mind soundness and unsoundness.' Dr Barnes cited beliefs in Mormonism, clairvoyance and mesmerism as proof that extremely unlikely concepts could be ardently believed in by huge numbers of perfectly sane individuals.

Dr John Conolly, too, told the Eyre Arms that Mrs Cumming was sane and more than competent to manage her financial affairs. He believed that the insane could suppress mention of their delusions, but not for very long: 'One never fails to bring it out,' he said. Appearing to contradict his own 1849 stance – that incarceration was necessary for all forms of mental unsoundness – Conolly strongly denied at the Eyre Arms that those who were simply of feeble memory ought to be put in asylums.

Dr James Davey, resident physician of the huge Colney Hatch county asylum north of London and a former assistant of Dr Conolly's, damaged his own career in allowing himself to be corralled by the lawyers into stating that anyone who did not believe in mesmerism and clairvoyance (as he ardently did) could be said to be of unsound mind. This extraordinary statement would be picked over sneeringly for many months in the medical press.

Adding an extra complication for the jury, Sir Alexander Morison stated that while he considered Mrs Cumming not to be insane, she was 'an imbecile', and therefore of unsound mind: 'There is a good deal of playful shrewdness about her in some respects . . . [but] she appears to me to be under the control of anybody that approaches her.' He was supported by Dr Edward Thomas Monro who testified that he had no doubt that she was insane, citing her suspicion of strangulation and of poisoning as proof. Yet under cross-examination, Monro admitted that he did not know that a noxious substance had been found in the bird-house sample, which could have explained Mrs Cumming's reaction.

Mrs Cumming was not well enough to attend the Eyre Arms after the first day, and so on the morning of Tuesday, 13 January the twelve members of the jury and Commissioner Barlow took themselves along to Gothic Villa. In the drawing room were Mary Moore and servant Esther Blake, along with one of Mrs Cumming's general practitioners, Dr Henry Caldwell; also present were one of her lawyers, Mr Southgate; Mr Petersdorff for the Inces and Hoopers; and a shorthand-writer. Even for a spacious St John's Wood drawing room, this was quite a crowd. The room was kept gloomy as the ophthalmia was raging again in the old lady's right eye, making her intolerant of light.

Commissioner Barlow addressed Mrs Cumming as if she were a small child, but the inquisitor's nonsense soon met with Miss-Havisham-like retorts.

Commissioner Barlow: 'You have not seen so many people for a long time?'

Mrs Cumming: 'No.'

'Do you remember seeing me in the year 1846 – it is some time ago?'

'I have not forgotten you.'

'This is a better house than you had at Belgrave Terrace?'

'Yes, it is.'

'You had cats there.'

'Yes, I had cats.'

'I think you had pigeons?'

'Yes, I had. If it was any mark of insanity to keep pigeons, there are a good many people who would be taken to the madhouse.'

The Commissioner asked a number of questions about her purchase of Gothic Villa and another house in Queen's Road, and in particular wanted to know the size of the mortgages.

'I do not know that I am authorised exactly to expose my private affairs in that way,' the old lady replied. 'Do not deem me impertinent to you, Mr Barlow.'

'May I ask the amount of money – the interest that is paid?'

'Why, I consider it, Mr Barlow, a private affair, and as I am persecuted so much about my property, I think it right to keep those affairs in my own breast. Do not deem me impertinent in giving that answer.'

'I understand you to say that you have been persecuted. What makes you think you have been persecuted? Who do you think to have persecuted you about your property?'

'My two daughters.'

'Anybody else?'

'No, not now.'

'You mean Mrs Ince and Mrs Hooper?'

'They have most grossly persecuted me. Wherever I go I am persecuted by them, the moment they find me out.'

'In what way do they persecute you?'

'By coming to my house and annoying me, and putting me in the position I am placed in at present when they get at me.'

'This house is a very comfortable one . . .'

'Yes, but I am not speaking of the house, I am speaking of the inquiry which is taking place with regard to my sanity.'

'You mean they took out a commission, in 1846?'

'Yes, they did.'

'Had not Mr Cumming something to do with it?'

'He had – it was so, nominally – they said he did it.'

Commissioner Barlow asked the old lady about the captain: 'Was he a person quiet, and of good temper? I am told you treated him with kindness sometimes, and sometimes not.'

'He is dead, and let all faults be buried with him.'

'Was he a free-living gentleman with ladies? Do you remember, because there is some allegation about his nurses?'

'He had some very bad nurses.'

'Are you quite sure of that from your own personal observation?'

'Yes.'

'You had no doubt about it in your own mind?'

'No, because I had ocular demonstration of it.'

'I do not like to ask you about that more minutely . . .'

'I could not enter into it for decency's sake – decency would not allow me.'

Commissioner Barlow now reverted to financial matters. It is not clear whether this hopping about was aimed at testing the intellectual reflexes of the old lady, or was attributable to the lack of method that seems to characterise Commissioner Barlow.

Of the rental for the house in Queen's Road that Mrs Cumming owned and leased out, he asked, 'How much is it – what do you get for it, I mean? Do you remember what it is a year?'

'I do, but my daughters make all inquiries to know how much this estate is, and how much the other, and that makes me more reserved now.'

'But I do not come here by order of your daughters.'

'No, I know you do not.'

Commissioner Barlow probed her about Robert Haynes: 'Do you have confidence in him?'

'The most implicit confidence.'

Barlow wanted to know how she had first met Haynes, and she was cagey about this, saying, 'I did not know that I was obliged to state the details.'

'I will not oblige you to say anything that you do not like, but still, these gentlemen [the jury] suggest that I should put questions to you, and they will draw their own inferences if you do not answer them. But at the same time I am bound to inform you that you are not compelled to answer any question which is disagreeable to you.'

She was then quizzed closely about the various solicitors she had used and dismissed over the years, and she recalled the order and the reasons perfectly.

One of the jurymen in the room stepped forward and asked Commissioner Barlow if the two women attendants could be asked to leave the room. After Mrs Moore and Esther Blake had left, the juryman explained that he had become concerned, 'because I saw one of the ladies looking at her'.

'They were not making any motion to me to teach me what to say,' said Mrs Cumming, aware of this tired old allegation of 'tutoring'. Ever proud of pedigree, she added: 'They are in a rank in society above that.'

The grilling continued – about Robert Haynes, and why Mrs Cumming retained him as a solicitor when she had dismissed so many others. It is clear that Barlow believed Haynes was profiteering from Mrs Cumming's predicament; but the old lady was unshake-able in her statements that Haynes had kept her fully updated on her income, expenditure and the market value of her various properties.

The room was growing gloomier and colder. 'May I poke the fire? I am afraid it will go out,' a juryman asked her.

'If you please,' she said.

'There are no coals – may I ring for some?'

'Yes, if you will take the trouble to ring.'

The servants' bell was rung and George Clarke came in. 'Some coals, George.' Clarke went away and came back with the coals and placed them on the fire, but Mrs Cumming grumbled that he had not brought a bellows: 'The fire has got so very low.'

'Where are your cats now?' Barlow asked. 'Are they upstairs in your bedroom, or in the kitchen?'

'I suppose they are in the kitchen. I very seldom go into the kitchen.'

'When did they cease to live upstairs?'

'Sir, they never lived upstairs – never. Whoever told you that told you a gross falsity.'

'Did they not live in your bedroom?'

'They came up to have their meals and then they were sent down again.'

'Do you not remember when the inventory was being taken of this house some moisture having come through the ceiling?'

'Not from the cats.'

'From something else?'

'The servants can best account for that.'

'Do you remember that evening when something came through the ceiling and you sent a servant up to look at it?'

Mrs Cumming did not reply. It is possible that the 'moisture' being referred to had been caused by her own physical infirmity. Mrs Cumming was alone with seventeen men, and may well have been feeling an agony of embarrassment as the questioning took this turn.

'Did the cats not dwell in your bedroom night and day?'

'No.'

Mrs Cumming then faced a series of detailed questions about various sums of money paid to her in connection with her Welsh property three years previously, and whenever she faltered over a precise date and sum, she was pressed repeatedly, as though she were on trial for her life. Her counsel did not intervene to protest at the questions raining down upon her. After minutes of persistent rapid-fire interrogation, she at last began to stumble in her answers. They appeared to have broken her at last and pierced through to a layer of confusion.

'You do not remember, do you?' coaxed Barlow, thinking he was being kind.

'I do remember perfectly well,' replied the old lady, 'but I do not know that anyone has a right to ask me these questions, because I am mistress of my own property and it is not a commonplace thing in the world to have your children to call you to account.'

A juryman piped up, 'Do you think she understands the position we are in?'

Barlow explained to Mrs Cumming, 'These gentlemen are under the order of the Lord Chancellor – they are summoned here.'

'To see my competency to answer their questions.'

'Your competency to take care of your property, or whether some person should not look after you and your property – take care of you and see that you are not imposed upon as to your health and property. That really is the object of these gentlemen.'

'That I am not?'

'They have not formed an opinion yet. I can do no more than suggest to you the propriety of answering the questions which are put to you. Your counsel, who are here, will check me if I do anything improper.'

A juryman said, 'That was the reason why I asked the ladies to leave the room, that you might speak more freely.'

'I am under no intimidation at all from them because they are intimate friends,' was Mrs Cumming's response.

'Your courtesy is very proper,' said another juryman.

'Who has been in the habit of hiring your servants?' asked Barlow.

'Myself.'

'Do you get characters [references] for them, for you seem to have been rather unlucky with your servants?'

'I was very unlucky when Mr John Ince used to send me servants, very unlucky.'

'When did he send you servants?'

'Some years ago.'

'Has he sent you any since I had the pleasure of seeing you at the Horns Tavern?'

'He has sent them here to me without my knowing they were sent by him.'

'You heard so afterwards?'

'I did.'

'If he sent them, he sent them for some purpose. But what makes you think the same from him more than from me?' Barlow had arranged for one Louisa Baker to be employed at Gothic Villa, to keep an eye on things for the Commissioners in Lunacy.

'Because I do not think you would have done such a dirty trick.'

'Why do you think he would do a dirty trick?'

'Because he is accustomed to do dirty tricks.'

'I do not like to condemn a man without cause.'

'I do not ask you to condemn him.'

'Could you tell me one or two dirty tricks he has done?'

'In taking Captain Cumming away from his own house. He got him there, and took his writing desk and overhauled all his papers when the man was not fit to be removed. He took his writing desk in a hackney coach.'

Barlow added, pointlessly, 'There were hackney coaches in those days. They are abolished now . . . Is there anything else you have to say against Mr Ince?'

'Nothing worth mentioning.'

'But you have had other things against him?'

'Yes, a good many other things.'

'Will you allow me to judge of them? Could you tell me one or two more?'

She did not reply. So he went back to investigating Robert Haynes, and the fact that Haynes now lived in a better house than this one, which he had sold to Mrs Cumming. 'Have you ever said that Mr Haynes is living in his present house on your money?'

'No, but I have been told that others have said so. And, amongst others, Catherine Ince has told everyone about the neighbourhood that I am kept a prisoner, and that Mr Robert Haynes is living upon my property.'

Barlow moved on to the broken arrangement of 1846 and asked her why she had reneged, and she replied, 'Because of course I would not consent to give up a whole loaf and take half.'

On several occasions Mrs Cumming had to correct errors of fact in Barlow's questioning and assertions. He became confused about the order of Mrs Cumming's peregrinations, mistaking her time in Maida Vale for her time in St John's Wood. 'I am in error, it was the other house,' he admitted. 'I am afraid I have misled you. I am given to error sometimes.'

'Yes, but you are not called to account for it as I am,' she said.

Barlow countered with, 'Yes I am, and rather roughly sometimes.'

The conversation now turned to the night that the police arrived at Herbert Villa in Maida Vale, and Mrs Cumming claimed that she had not screamed out of the window but that Rainey and Hickey had called the policemen, with whom they were on friendly terms, even allowing them to sleep at Herbert Villa.

'Do you mean the policemen were sleeping at the house?' asked the Commissioner.

'Yes, the servants had them in every night.'

'I do not want to doubt your word but what makes you think these policemen were sleeping in the house?'

'I am certain of it. They were there frequently.'

'Do you mean the same policemen that came in that night, or merely policemen generally?'

'I cannot tell you that for I was up in my room and very ill.'

'Did you not cry out at the window?'

'I called out when the woman Mary Hickey, I think her name was, no . . . Mary Rainey . . .'

Her confusion did Mrs Cumming no favours and she soon back-tracked on her accusation about the constables.

The cats slunk back into the conversation. Barlow asked, 'Are the cats in your house now?'

'No, not all of them.'

'Did you take the cats to Brighton at all?'

'Yes I did.'

'We are told there were four or five.'

'Ah yes, seven, or eight, or ten, I dare say you were told.'

Now the will – 'Can you tell me when it was you made it?'

'These things are so long ago, and never feeling in my own breast that anyone would have a right to call me to account . . .'

'You are of a certain age – you cannot tell when it was made, and who made it.'

'It was Robert Haynes.'

'Did you ever sign that will?'

'No, it was not signed.'

'You don't think it was signed?'

'I don't think it, I know it.'

Barlow established from Mrs Cumming that she had made the will while staying at Vauxhall with the Hutchinsons just after the Horns Tavern inquisition had finished. She had contracted bronchitis and had believed she was going to die. Only Robert Haynes was in the room when she dictated the will to him, and in it she left a significant sum to her solicitor and to his wife, whom Mrs Cumming could barely have had time to get to know. Haynes had made no objection to so unusual a bequest. But Mrs Cumming never subsequently signed this will; in fact, she burned it.

Next came a testy exchange in which Barlow, in error, attempted to convince Mrs Cumming that her own father had included the Hoopers and the Inces in his will. When the old lady became increasingly vehement in her denials of this, Dr Caldwell stepped in: 'I think, sir, she has been long enough under examination. I think this is somewhat confused.'

Mr Petersdorff, lawyer for the Inces and Hoopers, objected, 'I do not think she is fatigued.' The questioning continued and now turned to Mrs Cumming's dramatic encounter with her daughter Catherine.

'Did Mrs Ince come and see you at the Edgware Road?' asked Barlow.

'Yes. She pushed the servant almost downstairs to pounce upon me . . . Mrs Ince is very capable, I am sorry to say, of saying anything but the truth.'

'I want to speak to you a little about Mrs Ince presently.'

'The less the better, if you please.'

'Do you remember how long she stayed that first time she came to Edgware Road?'

'I could see her in the street, through the window of my drawing room, surrounded by policemen and a set of vagabonds round her, pointing to the house. That is very ladylike conduct . . . It was not a proper place for a person calling herself a gentlewoman to be surrounded by a parcel of policemen . . . She obtruded herself upon me and kicked up such a row that it made the house quite scandalous.'

Mrs Cumming knew she had overstated her case against Catherine in the past: 'I do not say that she attempted to strangle me, though that is what it is said that I did say.'

'What did you say? We will hear it from yourself as we may have been misled.'

'I was very much frightened when she came into the room, throwing the door open, running up to me, putting her arms round my neck, after the statement I received that Ince and her were taking

proceedings against me in court. Now that is a very strange thing if
you are taking proceedings against a person to come in a very cordial
way.'

'Why should you not put the best interpretation upon it, and
suppose that it was an act of affection?' asked the Commissioner.

'Affection, sir?'

'It is my duty not to set you against her, or her against you . . .
What proceedings had she taken, beside the original commission?'

'To get me into a madhouse, or to get my property . . . I never
mentioned that she strangled me, or wanted to strangle me, but I
said, and say again, it is a very strange way of behaving.'

Of Mrs Hooper, Barlow and the jury expressed the wish that there
could be affection again: 'Let us hope you will some day be reconciled,'
the Commissioner said.

'Never, never . . .'

They didn't like this – a family repudiated was unnatural. There could
not possibly be good cause for it. 'It's never too late, you know,' Barlow
said, as though addressing a dim infant. 'I want to exculpate your
daughters.' But he did not provide any proof of their innocence.

Similarly with the poisoning, Mrs Cumming now stated that she
had not alleged a murder plot against her but the fact remained that
a toxic substance had found its way into her household – Dr Barnes's
analysis had proved that that was so.

A juryman noticed that the old lady was becoming tired, and she
replied, 'Yes, I am very much fatigued.'

They started once more on the value of her Welsh property: 'Do
you know the annual amount of your property in Wales?'

'Yes.'

'Do you know what it is now?'

'Yes.'

'What is it now?'

'The same as it was then. Do not think this an impertinent or short
answer.'

'Certainly not.'

'They insinuate I have been squandering the money and the property, but if I had, how could I still have the same income from it?'

She refused to hand over to them the rent books that would
prove what she said was correct, pointing out that if she made such

private financial information public, it could be alleged that she was 'an imbecile' and therefore unfit to undertake business transactions.

The Commissioner changed tack again. 'Mr Ince, we understand, lost two of his children,' said Barlow.

'I do not know how many he has lost.'

'Do you remember seeing one?'

'I saw one of Mr Ince's and one of Mr Hooper's children.'

'Was there anything peculiar about one of Mr Ince's children?'

'I never made any remarks.'

'What did you say?'

'When I saw the child I said it looked a very pretty corpse. That was the expression I made use of . . . And the other of Mr Ince's children, I said it was very much emaciated, and so it was. It had suffered a great deal before his death.'

'Was there not one that you said was glazed?'

'Oh no! I cannot help smiling at that.'

'Did you ever say that?'

'No, so help me God!'

'Have you ever said it was like a waxen doll in a tailor's shop, or any phrase of that kind?'

'No, I have not. But it has been said so.'

'But you never said it?'

'On my oath.'

'But I do not put you on your oath, you know?'

'Oh sir, I am quite exhausted!'

A juryman said, 'We are here as kind friends to you. You may tell us as many secrets as you like because we are friends of yours.'

Commissioner Barlow suggested she have something to drink: 'A glass of wine, or brandy and water?'

Mrs Cumming didn't take the bait.

Then it was over for the day. Barlow rose and said, 'Good morning. I am afraid I have given you a great deal of trouble.'

'I am afraid I have given *you* a great deal of trouble,' Mrs Cumming retorted.

They were back at Gothic Villa three days later, and then again the following week, on the evening of Thursday 22 January. Again they grilled Mrs Cumming about mortgages, legal expenses and the behaviour of Robert Haynes. Again, she declared she would not answer questions that she believed were impertinent. A servant knocked and came in to light the gloomy room with candles. 'Would you like some light?' asked a juryman of Mrs Cumming.

'It is immaterial to me, sir.'

On and on it went, with Mrs Cumming occasionally stumbling but for the most part consistent in her answers to the repetitive questioning.

'Have your daughters ever tried to poison you?'

'Not to my knowledge.'

'Why can you not return to your natural affection for them?'

'That [the alleged poisoning] is not the reason I changed my affection for them.'

A juryman now pleaded, 'Will you allow me, as a friend, to make one suggestion? Dr Williams says that when you were at Bassaleg [Monmouthshire] you attended his church; the Reverend Mr Evans also says you attended his chapel. On those occasions you repeated that beautiful prayer of our Saviour, "Father, Forgive us our trespasses, as we forgive those who trespass against us . . ."'

'I have no enmity towards them.'

'I state this with the greatest affection towards you,' continued the juryman. 'God has put it that we are only to ask for His forgiveness of our sins, on the same ground that we are disposed to extend our forgiveness, not only to our children, but to all mankind.'

No answer.

'Should you like to see your daughters now?'

'No, I should not. I am in very bad health . . . I gave them money that I might have peace for the remainder of my days, and you see how much peace I have.'

'Can you account for the several thousand pounds that you received by the sale of property, and by mortgage and otherwise?'

'Yes, I can. I know very well. I have been persecuted so. And so I think that had better remain in my own breast until I am dead.'

'But that allows a suspicion to rest in the minds of other persons which you could remove immediately. We do not wish to take your property from you.'

'I do not suppose that as gentlemen you would.'

'We only ask it as a test of your accuracy in your accounts and of your being able to manage your own affairs.'

Silence.

'Do you know how many grandchildren you have?' asked another juryman.

'I cannot answer you that question for I have not seen them since two of them died.'

'Do you know that Mrs Hooper is very ill?'

'No, I do not.'

'Should you not like to see her?'

'I am very ill myself.'

'Have you no desire to see her, being ill?'

'No. I should be sorry to hear that she is ill.'

'She is very ill.'

'Indeed, I am sorry for it.'

'Would you rather that Robert Haynes had your property than your daughters?'

'No, and he never proposed such a thing to me . . . Mr Robert Haynes is not a particular friend of mine – he is my solicitor and has always treated me and behaved to me as a man of honour.'

Mrs Cumming once again slipped into silence when the Commissioner and the jurymen alleged that Haynes was nothing of the sort.

'What is the greatest offence your daughters have committed against you?' asked Barlow.

'Do you not think it any offence for daughters to persecute their mother, so that I cannot get a moment's peace, not anywhere I go? I am like a hunted dog, a vagabond.'

'You imagine it,' asserted a juryman.

'No, sir, no.'

'If you had them with you and experienced their kindness, you would not say so.'

'Ah, sir . . .'

And with that, it was over, and they bade her goodnight.

Back at the Eyre Tavern, each side delivered a lengthy summing-up. Counsel for Mrs Cumming said the case against her was no more than a concoction comprising the exaggerations of 'dismissed servants and disappointed lawyers'. Commissioner Barlow reminded the jury that the landmark judgments of Lord Eldon, Lord Chancellor between 1801 and 1827, had stated that non-lunatic unsoundness of mind, such as 'senile imbecility', also fell within the jurisdiction of an inquisition: the jury could bring in a verdict of 'imbecility' and consequent inability to manage affairs without declaring that Mrs Cumming was actually insane, or in need of asylum incarceration. It was important for it to be established as clearly as possible where eccentricity and caprice ended and derangement commenced. The Commissioner quoted Leonard Shelford, barrister and law writer, whose influential 1833 work, *A Practical Treatise on the Law Concerning Lunatics, Idiots and Persons of Unsound Mind*, stated:

> Derangement assumes a thousand different shapes both in character and in degree. It exists in all imaginable varieties, from the frantic maniac chained down to the floor, to the person apparently rational on all subjects and in all transactions save one, and whose disorder, though latently perverting the mind, yet will not be called forth except under particular circumstances and will show itself only occasionally.
>
> A sound mind is one wholly free from delusion . . . Weak minds, again, only differ from strong ones in the extent and power of their faculties; but unless they betray symptoms of a total loss of understanding, or of idiocy, or of delusion, they cannot properly be considered unsound.
>
> An unsound mind is marked by delusion, mingles ideas of imagination with those of reality, those of reflection with those of sensation, and mistakes the one for the other, and such delusion is often accompanied with an apparent insensibility to, or perversion of, those feelings which are peculiarly characteristic of our nature.
>
> The true criterion, the true test of the absence or presence of insanity, where there is no frenzy or raving madness, seems to be the absence or presence of what, used in a certain sense of it, may be comprised in a single term, viz, delusion.

Shelford's maxims on legal decisions about lunacy were frequently cited at inquisitions and gave a lucid framework for decision-making. But as often as not, juries did not appear to act in accordance with these highly respected points:

A. The law requires satisfactory evidence of insanity.

B. Insanity in the eye of the law is nothing less than the prolonged departure without an adequate external cause from the state of feeling and modes of thinking usual to the individual when in health.

C. The burthen of proof of insanity lies on those persons asserting its existence.

D. Control over persons represented as insane is not to be assumed without necessity.

E. Of all evidence, that of medical men ought to be given with the greatest care and received with the utmost caution.

F. The medical man's evidence should not merely pronounce the party insane, but give sufficient reasons for thinking so. For this purpose, it behoves him to have investigated accurately the collateral circumstances.

G. The imputations of friends or relations are not entitled to any weight or consideration in inquiries of this nature, but ought to be dismissed from the minds of the judge and jury, who are bound to form the conclusions from impartial evidence of facts and not be led astray by any such fertile sources of error and injustice.

Commissioner Barlow pointed out that the medical men were divided on Mrs Cumming's mental state, and that the jury ought to give greatest weight to the evidence of those doctors who had had the most amount of contact with Mrs Cumming. Barlow declared he had been most alarmed by Mrs Cumming's 'hatred' of her children and her refusal to answer fully the questions put to her about her property. The jury must decide whether her antipathy to her children was justified, or whether it arose from 'any morbid disposition'. Her love of her cats, he felt, could be discounted, as eccentricity; but her behaviour regarding her will was rather more alarming, and her moving from house to house also struck him as odd. And he was concerned at her rapid hiring and firing of solicitors.

The jury went out, returning one hour and twenty-five minutes later. They found that Mrs Cumming was of unsound mind, and had been so since 1 May 1846.

It was not the verdict that most had expected. *The Lancet* led the charge of the outraged: 'With the exception of the cats, the malady appears to have affected, in some way or another, all the living creatures connected with the inquiry.' The journal stated that if the public had been able to read the full transcript of the inquisition, it would have been even more shocked by the jury's verdict: it believed that the evidence had pointed in entirely the opposite direction. The Inces and the Hoopers had triumphed, said *The Lancet*, because of the dirt they had thrown at solicitor Robert Haynes.

However, Haynes failed fully to exonerate himself from the suspicion that he had sought to enrich himself at Mrs Cumming's expense. Lord Justice Knight Bruce, hearing one of the ramifications of the Cumming saga in the Court of Appeal, stated: 'From my judicial recollection of the facts of the case, from the condition of Mrs Cumming, her acts, *and her association with some persons* [my italics], I am most clearly of opinion that there never was a lady who more needed protection, and that the proceedings in lunacy were proper.'

Mrs Cumming, after years of outrageous fortune, was probably not as surprised by the verdict as everyone else. She was allowed to return to Gothic Villa to continue her decline into the grave. But the steel remained. Within a week she petitioned the Lord Chancellor and the Lords Justices of Appeal for a 'traverse' – a denial of the findings of the inquisition at common law, which would allow her to manage her affairs pending a third inquisition. Towards the end of March, the Lord Chancellor visited Gothic Villa, to establish for himself Mrs Cumming's psychological state – and to explain how expensive a traverse would be to implement. The old lady was adamant that the cost was immaterial to her. The Lord Chancellor reported that he had found her to be 'as rational and composed, free from heat, passion or violence as any rational person with whom I ever conversed. She understands how expensive it will be and so wishes to proceed.' He then remarked upon the huge cost of Mrs Cumming's sixteen days of humiliation at the Eyre Arms: the bill came to more than £6,000.

A fresh inquisition was ordered, and so it all started up again. Mrs Cumming had been allowed to keep Mrs Moore as her attendant-companion; she had also retained Dr Winslow, who begged each side to call off the fight, to allow the seventy-four-year-old whatever time she had left to be free of the anxiety of yet another hearing. The Inces and Hoopers deeply disliked Dr Winslow's presence but their attempt to have him replaced was thwarted by the Lord Chancellor. In fact, the Lord Chancellor made Winslow the old lady's gatekeeper. The family continued to haggle for all their own legal costs to come directly from Mrs Cumming's estate, and so once again, the nation was treated to the unwholesome sight of an accused individual being expected to foot the bill of her accusers. The only comforting fact was that the Inces and the Hoopers had almost bankrupted themselves in their attempt to obtain their mother's money; but this also meant that they simply could not now afford to back down.

What was also noted as odd by commentators was that during the 'traverse' – pending the preparations for the third inquisition – Mrs Cumming was permitted control over her affairs, with the sole exception that she could not transfer any of her property. However, any contracts she had signed after 1 May 1846 would later on be deemed by a court to have been void.

On and on Mrs Cumming battled, and her last miserable year of life was punctuated by visits from alienists, lawyers and Commissioners, each asking the same tedious questions. Dr Winslow and Mrs Moore were with her in her bedroom on Midsummer's Day 1853 when she died, with a mad-doctor in attendance attempting to discover how well her mind worked. She was telling him that she had forgiven her children, but no, she had no wish to see them again. Dr Winslow sat by as her final mumbling words were sifted for sense, or its opposite.

Peace at last in Kensal Green Cemetery. 'The merciful hand of death has removed a long-suffering victim to the manifold abuses of our lunacy legislation,' *The Lancet* announced, spotting the fairy-tale elements of the events:

> No case could demonstrate more urgently the necessity for vigorous and radical reform in the law that could permit such atrocities to be enacted. The case of the much-persecuted Mrs Cumming – a history in itself, a romance, but of that kind the truth of which is stranger far than fiction, but for its notorious reality – might be assumed to be a tale contrived for the express purpose of exposing the imperfections of the law of lunacy.

All that her tragic case had led to, continued the journal, was the passing of the 1853 Act for the Regulation of Proceedings under Commissions of Lunacy, which attempted to lessen the expense of inquisitions. A greater number of cases could now be heard without a jury, if so desired, speeding up the process. *The Lancet* remained unimpressed: 'True to his [the Lord Chancellor's] Chancery education, he would guard property with jealousy; the far dearer right of liberty is immolated without remorse . . . Without trial and without notice, by violence or by fraud, any person may be seized by the agents of a private trader, and incarcerated in a madhouse, on complying with certain easy formalities.'

Charles Dickens published *Bleak House* – with its brilliant attack on the deadly nature of Chancery delays and costs – in serial form, from March 1852, two months after Mrs Cumming was expensively declared insane; its final instalment appeared three months after her death. The new legislation may possibly have received some additional impetus from Dickens's devastating portrait. When the intention to slash lunacy inquisition costs was announced 'there was a decorous expression of applause in the body of the court', a newspaper reporter noted. However, the Act would prove to be not much of a memorial to Mrs Cumming's suffering. Ruinously expensive inquisitions could still take place, and, if anything, the streamlined system had the potential to increase malicious attempts to proclaim a rich relative a lunatic. (Indeed, the number of inquisitions soared after 1853, peaking in the 1880s.) Any number of Mrs Cummings could find their eccentricities or foul temper presented as unsoundness of mind by those who preferred not to wait until the hand of death delivered them a financial legacy.

Because Mrs Cumming died intestate, her daughters inherited the estate. However, the old lady had not wasted her final year: she appears to have booby-trapped her financial dealings, and many creditors began pursuing Thomasine and Catherine, who had been bequeathed a wonderful *Jarndyce* v. *Jarndyce* mess by their mother. In 1856 John Ince became a bankrupt, Catherine was being pursued for unpaid fees by snooping solicitor John Turner, and by 1860 the Cumming estate was barely sufficient to pay the costs of the suit of *Elliott* v. *Ince*, in which the compliant physicians and the proprietor of Effra Hall Asylum were seeking payment for their services in incarcerating Mrs Cumming. The Ince marriage foundered, and the couple separated, with an agreement that John Ince would pay Catherine £200 a year; when he failed to meet his quarterly payment to her in 1858, he was taken to court and lost the case. (How his mother-in-law would have chuckled.) John Ince died nine years later, aged sixty.

A month after her mother died, Thomasine arranged a post-nuptial agreement with her husband, in an attempt to avoid paying the trumpeter's many creditors. A court case of November 1856, to judge whether this agreement had been fraudulent, and therefore void, found in the Hoopers' favour, but by that time the couple were also being vigorously pursued by the hugely expensive counsel they had employed to pursue the lunacy inquisition. They were bankrupt in 1857, but were still living well, if their various Knightsbridge and Belgravia addresses are anything to go by; they adopted the surname 'Bayley' for some of the 1870s, possibly in an attempt to avoid creditors. The trumpeter died in the 1880s, but Thomasine made it into the twentieth century, dying aged ninety-three in 1906.

After the Cumming case, it was once again noted by most commentators how unsatisfactory it was that nineteen eminent medical men could give widely differing opinions of what constituted soundness of mind, tailoring their learning according to which 'side' in the dispute had hired them. One alienist had claimed that Mrs Cumming was a monomaniac, another that she was an imbecile, and yet another that she was perfectly sane. How could the public trust the judgements of a body of men who were in such theoretical conflict with each other? How safe was anyone when the experts had such divergent views of insanity?

6

'Gaskell is Single-Patient Hunting'

During the summer of 1846, York House – the asylum to which Mrs Cumming had been abducted that May – was also temporary home to one Martha Shuttleworth, whose dilemma was of a very different nature to Mrs Cumming's. At the end of July, Reverend John Clark Rowlatt, of St Peter's, Pimlico, was asked to visit the top-storey room of an otherwise empty and unfurnished house, at 10 Lower Eaton Street, Belgravia. Here he discovered fifty-five-year-old Mrs Shuttleworth, who lay naked on a urine-soaked bed under ragged bedclothes. She was emaciated, one of her legs was swollen, her pulse was weak and when Rowlatt addressed her, she was unable to make any sensible reply. Rowlatt called in Thomas Wilmot – the local surgeon who had recently certified Mrs Cumming – whose examination of Mrs Shuttleworth convinced him that she was insane. The two men established from the landlord, who lived next door, that the woman was in the care of one Dr John Quail, who left her alone for long periods of time. As there appeared to be no family or close friends to do so, the reverend now wrote out a lunacy order and Wilmot and another doctor signed certificates of lunacy. But when the carriage from York House arrived to take Mrs Shuttleworth away, Dr Quail appeared at the door, struggled with the doctors and shut himself and his patient inside the house. When the doctors and the York House keeper returned the next day, the landlord informed them that Quail, almost having to carry the enfeebled woman, had abandoned the house. Dr Wilmot rushed to the offices of the Commissioners in Lunacy and asked them how he was to proceed in a case where a private doctor claimed custody of a lunatic and refused to hand over the patient for asylum care.

Quail was a name that the Commissioners dreaded hearing. He was well known to the police, and had in fact been 'watched' off and on for six years. The Commissioners' own minute book refers to Quail as 'a dangerous lunatic', who since 1840 had been in and out of magistrates' courts for pestering Whitehall officials about a pension and remuneration he believed he was owed for his medical services to the Greek, Polish and Portuguese armies. Quail, a qualified surgeon, had been employed by the government to assist its allies and had been salaried to do so; but he believed that he was additionally entitled to a pension and had taken to menacing various officials in pursuit of this. He had turned up at the Commissioners' offices the previous autumn and told them a rambling tale of persecution of himself and one Mrs Shuttleworth by political enemies (the Foreign Office, in particular). He gave his address as 10 Upper Fitzroy Street, Fitzroy Square, and Scotland Yard Commissioner Richard Mayne promised Lord Shaftesbury that he would detail constables to keep a watch on Quail, though this was an expensive use of manpower.

The Commissioners in Lunacy encouraged Dr Wilmot to trace Quail and Mrs Shuttleworth but warned him that he was not entitled to use the certificates and lunacy order to commit a trespass or a breach of the peace. Although they believed the woman's life could be in danger, their cautious approach may have been a reaction to the controversial seizure of Mrs Cumming just three months earlier. The new lunacy law and its regime were only a year old, and it is clear from the documentation, and the contradictions and prevarications within it, that the Commissioners were feeling their way towards the correct way of implementing the new rules.

But then, the following week, Dr Quail himself turned up at the Lunacy Commission, presenting them again with his petition for a pension but now also complaining about being persecuted by Wilmot. The Commissioners demanded to know where Mrs Shuttleworth was, and when Quail refused to tell them, they handed him a formal summons for her to be surrendered to them. With Scotland Yard situated just the other side of Whitehall, a messenger was dispatched to dash round and ask Mayne to send a plain-clothes officer to follow Quail when he left the Lunacy Commission. PC Edwards tailed the doctor all over central London but late in the evening he lost him in a pub crowd in Norfolk Street, near Tottenham Court Road. Fortunately, Wilmot's own hired detective, a Mr Bradford, shortly afterwards located Quail at 19 Grafton Street, Fitzroy Square – a known brothel. This was where he was keeping Mrs Shuttleworth, who would later state that some women there had tried to make her drink alcohol and to sing 'queer' songs with them. When Bradford had attempted to speak to Mrs Shuttleworth at number 19, she simply pulled from her pocket a handkerchief with the astrological sign of Leo printed upon it and told him, 'This is my protector. While I have this, nothing can do me harm.'

The Commissioners in Lunacy and the Lord Chancellor were unsure how to proceed. Was it legal to enter a private house and remove from the custody of a registered medical practitioner a lunatic single patient, who seemed to have suffered neglect and abuse? What exactly were the powers – under the Act or at common law – for an asylum keeper to take custody of a certified lunatic? Robert Skeffington Lutwidge, the Commission's secretary, decided that the 1845 Act permitted Commissioners to enter premises and attempt an interview with a lunatic; so Commissioners Turner and Bryan Waller Procter went to the house in Grafton Street at five o'clock on 7 August, accompanied by two plain-clothes police officers, Dr Millingen of York House, and two of his nursing staff. But when the brothel keeper told them to go away, the party withdrew, unwilling to force entry.

Three days later, Bradford spotted Mrs Shuttleworth being removed in a cab. He pursued her and Quail across the City and as they crossed London Bridge he alerted two police officers, who seized them. The cab was full of luggage – they had been heading for the Dieppe packet boat.

Mrs Shuttleworth was conveyed to York House, where the Commissioners interviewed her and decided that she was 'a person of weak and unsound mind'. She told them that Dr Quail had frequently asked her for money and when she refused, sometimes he would kick and beat her. As proof, she showed the Commissioners her latest bruises. Her former solicitor, Mr Newland, confirmed that Quail had often called at his office trying to gain access to Mrs Shuttleworth's funds to invest in some wild speculations.

Quail repeatedly tried to see Mrs Shuttleworth at York House but was refused each time, the Commissioners telling him he was 'an improper person' to have charge of her. However, so ineptly had Mrs Shuttleworth's certificates and lunacy order been filled in, the Commissioners requested that a visit be paid to York House by the Lord Chancellor himself, because it had emerged that she was in fact a woman of some means. The Commissioners later wrote that Mrs Shuttleworth was found to be of 'imbecile mind and utterly incapable of taking care of herself or managing her affairs . . . she would wish to remain at York House where she was kindly treated and very comfortable.' Yet in the same month, her casebook reveals that she was threatening to smash windows at the asylum, alleging ill-treatment and neglect.

The enraged Dr Quail brought a habeas corpus case in November 1846, in order to regain custody of Mrs Shuttleworth. He alleged that she had been mis-certified into asylum care while he was providing – at her request – single-patient care. In his view, Mrs Shuttleworth was being illegally detained in an asylum on false certificates. In court, the two certificates and the lunacy order admitting her into York House were indeed found to have been technically illegal, as they were incomplete and contained many errors. Reverend Rowlatt and the two doctors told the judge, Lord Denman, that they had been so shocked by Mrs Shuttleworth's 'obscene and blasphemous' delusions that they had refused to put the full 'monstrous' particulars down on paper; her behaviour and conversation had been dirty and indecent in the extreme, they claimed, but they had not provided specific facts in the paperwork to back up this verbal assertion. Lunacy certificates and orders were public documents, but the need for euphemism could create problems for investigations of lunacy law breaches, when so many 'delusions' of troubled Victorians featured obscenity and blasphemy. Unseemly statements which had been screamed out in a padded room, or a darkened attic were often crucial evidence to justify incarceration, but were not easy for an official to write out verbatim, or to discuss in front of the public and the newspaper reporters at a trial or inquisition. As the century wore on, the urge to use an ever thicker linguistic veil risked greater compromise of the certification procedure.

Reverend Rowlatt, inexperienced in lunacy matters, had failed to answer sixteen factual questions on the lunacy statement, including those asking about the patient's age, gender and religion. Wilmot and the other doctor had simply scored out some of the printed form's rubric. Despite this, Judge Denman threw out Dr Quail's case, stating that Mrs Shuttleworth's detention at York House was legal and that the documentation's deficiencies had been solely technical. The bench had interviewed Mrs Shuttleworth during the trial and within minutes found her to be 'imbecile'. Denman had no patience for the tired old mangling of the liberty issue, pronouncing:

It would be an abuse not only of the substance, but of the very name of liberty, to confer it upon the person in question under circumstances which must render it a curse both to herself and others. The court reposed full confidence in the persons to whom her custody was confided by law; they would restore her to freedom whenever such restoration would be consistent with her own security and comfort.

Thanks to decades of progress, the modern asylum should be seen as a place of safety and refuge for those unable to care for themselves, he said.

When reports of the court case appeared in the newspapers, Mrs Shuttleworth's two sisters came forward, and told the Commissioners what Mrs Shuttleworth had been too enfeebled to reveal. In the late 1810s and early 1820s she had been the mistress of a scion of the wealthy Shuttleworth family, who, when he decided to marry another woman, had settled an income of £300 a year upon her. She had been born Martha Elizabeth Rhodes but now took the name Shuttleworth, as she believed herself to have been her lover's common-law wife. It was when her health and wits began to fail her in her late forties that she engaged the services of John Quail, who soon moved in with her. As she became more and more confused, her income was delayed and reduced to £100 by her trustees, who suspected that Quail was obtaining the money for himself, rather than spending it on her comfort and care. Mrs Shuttleworth became estranged from her sisters; we don't know the reasons for this, but Quail may have managed to engineer a row with her family, or simply kept Mrs Shuttleworth so well secreted that they lost all trace of her. Both her sisters insisted that she was not insane, and although her former solicitor, Mr Newland, considered her 'flighty', he too believed that she had been of sound mind. (It is possible, though, that five years with Dr Quail had driven Mrs Shuttleworth from 'flighty' to insane, as ill-treatment – and narcotics, if he had chosen to administer these – could have sent her mad.)

For reasons that are not clear, the Commissioners went against their family-first policy in the Shuttleworth case. Sarah Rhodes would make over fifty applications to the Commissioners to be allowed to remove her sister from York House to care for her at her home; all were refused. And only with extreme reluctance would Millingen permit visits by Mrs Shuttleworth's sisters. It is likely that the harsh view which prevailed was that the sisters had shown no interest in Martha while she was in Quail's care, and so should not be entrusted with her custody now. It is just possible that a more sinister motive could have made the Commissioners unwilling to allow Martha to rejoin people who had known of her rackety earlier life. Quail may possibly have been keeping hold of Mrs Shuttleworth as a potential crude attempt at blackmail against James Kay-Shuttleworth (soon to become 'Sir James'), who was one of Mrs Shuttleworth's trustees and also secretary to the Privy Council on education. It is clear from the Commissioners' archives that Kay-Shuttleworth intended to distance himself when the case came to light in 1846. He had been born simply James Kay, and took 'Shuttleworth' from his wealthy heiress wife, Lady Janet Shuttleworth, when they married in 1842. The faithless, deceased Mr Shuttleworth who had abandoned Martha had been a relation of Lady Janet's, and perhaps John Quail believed Mrs Shuttleworth's very existence could be used as leverage to get hold, at last, of the army pension he believed he deserved. It may be that the Commissioners feared damaging Sir James in this way. (Funnily enough, Sir James and Lady Kay-Shuttleworth made repeated attempts to add Charlotte Brontë to their social circle, after enjoying *Jane Eyre*, written in the very year that Sir James was panicking about being linked to an unsound, cast-off 'wife' of the Shuttleworth clan.)

In January 1848, Mrs Shuttleworth died at York House. An exhaustive coroner's inquest was held and Millingen's tale of her fatally ulcerated back and his failure to inform the family of the death without delay were deemed highly suspicious by coroner Thomas Wakley – a supporter of the Alleged Lunatics' Friends, many of whom came to the hearing. Once again, the legality of her lunacy certificates was discussed, with Wakley disagreeing with Lord Denman's view that they were valid: the nature of her hallucinations, no matter how obscene, ought to have been set down in writing. Millingen and his nurses were criticised for their conduct and for the level of care given to Mrs Shuttleworth; Millingen was additionally censured for not allowing her pen and paper to communicate with the outside world and for insisting on being present whenever the Commissioners came to see her. Although the verdict was that Mrs Shuttleworth died of 'debility and paralysis' and no negligence was established, Wakley used the hearing to question the implementation of the lunacy law. It had been correct to seize the patient from Dr Quail, he stated, but the running of York House left a great deal to be desired, and the Commissioners' procedures had a most unsatisfactory ad hoc feel to them.

Dr Quail too turned up at the inquest, claiming that he was owed £2,554 from the deceased, and providing the following note as evidence: 'London, August 11, 1842. I engaged Dr Quail in January 1842 as my medical attendant, at £300 per annum. On the 18th of June I thought fit to increase his salary to £500 per year, so satisfied was I of his kind and unceasing attention; I therefore promise that it shall be paid when it is in my power to do so. I am M. E. Eliza Shuttleworth.' Not surprisingly, Coroner Wakley instantly dismissed this claim.

John Quail relocated to the north-west of England, becoming a thorn in the side of the authorities there until his death in 1859 at the age of fifty-three. He was never punished for his neglect of Mrs Shuttleworth.

The Shuttleworth case had been one of the earliest test cases faced by the new Commissioners with regard to the 'single patient' – those lunatics who remained outside the asylum system, cared for either in their own homes or as the only lunatic in the house of another person who had designated him- or herself as carer. In trying to intervene to help Mrs Shuttleworth, the Commissioners had exposed the problematic nature of state intrusion upon private property and one-to-one lunacy care arrangements. (A similar uncertainty and reluctance to interfere in private life would also delay the imposition of legal safeguards against child cruelty and neglect by parents until the 1880s.) To inquire, visit, enter and inspect domestic premises where a single lunatic was kept risked the accusation of trespass and infringement of privacy; but to keep aloof might consign to murderous abuse unknown numbers of the mentally afflicted – or the perfectly sane who were nevertheless immured in their own home by a malicious family member. The single patient received none of the protection given to asylum patients (however scanty and ineffectual that might be). If no more than one paying patient were received, the house did not even need to be registered. One estimate in 1828 stated that around 5,000 individuals may have been in single care at that time; but the difficulty throughout the century was acquiring any accurate, useful figures for those confined in their own homes or in the home of another.

L UNATICS.—The immediate attention of all persons receiving to board or lodge in any house, (other than an hospital, a county asylum, or a licensed house,) or taking care or charge of a single person as a lunatic, idiot, or person of unsound mind, is directed to the 90th and 91st sections of the Act 8 and 9 Victoria, c.100; and notice is hereby given, that they will be required forthwith to make the necessary returns, and to observe the other regulations prescribed by the Act.   By order of the Commissioners in Lunacy,

R. W. S. Lutwidge, Secretary.

August 15, 1845

Upon their formation in 1845 the Commissioners in Lunacy had placed the above advertisement in the national newspapers requesting carers of single patients who were received for profit to send notification – with copies of certificates and lunacy order – of any lunatic on their premises to Lord Shaftesbury, so that he could place this information upon his Private Register of single patients. Only Shaftesbury, the Home Secretary, the Lord Chancellor and two Lunacy Commissioners – one medical and one legal – were permitted to peruse this list. The latter two, plus Shaftesbury, comprised the 'Private Committee', who would visit those single patients on an annual basis. The Commissioners were already pledged to secrecy and discretion in their work; the Private Register brought an even more occult aspect – and a vast new workload.

It soon became clear that the new arrangement did not work: there were simply not enough staff at the Commission, and single patients were scattered all over the country, making statutory annual visits difficult. Besides, there was huge under-reporting of home-based lunatics. 'The three Commissioners could not do the duty, and it was extremely awkward to have secrets within secrets,' explained Shaftesbury later. The furtive nature of the register had been devised to allay fears among the governing classes of public exposure of their private tragedies. It had, in fact, been a sop to the House of Lords, which had repeatedly rejected lunacy amendment bills that contained a clause requiring the inspection of single patients.

More than half of Chancery lunatics found insane by inquisition were cared for in single houses, and the Lord Chancellor's own team of visitors inspected premises and interviewed those patients once a year. But non-Chancery single patients could be visited only if they were known of, and fourteen years after the opening of his Private Register, Shaftesbury had to admit, 'We have spent years and years in endeavouring to learn [of them]. I am certain there are hundreds of persons called single patients of whom we have no knowledge whatever.' By this time, just 124 notifications had been received, and this was widely believed to be but a small fraction of the true total.

Care given within the family attracted no official scrutiny. If a spouse wished to confine a spouse, a sibling a sibling, a parent a child, or vice versa, no lunacy certificates, notification or inspection were required, as these patients were not kept for profit. Families were deemed to be the appropriate people with whom the insane should reside. Husband and wife were legally bound to care for each other – in sickness and in health – and parents and children were also regarded as having a 'natural' mutual obligation. Sibling relationships attenuated this sense of natural responsibility; in-laws stretched the notion yet further. The law permitted the family to take the steps it considered necessary to keep a lunatic safe, and to keep others safe from the lunatic. However, confinement and physical restraint had to be 'reasonable', and anyone locking away a harmless unsound person could be prosecuted for illegal imprisonment and ill-treatment – even if the prisoner was a blood relation. Needless to say, the authorities would have to know of the lunatic's existence before any such action could be taken.

Accidental discoveries of a hidden lunatic, such as that of Mrs Shuttleworth, would, from time to time, induce in the national psyche an anxiety that there were likely to be hundreds more who would never be found – in all classes and all locales. Someone in the Devon village of Lewtrenchard approached a local Poor Law officer, William Perry, with fears that a lunatic was being kept in poor conditions in a disused part of an old mansion, called Orchard, which at the time was operating as a farmhouse. Perry went to Orchard on 27 March 1851, knocked on the door and asked to see the farmer-owner, John Yeo. A servant explained that Yeo was not at home, and although

Perry had no legal right to enter and search the premises, the servant let him in and led him down a narrow passageway that terminated in a strange wooden room. The servant unbolted the door and raised his candle. As Perry's eyes adjusted to the gloom, he saw a naked man sitting on a small raised platform serving as a bed, which was covered in urine-soaked straw and a piece of canvas for a blanket. His beard and hair were long and filthy, his finger- and toenails untrimmed, and around his left ankle was a large metal ring, attached to a chain that was riveted to a beam in the ceiling. The wooden cell was seven feet by five, and the only light came from a small hole in the wall, barred with iron frets.

Perry went to fetch two magistrates and a doctor, and as they carefully examined the man, John Yeo returned home and told them the story. The confined man was Charles Luxmore, Yeo's brother-in-law. 'He was always weak in the head and strange in his conduct,' Yeo told the magistrates. 'His mother says he was of weak intellect from childhood.' He had been a blacksmith and while he was still a young man his behaviour had become of concern and he experienced episodes of mania. In 1838, 'thinking that he would otherwise get into some mischief', Luxmore's father had constructed this cell of wood at the family farmhouse at nearby Germansweek, and had fashioned the leg-iron and chain to restrain him. The years passed, Yeo married Luxmore's sister, the parents became bedridden, and Yeo inherited the problem of Charles. None of the other Luxmore children had wanted anything to do with him. Mr and Mrs Luxmore asked Yeo to care for Charles in the same way in which they had, and when Yeo and his wife moved to Orchard, the wooden cell had been taken down at Germansweek and reconstructed as an annexe to the old mansion – stuck out on the end of a wing. In the cases that made it into the public record, the extremities of a building – its attic, cellar, most far-off chamber – were often the sites of deposit for the family secret.

The magistrates asked Yeo why he had not yielded up Charles to asylum care: if he had been unwilling to pay for a private asylum, there was the huge new public facility at Exminster. Yeo explained that the Luxmores received £30 a year as an annuity from the lunatic's uncle, and Yeo believed that if Charles had gone into Devon County Asylum, they would have had to pay for at least some of his care (with the parish paying the rest). 'Sometimes he is violent, and sometimes he is quiet for a long time,' said Yeo, explaining the chain. The reason Charles was naked was that he tore any clothing put upon him; and at the previous Christmas they had given up shaving him and cutting his hair because he had grabbed the razor and slashed at Yeo and the servant.

Charles was cut free from the chain and assisted into a covered cart, being unable to walk unaided. He was taken to Devon County Asylum, the 800-bed institution that had opened in July 1845. Here, Dr John Charles Bucknill, one of the eminent alienists of the day, was medical superintendent; the newly invigorated county asylum system offered far larger scope than the private asylums for the study of lunacy in all its varieties, and many brilliant men would therefore choose to work in the public system. Bucknill described Charles as 'remarkably amiable, quiet and inoffensive'. He oversaw the slow, careful removal of the thick metal ring around his ankle.

Something had to be done about John Yeo – but what? What law had been broken? How had the Lunatics Act been flouted? The Devon magistrates wrote to the Commissioners in Lunacy that there appeared to be nothing in the 1845 Act 'to render the parties implicated liable to punishment'; they guessed that Yeo's harbouring of Luxmore could only be 'a misdemeanour at common law'. The Commissioners prevaricated, requesting more information on the case and wondering whether the local Poor Law officers could be blamed for not finding out about the recluse of Orchard farmhouse earlier. In an increasingly testy set of letters, the magistrates and Commissioners passed the buck back and forth. Finally, a report was sent to Home Secretary Sir George Grey, which included Bucknill's upbeat report on Luxmore's health – he had shown no signs of physical injury, his cough had proved not to be consumptive, he was now happy to wear clothing and be groomed. Grey's scrawl on the documentation's envelope reads: 'It is impossible to doubt that the treatment of this poor man amounts to a misdemeanour of a very aggravated description. As to the propriety of a prosecution, the Commissioners might exercise their discretion.' Just what they didn't want to do.

The prosecution of John Yeo, for the common-law misdemeanour of volunteering to look after a lunatic and failing to do so properly, took place at the end of July 1851. Dr Bucknill used the opportunity to advertise the wonders of the county asylum system, detailing the progress Luxmore had made since his admission: 'The lunatic has been very quiet and tractable since I have had charge of him . . . He is good tempered and perfectly harmless.' But this could also suggest that the thirteen years in a darkened cell had not wrought half as much damage as the prosecution would hope to demonstrate. Indeed, Yeo's servants testified that Luxmore had been well fed and kept warm; his episodes of violence, they said, entirely justified the use of the chain. The local vicar revealed that he had known all about the situation, and had even deigned to look in on Luxmore while visiting the Yeos. 'There was a terror in the neighbourhood about him,' the clergyman said, prompting many to wonder why none of the locals had come forward earlier to raise the alarm and have Luxmore removed from their vicinity. It was also put in as evidence that Yeo had had the burden of care placed upon him by his parents-in-law; the blood relatives had distanced themselves, but Yeo had attempted to do what he could to help, while struggling to run his own small farm. Should a man be punished for taking such duties upon himself?

The judge, Justice Coleridge, thought so, noting Yeo's unwillingness to contribute financially to any better quality care provided by the county asylum. Coleridge declared: 'Any man who took upon himself voluntarily to interfere with the liberty of his neighbour must do it under all responsibility . . . It never was the law, and God forbid it should be, that an individual might take upon himself the custody of a lunatic . . . and then, even from innocent motives, chain that lunatic up for a series of years, without regard to his situation.' If, as the defence had claimed, the family had great affection for Charles, 'a more unfortunate mode of showing it, he had never heard of'.

Yeo was sentenced to six months in prison, but Coleridge spared him the house of correction, sending him instead to the less punitive common gaol. Coleridge was keen that the Luxmore case should act as a warning to people who did not come forward with their insane family member yet were manifestly unable to provide adequate comfort and humane treatment within the home. The message was that a layperson was not competent to diagnose or treat the insane; ignorance and local custom ought now to be giving way to trust in the well-funded and humane new asylums. But resistance to asylums could be deeply felt in many communities. County asylum superintendents throughout England and Wales were aware of the refusal of local people to hand over escapees. Attendants seeking to recapture Rees Williams, a pauper lunatic who escaped from his warders at Briton Ferry asylum in South Wales in early 1846, were fought off by a crowd who gathered about Williams's home, where he had fled after being helped over the fifteen-foot-high asylum wall by a fellow patient. Police officers had to go in large numbers to re-take Williams, and the local magistrate wrote that 'a general prejudice existed against lunatic asylums, and the friends were disposed in most cases to assist escapes and screen patients'.

F OUND, wandering about in the parish of Bowness, in Cumberland, on the 6th October instant, a FEMALE LUNATIC, supposed to have escaped from a private asylum. She cannot tell her name, but has been heard to mention Liverpool. She is about 50 years of age, hair gray and cut short like a man's, gray eyes, strong masculine features, and speaks with a Lancashire accent; hands and face freckled. She was dressed in a blue print gown, neatly made, and apron to match, white cotton stockings marked "E.G.," and lasting boots, black silk shawl with fringe, fine black and white tartan woollen shawl, and long-haired boa, worked cap trimmed with yellow, and Tuscan bonnet with white ribands. She is supposed to have been in the neighbourhood since the 15th of September last. Further information may be obtained by application to Mr. T. H. Hodgson, Courts, Carlisle.

A remarkably similar case to the Yeo–Luxmore scandal, four years later, showed a tougher reaction by the Commissioners in Lunacy. Following the Yeo conviction, they seemed to have felt more optimistic about going ahead with a prosecution; in addition, an Act of 1853 gave greater powers to magistrates to examine and institutionalise lunatics other than the 'wandering lunatics' found in public spaces. (Advertisements such as the above, in The Times, in October 1845, were sometimes placed when a 'wandering lunatic' was discovered.) An Englishman's home was his castle; but if he chose to make a dungeon within it, and keep a lunatic, the state could now more confidently enter and explore if there was prima facie evidence of false imprisonment or abuse. In April 1855 local rumour had led a Poor Law official, magistrates and a doctor to the Devon home of Anthony Huxtable,

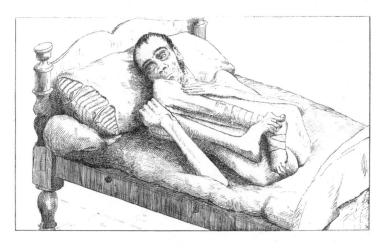

Edward Lancey in the Devon County Asylum at Exminster following his rescue from his brother-in-law's home; he had been kept in a darkened room for many years. Lancey's condition reportedly improved significantly in the public institution.

a farmer. Here, in the village of Bratton Fleming, in a small, stinking, darkened, ground-floor room at the end of a passage, lay Edward Lancey, on a low bed, semi-naked. Lancey was Huxtable's brother-in-law, and Huxtable, a widower with several children to care for, had been bequeathed the care of Edward by his in-laws; he had kept Lancey in that room for seven years. The farmer received £21 a year for his care – each of Huxtable's late wife's three sisters paying him £7 – and he admitted that he relied on that cash to be able to feed his family and pay the rent. As in the Luxmore case, none of the blood family had taken on the burden of care, once the lunatic's parents were no longer able to do so.

Lancey lay on the bed with his knees drawn up to his chest. He hallooed and sang throughout the magistrates' visit, and was unable to respond to questions put to him. Huxtable said that Lancey would tear any clothing and break items; he was also doubly incontinent, so that it was impossible to keep him clean twenty-four hours a day. Huxtable was very unwilling to let go of his brother-in-law and only with reluctance brought forward some items of clothing – including two petticoats – in which Lancey could decently be transported to the Devon County Asylum.

Dr John Charles Bucknill (1817–1897) was the superintendent of the Devon
County Asylum and promoted its use among the poor of the county.
However, later in life, he changed his mind, and argued that home-based care
was superior to institutionalisation.

Here, Dr Bucknill found that he was emaciated and had fractures
to both shin bones. Lancey could not straighten his legs and would
be unlikely ever to walk. 'His mental condition was that of chronic
mania – the faculties of the mind were deficient but not lost,' noted
Bucknill. At the court case three months later, and once again
promoting county asylum care, Bucknill revealed that Lancey's
mental state was now 'considerably improved . . . He was at first
noisy, anxious and timid, having a most anxious and wistful expression of face.' Contradicting Huxtable's assertion that Lancey was
hopelessly dirty, the doctor stated that he was from the start quite
capable of indicating that he needed to use the privy and was able
actively to help staff keep him clean. Bucknill also denied that Lancey
had violent tendencies. The doctor rejected the argument that
Huxtable had struggled to work his farm and pay adequate attention
to his charge, whom he had willingly taken on in return for a fee.
Bucknill did not hesitate to use the word 'imprisoned' of these
home-care cases, which he felt were all too common in the rural
parts of the West Country and Wales. Ignorance of the help

available and prejudice against the asylum were no excuse for this type of barbarity, he believed.

The judge, Mr Justice Compton, disagreed. He stated that the case had not been made that Huxtable had wilfully mistreated and neglected his charge. No proof had been given that Lancey was in any worse condition when discovered than when Huxtable had first taken charge of him seven years earlier (the broken shin bones seem to have been overlooked by the judge). And there had been no false imprisonment, as 'the lunatic was a prisoner by nature'. The jury agreed and returned a verdict of not guilty.

The Yeo case of 1851 had strongly suggested that a brother-in-law was not under a 'natural' obligation to take upon himself the care of a lunatic in-law: he had entered into the situation voluntarily, and so was bound to perform his duties properly. However, Justice Compton seems to have believed that the opposite was the case: the very fact that Huxtable, a struggling farmer, had the care of Lancey delegated to him meant that he was entitled to more sympathy than a blood relative. The Lancey siblings had not bestirred themselves to help their insane brother, and Huxtable had undertaken their 'natural' duties for them.

The failed Huxtable prosecution of 1855 was a setback for the Commissioners, and to promoters of the county asylums, such as Dr Bucknill. Prosecutions would continue to be brought, where there was prima facie evidence of abuse or neglect; but in less clear cases, gentle and then firm personal persuasion was the Commissioners' preferred method, to encourage families either to place their relative in an asylum or to agree to being periodically inspected by a medical man or a Poor Law official.

In the Huxtable case, it had been the local vicar who called in the authorities; rumours had come to his ears, he explained. Clergymen were often the breakers of the spell of silence and secrecy within rural communities where a lunatic was concealed. In urban areas, it was the public who frequently alerted the authorities to the possible harbouring of uncertificated people, both family members and single patients detained for money. Screams, shouting and strange comings and goings prompted town-dwellers to come forward to have the mystery investigated. Mr Chalk of 78 Warwick Square, Pimlico, told the Commissioners in Lunacy of the disturbance caused by the loud cries of a female lunatic confined at the house of surgeon Thomas Blanchard, next door at number 79. In February 1847, the Commissioners instituted a special inquiry and discovered that Blanchard was charging £80 a year to board one Miss Kidston, who had never been certified and who 'never went out of the house, owing to her noisy propensities, being obscene in language and violent in gesture'. The surgeon was summoned to the Commissioners' office where he was made to promise to have Miss Kidston certificated and to have her added to the Private Register.

The Commissioners were keen to maintain a mixed economy in lunacy care, recognising that a discreet single-patient set-up could be of particular benefit to the wealthy; they were also reluctant to interfere in the free trade of lunacy – that would be an assault upon the business ethic. Lord Shaftesbury himself chose to avoid the asylum system for his epileptic son, Maurice, instead lodging him in 1849 as a single patient with a family in Lausanne. John Perceval would doubtless have been stunned if he had read this diary revelation by Shaftesbury: 'Epileptic fits are treated like madness, and madness constitutes a right, as it were, to treat people as vermin.' Shaftesbury agonised over what would become of Maurice when he and his wife died – a common source of distress for those with mentally troubled dependants. It was, after all, the wishes of elderly in-laws that had created John Yeo's and Anthony Huxtable's dilemmas. Maurice never did come home, despite his father acknowledging that 'separation and solitude have done nothing' for him.

Throughout the Commissioners' minutes, boarders of single patients were urged to observe the lunacy laws and to ensure that conditions were optimal. 'We have endeavoured year by year to do things by persuasion until I have lost all patience,' Shaftesbury revealed in 1859. 'We have erred on the side of lenity in respect of licensed houses and those who receive single patients, and I am very sorry for it.' But he felt that public opinion was still not ripe for state officials routinely to enter domestic spaces unless there were grave allegations of wrongdoing.

It is clear that, privately, it wasn't just Shaftesbury who lacked full confidence in both the private and the public asylum system that the Lunacy Commission oversaw. In August 1857, Commissioner

Sir Alexander Morison (1799–1866) was one of the elite alienists with a large, lucrative and very discreet practice relating to single patients. Along with Drs Alexander Sutherland, Edward Thomas Monro and Forbes Benignus Winslow, Morison would board very wealthy alleged lunatics in private homes, but failed to register these patients with the Commissioners in Lunacy. Critics would accuse Morison of certifying 'difficult' children of the wealthy on the mere say-so of their parents.

Bryan Waller Procter wrote to John Forster – Commission Secretary, from 1855 – requesting a recommendation for single-patient care for a friend of his, one Mr Strickland, who was shortly to go abroad and needed to place his unsound son. Procter wrote that, ideally, a public institution should have separate wards made available for paying middle- and upper-class patients, which strongly suggests that Procter secretly believed that the private asylums were not up to scratch; the desire for the state system to set aside private wards for fee-paying patients would become increasingly urgently voiced in the second half of the century. Procter asked Forster to lend him the 'Private List', as he wanted to see whether a Miss Bailey of

Tavistock Place, Bloomsbury, was on this register of trustworthy and discreet keepers of wealthy single patients. Back in 1842, William Makepeace Thackeray had asked Procter to recommend a good private asylum for his wife Isabella, who had become mentally ill. The author visited the asylum that Procter believed to be the best, but later wrote that it 'makes me quite sick to think of even now. He [Procter] shook his head about other places.' Thackeray decided instead to place Isabella in single-patient care in Camberwell, where she lived until her death in 1894.

Thackeray has been criticised for placing his wife in an obscure South London lodging under no particularly eminent alienist, but Procter may well have pointed out to him that the exclusive end of the market was no guarantee of humane and companionable confinement. Two of the century's biggest names in mad-doctoring, Alexander Sutherland and Sir Alexander Morison, routinely failed to register their many single patients with the Commissioners, and for many of the confined, little attempt was made to provide them with appropriate company or mental stimulation. Abusive attendants blacklisted at asylums were often employed to guard wealthy single patients; and drugging, bleeding and head-shaving appear to have been carried on against them; many had been confined on the mere say-so of parents, who had asked Morison to 'straighten out their wayward children'. Dr James Crichton-Browne was one of the three Lord Chancellor's Visitors in Lunacy who in 1877 inspected the 336 Chancery lunatics in single care (a further 676 were in asylums). Among the cruelties he uncovered were a woman tied to a chair by a rope and another shut in a darkened room for three months. He witnessed wealthy patients being brought into asylums from home care with broken bones, the marks of flogging upon them, covered in bruises and sometimes delivered in ropes or in strait-waistcoats. Crichton-Browne believed that greed and indolence were much more likely to pass undetected in a private home, even within a family, than in an asylum. An expensive single house, overseen by a top doctor, ought to have offered the best lunacy care possible, but it seems that abuses in this sector went on in defiance of the inspectors. '[Commissioner] Gaskell is single-patient hunting,' John Forster wrote to Procter about a fellow Commissioner whose quest to unearth these lodgings was made harder by the blatant refusal of men like Morison to reveal the existence and whereabouts of their single patients when requested by the Commissioners.

L UNACY.—A Married Medical Man, in one of the midland counties, having long experience in the treatment of the insane, wishes to RECEIVE into his house a High-class RESIDENT PATIENT. The house is large and commodious, and has attached to it gardens and pleasure grounds, comprising nearly four acres, with a large extent of surrounding grass land. A quiet and harmless patient, whom it may be considered inadvisable to place in a public institution, would find here combined the ordinary associations of home with skilled management.— Address "Medicus," care of W. H. Smith and Son's bookstall, railway station, Charing-cross, London.

If the alienist elite appeared to remain safe from state censure, those on the fringes of the medical profession might face disproportionate scrutiny. On 10 February 1882, two Marylebone butchers were standing in Devonshire Place when a carriage drew up. They watched as a slender, fair, young man, wearing no boots or hat, and with his hands tied, was manhandled out by four people and up the steps of number 39, calling out, 'Oh you devils, let me go, I am no more mad than you are!' He spotted the two bystanders and cried, 'They are trying to kill me!' The butchers found a police officer and a watch was placed on the premises. Before long, Mrs Talbot of number 38 reported that she heard the sound of groaning coming from next door on successive mornings, which made her think there was someone living there who was 'mentally afflicted'. The police officers reported the case to the Commissioners in Lunacy, who asked alienist Dr George Blandford to investigate. When Blandford was reluctantly admitted into the house, he was shown up to a large, airy, clean and well-furnished attic suite, where he found one Mr Winn. The man refused to give his first name, but it emerged that he was one of the aristocratic Winns of Warley Lodge, near Brentwood in Essex. Winn had rented these rooms from Dr George Fenton Cameron so that he could spend time with his elder brother – the chap spotted by the butchers – who was in a 'nervous state'. Winn thought that being in London might distract his brother and raise his spirits. The patient was under the care of Dr Duncan Herbert Wilson, of Brook Street, Mayfair, a homeopathist, 'who is unfavourably known in this department', the Commissioners in Lunacy curtly noted. They were not likely to have thought well of Dr Cameron either, who was one of the first promoters in Britain of massage as a therapeutic treatment for all sorts of problems, physical and psychological.

Winn the younger worked by day in a solicitor's office, and hired a servant to be with his brother while he was at work. When Dr Cameron turned up, he refused to tell Blandford the Winns' first names, or any other information. He said he had no intention of certifying the elder brother, as he did not believe him insane under the terms of the Lunacy Act. Blandford thought quite the reverse, after finally being granted the right to interview him alone: the elder Winn was 'trepidatious' in the extreme, admitted that he would only go out in the London streets at night because in the daytime everyone looked at him, and was clearly unsound, in Blandford's view. 'Masturbation was the cause of all this,' wrote Blandford to the Commissioners, failing to substantiate this most interesting assertion.

The Commissioners wrote to the Attorney-General to find out what grounds there might be for prosecution of Dr Cameron, and were told that there were none. The younger Winn had merely rented rooms without paying for any care from Dr Cameron – and therefore the elder Winn could not be described as a lunatic being kept for profit. Cameron was acting as nothing more than an ordinary landlord, while the servant who was with the elder Winn in the daytime was not fulfilling the role of a keeper. The Commissioners seem to have been spoiling for a fight with an 'alternative' practitioner, but this time, they were thwarted.

So, now – mad wives, in the attic; or sane wives to be driven mad. They are our most potent image of nineteenth-century lunacy, largely thanks to *Jane Eyre*'s Bertha Mason, slightly less so to Laura Fairlie in *The Woman in White* – drugged, housebound then asylum-bound by her money-obsessed husband. The 1938 Patrick Hamilton play *Gas Light* – filmed in 1944 with Ingrid Bergman being driven close to distraction by Charles Boyer, as the dastardly husband, in Pimlico, in 1880 – revived and reinvigorated the image of Victorian womankind's mental distress in the face of unbridled male power. Feminist academics picked up this ball and have run with it, for the past thirty-five years or so, heroically retrieving from unjust neglect Victorian women's novels, diaries and poetry and placing them centrally in any serious consideration of the period. And there, perhaps, lies a problem. By privileging literary work over other less accessible, less pleasure-giving sources of information about lived experience, some distortion has crept in. If we call up the shade of Wilkie Collins, he can explain. In 1877, in answer to an interviewer's question about the origins of *The Woman in White*, published in 1860, he said: 'The victim to be interesting must be a woman, to be very interesting she must be a lady, [and] as there is a person to be injured – innocent and beautiful, of course – there must be a villain.' Hamlet and King Lear notwithstanding, it is a woman in psychological peril that attracts mass audiences and mass readerships.

Charles Reade found this out when he published *Hard Cash* in 1863, which featured as its hero Alfred Hardie, wrongfully incarcerated in a lunatic asylum by his villainous father, who plans to grab Alfred's £14,000 inheritance. Reade drew heavily for his plot on the Richard Paternoster case of twenty years earlier, and the case of Edward Fletcher, who in 1858 had been confined in an asylum by his greedy uncles (see Appendix 3, p. 395). Reade also cited the 1851 *Mathew* v. *Harty* case in Dublin, a real-life plot in which fact was more hackneyed than any fiction would dare to be: after being freed, the alleged lunatic, a young man, sued the elderly doctor who had certified him, and in the dock the doctor revealed himself to be the boy's long-lost father. Reade was a campaigner against many social abuses, and did not hesitate to use his novels as a blunt instrument – which led to him being denigrated in some quarters as 'the novelist with a purpose' and a 'newspaper novelist'. Lunacy law abuse was perhaps his most passionate cause, and he gave shelter to a number of individuals on the run from the mad-doctors. The heavy traffic between fiction and fact meant that while the newspaper novelists and the Sensation novelists* took plots, characters and atmosphere direct from life, they in turn were referred to and quoted in official documents and newspaper commentary on real cases. Verdicts unguessable, personas hidden or multiple, secrets in peril of exposure: these fill the records of disputed lunacy cases as well as the novels and plays of mid-century.

Hard Cash, which Reade subtitled *A Matter-of-Fact Romance*, became a touchstone for commentators on lunacy disputes, and in that sense it was an influential book. However, the novel's serialisation in

---

* Let other pens dwell on the Sensation Fiction of the 1850s and '60s. There is a very healthy strand of literary studies that has produced some excellent work on the genre, and I have little to add that is new, *Hard Cash* and *The Woman in White* excepted.

Charles Dickens's magazine *All the Year Round*, starting in June 1862, caused circulation to fall as readers failed to see the allure of a story of a sane man being mis-certified and maltreated in an asylum. While confined, Alfred endures sexual advances from two asylum attendants – Mrs Archbold and Babyface Biceps, a strapping great nurse – which turned the collective stomach of *All the Year Round*'s readership. Forty weeks and 275 pages later, Dickens insisted that *Hard Cash* be brought to a hasty end, and the denouement is achieved at breakneck pace. Alfred Hardie's plight was of interest to no one, and besides, Reade seemed to be impugning one of the mad-doctors Dickens most admired – Dr John Conolly. By the end of the century, Reade was unread and 'perchance half-forgotten', as one acquaintance of his regretfully stated.

So we do not know *Hard Cash* today; nor the excellent Wilkie Collins short story 'Fatal Fortune' (1874), based on the true case of a mis-certified, eccentric and very rich young man who wished to marry

Novelist Charles Reade (1814–1884) championed the plight of the wrongly confined in his controversial 1863 novel *Hard Cash*, in which hero Alfred Hardie is placed, sane, in an asylum.

against his family's wishes. Now, as then, mass readerships (and audiences) reject stories that feature a highly strung or unorthodox male as a victim of lunacy conspirators. 'Torture the heroine' was the formula that nineteenth-century playwright Victorien Sardou recommended in the search for a crowd-pleasing entertainment. It is still ladies that we like to see, 'going mad in white satin' – Richard Brinsley Sheridan's hilarious skewering of a theatrical cliché in his 1779 play *The Rivals*. 'Going mad in white satin' shows that the bonkers pretty girl, or emotionally fragile young heroine, was a well-established literary 'type' that could not fail to pull the punters in.

Ophelia can probably be blamed for much of this; she is exquisitely sensitive, intelligent, high-born, and is confronted with the murder of her father and rejection by her lover. The loss of her wits is not only understandable but laudable: it is a mark of her refinement and the depth of her love – and she stays beautiful throughout. No one wants to go mad like Bertha Mason, though. 'It snatched and growled like some strange wild animal . . . The clothed hyena rose up, and stood tall on its hind feet': the scene in the Thornfield attic is perhaps the most vicious depiction of an insane person to have been committed to paper. Charlotte Brontë places her readers in the position of the penny visitors who came to gawp at Bedlam; few mad-doctors, even the hardest hearted, ever wrote of their charges in this language. Bertha is descended from a line of 'idiots and maniacs through three generations', as Mr Rochester tells Jane, and her life of heedless sensual indulgence led her prematurely but inexorably into the full-blown raving insanity that was her inheritance. The purple-faced, shaggy-haired, corpulent, murderous beast of the upper storey is the product of a vicious lust- and drink-filled earlier life – behaviour dictated by the tainted Mason blood running in her veins. She was first a moral maniac, and then her intellect collapsed.

Where did Bertha spring from? Most answers tend to be as crudely reductionist as any mad-doctor dabbing his scalpel into brain matter to try to find the seat of a delusion. *Jane Eyre* is endlessly rich in rereading because Brontë's writing hand was hooked up to a wilder part of her own mind. This is why her novel has been forced repeatedly on to the psychoanalyst's couch, and a mini-industry in academia has larded multiple meanings on to each and every scene and protagonist. Brontë herself tried to explain how the imagination worked:

> . . . this I know, the writer who possesses the creative gift owns something of which he is not always master – something that, at times, strangely wills and works for itself. He may lay down rules and devise principles, and to rules and principles it will perhaps for years lie in subjection; and then, haply without any warning of revolt, there comes a time when . . . you have little choice left but quiescent adoption. As for you, the nominal artist, your share in it has been to work passively under dictates you neither delivered nor could question – that would not be uttered at your prayer, nor suppressed nor changed at your caprice. If the result be attractive, the World will praise you, who little deserve praise; if it be repulsive, the same World will blame you, who almost as little deserve blame.

(Forty years later, Wilkie Collins, in response to being asked about the creative process, replied in a similar mode: 'My perverse brains set to work without consulting me,' he told the *Ladies' Treasury* magazine.)

Among the storms that the pseudonymous publication of *Jane Eyre* created in 1847, the depiction of Mrs Rochester brought an element of 'blame' that Brontë had not anticipated. In response to reviewers who had described Bertha as 'shocking', Brontë wrote:

> I agree with them that the character is shocking but I know that it is but too natural. There is a phase of insanity which may be called 'moral madness', in which all that is good or even human seems to disappear from the mind and a fiend nature replaces it. All seems demonised. It is true that profound pity ought to be the only sentiment elicited by the view of such degradation, and equally true is it that I have not sufficiently dwelt on that feeling; I have erred in making *horror* too predominant. Mrs Rochester indeed lived a sinful life before she was insane, but sin is itself a species of insanity: the truly good behold and compassionate it as such.

More immediately problematical, Brontë was told that she might have caused pain to Thackeray, to whom she dedicated the second edition of the book. Brontë had known nothing of his wife's mental state and her single-patient confinement, and was mortified to learn that her harsh depiction of Mrs Rochester might be read, by those in the know, as a reference to the mysterious Mrs Thackeray. Others believed that 'Currer Bell' (the name under which the novel was originally published) was really Thackeray's governess, who had fallen in love with the master of the house when his wife had gone mad. Fortunately, he had not been perturbed by the rumours, and the friendship between the writers continued.

In the late 1840s readers would have understood that Mr Rochester's refusal to place Bertha in an institution was a mark of his nobility, not perversity, or brutality. As we have seen, even in the most exclusive private asylum, a violent patient might have been subjected to the strait-waistcoat and the cold-water treatment, and – even though they were no longer permitted by the Commissioners – to manacles, the darkened room and other types of restraint. Home-based care would therefore have been seen as the option of a hero, not a scoundrel. In his words, Bertha was Mr Rochester's 'filthy burden' and not to be palmed off on strangers. She was also his punishment for his failure to go against his father and brother, whose greed for Bertha's £30,000 dowry had coerced him into the match fifteen years earlier. It was punishment, too, for his youthful vanity: he had rushed into the alliance partly because he was so flattered that the beautiful and rich Miss Mason favoured him over all the other young men in Spanish Town, Jamaica.

Why did he not seek a parliamentary divorce? Bertha's adulteries alone gave him the right to this. Lunacy was not grounds for divorce, so long as the spouse had been sane at the time of the wedding; and Brontë cleverly suggests that Bertha probably was incipiently mad at the point of the marriage, but that Rochester would have had no chance of proving this. More importantly, the first readers of *Jane Eyre* will have understood that to force a raving wife through the process of a divorce on the grounds of adultery would have been cruel and 'unmanly'; he would have to be able to prove that Bertha had known of the consequences of her adulteries at the time she had committed them. Less honourably, it would have made public the very shame that Rochester was seeking to conceal.

Brontë insists that we understand his impulse to decontaminate, and rejuvenate, himself with the woman who least resembles Bertha, Blanche Ingram, Céline Varens and all the other black-haired coquettes with whom he has dissipated himself. Mr Rochester's moral lapse was not locking his mad wife in the attic, but his perfectly understandable intention to commit bigamy, and to practise a deception in order to secure the real love that he had found in Jane.

Regarding Bertha, he had sought to 'bury her in seclusion', and his other home, Ferndean Manor, was indeed more isolated; but the damp of the woodland in which it lay would have polished Bertha off; Thornfield's third-storey 'secret inner cabinet' was the solution. So that she would have permanent, personal care, he hired Grace Poole from the Grimsby Retreat, where her son was the keeper – 'Retreat' indicating an advanced, humanitarian, Quaker-inspired institution, where physical restraint was minimal. Grace has the wherewithal to tie Bertha to a chair once in a while, but for the most part, Bertha is free to scuttle around in her 'goblin cell'. Unfortunately, she gains herself a little more freedom than that, and Grace's understandable solace-seeking in gin-and-water leads to the eventual catastrophe. Only Mr Rochester, Grace, Grace's son, Bertha's brother Richard, and the surgeon, Carter, ever knew of the lunatic wife up at the hall, although there had been local rumours. 'Who or what she was, it was difficult to conjecture,' a local man later tells Jane. Even Wood, the vicar, the usual repository of such parish secrets, had known nothing of Bertha.

In 1979, Sandra Gilbert and Susan Gubar published their famous theory – that Bertha is Jane's alter ego: a personification of the rage engendered by pent-up female energy, especially sexual energy. But despite Gilbert and Gubar's sophisticated comparisons of the patterns of metaphor and imagery common to Jane's experiences and Bertha's story, Bertha actually appears to be – among other things – a figure who shows the potential fate of a woman who in her early life failed to assert herself (as Jane asserts herself) and who took refuge in commonplace thoughts, activities and appetites. Bertha sought freedom in promiscuity and drink, but Jane knows, as Mr Rochester has learned, that that kind of libertinism is an illusion of freedom – for man as much as for woman. If Bertha is an echo of anyone in the novel, it is surely Blanche Ingram – the vacuous, conventional drawing-room beauty that Bertha herself once was, in Spanish Town. Bertha is what happens when you have no true sense of a self, and the language used to describe Blanche and Bertha (in her youth) also bears comparison – they are raven-ringleted, dark-eyed and magnificent, imperious for no good reason; and the Dowager Ingram, Blanche's mother, is already exhibiting Bertha-like physical attributes: her features are 'inflated and darkened' and her eye is 'fierce'.

Bertha at Thornfield was being as well looked after as was possible in the early decades of the nineteenth century, though it isn't easy for modern eyes to spot this fact. The depiction of a woman confined in her husband's home brings a sense of unease. No law had been broken by Mr Rochester, and he had not forsaken his wife in her sickness; but Brontë nevertheless plays on the idea that some transgression has taken place. Newspaper and parliamentary bluebook revelations in the early 1840s, of relatives hidden away in sheds, cells and remote chambers, created a similar frisson, or shudder, for anyone who read them, even when it was clear that the family was often doing what it believed to be the best. And so the madwoman in the attic remains a troubling figure, no matter how hard we try to explain her. Three decades after publication, *Jane Eyre* was still the point of reference for those addressing the problem of family confine- ment and its potential for abuse. In 1879 the *British Medical Journal* worried that there was still 'no law to prevent a Mr Rochester from locking up his mad wife in the attic of a mansion, with a keeper, as described in *Jane Eyre*'. Government attempts to persuade people to offer up their lunatic spouses, children, parents and siblings for certification and inspection had been a failure. Families still preferred secrecy.

Yet two horrific cases – one from the mid-1860s, the other from the mid-1870s – kept fresh the public anxiety about family confine- ment, and that of wives in particular. On a summer day in 1864, Mrs Rosalind Hammond tore a strip of wallpaper from the bedroom in which she had been imprisoned by her husband and two maidservants for the past two years; she wrote upon it using a pencil that had been accidentally left in the room and tossed the paper through the bottom of her iron-barred window at Laurel Cottage in Peckham Rye, south- east London. It fluttered into the path of a passer-by, who looked up and saw her at the window, and then alerted PC John Spinks. Gaining entry to the bolted and chained house, Spinks found Mrs Hammond emaciated and in a wretched physical condition, though rational and able to tell her story coherently. Later that day, at the magistrates' court, she explained that her husband Edward, a doctor, and maids Emily Wakeman and Eliza Allen had imprisoned her when she had discovered that Wakeman and Edward were lovers. The maids dressed themselves in Mrs Hammond's clothes and jewels, pawned her other belongings and rode out in her carriage. Each had beaten her when she had tried to escape; on one occasion they had goaded her drunken husband to assault her with his fists. Looking out from her window, she was too afraid to make a sound when she saw neighbours coming and going; she watched her child playing in the garden but was scared to communicate with the little girl. She was plied with brandy and morphine and degenerated into a passive state. She gave birth to a child in the room in July 1863, and was attended by a Dr Nine, who does not appear to have asked any questions about the unusual set-up, and she was unable to alert him. The baby lived just a few hours.

At the subsequent trial, in September 1864, Dr Edward Hammond pleaded guilty to illegally imprisoning and ill-treating his wife. Sentence was deferred for a few weeks, and when he came back to court, Hammond told the judge that he was willing, as part of a judicial separation, to return to his wife half of the large fortune that she had brought to the marriage. The judge was outraged and said that he should give the entire sum back to her and sentenced Hammond to twelve months' hard labour. Hammond was astonished at the severity of the sentence. In a verdict that angered the public, Wakeman and Allen were acquitted for lack of evidence. The *Times* editorial asked who could believe that 'a woman of station could be shut up in England in her husband's house without the possibility of release? The supposition was too absurd to be entertained.' That particular plot line in *The Woman in White* had, *The Times* continued, been 'ingenious' but 'improbable . . . and the novelist was discredited for making it the foundation of his tale'. Yet in Peckham Rye, the newspaper pointed out, the unlikely Sensation plot had actually occurred.

In 1877, the Penge Mystery, also known as the Staunton Starvation Case, linked another London suburb to marital imprisonment. Harriet Richardson was described by her mother as a 'natural' – perhaps today we would describe her as someone with 'learning difficulties'. Harriet, aged thirty-four, was worth £3,000, with a far larger sum to come upon the death of her mother (who had remarried and was now Mrs Butterfield). The family had assumed that no man would ever want to marry Harriet, but when, in 1874, debonair and glib Lewis Staunton began to pay court, Mrs Butterfield panicked. She asked a doctor if he would certify Harriet as of unsound mind, thereby making any marriage she might contract legally invalid. The doctor refused to do so, claiming (incorrectly) that Harriet did not fall within the category of 'unsound' as described in the Lunacy Act; and in any case, there would be nasty gossip – it would be said that Mrs Butterfield was more interested in protecting the family fortune than the welfare of her child. This doctor's refusal (calamitous, as it turned out) gives the lie to the notion that any doctor would happily sign away liberty for a fee. Indeed, one line of defence made by the alienist profession at the time was that the increasing suspicion under which they operated would cause physicians to shy away from putting their name to any lunacy certificate.

Mrs Butterfield then appealed to the Lord Chancellor, but this too failed. Lewis Staunton acted swiftly and the couple married before Mrs Butterfield could find any other solution. Staunton now removed Harriet to a farmhouse at Cudham in Kent, where he imprisoned her in a back bedroom, while he, his lover Alice Rhodes, his brother Patrick and sister-in-law Elizabeth embezzled Harriet's money. As Mrs Butterfield tried continually to find out where her daughter was, the Stauntons and Rhodes deliberately starved Harriet and the baby she had given birth to in March 1876. Shortly before their deaths, mother and child were transported to 34 Forbes Road, Penge, the dying infant being dumped at a hospital on the way. Harriet died weighing 5st 4lb, and when a local nurse came to lay out the body, she found the skin deeply filthy – like the bark of a tree, she said – and Harriet's hair full of lice. She alerted a doctor and magistrate, and the Stauntons were taken into custody.

All four were found guilty of wilful murder and sentenced to hang, but the verdict proved controversial. Many medical men believed that the evidence in fact indicated death from typhus, not starvation; they signed a testimonial stating that the judge had misunderstood the science and had misdirected the jury. There was public outrage when the Home Secretary, acting on the testimonial, commuted the three Stauntons' sentences to penal servitude for life and Alice Rhodes was given a free pardon.

In the Hammond and Staunton cases, the law punished the wrong-doers (though the public would have wanted far harsher retribution). Both women had been illegally confined, since neither was insane; both had been physically maltreated, which even a husband was not entitled to do. The first woman to shout very loud about what the mid-century paterfamilias could do, with regard to incarceration, is the subject of the next chapter.

7

The Woman in Yellow

Edward Bulwer-Lytton is remembered today for two things only: the opening line of one of his works of fiction – 'It was a dark and stormy night'; and having his wife confined to an asylum in controversial circumstances. Very few Victorians would have guessed at his almost total eclipse in the twentieth century. Bulwer-Lytton (1803–73) was one of the era's best-selling, highest-earning authors; a novelist, poet, playwright, historian, MP and statesman; necromancer, ostentatious setter of trends both literary and sartorial, owner of Knebworth House; and from the mid-1830s to the late 1860s one of the most powerful and influential men in the country. This was the writer Charles Dickens idolised above all others and whose innovations had profound effects on Gothic fiction, crime fiction and what we today call 'science fiction'. But his flatulent, mouldy prose style places him alongside G. M. W. Reynolds, Harrison Ainsworth and Charles Reade as a literary lion who ceased to roar beyond his own lifetime. It was rare for Dickens's acuity on such matters to fail him; but he seems to have been blinded by the dazzle of Bulwer-Lytton.

Here he is in April 1826, aged twenty-two, at a tea party at a fashionable house in the West End: glittering golden ringlets fall to his shoulders, his shirt is a riot of lace and embroidery, with turn-back cuffs that pre-empt a fashion craze by ten years; his boots are as shiny as a looking-glass; he is affecting a Byronic world-weariness. This description was supplied by Rosina Wheeler, who had just entered the room, and of whom his mother, nudging her son, had said, 'Edward! What a singularly beautiful face!' Miss Wheeler, for her part, later wrote that Edward's mother's turban had looked like a pile of strawberry baskets heaped up at Covent Garden market, and that taken as a whole, she had the appearance of 'a galvanised rag bag'.

Rosina Wheeler was becoming noted in London drawing rooms both for her beauty and for her savage, seemingly uncontrollable urge to mock. Even her friends called her 'The Asp'. One observer wrote of her 'white shoulders, abundant hair, grace in the figure . . . It was not difficult, however, to perceive . . . something that gave disquieting intimations concerning the spirit that looked out from her brilliant eyes – that he who wooed her would probably be a happier man if content to regard her as we do some beautiful caged wild creature of the woods, at a safe and secure distance.' She was a brilliant mimic, in speech, action and on paper, and she was surely tittering four months later when she received from Edward the following reply to a letter of her own. She had written to her lover (they had consummated their relationship very quickly, in the summer of 1826) offering to end their engagement because of his mother's disapproval: if he married too early and without Mama's consent, it might threaten his highly promising literary career. Edward replied to Rosina's letter: 'Hate *you*, Rosina!? At this moment the tears are in my eyes, my heart beats audibly! I stop to kiss the paper consecrated by your hand – can these signs of love ever turn into hatred?' And so on for Romantic reams. Two months later, following a row with his mother about his infatuation with Miss Wheeler, he wrote to one of his confidantes, in the style for which we now un-celebrate him: 'It is a dim, heavy, desolate evening, the trees quite breathless, one deep cloud over the sky, the deer grouped under my window, and the old grey tower of the church just beyond.' The reason for his picturesque misery was that, as Miss Wheeler had advised, he had broken off the engagement from a sense of duty to his mother. One month later, however, word reached him that Miss Wheeler was ill in London and he rushed to her bedside, where he swore that, Mama or no, poverty or no, literary obscurity or no, they must marry. Twenty years later he refashioned this episode, erasing Miss Wheeler's reluctance and his own foolhardiness: 'I married my wife against all my interests and prospects, not from passion, but from a sense of honour. She had given herself to me nearly a year before, and from that moment I considered myself bound to her.' Small wonder that in later years Rosina would refer to her husband habitually as 'Sir Liar'.

Rosina Bulwer-Lytton, née Wheeler, painted in the 1830s.

'If you marry this woman, you will be in less than a year the most miserable man in England,' Mama told her son, who later went on to be a huge believer in clairvoyance. Mama made one last attempt to prevent the match, having parochial records searched in order to prove that Miss Wheeler was a good deal older than she claimed. How could a young lady have such devastating self-assurance, be so very well (self-)educated, so articulate? But Miss Wheeler really had been born in November 1802, and so the marriage went ahead, on 30 August 1827 at St James's Church, Piccadilly. Edward's mother did not attend and instantly withdrew her son's allowance (though she stopped short of disinheriting him). He still had an income from the small lump sum that had been left to him by his father, who had died when Edward was four years old, and Rosina brought an inherited income of £80 a year to the marriage. But this was not enough to live fashionably without incurring debt.

The couple appear to have been fairly happy in the early months of their marriage; or if they weren't, each of them uncharacteristically failed to mention it. He was her 'Pups', and she was his 'Poodle'. A prize-winning student poet, Bulwer-Lytton had published five reasonably well received volumes of Byronic poetry, and one politely, unenthusiastically reviewed novel, *Falkland*, which appeared in the year of his marriage. Now, in their relatively inexpensive rural retreat near Henley-on-Thames, he set to work, to earn money and glory. With energy that his wife would later consider diabolic, he averaged a substantial book every ten months or so. His intense labour, his desolation at having been cast aside by his mother, his anger at having to watch his spending, plus his naturally foul temper and self-absorption, before too long caused antagonism between the couple. Rosina made few complaints in the first four years, despite noticing some extremely unpleasant aspects of married life that she probably had not anticipated. She wrote light-heartedly to a friend that her husband had laid down many rules about what she was and was not allowed to do. His literary work required him to be alone and quiet for much of the day – that much she understood; but when he did find leisure time, he was off up to London, to the theatre or to literary gatherings, and so she saw very little of him.

Their first child, Emily – known as Little Boots in her infancy – was born in June 1828 and her father immediately sent her off to be wet-nursed by a farmer's wife, several miles away, which caused Rosina great distress; she had been ill following the birth and had been unable to suckle, but would have preferred a wet nurse to have come to live in. Her husband and his supporters, however, would later maintain that she had shown no maternal feelings. When their second child, Robert ('Teddy'), was born in November 1831, Rosina appeared to have understood that she was only to be a distant presence in her own children's lives. She was not to descend to the middle-class cult of domesticity and intimacy with one's offspring. She bought a lapdog, a Blenheim spaniel called Fairy, for companionship; her husband had a Newfoundland called Terror. Both children would later say that they feared both their parents and felt that they must on all accounts avoid annoying or causing offence to the dogs. Emily and Robert had to address their father as 'Mr Bulwer'. This distance between parents and offspring was quite normal in Society circles in these years and it is difficult to establish whether Rosina truly didn't care about her children or whether she was simply fitting in with expectations of upper-middle-class motherhood. These would change as the century wore on, leaving her vulnerable to accusations that she had been cold and indifferent.

Edward Bulwer-Lytton: his wife alleged that gentlemen grew facial hair in order to disguise the villainy that their facial features revealed.

Bulwer-Lytton's second novel, *Pelham*, was a huge commercial and literary success and ensured that publishers paid good sums for its follow-ups. The publishers' advances allowed him to buy 36 Hertford Street in Mayfair, within which he reconstructed a Pompeiian room. His natural extravagance re-erupted, and although he had raged at Rosina's outlay on clothing, he bought himself such treats as a huge bronze of Apollo and two Louis XIV clocks. Restlessly he sought out, bought and sold on properties in London and the home counties. What Rosina did not know at the time was that some of these were abodes of love for his mistresses, the most significant being one Laura Deacon, with whom he had three children.

In 1831 Edward was elected MP for the rotten borough of St Ives in Huntingdonshire, in the Whig interest, and when this seat was abolished, he became the member for Lincoln until 1841, when he left parliament. Rosina would claim that he had only been able to scrape together the income of £300 a year required of a parliamentary candidate because of the inheritance she had brought to the marriage. However, this seems unlikely, as by 1831 he had begun to earn money from his novels – and if he could bring Pompeii to Mayfair, he could surely afford a seat in Westminster. He promoted two causes very effectively in the House of Commons: the first was copyright legislation, to benefit writers and dramatists, and his speech in support of the Negro Apprenticeships Bill was said by Irish nationalist MP Daniel O'Connell to have been one of the best he had ever heard in the House. The legislation, passed on 1 August 1838, was devised to counter slave-owners' attempts to enforce twelve-year 'apprenticeships' upon freed slaves – a tactic to delay the loss of free labour that abolition had caused.

At home, he was proving to be less egalitarian. When Rosina was eight months pregnant with Emily, her husband had her up and down the library stepladder to fetch and read to him volumes of *The Newgate Calendar*, as part of his background research on criminals and lowlife. She claimed that when at last she said she was too weary to help any more, he kicked her hard in the side of her torso. There were no witnesses to this incident; but one day in July 1834, in the dining room of Hertford Street and in front of Rosina's maid, Rosetta Byrne, Bulwer-Lytton – whose hearing was poor – failed to hear his wife reply to a comment of his and shouted: 'Why didn't you answer me? Damn your soul, Madam! I'll have you know that whenever I do you the honour of addressing you, it requires an answer!' He then rushed at her with a carving knife, and when she screamed, he leapt upon her – 'like a tiger,' in Mrs Byrne's words – and bit deep into her cheek. Her screams brought the menservants into the room and Cresson the cook broke rank and etiquette to pull his employer off his wife. Bulwer-Lytton fled down Piccadilly. He later wrote an extravagant apology: 'You have been to me perfection as a wife, I have eternally disgraced myself, I shall go abroad, change a name which is odious to me, take £200 a year, and leave you all the rest.' Rosina treasured this letter, not for its emotional content, but as proof that he had considered her to have been a good wife, and that he had admitted to the assault. He would later publicly deny both these things, and she liked to know that she had the means with which to prove him a perjurer. 'The pen is mightier than the sword,' Bulwer-Lytton would write in his 1839 play *Richelieu*, and Rosina enjoyed the knowledge that she could run him through one day with his own written lies.

The existence of Laura Deacon was brought to Rosina's attention by a friend, and later she learned of various other amours of her husband's. When she retaliated by flirting with a Neapolitan prince during a trip to the Italian city, Bulwer-Lytton slammed her face against the stone floor of their palazzo. What's more, it is likely that in the following sentence of Rosina's she is indicating that her husband sodomised her, when she writes of the 'other little incidents which women cannot tell even to their lawyers; and which very young women, however disgusted they may be at them, are still not aware that they have legally a right to do so'. While rape within marriage was legal, sodomy would come under the heading of 'cruelty', if a wife should wish to consider divorce proceedings – also having to prove that her husband had been adulterous for her action to be successful. 'Marriage is Saturnalia for men, and tyranny for women,' Rosina concluded.

Her own mother could have told her that: Rosina was the estranged daughter of Anna Wheeler, an Irish socialist and early feminist, who had published her thoughts about the subjection of women. But Rosina had disliked both her parents, and after their marital separation she had not enjoyed growing up in the radical, free-thinking circles in which her mother moved. By the mid-1830s Rosina had found out for herself that the marriage laws were grossly unfair to women.

Emily ('Little Boots'), the Lytton's first child.

She also now felt she understood the workings of the 'infernal machine of occult power', as she later described the male systems of patronage. The institutions of the state – the state that made such a loud noise about liberty – were staffed, or stuffed, by men who had toadied for other men, or who were keeping their masters' nasty secrets quiet, or who had simply proved themselves to be jolly good fellows at school, university or club. Male-controlled British public life was a 'consecrated palladium of puffery and party', Rosina decided. She observed that although many of these men may have felt dislike and contempt for each other in private, in public there was an understood system of homage, deference and payback for past favours and silences maintained.

As wealthy and well-connected people, the Bulwer-Lyttons could have petitioned parliament for a divorce, twenty years ahead of the Matrimonial Causes Act that would make divorce a civil matter (taking place in the new Divorce Court) and less expensive, and thus available to those in (slightly) humbler circumstances. Her husband suggested such a move, but on condition that Rosina admit to infidelity (although there is no suggestion that she had ever done more than flirt with anyone) and that she would stay silent about his own adultery and his assaults upon her. (A husband could sue for divorce purely on the grounds of his wife's adultery, but a wife had to be able to prove her husband's adultery plus one other factor, such as extreme and repeated cruelty, desertion, incest, or sodomy with another male; this double standard was controversially left unchanged by the 1857 Matrimonial Causes Act.) Rosina refused to accept the terms, and instead, a deed of separation was drawn up. Rosina requested £600 per annum, plus £100 each for Little Boots's and Teddy's education – a sum she felt was reasonable, given that her husband was by now immensely independently wealthy (earning an estimated £3,000–£4,000 a year) and in line to inherit Knebworth House from his mother. But Edward rejected this sum, and although he said that he would be willing to part with £500 a year, when the deed of separation was placed before Rosina on 19 April 1836 the amount had been reduced even further, to £400 a year plus £50 for each child. This was a respectable middle-class income, but it was inadequate for a fashionable lady, with appearances to keep up and a love of the flashy. What is more, Rosina felt that the sum did not reflect the financial and practical contributions she had made to the nine-year marriage. But Rosina wanted her freedom and so she accepted, in the belief that she could supplement the £400 by wielding her own pen. She knew that she was clever and wrote well; she claimed she had contributed hugely to *Pelham*, *Paul Clifford*, *The Disowned*, *Devereux*, *Eugene Aram* and *Godolphin* – the early-career novels that had earned Bulwer-Lytton so much acclaim and cash. She was also glad that he had allowed her to keep the children at a time when many men took full advantage of the laws of the country that recognised no rights in a mother.

Rosina left England for her native Ireland, and to begin with, she lived there happily with the children and with her companion, Mary Greene. But when Bulwer-Lytton learned, in 1838 – the year in which he was created a baronet – that his wife had become romantically close to a married Dublin man, he won custody of ten-year-old Little Boots and six-year-old Teddy. He entrusted their care to Mary Greene, now estranged from Rosina, and visited them once each year for a week. His payments to Rosina now became irregular.

Rosina began her own literary career with the novel *Cheveley; Or, The Man of Honour* (1839), a satirical attack on her husband, his mother's family and Bulwer-Lytton's friends and supporters. Rosina's prose (much of which is now available online) is extremely tiring to read – a hurricane of images and metaphors, subclause upon subclause, and the main thrust of her sentence often not revealed until the very end. However, within the tumble of words are to be found many gems – odd aperçus that feel fresh and unusual. For example, in her autobiographical work *A Blighted Life*, she writes:

> The next day, Dr Roberts, whom I had known a long time, called upon me. He had just had the supreme felicity of becoming Lord Palmerston's medical attendant, and is just the smooth, mellifluous, double-dealing, Jesuitical personage, who would be happy to accept a reversionary emetic from any of the peers or peeresses whom he attends, (or) though an infidel, to do any amount of canting with Lord Shaftesbury in Exeter Hall in the morning or any amount of pimping for Lady Shaftesbury all the evening. The dear Conservatives having fallen upon evil days, via their Colonial Secretary, was of course nuts to the dear Whigs, though as far as any amount of dirty work, back-stair climbing, and

athletic, indefatigable, political, and every other sort of jobbery, the two parties are in reality 'one concern'; and having the same 'bonnets', during their alternate ins and outs always know the exact thimble the pea lurks under.

A Blighted Life was revelatory of the bedroom habits of the nineteenth century's 'respectable' classes. It was suppressed when it first emerged, in 1867, and when it reappeared in 1880 most of the people whose peccadilloes were referenced were no longer around to protest.

Her husband hit back with the poem *Lady Cheveley; Or, The Woman of Honour*, which included the lines:

> Oh! when you find in her who bears your name,
> The cold remorseless sland'rer of your fame,
> Then if you grieve, grieve silent and alone . . .
>
> . . .
>
> Smile while the traitor wife, the fire-side spy,
> Weaves the base slander, and the specious lie.

To which Rosina replied:

> Here, still lies, my Lord Lytton, – at last in a fix!
> Being too stingy to pay, his fare o'er the Styx.

Moving from Dublin to Bath, to Paris, to Florence, to Geneva, Rosina continued to publish parodies of Lytton's work and thinly veiled, near-libellous tittle-tattle about the circles in which the couple had moved. Her anger and sense of injustice was ratcheted up by Bulwer-Lytton's increasing renown, wealth and celebrity. In 1843 Mama died and her son inherited Knebworth House. Rosina took advantage of her right to be called Lady Lytton, partly because she hoped that sharing his name and rank might help her in her battle to stay in print, and partly because she knew how much he would hate her doing so. Her husband had used his immense influence to ensure that her novels were either ignored or attacked in the periodical press; he also let it be understood that any publishing house or bookseller who dealt with her work could expect trouble. Lord Lytton would later deny in a court of law that he had ever tried to prevent her writing; but Rosina owned another treasured note in her husband's handwriting, written in 1839 and stating that he would 'ruin' her if she published any more books.

Rosina had few supporters of any influence, but it is interesting to note that three of the age's most intellectual writers – Walter Savage Landor (1775–1864), Thomas Carlyle (1795–1881) and George Sand (1804–1876) – sympathised with her and disliked her husband. All, however, wisely realised that they needed to be circumspect in doing so. Landor had offered Rosina friendship and advice in 1838 as she was losing the children, but was in no doubt of the power that Bulwer-Lytton possessed within the tiny and treacherous world of letters. Landor was embarrassed to find himself the dedicatee of *Cheveley*, and asked Rosina not to identify him with her camp; surprisingly, for one so prickly, she did not take offence at this. Thomas Carlyle and his wife Jane, meanwhile, tried to find a publisher for Rosina's novels and soon discovered the pressure that had been brought to bear by Bulwer-Lytton to suppress Rosina's books. Writing four years after the separation, Carlyle was amazed that so many people took Bulwer-Lytton at his own estimation: 'It will be a rather tragical fate for this poor Bulwer, I think . . . He is certain before many years to be universally found out and proclaimed as a piece of pinchbeck [imitation gold].'

When Lady Lytton returned to England in 1847 she tried repeatedly to get her allowance increased, or at the very least paid on time, and to have the debts she had run up paid off. Lord Lytton would not comply. Lady Lytton had not seen her children for nine years. She understood that Emily lived with her father at Knebworth as his literary handmaiden, and she claimed that Emily spent her days exhausting herself in translating German works, since Lord Lytton wasn't bright enough to learn the language. Though her father was immensely wealthy, Emily owned one day dress and one evening dress, and constantly had to patch up her gloves and shoes. Little Boots was nineteen years old, and her wretched life was drawing to a wretched close. In 1848 her father placed her in a down-at-heel boarding house in Pelham Terrace in the London village of Brompton when she was dying from typhoid, with an elderly hired nurse as sole carer. No explanation was ever forthcoming for why her father had sent her away from Knebworth to die in these surroundings; his mind was strange and superstitious enough to give credence to the idea that he may have seen a good omen in the choice of Pelham Terrace, as his novel *Pelham* had marked the change in his own fortunes.

When Lady Lytton learned of Emily's whereabouts, she moved into the boarding house, together with maid Rosetta Byrne, renting the room above her daughter's. The nurse – acting on the orders of Lord Lytton and Dr Marshall Hall, the physician he had hired to treat Emily – told Lady Lytton that she must not make herself known to her daughter, arguing that the shock of seeing her mother after all these years would instantly kill the delirious girl. But Lady Lytton bribed the nurse and the landlady to allow her to look in at Emily during one of her spells of unconsciousness. She saw that the shabby room was so small that the bedstead filled it; even the nightdress Emily was dying in had had to be borrowed from the nurse. Lady Lytton sat outside the room on the staircase all night, listening to her daughter's fevered moaning. Lord Lytton had been told of his wife's presence in Pelham Terrace and had instructed his son Robert to accompany Dr Hall to the house and to throw Lady Lytton out into the street. When they turned up to do his bidding, they found Lady Lytton still sitting on the stairs. At some point during the row that ensued, Emily died.

Each parent used this tragedy as ammunition against the other: Lord Lytton said his wife's appearance in the sickroom had finished the girl off. Lady Lytton claimed that her husband had killed the girl by hiring a disreputable quack who had 'murdered' Emily with his incompetence and neglect. She wrote to Dr Marshall Hall: 'The actual cause of her death was your gross ignorance, only to be equalled by the coarse and inhuman brutality of your manner. I shall ever look upon you and proclaim you as her murderer.' When the apothecary Dr Rouse, who had been assisting Dr Hall in caring for Emily, cut his own throat and died a fortnight later, Lady Lytton claimed that he had done so in recognition of the fatal effects brought about by the bleeding and the starvation of her daughter that Hall had recommended and which Rouse had obediently carried out.

With Emily's death, Lady Lytton's rage grew ever more intense. She began a campaign of bombarding her husband and his friends and associates with obscene and libellous letters – the obscenities often scrawled across the envelope to give extra publicity to the allegations within. Sadly, very few of these envelopes appear to have survived to show whether Lady Lytton used good old Anglo-Saxon or the more high-flown filth of the letters' contents. One that has survived reads: 'To be forwarded to the Reptile Sir Liar Coward Bulwer Lytton Fenton's Hotel St James's London'. The letters contained allegations about mistresses, illegitimate children, and in the case of William Loaden – Charles Dickens's lawyer and an associate of Lord Lytton – the accusation that he was intimate with his own sister in order to spare the expense of a mistress. Her grandson would write in 1913 that reading the correspondence years after her death had been like 'opening a drawer full of dead wasps. Their venom is now powerless to hurt, but they still produce a shudder and feeling of disgust.'

Attorney-General Alexander Cockburn (with whom Lord Lytton had been close friends at Cambridge) and politician, lawyer and thrice Lord Chancellor Lord Lyndhurst ('a superannuated adulterer') were among the recipients of her abuse. A letter to her own son was addressed 'To that white-livered little reptile Robert Lytton'. But her favourite target among her husband's cronies was 'that Dunghill divinity', that 'Pothouse Plutarch', 'that patent humbug, Mr Charles Dickens'. She detested what she saw as Dickens's sham philanthropy and concern for orphans, cripples, chimney sweeps, crossing-sweepers and any other representatives of the picturesquely downtrodden, which served to build him up as a champion of the oppressed at very little personal cost. In the age of cant, Lady Lytton regarded the 'popularity hunters' as particularly sickening. She believed that a hard little heart beat within Boz. What is also likely to have rankled was Dickens's immense success while his 'clique' had done all it could to exclude her from the world of letters, along with anyone else they chose to snub; the acclaim for Lord Lytton's novel *The Caxtons*, published in the year after Emily's death, cannot have helped her mood: 'After twenty-five years' bitter experience, [I know] that wherever the literary element enters, there camaraderie, expediency, claptrap, treachery, moral cowardice and concrete meanness are sure to follow.' She believed that Dickens and her own husband had both had to cultivate plentiful facial hair in order that their features could no longer betray to the observant the villainy expressed in their physiognomies. Regarding the hirsuteness of Victorian gentlemen, Lady

Lytton stated that beards, moustaches and sideburns hid terrible things about a man's soul. 'One has only to look at his [Lord Lytton's] hideous face and that of that other brute Dickens to see that every bad passion has left the impress of its cloven hoof upon their fiendish lineaments.'

She took snobbish delight in pointing out Dickens's humble start in life, and his early career as a legal and parliamentary shorthand reporter. In the first week of May 1851 she wrote to him to point out his 'vulgar parvenu extravagance' and reminding him that he had been hitherto a 'penny-a-liner'. When Lady Lytton learned that there was to be a performance of her husband's play, *Not So Bad As We Seem*, with Queen Victoria as guest of honour and the Duke of Devonshire as master of ceremonies, she wrote to Dickens that she intended to be there too, to pelt the Queen with rotten eggs and the players with rotten fruit: 'Sir, As it is my intention to attend the Fooleries at Devonshire House on the 16th to disseminate not indeed Bills of the Play, but a True Bill, of its Ruffianly and Blackguardly Author, and also to suggest that in consideration of the disreputable set who are to act it, the title of this farce be changed to "We're even worse! than we seem!, or the real side of our character . . ."' She told Dickens it was outrageous that he was putting on such an entertainment, 'considering that your father and one of your children have not been a month buried!! I should have thought that common decency (for common feeling I know you don't possess) would have made you abstain from making an ass of yourself on this occasion . . .' As for Victoria: 'Shame on the little sensual, selfish Pigheaded Queen.' Dickens arranged for his favourite pet policeman, Detective Inspector Field ('who is used in all sorts of delicate matters, and is quite devoted to me,') to be at Devonshire House on the night of the play to thwart any attempt Lady Lytton might make to disrupt proceedings. In the event, she did not try to enter, and the evening was a bit of a damp squib all round, with some saying the performance had been 'Not So Good As We Expected'.

In 1851 Lord Lytton joined the Conservative Party and the following year he entered parliament again, as MP for Hertford. His change of political horses had come about partly because of his close friendship with Disraeli and partly as a result of his increasing disgust at the venality and banality of the mercantile middle classes ('wretched money-spiders', as he called them) who tended to support the Liberals. He had also been shocked by the revolutions on the Continent in 1848 and he coined the phrase 'The Great Unwashed' for the labouring classes and unemployed. Lady Lytton, by contrast to her husband, was beginning to fail to keep up appearances, living in a cottage in the Fulham Road, West London, and then, in order to live even more cheaply, heading for Llangollen in north-east Wales, before moving into a hotel in Taunton. She later alleged that two attempts were made to poison her (or at least to introduce a soporific into her soup) at Llangollen by emissaries of her husband; and that when she became too suspicious for anything to be put into her food or drink, they tried to entrap her into a lunatic asylum, with her various eccentricities being worked up into a tale of lunacy.

There were no independent witnesses to these events, and it is tempting to see the allegation as a wild attack on her husband. However, there is documentary evidence which confirms that Lord Lytton arranged surveillance on his wife. As early as 1839, John Forster, a close friend of Dickens and Lord Lytton, and later to become a Commissioner in Lunacy, was sent to Bath by Lord Lytton to gather information about Rosina, who was living there at that time and had just published *Cheveley*. Forster wrote to her husband on 4 September 1839, stating that he had been very cautious in his investigation, 'for it would have been highly indiscreet in me to have made formal inquiries, even of [their mutual friend, Walter Savage] Landor'. Forster didn't appear to have come up with anything dramatic that could be used against Rosina, except for her careless spending habits and her friendship with the married man from Dublin. Thomas Carlyle thought that he detected a rapid cooling in Forster's affection for Lord Lytton in the early 1840s, and it is possible, though not provable, that Forster was beginning to resent being asked to undertake such underhand tasks. The coolness didn't last long, though, and Lord Lytton came to lean heavily on Forster for the latter's training as a lawyer, asking Forster to double-check the legal possibilities or likelihoods of some of the plot devices for plays he had in mind. He needed to know about the mid-nineteenth-century bureaucratic realities of such matters as marriage licences, birth certification and probate processes, in order to create a storyline or to muddy up a mystery. Lady Lytton detested John Forster, nicknaming him Jackal Fudgster. He, in turn, had reasons for loathing her; Forster had been engaged to the poet Letitia Landon in 1838 and believed that Rosina had spread rumours about an intrigue that Landon may have enjoyed with another man. When Forster confronted his fiancée, Landon broke off the engagement.

In a separate incident, in 1839, Lord Lytton's solicitor wrote to his client, presumably in reply to a request for advice, to state that if Rosina did begin to behave outrageously through drink, 'it may be both wise and merciful to place her under personal restraint'. Unsoundness of mind caused by dipsomania would indeed have made Rosina eligible for at least a short stay in an asylum. Alas for the conspirators, Rosina did not drink to excess on a regular basis. They would have to bide their time.

By 1853, Lady Lytton was living at the Giles Castle Hotel in Taunton (incidentally the same hotel in which eight years earlier the Agapemonite triple marriage had been decided upon). The hotel's owner, Mrs Clarke, remained devoted to her despite the arrears that Lady Lytton was building up; Mrs Clarke accepted that the debt was caused by the sporadic and inadequate payments by Lord Lytton. Private detective Henry Trenchard had been commissioned by Lord Lytton to spy on his wife; alas, Trenchard's reports stated that she led a very secluded life and was of regular habits, and that all her visitors were unremarkable. Although she was said to have a temper, 'her general behaviour in the hotel does not of itself justify' any assertion that she was of unsound mind. Trenchard had followed her around Taunton but all he could note was that she 'very much disfigures her face with paint'.

In May 1858, Lady Lytton heard that her husband was to be made Secretary of State for the Colonies. As he rose and rose, she was continuing to dwindle. She decided to take action, as she later wrote:

> The month of June 1858 had arrived, and the Hertford election was to take place on the 8th, a Wednesday, I think. The Sunday before, I was in bed with one of my splitting headaches, from ceaseless worry of mind and want of rest. I got up, and in a perfect agony prayed to God to direct me, to send me some help in my cruel, cruel position. I went

back to bed exhausted, and the sudden thought struck me, I would go
to the Hertford election, and publicly expose the ruffian.

With the help of Mrs Clarke, Lady Lytton had posters printed, which
read: 'Lady Bulwer Lytton requests the Electors of Herts to meet her
at the Corn Exchange this day, Wednesday June 8, 1858, before going
to the Hustings.' Armed with these, she and Mrs Clarke made a long
and complicated journey, involving post-horses and the railway, to
Hertford ('a dirty little mean town'), arriving at five in the morning:
'My head was burning and I had the cold shivers.' They booked themselves into the Dinsdale Arms and before getting some rest, Lady
Lytton paid the inn's shoeblack ('the boots') a sovereign to plaster the
town with the placards before full daylight, which, she reported, he
did wonderfully well. She then took a bath and dozed until 11.30 a.m.

It was a scorching, windless day, and Lord Lytton's hustings were
set up in a rural spot on the edge of town, but very close to Cowbridge
House, the home of Stephen Austin, the supportive editor of the
Hertford Mercury. Lord Lytton was on the platform with friends and
associates, including his son, Robert. The reporter from the hostile
Daily Telegraph wrote of the 'pretty ladies' in the crowd – 'a few open
carriages full of enthusiasm and crinoline'. As Lord Lytton was
approaching the end of a very long speech, one of the men on the
hustings saw in the middle distance an alarming figure advancing
across the grass. It walked determinedly, and as it came into focus he
saw that it was a woman wearing a deep yellow dress – the colour of
the Liberals – and carrying a yellow parasol and a green fan; her hair
appeared to be dyed yellow and her face heavily rouged. 'Your wife
is here!' one of his associates cried to Lord Lytton, whose deafness
meant that this had to be said three times; in fact, he thought he was
being told that his sister-in-law, Lady Bulwer, had turned up, and was
answering 'How very kind of Georgina to come!' when Robert
screamed in his ear, 'My mother is here!' Lord Lytton turned white
and appeared to stagger backwards. The crowd parted to let the
extraordinary yellow figure pass, and she stalked to the foot of the
ladder, mounted the platform and declared, 'Fiend, villain, monster,
cowardly wretch, outcast! How can the people of England submit to
have such a man at the head of the colonies, who ought to have been
in the colonies as a transport long ago?'

What happened next is reported in two different versions by onlookers: some say Lord Lytton almost swooned upon the platform, but managed to get down the ladder and into a waiting carriage, in which he fainted good and proper, as the driver galloped him back to Knebworth. Lady Lytton claimed that he jumped the palings into Mr Austin's garden and ran across the flowerbeds, trampling the flowers, then locked himself into Austin's dining room.

There is a variant, too, regarding Lady Lytton's apparel. Robert told John Forster that he had spotted 'a prodigiously large woman, dressed entirely in white, with a white parasol'. Quite a while later, now calmly able to give his own view, Lord Lytton himself believed it had been white – 'an elderly woman in a gay white dress, holding a white parasol, her face daubed with the coarsest paint, her eyebrows strangely blackened, forcing her way, gesticulating and gibbering . . .' White is the colour emblematic of lunatics, as it is for ghosts; it is instantly other-worldly. But a yellow Lady Lytton somehow has the greater power – odder, creepier, as she hove into view across the fields, flapping her fan, which contrived to remain green in all accounts.

From the hustings, Lady Lytton addressed the crowd, for over an hour, about her husband's many shortcomings. 'The moment the cowardly brute took to flight,' she wrote later,

> the mob began to hiss and yell and vociferate, 'Ah! He's guilty, he's guilty, he dare not face her. Three cheers for her ladyship.' As soon as silence was restored, I turned to the crowd, who roared, 'Silence, listen to what Lady Lytton has to say.' Whereupon I said, 'Men of Herts, if you have the hearts of men, hear me.' 'We will, we will, speak up.' . . . I then went on to tell them that their member's last conspiracy was to make out – because I dared to resent, having no brother to horsewhip him for his dastardly persecutions, and sending his infamous street-walkers to insult me – that I was quite mad, in order to incarcerate me in a madhouse. Cries of 'Cowardly villain' . . . But I need not bore you with my speech, nor their plaudits, or the way in which they cheered and wanted to draw me back to the hotel, which, thanking them cordially, I implored them not to do, as I had to go by the 3 o'clock train. Nor need I tell you how the roofs of the houses were covered with people, as well as the windows, waving handkerchiefs, and crying 'God bless you,' when I went.

Lady Lytton was spot on with her allegation that there was an orchestrated campaign to ignore or malign her and to puff and protect her husband. *The Times* was edited by John Delane, a friend of Dickens and Forster, and the newspaper employed Lord Lytton's brother Henry as a foreign news contributor; protection of Lord Lytton is highly likely to be the explanation for the very odd exclusion of any mention of Lady Lytton's hustings appearance from that newspaper. However, she found an unexpected new ally – the *Daily Telegraph*, which had been founded three years earlier to target and call to account certain sections of the establishment. Ironically, its creation had been hugely assisted by Lord Lytton's parliamentary support for the removal of the stamp tax on newspapers: the *Daily Telegraph* was the first 'penny paper' to achieve success following the repeal of the tax. It would go on to reproduce in full the column inches of pro-Lady Lytton coverage in the Somerset newspapers.

Lady Lytton and Mrs Clarke were back at their Taunton hotel by the early hours of the next day, and Lady Lytton was ill in bed for the following two days. At 11 a.m. on 11 June, a servant came to her room presenting the card of one Dr Frederick Hale Thomson, of 4 Clarges Street, Piccadilly. Just as Lady Lytton was saying that she wanted no visitors as she was unwell, Mrs Clarke rushed up and urged her to lock herself in. Mrs Clarke then stood across the doorway as, moments later, the doctor, a nurse and lawyer William Loaden mounted the stairs. Loaden shouted that he would kick the door in, but Rosina called out that there was no need as she had no fear of them. So just as she was 'sitting up in bed, arranging the frills of my night things', in strode Dr Hale Thomson, a little man with black hair and dark eyes; he was known to his friends as Bullet-Proof Thomson, for his success in duelling. He was accompanied by a six-foot-tall 'giantess' of a woman. They sat either side of her bed, and the doctor took her pulse and engaged Lady Lytton in lengthy conversations about national and European politics and the political views of Lord Lytton – subjects of which she was knowledgeable but which signally failed to excite her. He took her pulse at several times during the chat, raised her eyelids to look at her pupils and examined her teeth. After about an hour, Dr Hale Thomson went into the room next door, and Lady Lytton heard male voices conferring, one of them Loaden's. She later learned that he was interviewing the hotel staff individually to find out if Lady Lytton had ever been unkind or violent to them. They all said no.

Lady Lytton later wrote that the doctor came back into the room at about five o'clock and said to the giantess, 'Well, I don't know. I think I never saw anyone in sounder mind or body. What do you think?' The giantess, wiping away tears, replied, 'Why, really, sir. I do think this is one of the cruellest outrages I ever witnessed or heard of.' 'Humh,' said the doctor, and went out of the room again for another two hours. When he came back he showed Lady Lytton some letters she had written to her husband and to Loaden four years earlier and said to her, 'Now, Lady Lytton, I want you to oblige me by writing me a note, stating what terms you will accept from Sir Edward, to never again expose him as you did at Hertford on Wednesday.' She protested that all she had ever sought was £500 a year, and for the payments to be made on time and in full; also for £2,500 of debt run up over the past twenty-six years to be paid off, and a written promise by her husband never to persecute her, and to allow her to publish and to live where she liked. She said she had gone to the Hertford hustings mainly to show the public that she was neither dead nor raving mad, as she had heard that her husband had been telling these lies. Dr Hale Thomson seemed happy with this, and said that he would leave at once for London and that he hoped to be able to provide her very shortly with a new legal document that would ratify the annual sum of £500, to be paid punctually. Mrs Clarke told Lady Lytton that the doctor seemed to be trustworthy, and so Lady Lytton allowed matters to stand at that, and the visitors left. What she hadn't known was that a second asylum attendant and a carriage and four belonging to that establishment had been parked opposite the hotel, in preparation for her removal, which it had been assumed would be a simple matter.

Ten days later, Lady Lytton had still not heard from Dr Hale Thomson, and her two letters requesting to know whether Lord Lytton had agreed to her demands had not been acknowledged. So with Mrs Clarke and an old friend, Rebecca Ryves, she travelled up to London, arriving unannounced at the doctor's house in Clarges Street at noon on 22 June. Dr Hale Thomson welcomed them, invited them to stay for dinner but evaded her questions about whether an agreement had been reached. Lady Lytton said she would return at six o'clock and that if her husband had not assented to her demands in writing by then, she would go to a magistrate with the letters she had in her possession that proved him to be a double-perjurer. This brinksmanship proved to be unwise.

When she took a carriage back to Clarges Street at six, she spotted an 'impudent-looking, snub-nosed man, who was walking up and down, and stared at me in the most impudent and determined manner'. The folding doors in Dr Hale Thomson's drawing room were closed; earlier they had been fully open. From the partitioned-off space, Lady Lytton could hear the murmuring of low voices. The doctor kept her waiting half an hour, and then walked in with a 'tall, raw-boned, hay-coloured-hair Scotchman', an apothecary by the name of George Ross, who kept a pharmacy in Fenchurch Street. Lady Lytton tried to leave but in the hall her way was blocked by alienist Dr Robert Gardiner Hill and by the snub-nosed impudent man from the street (who turned out to be Mr Ross's assistant), two asylum nurses, one of them a 'great Flanders mare of six feet high' (it helped if madhouse nurses were substantially built), and Dr Hale Thomson's 'very idiotic-looking footman'. Seeing this 'blockade', Lady Lytton exclaimed, 'What a set of blackguards!' and Dr Hale Thomson – who had, as she put it, 'that horrible mad-doctor's trick of rolling his head and never looking at anyone, but over their heads, as if he saw some strange phantasmagoria in the air above them . . . wagging his head, and phantom-hunting over mine, with his pale, poached-egg-unspeculative eyes' – said, 'I beg you'll speak like a lady, Lady Lytton.' She turned back, and opening the folding doors in the drawing room, from where she had heard the murmuring, she found her husband and lawyer Loaden. 'You cowardly villain,' she said to Lord Lytton. 'This is the second time I have confronted you this month. Why do you always do your dirty work by deputy, except when you used to leave the marks of your horse teeth in my flesh, and boldly strike a defenceless woman?' Whereupon, her husband rushed down the back stairs and out into Clarges Street.

Miss Ryves challenged the ambushers to try to detain her, which of course they could not, and so she went outside, where she asked the first young man she saw – waiting at the corner of Piccadilly – for help in fetching a cab to rescue her friend who was about to be abducted to a madhouse. The pale young man whispered, 'I am very sorry, I can't interfere.' It was Robert Bulwer-Lytton. 'Talk of novels!' expostulated Lady Lytton in her written memories of that day.

Miss Ryves asked two policemen to intervene, but when they entered number 4 they were presented with the certificates signed by Dr Hale Thomson and the apothecary Ross and so supported the removal of the patient. Lady Lytton said she would not put up a struggle but that her accusers would regret what they had done. Mrs Clarke warned them that a public investigation would follow, but she was laughed at, and Dr Hale Thomson remarked that Lady Lytton had no friends, and that Sir Edward 'is at the top of the tree'. 'You'll see,' replied Mrs Clarke.

While Miss Ryves returned to Taunton, taking with her the incriminating letters, Mrs Clarke was allowed to accompany Lady Lytton. The carriage that had been sent by the asylum took the party through Hyde Park, where Lady Lytton claimed that she saw friends out for drives, or strolling in the park, and that some of these recognised her and waved kisses, in ignorance of the nature of her journey and fellow passengers.

Wyke House in Brentford, Middlesex, was an early-eighteenth-century mansion, used as an asylum from the mid-1840s. It was controversially demolished in the early 1970s.

She was deposited at Wyke House, in Brentford, Middlesex, an eighteenth-century mansion in thirty acres of garden and 'pleasure ground'. She was shown into a large but low-ceilinged bedroom, its windows nailed shut except for an allowable three inches at the top, and with two female keepers present. Through the window Lady Lytton saw thirty to forty female patients gathering strawberries in the grounds. Dr Gardiner Hill entered and suggested that she take a walk in the warm evening air. She was having none of this: 'Mr Hill, I sent for you to order you to remove those two keepers from my room for I am not mad, as you very well know, and I won't be driven mad by being treated as a maniac, and as for walking out, or associating with those poor creatures out there, if they really are insane, I'll not do it, if I am kept in your madhouse for ten years.' 'Madhouse, madhouse, nonsense!' was Dr Hill's response. 'Lady Lytton, this is no madhouse, and those are my children.' Dr Hill based his regime on the illusion that this was a family home and that the patients were there as house guests and could move freely among Mr and Mrs Hill and their ten noisy children.

The doctor left with the two attendants, but alarmingly, he locked the door behind him. Half an hour later a girl of fourteen came in with tea and strawberries. This was Hill's eldest daughter, Mary, whom Lady Lytton instantly adored. 'How he and his odious vulgar wife came by such a child, I can't imagine,' she wrote. '[Mrs Hill is] a thoroughly vulgar, selfish, inane "British female", as they very properly and zoologically call themselves.' Lady Lytton was very proud of her Irish ancestry, and ever aware of her own social rank, she spent her time in captivity tripping over Mrs Hill's dropped 'h's'.

At night-time, more unexpected privation: she was allowed only two inches of candle by her bedside, to prevent attempts at self-immolation. In the morning, she found how very bad the water was at the asylum, which was a problem, because it was proving to be an extremely hot June, and despite the palatial proportions of Wyke House, the asylum was stuffy and oppressively hot.

Dr Hill's memories of Lady Lytton's first day at Wyke House were rather different. His journal records her using violent language and attempting no control over her feelings. Upon arrival she had made 'gross and calumnious charges against persons of high rank', and more specifically mentioned instances of 'unnatural connection' between her husband and Disraeli. Not for the first time, a lady was considered unsound because she conversed without inhibition about sexual matters. She 'speaks of it openly', wrote Hill, and 'did not appear to be the least ashamed when relating the circumstances to my wife'. Sometimes sobbing she would talk 'in the most disgusting way and charging innocent and virtuous women with unchaste and licentious conduct'. Lady Lytton was well aware of this double standard: 'In this highly moral country (very!) there is no amount of vice not only tolerated but admitted in men; it being only considered horrible for a woman! and more especially a victim wife, to allude to such things, especially when . . . elles appellent un chat un chat.'

Inverness Lodge, photographed in the 1930s, when it had become a British Legion club.

Lady Lytton would claim that Dr Hill sent all his other patients down the road to his own large private home, Inverness Lodge, and that she had the villa all to herself. Many private asylum keepers who had leases on more than one building would decant and shuffle patients in this way – a relatively informal arrangement that was acceptable to the Commissioners in Lunacy so long as conditions at each building met their standards. But it seems much more likely that Dr Hill moved Lady Lytton to Inverness Lodge and kept his lunatics in the villa, because, though roomy, Inverness Lodge would have been a tight fit for forty patients, twelve Hills, plus servants and attendants. Certainly, her letters to Rebecca Ryves are headed 'Inverness Lodge'. Dr Hill would turn out to have one very good reason to keep Lady Lytton in his own home rather than in the asylum proper.

Dr Hill gave her use of a maid, Sparrow, incongruously strapping and dark; but it was his daughter Mary that she preferred to spend most of her time with, along with a fat, friendly tortoiseshell cat, and a cow that she claimed Dr Hill left out in an arid field in full sun. She and Mary worked hard at the nearby pump to give the cow some water, which, according to Lady Lytton, was seen by Dr Hill as further evidence of her unsound mind. Mary Hill and Lady Lytton took long rides together in a brougham, including trips to Acton, Hanwell, Isleworth and on one hot July dusk, to Richmond Hill, to look at a beautiful sunset. On no occasion did Lady Lytton attempt to escape.

The practice of mixing family and patients had many drawbacks, even for a man as facilely genial as Dr Hill. His own diary revealed his disgust at one Mrs Burkitt, whose 'feelings are quite perverted. She whistles as she sits at cards, and sometimes makes use of expressions before my children which are quite horrifying . . . I have every reason to believe that if she had unconditional liberty she would be extremely dangerous.'

Dr Hill kept notes on Lady Lytton's habits. She would rise each day at around 11 a.m. or noon and preferred to stay in her room when she had no carriage rides organised. She used a great deal of rouge and refused to allow anyone into her room while she was dressing and making herself up. She regularly made abusive comments about John Forster, saying that he was 'drunk every day of his life', which Hill took to be proof that she was delusional. As was her claim that not long ago she had bought a diamond bracelet for twenty guineas (in fact, such a purchase would not have been out of character). Her other fantasies, Hill believed, were that her husband had bitten into her cheek, and that an attempt to poison her had been made at Llangollen. During another conversation, Lady Lytton told Hill that her husband had boasted to her that he had had the run of London brothels before he was thirteen years old, and had told her that 'a man had a right to have connection with his own daughter if she was pretty enough'. On 11 July she shouted about Disraeli being a sodomite so loudly that the servants had to run around closing the windows in case passers-by in the street should hear.

After around ten days' incarceration, Lady Lytton was visited by Bryan Waller Procter and Dr Samuel Gaskell from the Lunacy Commission. All Commissioners in Lunacy, wrote Lady Lytton, were 'patent humbugs', with the exception of seventy-year-old Procter, who had been a Commissioner since 1832. He was now on the colossal salary of £1,500 a year, though his health had been damaged by his gruelling schedule of visits to the nation's asylums. In Lady Lytton's snooty view, Procter was 'by far the best and most gentlemanlike' of the Commissioners; she didn't appear to have known how very friendly Procter and his wife were with her husband. Procter listened carefully to Lady Lytton's story but told her that he had been shown her obscene messages to Lord Lytton and his friends (many of whom were also friends of Procter): 'Those letters, I confess, startled me.' She startled him further by repeating the sodomy allegation and speaking of a seraglio of boys in an Eastern land made use of by Disraeli; she also told him that her husband often surrounded himself at Knebworth with women dressed up as men.

The visitors wanted to know why she was accusing Dr Marshall Hall of being her daughter's murderer. Lady Lytton pointed out that she had made her accusation ten years ago, to the doctor himself, and that it was very odd that only now was it being put forward as evidence of her unsoundness of mind.

Dr Hill asked why she had been so insistent on Lord Lytton's level of maintenance to her: 'I must really say, Lady Lytton, that I think you are unreasonable to Sir Edward, for £400 a year is a very good allowance.' 'It might be for a mad-doctor's or attorney's wife,' she retorted, 'and even then, they might be so very unreasonable to want it paid in coin instead of promissory notes [IOUs].'

Lady Lytton asked Dr Hill directly if he had ever seen anything during her time with him that suggested she was not sane. 'I'd rather not give an opinion,' he replied. She pointed out that Dr Hill must have believed her to be of sound mind, otherwise he would not have allowed his daughter Mary to be alone with her for long spells. Dr Hill did not respond. He simply cleared his throat and reminded the visiting Commissioners that they must not be late for their train.

Two more visitors came to Wyke House later that week: Dr John Conolly ('who would sell his mother for money', and, worse, was admired by Charles Dickens) and Dr William Charles Hood of Royal Bethlehem Hospital. Hill wrote in his journal that, after the pair had left, Lady Lytton had expressed a wish to cut Hood's throat; before too long, Hill would be in a similar frame of mind with regards to Hood.

Hood was the well-regarded superintendent of Bethlehem – the new broom who had come in following the Peithman scandal (as told in Chapter Three). Even John Perceval thought highly of him. Yet he would not have done so had he known of Hood's role in the Lytton affair: the thirty-four-year-old physician had been sent by Lord Lytton to find proofs of his wife's madness. Lytton had written to Hood to ask him to 'examine as carefully and pathologically as you can her physical state, ascertain if her heart be sound or not . . . I also believe [there may be] uterine disease, such as cancer or tumour . . . Uterine disease . . . is in itself so often a concurrent malady with cerebral afflictions or morbid delusions of imagination and that . . . would form an additional evidence of diseased intellect.' Hood's reply does not appear to have survived, but no gynaecological slander was subsequently used against Lady Lytton.

Lady Lytton's solicitor had requested that the Commissioners allow him to see the certificates and lunacy statement that had led to her confinement at Wyke House. He now informed Lady Lytton that the certificates had stated that both her parents had died mad – in fact, neither had. It was also claimed that she had attempted suicide and that she was a drunkard – again, both allegations were untrue. Other matters set down as evidence of her unsoundness were her allegation that her husband had committed sodomy with Disraeli; that he had paid *The Times* not to publish details of what had happened at Hertford; that Dr Marshall Hall had been paid to put a swift end to Emily's life; and that she believed that the Somerset yeomanry would rise up and march if she were disappeared into an asylum.

The certificate and statements were clearly of highly questionable validity. Lord Lytton's position looked even more vulnerable when it was borne in mind that the only doctors a man of his stature and influence had been able to procure to undertake the certification were an obscure Fenchurch Street pharmacist and Dr Hale Thomson, who had not enjoyed an illustrious career, having several times come close to being sacked from the Westminster Hospital for incompetence. But Lady Lytton was to hear nothing more from the Commissioners in Lunacy. Appealing to the Lord Chancellor himself would have been pointless, since that post was at the time being filled by Sir Frederick Thesiger, another good friend of Lord Lytton; as was Lord Shaftesbury, the head of the Lunacy Commission. It was no bizarre delusion of Lady Lytton's that many of the powerful men who could have helped her were either part of Lord Lytton's social circle or had good reason not to rebuff or offend him. By now she had been able to work out another possibly sinister connection. Dr Hill was a native of Lincolnshire, and in 1835 he had been employed as house surgeon at Lincoln's large county asylum, becoming a hugely popular figure in the town and eventually its mayor. And who had been MP for Lincoln until 1841? Lord Lytton.

Dr Hill's predecessor at the Lincoln county asylum had already abolished the use of strait-waistcoats, iron whole-leg hobbles, hand-cuffs, finger-confining instruments and manacles. Dr Hill improved still further the conditions and treatment of the insane at Lincoln and gained national fame for his advanced methods. Dr John Conolly came to visit Lincoln and took careful notes on the regime there. Dr Hill believed that kindness was the most effective way to maintain order within the institution and that it offered the best chance of effecting a cure. He was convinced that 'non-restraint' diminished the number of escape attempts and suicides. He admitted that there were incidents of violence by patients within the nation's asylums, but that one could stand on London Bridge for an hour each day and see black eyes everywhere – they were considered to be perfectly normal. He asked: 'If Liberty generates such trifles, who is the man so thin-skinned as to shudder at its occasional manifestation among the insane?'

Nevertheless, kindness and courtesy at Inverness Lodge were of little help to someone who had been wrongfully confined. Lady Lytton's appetite fell away because of her anxiety, and the quality of her sleep was poor too. When she closed her eyes, the scene in Clarges Street arose in her mind. 'I feel my health is giving way,' she wrote to Rebecca Ryves. She awoke on the morning of Saturday 10 July 'from one of those terrible dreams which have now haunted me for a fortnight, dreams that I am escaping over high walls and house-tops'.

Dr Hale Thomson and apothecary Ross's faces, swathed in swirling veils of black crêpe, pursued her, and each time she ran, they would re-form themselves in front of her, and she was being chained down in a dark, deep dungeon when she woke in a sweat to the perfectly mundane horror of Inverness Lodge, Brentford. As she later wrote, if you keep someone locked up in Buckingham House or the Palais des Tuileries, a palace will nevertheless become a dungeon. It was the function of the asylum that terrified, not its physical manifestation.

Meanwhile, in Somerset, Lord Lytton and solicitor William Loaden had come to the Giles Castle Hotel and demanded that Mrs Clarke hand over all of Lady Lytton's papers. Mrs Clarke ('my Koh-i-noor', 'my deputy tigress') refused, and when voices became raised, a commercial traveller who overheard the argument insisted on seeing the men's written authority for their demand. When they failed to produce it, he called a constable and had them ejected.

So angry were the townsfolk, when they heard from Mrs Clarke and Miss Ryves of what had taken place during the visit to London, that a public meeting was convened at short notice, chaired by one Mr W. R. Hitchcock. Various speakers wanted to place on record that during her three years of living in Taunton, Lady Lytton had never shown any signs of unsoundness. The meeting resolved:

> 1) That the removal of Lady Bulwer-Lytton to a lunatic asylum, or other place of confinement, and the circumstances under which she was incarcerated therein, call for a public expression of alarm for the rights and liberties of the subject, and particularly of distrust of the treatment to which her ladyship is said to have been subjected.
> 2) That a committee be now appointed to watch the result of the extraordinary measures reported to have been adopted in Lady Lytton's case, to the end that the public mind may be satisfied, through their report, that in her ladyship's case justice may be done.

This wasn't quite the rising of the Somerset yeomanry that Lady Lytton had predicted. Still, the *Somerset County Gazette*, while acknowledging 'her undoubted peculiarities of temper' and admitting that she was 'unamiable', haughty and capable of harsh words, devoted entire pages to the outrage committed against one of its citizens. The abduction into the asylum had been how the French *ancien régime* and their Bastille had operated, said the *Gazette*: was Lady Lytton to be the modern-day Man in the Iron Mask? The newspaper called for a public inquiry to be held before every lunacy certification, stating that 'only a nation of savages' would have the sort of admissions system prevalent in England. 'So strongly do the plot and detail savour of the "atrocious fraud" and "abominable conspiracy" of the modern romance writer,' the *Gazette* editorialised, 'that one might easily imagine it to have been the sole invention of such a genius.' Which of course it was: Lord Lytton had plotted his wife's disposal just as he plotted his novels and dramas. But how infuriating that real people would not oblige him by acting and speaking as he dictated.

The Somerset readers were outraged, and some of them (or was it the sub-editors?) staggered recklessly into verse. The following poem appeared in the newspaper on 19 July 1858: 'Thoughts suggested and put together after perusing the leading article in the Somerset County Gazette of last week'

> I call thee, Byron, from the shades,
> Thy genius must not sleep;
> A woman's wrongs claim sympathy,
> Wrongs cruel, poignant, deep.
>
> Thy power impart, thy spirit send,
> Great poet of your day!
> Give me thine arrow with its sting,
> To mark oppression's sway.
>
> Freedom has suffered violence,
> (The story shall be told),
> Freedom so dear to British breasts,
> More precious far than gold.
>
> Freedom, the Saxon's liberty,
> 'Delight of human kind';
> Her fate is worse than servitude,
> Not such do martyrs find.
>
> The rack, the harrow and the wheel,

These are the martyr's doom;
But woman, not bereft of sense,
Is driven wild with gloom.

Sane, but eccentric in her ways,
And who has not some whim?
A wife in durance sad is held,
The husband's boat to trim.

Sailing thro' life, o'er rocks, o'er shoals,
With misery at the helm,
She only sought a kindly shore,
Where Plenty had its whelm.

She did but ask, what Reason shewed
A just and fair attorn,
The dower she brought, with recompense
For past neglect, past scorn.

Drifting unheeded and alone,
Desperate in her course,
A flag she hoisted full mast high,
The signal of distress.

The signal, too, for cowardice
To work its cunning woof;
A whirlpool is the victim's fate,
No harbour her behoof.

Shame on the dastardly design!
War to th'accomplished deed!
Rouse fathers, mothers, children, friends,
'Tis time your hearts should bleed!

Rouse, and assert Old England's boast
With indignation rife;
From Orkney to the Scilly Isles
Cry 'Liberty in Life!'

[PRICE ONE PENNY.]

EXTRAORDINARY NARRATIVE

OF AN

OUTRAGEOUS VIOLATION OF LIBERTY AND LAW,

IN THE

Forcible Seizure and Incarceration of Lady Lytton Bulwer,

IN THE GLOOMY CELL OF A MADHOUSE ! ! !

AND THE PROCEEDINGS TO OBTAIN HER RELEASE.

[Lady Bulwer Lytton's first interview with her Solicitor, in the dismal dungeon of Bedlam.]

WITH EXCLUSIVE DETAILS OF SIR E. B.'s AMOURS IN THE ALBANY—THE
DELICATE DISCOVERY BY HER LADYSHIP,

THE CAUSE OF THE SEPARATION,

With many curious particulars, never before published.

ADDRESS OF LADY BULWER TO THE ELECTORS OF HERTFORDSHIRE.

LONDON: PUBLISHED BY W. JAMES AND CO., 34, BOOKSELLERS'-ROW,
ST. CLEMENT'S, STRAND,
AND SOLD BY ALL VENDORS OF NEWSPAPERS, &c.

This pamphlet on the 1858 abduction of Lady Lytton makes use of extremely outdated Gothic tropes – Gothic was resorted to frequently in imagery and prose by those addressing the wrongful confinement issue. The artwork here may also be referencing Lord Lytton's 1828 novel *Pelham*, in which the (sane) heroine is discovered by the hero locked in a madhouse dungeon cell. Lady Lytton claimed that she had suggested that particular plot twist to her husband, thirty years before her own incarceration.

Many national newspapers were also reporting with horror the incarceration of Lady Lytton, and at the head of the pack was the *Daily Telegraph*, which condemned Lord Lytton and Derby's government in strong language. Rebecca Ryves had written to all the newspapers with a full account of the seizure of Lady Lytton, but not surprisingly, *The Times* refused to print anything on the subject; the organ that was usually so loud in its criticism of lunacy law never once mentioned the Lytton affair. But in the *Telegraph*, 'The right honourable novelist' was portrayed as a traitor to his original Radical Liberal roots, a man whose hauteur prevented him from treating his electorate as anything but children: 'He is an enemy to reform; his name is not associated with a single meritorious public act . . . He is an amazingly amusing story-teller; he knows how to interest young ladies in Italian poisoners, to idealise the corruption of Pompeii . . . agitating with his eloquence broad billows of crinoline.' This was not entirely fair: the causes that Lord Lytton had effectively championed had been slave emancipation and the law of copyright (as we have seen), the abolition of the stamp tax, prison reform and open competition for places within the Civil Service (odd, though, for a confirmed nepotist). On 21 July, the *Telegraph* reported that it had received a huge number of letters from readers, proving that Lady Lytton's plight was of national significance – international significance, even, given that it was the Secretary for the Colonies who stood accused of this assault upon the liberty that Britain claimed to be exporting around the globe.

The plot was backfiring spectacularly on its author, and his poorly constructed storyline was at the mercy of the critics. News had reached the Carlyles of the hustings furore and the incarceration. 'The case looked very bad against Bulwer,' wrote Jane Carlyle to her husband. Thomas Carlyle declared that Lady Lytton was 'no more mad than I am, – tho' unwise, ill-guided to a high degree, and plunging wildly under the heavy burden laid on her'. He knew that Lady Lytton's behaviour could be called 'mad' in 'common speech', in the sense of excessive, disproportionate and rash; but Carlyle believed that this was 'folly', not madness, because unlike an insane person, she was capable of changing her ways. Carlyle felt pleased that he had thus worked out the answer to the universally perplexing question of what constituted madness and what did not: 'I found that if you cd conceive a change of heart . . . it wd entirely cure her; whereas it wd do nothing at a real madman . . . nothing, but alter the figure of his madness. This, for the first time is a real distinction I have hit upon in that abstruse matter.'

Lord Lytton's mood and health both suffered, and one of his clerks at the Colonial Office described him in these weeks as 'insolent, rude and feckless', while Thomas Babington Macaulay wrote that he was 'if not deranged, so much overworked as to be quite hors de combat'. Lord Lytton repeatedly tried to resign his post as public anger about what he had attempted to do to his wife increased. Lord Derby refused to allow him to do so, at a time when political talent was not abundant. So Lord Lytton was condemned to high office for the time being. Those who know about these things believe that in his year at the Colonial Office Lord Lytton achieved a great deal; but it is irresistible to quote the man who had locked up a sane woman saying, of the pink patches on the map, 'If we give up these places, they will gradually relapse into primitive barbarianism.'

The Lytton children had been born to be cannon fodder for their parents. Poor Emily had only managed nineteen years' service before expiring, but there was still Robert. Now Lord Lytton pushed this important pawn into the game. Lady Lytton had let it be known via her solicitor that she was intending to use the one-year-old Divorce Court to air all the filthy underlinen of the marriage (although quite how she would have managed this, having the status of certified lunatic, is difficult to understand). Lord Lytton sent Robert along to work out a compromise. Dr Hill entered her room and 'began tapping that bay window of a paunch of his'; behind him stood a terrified Robert. For three hours, often in tears, Robert pleaded with his mother to abandon her plans for legal action. He had been told to offer Lady Lytton release from the asylum to a life of comfort, with Robert, on the Continent, and the sum of £500 a year to live on. In return, she would have to sign a perpetual truce, guaranteeing that she would no longer persecute Lord Lytton in person or in print. Having guessed that there must be real trouble brewing for her husband if he would stump up £500 a year, Lady Lytton agreed to these terms but now demanded £1,000 a year. Robert reported back to his father, and shortly afterwards lawyer Edwin James and Dr Forbes Benignus Winslow came to Inverness Lodge. The latter was there to ratify Lady Lytton's removal from the asylum – to let the world know that she was of sound enough mind to go free. Edwin James and 'the dulcifluous Dr Forbes Winslow' told her that her husband had agreed to the thousand a year and then left. At three in the afternoon of Saturday 17 July 1858, after twenty-five days in captivity, Lady Lytton was a free woman.

She made a brisk shopping trip on that very hot evening, ate a rushed meal in a Belgravia hotel, took a train to Dover and reached Calais on the Monday morning.

On that same morning, most of the national newspapers dutifully published a letter from Robert, written from his father's house at 1 Park Lane. Robert stated that after conferring with Lord Shaftesbury, and in accordance with his father's wishes, he had decided that foreign travel was the best form of care for his mother. Robert stated that she never had been placed in an asylum, but had simply spent some time in the private residence of a medical man, living among his family. (This is the significance of Dr Hill shifting Lady Lytton from Wyke House to Inverness Lodge.) Robert continued that during this stay, which had been entirely misrepresented in some sections of the press, his father had only sought the best medical opinion available in order that Lady Lytton should not be restrained a moment longer than was strictly justifiable. Below Robert's letter were printed the weasel words of two doctors in a tight spot. John Conolly informed the world that Lord Lytton's course of action had been entirely justi-fied, and that he was happy with the arrangements Lord Lytton had made for Lady Lytton to be with her son and companion Rebecca Ryves. Dr Winslow wrote that his interview with Lady Lytton had permitted him to proclaim that she could be freed from restraint, and, he added, 'I think it but an act of justice to Sir Edward Bulwer-Lytton to state that . . . the course which he has pursued throughout these painful proceedings cannot be considered as harsh or unjustifiable.' Privately, though, the incident had worried Winslow, who feared that suspicions of mis-certification damaged the standing of English doctors. As we will see in the next chapter, his own high reputation was suffering a great deal at this time.

The pen certainly hadn't been mightier than the sword in poor Robert Lytton's hands. Commentators soon pointed out various inconsistencies in the case. To start with, Conolly's and Winslow's

Robert ('Teddy') at the age of eighteen.

'certificates' made no reference to those concocted by Dr Hale Thomson and apothecary Ross, by which Lady Lytton had been forcibly seized. Moreover, why did Robert append Winslow and Conolly's opinions while arguing that Lady Lytton had never been in an asylum but in a private residence? Why, when she was restored to liberty, was she spirited out of the country at high speed? And why had the Commissioners in Lunacy spoken not one word on the matter? 'An Englishman' wrote to the *Daily Telegraph* to say, 'The more enquiries we make into the matter, the more convinced we are that a great wrong was attempted, and has now been glossed over.'

It was always Lady Lytton's contention that this group of powerful men protected each other and performed each other's bidding. The documents that Robert Lytton collected together and safe-housed at Knebworth, plus the huge Bulwer-Lytton correspondence files at Hertfordshire Archives and Local Studies, contain proof that this was no delusion. Not only was John Forster up to his neck in it, Lord Shaftesbury himself had connived at a scheme that was illegal as well as unethical. Forster had been secretary to the Commissioners in Lunacy since 1855, and in 1861 would become a Commissioner himself.

It started with a row in March 1859 about foul-mouthed Mrs Burkitt and the Commissioners' suggestion that Inverness Lodge was not a 'suitable abode' for this lady, and their description of Hill's home as 'a lodging house'. Ever prickly, Hill wrote a furious letter to John Forster, pointing out how very helpful he, Hill, had been in the matter of Lady Lytton: 'I have written evidence to show that Lady Lytton was placed in confinement by your advice and the Commissioners', long before the certificates of lunacy were signed. I should not have alluded to this matter if I did not feel that there was a prejudice against me. Indeed, I have been so worried of late that it has affected my health and I am becoming careless as to the result. I begin to think that a man had better break stones than have the care of lunatics.' Lord Shaftesbury himself wrote to Hill to state that Forster had shown him this vaguely blackmailish-sounding letter; Shaftesbury summoned Hill to his office to reveal this 'written evidence'. Hill noted in his journal on 12 March 1859, 'Received also a most insulting letter from Mr Forster', in which Forster called Hill's allegation 'a wicked and calumnious falsehood'. Hill replied to Shaftesbury that he would be happy to come along with the documentation but that he would be bringing his lawyer with him. To Forster, Hill wrote that 'the language with which you conclude your note is so utterly beneath the notice of a gentleman that I should find it derogatory to myself to reply'.

Forster protested that he was willing to swear an oath that he had never made any comments about Lady Lytton's 'malady' prior to her being placed in confinement. Hill retorted that 'if that was the fact, he was a most wicked liar'.

Now Dr William Charles Hood began to make a sinister intervention, as he attempted to get hold of the paperwork that Hill believed would prove Forster's key role in the plot. Over dinner on 18 March, Hill claimed that Hood soothed him by saying that Sir Edward 'would protect me against any attack by the Commissioners' and would 'give me something that would make me independent of the Commissioners for the future'. When this attempt at a pay-off failed, Dr Hood 'gave me to understand that if I did not accede to this proposition then I was a ruined man. I told him I might as well be ruined at once as by degrees . . . I told him that I had been completely sold by Sir Edward BL.' Hood informed his powerful crony, Lord Lytton: 'I have not at present altogether succeeded with Mr Hill. He is more stubborn than I anticipated . . . I shall adopt other measures and am determined not to be defeated.'

Hill copied out the incriminating document in his diary, in case Hood should somehow be able to get his hands on the original. This letter – from Forster to Lord Lytton, dated 9 June 1858 – began with Forster stating that Shaftesbury had just told him of the hustings horror and that Lady Lytton had addressed the crowd in a 'most violent and excited way . . . her words . . . were those of utter insanity . . . Lord Shaftesbury knows I am writing this to you, and desires me to tell you that there can be only one impression as to the wretched exhibition made by this unhappy person – a full justification of yourself in any measure you may now think it right to take.' Forster wrote that Shaftesbury's very words about the hustings incident had been: 'It is very fortunate . . . it puts him [Lord Lytton] quite right. I am sure it will be satisfactory to you [Forster] to know this.' A letter of 29 July 1858 from Shaftesbury to Lord Lytton reveals, 'I am quite convinced that your course was just and necessary in placing Lady L under care and treatment.'

Another letter, from Forster to Lord Lytton – and unknown to Hill – exists: when Lytton had asked Forster's advice, long before the hustings, about what could be done with his wife, Forster had replied, in October 1857: 'Pray, pray be careful in what you do as to the matter you mention . . . I have long been convinced that she is insane, but it is a case belonging exactly to the class which it is most difficult to get medical men to certify.' However, elsewhere, Forster had described Lady Lytton as 'more bad than mad'.

Forster also suggested to Lytton that certain technical matters should be kept in mind if the plot was to go ahead: Forster tells his friend that 'in cases where there is method and infuriatingly mixed, reason and madness, you [must] act wisely in making the attempt . . . Success ought to be next to a certainty before you do so. That makes this difficult, to my thinking, and sending medical men expressly from London, who must do this thing by a kind of coup de main, if at all – hit or miss [writing becomes illegible]. I should have thought that the wisest course would have been to instruct reputable medical men in the neighbourhood who, being on the spot, might watch the opportunity.' Forster instructed his friend on no account to be the person who signed the lunacy order, as Lord Lytton must not appear in the matter 'until success is absolutely obtained'.

Forster actually thought that single-patient care, with one of the cele-brated and discreet alienists (Sutherland, Winslow and Monro were all cited), would be a safer way of avoiding exposure. These lines are damning proof of Lady Lytton's suspicion that the very authority charged with ensuring that no sane person could be placed in an asylum or single-patient lodgings had approved her seizure, months before any doctor had even interviewed her. These men really were As Bad As They Seemed.

Lord Lytton's response to this proof? He simply replied that the document that Hill possessed was a forgery. However, George Ross, the Fenchurch Street apothecary, now entered the fray, stating that Hill's evidence accorded with his memory of how the incarceration had been pre-arranged.

Solicitor William Loaden threatened Hill with litigation if the doctor did not hand over the paperwork; Hill replied to Loaden that it was he who was the injured party, and would do whatever he thought best for his own defence. An independent legal opinion was sought, and after having listened to the tales of the various parties, the lawyer backed Hill, confirming that he had nothing to fear from any court action.

Yet the Lytton business would hardly ever be mentioned in connection with Dr Hill, even by his enemies. Posterity has attributed his

John Forster (1812–1876), secretary to the Commissioners in Lunacy from 1855, and, from 1861, a full Commissioner. Forster was Charles Dickens's close friend and literary adviser, Lord Lytton's close associate and was nicknamed 'Jackal Fudgster' by Lady Lytton, in whose incarceration Forster played a role.

flight into insignificance to another cause altogether: an increasing peevishness at having been largely written out of the story of 'non-restraint'. His repeated attempts (entirely justified) to publicise his large role in the humanitarian treatment of lunatics was coming to be seen as tiresome and graceless. Dr John Conolly had adapted Hill's methods for use at the huge Middlesex County Asylum at Hanwell, and the glory and fame had gone to Conolly, not Hill.

As soon as he could abandon his Downing Street office, Lytton fled to a Continental spa to recuperate. Those who detested him did so more strongly; but some of his closest friendships suffered damage too. When the conspiracy collapsed, Lord Lytton suggested that the idea to confine his wife had been John Forster's, and a letter from Forster to His Lordship indignantly (and erroneously) insisted, 'I was not your "adviser".' In a letter dated 14 March 1859, a panicked Forster told Lytton that if the true sequence of events were to be discovered, 'It would be a momentous scandal, and would require a public inquiry into the lunacy laws and practice . . . I know the line I took all through. I cannot be mistaken as to the general character of the views I held and suppressed . . .' The friendship did not mend fully until the mid-1860s. It is not much credit to Forster that it mended at all.

Even Dickens appeared to cool towards Lord Lytton. The editors of the Pilgrim edition of Dickens's correspondence noted that a letter from Dickens dated 11 June 1858 (eleven days before the abduction of Lady Lytton) opened with 'Sir Edward Bulwer-Lytton'. In a footnote they make the point that, 'It seems impossible that Dickens should address an old friend so formally.' The message was to decline a dinner invitation with Lytton on 26 June. Perhaps Dickens knew of the outra-geous plans and was indicating his disapproval.

There has been speculation about whether Dickens himself ever contemplated the madhouse for his wife Catherine, from whom he was controversially about to separate. Descendants of Dr Thomas Harrington Tuke, superintendent of Manor House Asylum in Chiswick between 1849 and 1888, are believed to have seen correspondence in which the novelist asked Tuke to investigate the possibility of having his wife committed to Manor House. Allegedly, Tuke, in reply, refused, on the grounds that there was no evidence that Catherine was of unsound mind. The original letters were handed to a researcher in the 1970s and have been missing ever since; as no copies were ever made, this story cannot be verified. Dickens, for his part, made a huge bonfire of much of his correspondence on 3 September 1860, possibly immolating evidence of such a plan. In a surviving letter to his confidante Angela Burdett-Coutts, dated 8 May 1858, Dickens wrote of his wife that 'her mind has, at times, been certainly confused'. He claimed that Catherine took no interest in the children – an accusation not uncommon against women who were the subject of lunacy investigations, as we have seen; the Dickens children themselves denied that this was the case. But a full-blown lunacy panic – of which Lady Lytton's story was just one part – was taking place in 1858, as the Dickens marriage disintegrated; and so it is difficult to accept that the nation's most popular fireside companion would have been so unwise as to risk mass opprobrium by attempting to have certified a quiet, dull, withdrawn, nervy woman who was, moreover, popular with many of Dickens's friends, not least John Forster. Lord Lytton's experience had shown how fraught with danger such an attempt could prove. Dickens's concerns in the correspondence that has survived were that Catherine should live where, and with which family members and companions, she wanted. (In the event, the separation allowed her £600 a year.) Until the Tuke letters turn up again, Dickens must surely be permitted the Scottish verdict regarding any madhouse plot of his own.

Things didn't go well in France, of course. Lady Lytton suspected Robert and Rebecca Ryves, her companion, of reporting stories about her back to Lord Lytton, and of trying to get hold of the perjuring letters. His father suspected that Robert was now taking his mother's side and Robert almost broke under the strain of being vilified by both his delinquent parents. His mother later wrote that when Robert wished to discuss family matters with her, he would turn pale and look around him furtively, 'as if the very birds in the air would carry his words back to Park Lane or Downing Street'. Lord Lytton reprimanded the pair for spending too much money, and Lady Lytton quickly discovered that her £1,000 a year had been reduced to £500. She also learned of Robert's letter to the press and its attempt to exonerate Lord Lytton, and realised that she had been 'smuggled abroad in such electric telegraph haste' as the best means of shutting her up. After five months, their life together had become unbearable and Robert abandoned his mother. They would never see each other again.

Lady Lytton came back to England a few months later. She, too, was in breach of the agreement and continued to send abusive letters to her husband; but Lord Lytton knew now that the best course was not to respond. When Wilkie Collins published *The Woman in White* in novel form in the August of 1860, she wrote to him: 'The great failure of your book is the villain; Count Fosco is a very poor one, and when next you want a character of that sort, I trust you will not disdain to come to me. The man is alive and constantly under my gaze. In fact, he is my own husband.' Collins, who was on friendly terms with Lord Lytton, forwarded the letter to Knebworth. His Lordship's thoughts on this are not known; but we do know that he believed *The Woman in White* to be 'great trash'.

Lord Lytton was indeed weirder than Fosco. His interest in the occult was now consuming more of his time and energy, and he had regular conversations with Little Boots and Shakespeare, attempted to raise from the dead Apollonius of Tyana on a Regent Street rooftop, and completed detailed horoscopes of Mr Gladstone (predicting he would always be a solitary creature) and of his old friend Disraeli. Haughtier than ever, he once refused to continue a seance with a medium because she dropped her 'h's.

Despite (perhaps because of) his by now extreme deafness, Lord Lytton entered the House of Lords, where he voted on the Second Reform Bill, presumably not having heard a word of the debate.

In 1867 Lady Lytton sent a manuscript copy of her autobiography, *A Blighted Life*, to a lawyer and, it is believed, to Charles Reade. The author of *Hard Cash* had corresponded with Lady Lytton and suggested to her that it was John Forster who 'had whispered into her husband's ear what facilities the lunacy law affords for disposing of an inconvenient wife'. She later suspected that the manuscript was copied by the lawyer, who then published it in a small print run. It was so filled with libel that she had to publish a pamphlet denying that she was the book's author; it did not re-emerge from its suppression until 1880, two years before her death at the age of seventy-nine in Sydenham, South London.

To her delight, Lord Lytton had predeceased her in 1873. Robert subsequently raised her allowance to £700 a year. But she was not to be mollified, leaving instruction 'that he should never desecrate the grave of the mother he had so cruelly betrayed and inhumanly neglected, by any tombstone verbiage, or any impious posthumous sentimentalities in poems or magazines'. Poisonous to the very end – and then beyond.

The Lytton scandal is one of the earliest of the nineteenth-century lunacy panics that identified women's rights as deserving of particular mention. Where before, simple gender-blind justice, or, alternatively, the chivalrous/patronising need to take extra care of the ladies, had been called upon by those defending liberty, this time, a 'feminist' perspective is evident. Take the following letter, which was sent to the editor of the *Taunton Courier* on 24 July 1858 and was entitled 'From a happy wife who pities a persecuted one'. It is quite possible that it was written by Lady Lytton or by one of her supporters (the handwriting is not hers, but the syntax has elements of her style). It hardly matters, though, who the author was, because it is the rallying cry that is of note:

> My proposal is that women should for once show their esprit de corps (in which they are usually so lamentably deficient as to countenance and even admire the very men who trample on all social and family duties) and enter into a penny subscription throughout the length and breadth of England, in order to enable Lady Bulwer to obtain legal redress for the false imprisonment of the very worst sort . . . Let no pennies be levied on the labouring classes, who not having husbands with £8,000 a year are not likely to meet with similar injustice – neither let us ask aid from the higher classes, who look on and smile at fashionable delinquencies, but let the middle-class women unite to show a sense of their sister's wrongs.

On the same day that this letter was composed, Stephen Austin, editor of the *Hertford Mercury*, who had shifted his allegiance from Lord to Lady Lytton, took up this aspect of the subject. The newspaper's editorial stated: 'In this country, a man is not master of his wife, in the sense that he may do to her what he pleases, or dispose of her in whatever manner his fancy or his passion suggest. A woman has rights which may not be invaded, even by her husband.' This wasn't correct, in fact, as the editor ought to have known (and as the Harriet Price habeas corpus case, mentioned in Chapter Four, would prove): husbands did have the basic right to the possession of the body of their wives. But physical assault was, as the newspaper pointed out, a public wrong, and if a third party were willing to act as prosecutor – where a wife felt unable or unwilling – the attack was treated in the courts as a public matter, not a privileged incident behind closed doors.

The family, the *Mercury* argued, did not have the right to flout the law and put an individual's liberty at danger. It was simply not good enough for a cloak of secrecy to be drawn across lunacy issues by invoking the sacred nature of domestic privacy:

> It is impossible to conceive a more grievous injury than . . . the imprisonment of a sane woman in an asylum . . . Whether we call them euphoniously 'retreats for the mentally afflicted', or prisons for the mad, they must necessarily be places of unutterable horror to the sane immured within their walls; nor could malevolent ingenuity devise a more frightful and audacious scheme of vengeance than to convert them into bastilles to silence troublesome complainants and blot out the obtrusive record of domestic wrongs.

The Victorian paterfamilias no longer had a clear run at it. Women could, and did, avail themselves of the new Divorce Court (albeit on a very uneven playing field); and whereas before the 1857 Matrimonial Causes Act, just one per cent of divorces had been granted to a wife, after 1857 that figure soared to 25 per cent. Agitation for full property and civil law rights for married women was under way, despite persistent blocking of such moves by the House of Lords. Lady Lytton could have joined in and used her powerful pen to assist the various campaigns for women's rights, had she not poured her energies into her solitary vengeance upon His Lordship and his cronies.

8

Juries in Revolt

Lady Lytton's was just one of four scandals that led to the 'lunacy panic of 1858'. The summer and autumn of that year were to bring to light yet more frightening stories of Britons – from high-born to humble – being 'disappeared' into a lunatic asylum. By the end of the year, the demands for a Select Committee into the operation of the English lunacy laws could no longer be withstood, as inquisition jury after jury refused to equate bizarre, perverse, even violent, behaviour with insanity. The make-up of the 'special juries' had not changed: it was still the same set of men, predominantly Middlesex magistrates, who were gathered together to decide where eccentricity shaded off into lunacy. But in 1858, a shift in sentiment appeared to take place among jurymen.

Six days after Lady Lytton's coerced voyage to the Continent, a lunacy inquisition opened in York. On Friday 23 July, twenty jurymen and Commissioner Francis Barlow met in the magistrates' room at York Castle to hear a story that they, and most newspapermen, would consider to be the melancholy tale of a love gone wrong. These eminent local men, charged with a task of high seriousness, were strongly affected by the testimony they heard, reflecting a culture in which, as historian G. M. Young noted, 'ministers sometimes wept at the table; when the sight of an infant school could reduce a civil servant to a passion of tears . . . an age more easily touched, more easily shocked . . .'

Charles Turner, Harrow-educated and from a wealthy family, worked as the official assignee of the Liverpool Court of Bankruptcy – a highly respectable legal position, passed on to him by his father, also called Charles. He fell in love with Mary Jane Hepworth, seventeen years his junior, who came from a humble background and was unable to read or write. Turner was afraid that his father would disapprove and so the relationship was clandestine. Mary Jane became pregnant with their daughter, Ellen, in 1839 but Charles did not marry her until 1844, and he kept this secret from his family. They moved across the Mersey, to Bebington in Cheshire, where they lived happily for a while. However, Charles's job required him to be away from home a great deal, and as he was a good-looking man, in his early forties, Mary Jane strongly suspected that women were very attracted to him. For his part, Charles claimed that he was always 'passionately' attached to his wife, and watched as she flourished – learning to read and write and becoming 'a woman of some accomplishments', in his words.

Their marriage became hellish within two years, with Mary Jane accusing Charles of infidelities with just about every female he met at the hotels and boarding houses he used when travelling on behalf of the court. Then, on 2 December 1846, one of their rows became violent. Mary Jane screamed and spat at Charles and attacked him with a stick. When he took the stick away from her and struck her with it, his wife threw herself out of the first-floor window, breaking a leg. After this incident, he told his father and his family's social circle about the marriage. As he had feared, they were not pleased; his wife's violence and irrationality were only to be expected, was their snobbish reaction to his allying himself to someone low-born.

The rows continued. A policeman confirmed that during a very noisy argument – and presumably neighbours had alerted the constable – Charles had instructed the servants to take no orders from their mistress, only from him. At the height of another quarrel, servants heard him shout at Mary Jane that she was 'a strumpet', and on another occasion he shouted that 'he had found her in the dirt, and he would leave her back there'.

The couple were cruising on a steamboat on Lake Windermere one summer day, when Mary Jane accused Charles of having been looked at by another woman; she attacked him in front of the other passengers. Then, on 1 June 1850, on an outing to the Menai Bridge, a woman passed the Turners, and Mary Jane insisted that Charles had appreciatively returned the woman's gaze. At home, the row continued, and Mary Jane picked up the poker in the parlour; the blow that she crashed down on Charles's handsome head fractured his skull.

She was arrested and put in Birkenhead Gaol, but Charles, bed-bound for weeks, forgave her and declined to prosecute, and so she was released. Mary Jane drank heavily during his recuperation and attacked him in bed; she had to be pulled off by the servants, with whom she accused Charles of being intimate.

And so it went on for three more years, until a separation was agreed. Mary Jane was to receive £200 a year, to be paid to her quarterly by a trustee, solicitor Thomas Pemberton. Charles went back to live in Liverpool; Mary Jane moved to York, then to Bath for four and a half uneventful years, and finally to Scarborough, where she lived servantless in a small and inexpensive cottage. By living frugally and investing wisely during these years, Mary Jane built up savings of £700. Charles kept in touch with his wife and when he noticed during one visit that she was looking very ill, he took her on a tour of Scotland and the English Lakes to improve her health. She seemed to have calmed down considerably, he thought, despite one outburst, when she shouted that when they were apart, his behaviour was driving her 'mad' – an accusation he did not understand. And when she made a claim that someone was trying to poison her, with fish as the vehicle for the dose, he chose to ignore it. He would later say that he had remained heartbroken at the failure of the marriage, and once wrote to her: 'My dearest Mary . . . If you love me one-tenth part as much as I love you, you will come to me in comparative poverty, rather than live apart.' It is difficult to understand his reference to 'comparative poverty' as his salary will have been substantial. He enclosed a portrait of himself with the letter. But no resumption of married life took place.

At four o'clock in the morning of 19 December 1857, Leeds surgeon William Hey was woken by hammering at his door. When he dressed and went downstairs to open it, he found a policeman and Mary Jane Turner, who was carrying two wooden boxes. She told Hey she had terrible pains in her bowels and believed she had been poisoned while taking tea the night before with her sister, her sister's husband, and friends of theirs. Mary Jane had travelled to Leeds from Scarborough the previous day. Her sister later confirmed that she had not been best pleased when Mary Jane had turned up unannounced at her

Headingley home, though she and her husband had given her supper and a bed for the night. Mary Jane had left the house in the early hours and found the policeman, who had taken her to the surgeon.

Hey examined her briefly and prescribed something for her stomach pains. Mary Jane urged him to analyse the contents of the two boxes she was carrying. Inside them, Hey found four jars. Within these were faeces, urine, vomit and a lump of butter.

None of the four substances contained any poison, Hey established, but Mary Jane was not happy with this finding and angrily said that she would send them to a specialist in London, but changed her mind twice about this. She eventually left the surgeon's house with her boxes, appearing to need no further treatment.

Later that day her brother-in-law in Headingley, Mr England, telegraphed to Charles Turner about Mary Jane's extraordinary behaviour. Mary Jane also wrote to her husband asking him to visit her in Leeds as two 'cold-blooded murderers' had tried to poison her, first at Scarborough and then at the Englands' home. Would he help bring the guilty to justice? She reassured Charles that she still loved him despite 'the insult, cruelty and injustice' she had received at his hands.

Charles later claimed that he was at this time very ill, and as his recovery could not wholly confidently be predicted, he placed matters in the hands of a clergyman friend in Rock Ferry, Reverend Thomas Fisher Redhead; the reverend had also become the guardian of the Turners' daughter Ellen during the troubled marriage and later separation. Redhead travelled to York to look for Mary Jane at the temporary address she had left with surgeon Hey. He was told that she had taken herself off to a pharmacist's shop in Coney Street, where he found her trying to buy an emetic. Her clothes were disordered and the pharmacist told Redhead that she had just cut off her stays with a knife. She claimed that she had been poisoned the night before at York's Royal Station Hotel, and then she rambled that her husband, the Englands and Redhead had poisoned her too.

Redhead led her away from the shop and placed her under the care of surgeon William Procter (no relation to Bryan Waller Procter), who agreed to make sure she did not harm herself or others. Mary Jane had found lodgings in York for herself and her precious boxes with one Mrs Potter in De Grey Street. She told her landlady that she would henceforth eat only dry bread, in order to thwart attempts to poison her. During his visits over the next two days William Procter twice found Mary Jane trying to make herself sick in order to obtain samples to prove that Mrs Potter was poisoning her. Then on the night of 23 December a policeman found her crying in Minster Yard, and she told him that she had had to flee her landlady in the middle of the night for fear of poisoning. She became louder and more agitated and the constable took her to the police station and contacted Procter, whose name and address Mary Jane had given him. Arriving with a second medical man, Dr North, Procter wrote a certificate for her admission into Acomb House Asylum, York, where she was received on Christmas Eve.

Acomb House Asylum in Acomb, York. Despite Mrs Turner's deliciously Gothic-sounding escape from the dark attic room, the building is of only two storeys, and 'attic' simply meant the upper floor.

Neither Redhead nor her husband were told of this. And although the confinement was brought to the attention of solicitor Charles Pemberton before the year was out, he ignored the information, continuing to pay promptly into her account her quarterly separation money. He would later claim that he very much regretted his initial lack of curiosity and compassion.

Acomb House was run by surgeon-proprietor John William Metcalfe, aged thirty-nine, assisted by nurse Harriet Atkinson, aged twenty-six, whom Metcalfe would marry on 23 February 1858. Metcalfe was the son of a Yorkshire curate and had previously been medical superintendent of York's county asylum; Harriet was the fourth daughter of a Yorkshire gentleman. Acomb House – or Acomb House Retreat, as Metcalfe sometimes styled it – charged a hefty weekly fee of three guineas, plus extra charges for wine, beer and laundry.

When Mary Jane Turner was delivered to him, Metcalfe noted 'a want of collectedness about her'. The patient had told him she was glad to be at Acomb House as a place of safety from those who wanted to poison her. 'I find Mrs Turner to be specious, mendacious, ignorant and beastly,' Metcalfe wrote in his casebook. He repeatedly addressed and referred to Mary Jane as 'whore'; more elaborately, 'a sanctified pious whore'. He often forced her to strip in front of him and when she refused, he told her, 'You have stripped before many men before now . . . You whore, I am up to all the tricks of a whore.' As punishment she was then locked in a small, dark, cold room for up to fifteen hours at a time with nowhere to 'perform the offices of nature'.

Mary Jane was not allowed pen and paper, in contravention of the lunacy laws. However, on the day after the Metcalfes' wedding, she escaped from Acomb House, and walked the twenty-four miles to Leeds. She wrote to Charles Pemberton:

Dear Sir, I write to inform you that I have made my escape from the asylum last night. I have been very cruelly treated by them, and very cruelly treated and neglected by your not coming to see [for] yourself to ascertain whether there was any foundation for such accusations, and such a tone of unkind treatment and cruelty. Excuse me, my dear sir, when I say I think it was your duty, as my trustee, to come and see me. It was very cruel of you and Mr Turner to leave me there three months without taking the slightest notice of me, instead of coming to see me yourselves . . . Come to me the moment you receive this note. Remember it is a woman, a woman's mind, you have got to save from destruction, for if I am detained any longer where I am now, I shall break my heart.

Pemberton immediately tried to see Charles Turner, but was referred instead to Charles's own solicitor, Mr Norris. When Norris tried to fob him off, saying, 'Oh she is mad', Pemberton claimed that he replied to Norris, 'She is no more mad than I am.' But Norris did not appear to want to become involved in the matter. Charles Turner himself would always be mysterious about when he had become aware of Mary Jane's complaints about her treatment.

Mary Jane was recaptured after a week and was put in the dark 'attic' room at Acomb. But three weeks later she knotted together her bedsheets and lowered herself from the window. She walked into central York and took lodgings at Mrs Sargison's in Little Blake Street, having first borrowed £5 (source of loan unknown; an Anne Catherick–Walter Hartright scenario?) and bought herself a bonnet.

Her whereabouts were discovered within a few days, and on the night of 2 April Metcalfe broke down the door to her room. The asylum keeper had brought along his wife and his groom to assist him in the recapture, which became a violent struggle, the most nationally notorious aspect of which turned out to be the extent of Mary Jane's undress: what would most perplex and horrify newspaper reporters and readers was whether Mary Jane had simply had the sleeve of her cotton chemise torn off by Metcalfe or whether she had been dragged naked from the bedstead that she clung on to, and carried between the two men into the Acomb House carriage. As with the Nottidge and Cumming seizures, the refusal to allow a lady fully to dress herself (including headwear and proper outdoor shoes) had a huge significance. The concern was more than simple prurience (though that aspect shouldn't be ignored): for many in those years, what seemed to be under attack in such episodes of rough handling was not just a lady's liberty, but her right to avoid indecent and improper circumstances. In a culture unwilling to confront rape and sexual assault directly – unless both victim and perpetrator were of very low social status – perhaps such enforced immodesty in dress was emblematic of a far more serious violation of a woman's privacy and physical integrity. In the Turner case, Mary Jane's nudity and being called 'a sanctified pious whore' were given the same weight as beatings, starvation, cold showers and all kinds of viciousness in the long and grim record of asylum atrocities. Mary Jane would later claim that Metcalfe's conduct towards her had been far worse than had been indicated; it could be that nudity was standing in for something that she was too ashamed to allege openly.

Charles Pemberton attempted to visit Mary Jane for the first time when she was returned to Acomb House from York, in mid-April. However, Metcalfe told Pemberton on the doorstep, in a 'most unkind manner', that he would not allow the solicitor to see her: the only visitors who were permitted interviews were the individuals who had consigned the patient to the asylum, or the local inspecting magistrates. In order to check the legality of this assertion Pemberton travelled to London to see the Commissioners in Lunacy. In fact, he was able to lay the case before Lord Shaftesbury himself, who assured the solicitor that if he put the matter into writing, Shaftesbury would insist that Metcalfe granted him four separate interviews with Mary Jane, to last four or five hours each. Pemberton additionally filed a writ against Charles Turner on Mary Jane's behalf because Charles had applied to have the Acomb House fees paid out of his wife's annual allowance, instead of being billed directly to him. The Master of the Rolls suspended these proceedings, pending a full lunacy inquisition.

The Commissioners in Lunacy visited Mary Jane at Acomb House on 28 May, five months after her committal; but during their talk, Mary Jane did not speak of her maltreatment. When asked later about this curious omission she explained that as soon as she knew there was to be an inquisition, she decided to withhold her evidence of abuse until the full hearing. But she did make an allegation of poisoning: as late as May 1858, Mary Jane had become distressed and violent at the belief that the beer she drank at Acomb House had been tampered with.

When the York Castle inquisition began, Mary Jane had a long sotto voce conversation with Commissioner Barlow at the far end of the room, which reporters and onlookers strained – and failed – to hear. When she was ready to address the court proper, she was described as 'a lady rather above the middle stature, of good carriage and pleasant features. She behaved with the greatest propriety throughout the inquiry . . . Her story was connected and unvarying.' Mary Jane insisted that all the doctors who claimed she was insane had been wrong. She admitted making the poisoning allegations in the latter part of 1857, but explained that she had at that time been ill and 'in difficult circumstances'. Barlow failed to draw from her an admission that her claims of poisoning had continued for months after her incarceration.

York surgeon Dr Simpson had undertaken ten interviews with Mary Jane at Acomb House, starting on 12 July 1858. He told Barlow and the jurymen that while her conversation was now more rational and consistent than it had been, he nevertheless believed that she was still of unsound mind and should therefore stay in asylum care. Dr Simpson believed that her delusion about poisoning was as strong as it had ever been and he suspected that she was now working hard to avoid using the word 'poison' – a common phenomenon among the unsound who were desperate to prove their sanity. Dr Simpson's point of view, then, left no way out for the incarcerated: those who mentioned their delusions were deemed to be 'mad', and those who failed to mention them were deemed to be 'mad' and cunning.

Two more doctors testified to her unsoundness of mind. Dr Caleb Williams, an eminent local physician associated with the Quaker-founded York Retreat since 1824, had interviewed Mary Jane nine times in the past few days and found her to be delusional and unsound. With asylum care, he estimated, she could fully recover her wits in six to eighteen months' time. Dr Swaine, the medical visitor at Acomb House, and one of the magistrate-appointed visiting physicians to the West Riding's lunatic asylums, also believed that she was as unsound as she had been upon admission.

On Mary Jane's side, Dr George Wilkin said that he had spoken to her the night before at the Royal Station Hotel in York, in a room set aside for these rather desperate-looking last-ditch interviews. He testified that she seemed to be perfectly able to manage her affairs. Dr Wilkin believed that delusions could not be suppressed: they came pouring out as soon as you touched 'the chord', as he put it, and he had not managed to get Mary Jane to mention poisoning, despite his repeatedly touching that chord during the interview.

John Owen had for thirty-four years been the keeper of Tue Brook Asylum near Liverpool. He too had spoken with Mary Jane at the Station Hotel and had found nothing unsound about her – she had been entirely coherent and rational. Owen believed that cruel treatment increased 'erroneous impressions', and that quiet and kindness were essential to removing delusional thoughts. Under cross-examination he stated that a lunatic would indeed be able to suppress mention of delusions for one or two interviews; but despite this, he was sure that Mary Jane was sane.

A letter was then read out by Mary Jane's counsel, written by the patient when she was at Acomb House, in which she (correctly) stated that Metcalfe had £57 of hers in his keeping that she felt should be in her possession so that she could earn interest on it. This was offered to the inquisition as proof that she was capable of managing her affairs.

John William Metcalfe's admission to the inquisition of his use of foul language and behaviour astonished the onlookers. He made no attempt to lie his way out of trouble, perhaps because his own case-book notes on Mary Jane ('specious, mendacious, ignorant, beastly') were documentary proof of his appalling attitude towards the patient. Metcalfe confessed that he had called her a whore, had not left the room when she undressed and had once seized her by the neck and thrown her to the ground, though he denied having ever beaten her. He said that excessive force had not been used to remove her from her lodgings in Little Blake Street after her second escape; that when she had cried out, it had been an expression of rage, not pain; and that his wife had been present throughout, so he was clearly not about to attempt anything improper. Metcalfe made little attempt to justify himself, except to say that he had regarded Mary Jane as troublesome and that he had other patients to think of when she was refusing to do as she was told. No complaints had ever been made against him, he said, and the Commissioners in Lunacy archives do not reveal any previous history of mismanagement or cruelty concerning Metcalfe. In fact, Commissioner Bryan Waller Procter – in a letter that belies his reputation for humanity and gentlemanliness – wrote to John Forster, 'It is perhaps best, on the whole, that we should prosecute. But I am sorry for the man, who has had to deal with a woman of a decided character, in many ways.'

When Charles Turner stood up to testify, Edwin James, counsel for Mary Jane (and Lady Lytton's old enemy), asked him, 'You would be sorry to have her called a "sanctified pious whore"?' Charles replied, 'I should be sorry to hear her called anything at all.' By her husband's request, Mary Jane had been temporarily liberated from Metcalfe's institution for the duration of the hearing and had been permitted to stay under Pemberton's protection. 'Convey my gratitude to Mr Turner,' Mary Jane rather formally said to his solicitor.

Charles revealed to the jurymen the distressing details of how the marriage had failed and of the violent assaults he had been subjected to, because of Mary Jane's jealousy. He strongly denied Edwin James's insinuation that he would be £800 better off if his wife were to be declared a lunatic, because he would be made a member of the committee in charge of her estate and the asylum fees would become chargeable to her own savings, not to his separation payments. After Pemberton and Shaftesbury's intervention, Mary Jane had been able to write to her husband from Acomb House. She sent Charles twelve letters, of which he destroyed ten, for reasons he would not reveal to Edwin James. But in one of them she accused Charles of having had her locked up for financial reasons. The rest of the letters, Charles told the inquisition, had been kind, coherent and affectionate, though he felt that certain paragraphs had been dictated to her by Pemberton, in order to make Mary Jane appear sane. (Both patient and solicitor said that this was not true.)

During his two-hour summing-up on the second day of the hearing, Edwin James heavily implied that, although a basically good man, Charles had raked up unpleasant private marital matters in order to try to prove Mary Jane's insanity. Was a woman to be deemed insane because she was jealous and angry? He had kept her as his mistress for years before marrying her, was then absent for long spells, and had on one occasion told their servants not to obey any instructions from their mistress. No wonder she had been roused to physical anger. Women's passions were warmer than those of men, insisted James, appealing to the chivalry of the all-male jury. Should she be 'immured' just for those two acts of violence? he inquired of them (appearing to hope that the broken skull could be passed off as ordinary anger).

It was more difficult to pass off her beliefs that she had been poisoned as compatible with a sound mind: this was a woman who had travelled from town to town with a box of bodily substances, claiming that a variety of relatives and acquaintances were trying to kill her. But surely, claimed James (pushing his luck), this was the sort of suspicion that had crossed 'all of our minds when we have felt unwell'. And he was certain that she no longer laboured under this mistaken impression. His appeal cleverly played upon the heightened wariness of the mid-Victorian mind following the infamous case of the Rugeley Poisoner, the respectable William Palmer, executed in 1856 for poisoning various equally respectable family members and friends; two years later, the poison panic was still unsettling some people.

James set up an Aunt Sally for the lunacy certification. He claimed that Reverend Redhead had been a very unwise choice of person for Charles to have turned to for help. He painted Redhead as a slippery customer: not only had his affidavits provided two conflicting accounts of the druggist's shop incident, but James claimed that the reverend had subsequently travelled to Scarborough, 'broken into' Mary Jane's cottage and seized and sold off her belongings, handing the proceeds over to Charles. Moreover, James heavily implied that Redhead and his wife had become so fond of the Turners' daughter, Ellen, that the reverend wished Ellen's mother entirely out of the way. Charles may well have been seriously ill at the time of Mary Jane's certification, but Edwin James nevertheless summoned up the spectre of a husband who saw the asylum as granting him relief from a troublesome wife and employed Redhead to make all the arrangements.

Working himself up to his finale, James made a crude appeal to domesticity and paternalism, which failed to express much of the reality of the Turner case: English womanhood must be liberated from the dungeon (or attic) of such a brute as Metcalfe. He called upon the 'fathers, husbands and brothers' of the jury to give their verdict in favour of the lady, 'and then they would go to their homes with satisfied conscience, and in quietness and peace would lay their heads upon their pillows'.

Commissioner Barlow sent the jury out, telling them that he would need the agreement of at least twelve of the twenty jurymen. He told them that it could be accepted that Mary Jane had been of unsound mind last December, and so the question for them to consider was whether she had 'recovered her intellect'. Whatever they decided, 'considerable caution' would be required with regard to any future treatment – they would not be condemning her to Acomb House if they were to find her insane.

Half an hour later, the jury returned the majority verdict of thirteen to seven that Mary Jane was of sound mind. John Clough, the foreman (who had not been among the thirteen), also handed in a note expressing their disgust with Metcalfe's behaviour, and praying that the Commissioners in Lunacy would see fit to punish him.

This looks a rather perverse verdict – Mary Jane had still not stopped talking about widespread attempts to poison her, as late as six weeks before the opening of the inquisition – and is likely to have been a protest vote against inhumane treatment. It appears on the face of it similar to the actions of juries at many criminal trials of the early decades of the century, who had increasingly refused to bring in a guilty verdict when a property crime with no accompanying violence carried the death sentence. This behaviour by juries on capital cases had significantly contributed to the erosion of the Bloody Code. The Turner verdict may well show a jury refusing to condemn an unsound individual to the type of incarceration that Acomb House exemplified.

Mary Jane became a national heroine, and for the next month or so, her experiences at Acomb House filled newspapers and periodicals. By downplaying, or overlooking, her use of the poker to break her husband's skull in 1850, the press was able to fashion her into a more sympathetic victim of the lunacy laws than Lady Lytton. Her jealousy had been caused, they believed, by her being too loving a wife; the knotted-sheet escapade and the long walk to Leeds showed pluck, spirit, a love of liberty; and at the York Castle hearing, reporters had admired her dignified stoicism. What gave the story an extra frisson was the fact that Mary Jane's sufferings had come to light by chance: if Pemberton had not had the good fortune to have come across Lord Shaftesbury himself that day at the Commissioners' offices, and Charles Turner hadn't chosen to challenge how the asylum fees were paid, then Metcalfe's cruelties would not have emerged. So how typical of English asylums was Metcalfe's cruel regime at Acomb House? Was it a one-off, or representative of asylum life? The nation pondered these questions throughout late July and August 1858.

Could a Metcalfe simply break into English homes and steal away our English wives and declare them madwomen? *The Standard* wondered. The *Derby Mercury* pointed out that Mary Jane's mind must, in fact, have been uncommonly sound for her not to have disintegrated under six months of appalling treatment. To avoid the recurrence of such an error, the newspaper argued, a jury ought to see an alleged lunatic before incarceration and not after – the very procedure that the Alleged Lunatics' Friend Society had been demanding for twenty years.

The *Morning Chronicle* savaged the bureaucrats, stating that the Lunacy Commission's annual reports 'show that everything is *couleur de rose*' in the nation's madhouses. The Commissioners, the newspaper pointed out, restricted themselves to highlighting the occasional case of mechanical restraint or the problematic legal wording of a certificate. These instances elicited minor punishments and were only publicised 'for the purpose of disarming suspicion', the *Chronicle* sneered. What the Commission reports dealt in were 'easy platitudes . . . soothing generalisations . . . [and] . . . gratifying averages'. If Acomb House were not immediately shut and Metcalfe prosecuted, the Commissioners must be considered to be nothing more than 'an ambulatory sham', one provincial newspaper argued. The mass-market *Lloyd's Weekly Newspaper*, on the other hand, could not get one particular image out of its mind: 'Madwomen to lie nude upon straw!' (Straw had never come into the story.)

One week after the verdict, Lunacy Commissioners James Wilkes and Robert Skeffington Lutwidge opened an inquiry into Metcalfe's behaviour, at the Royal Station Hotel in York. There was uproar when Lutwidge announced that the hearing was to take place behind closed doors, as any evidence given could prove to be prejudicial to a future criminal trial. The *York Herald* was just one of many newspapers angered that a veil was being drawn across a matter of supreme public concern: 'No act could be more indifferent to, or defiant of, public opinion. The case is the subject of conversation in all circles and classes, and every man amongst us, when reflecting upon the inviolability of his personal liberty, regards it as one of tremendous social importance.' Yet somebody inside the room leaked details to the *Herald*, which were swiftly repeated in other newspapers. It transpired that Mary Jane had spoken for over four hours to Lutwidge and Wilkes about Metcalfe and his attendants committing 'bodily torture' upon her, of beatings, persistent verbal abuse and being kept alone in darkness. Mrs Sargison, her York landlady, confirmed to the two Commissioners the violence of Mary Jane's recapture at Little Blake Street on 2 April. Metcalfe's wife Harriet and attendant Merindah Hall denied all the allegations, with the exception of one incident, when Metcalfe pushed Mary Jane to the floor.

The Commissioners decided to prosecute Metcalfe at the winter assizes at York. But the asylum keeper and his wife fled to the Continent, and so it was in his absence that on 9 December a verdict was returned against him for assault, but only as a 'misdemeanour'. The most serious part of the charge – beating and wounding – was 'not found' by the grand jury. It had been a sloppily put together case, and the judge, Mr Baron Watson, when asked for a bench warrant to apprehend Metcalfe, said that he had neither depositions nor an affidavit, and was not willing to proceed on the reports of newspapers alone. He was eventually persuaded to issue the warrant but Metcalfe never did return to England to stand trial; the Census of 1881 lists him living in Jersey, aged sixty-two, describing himself as 'in the medical profession, not practising'.

The huge press furore of 1858 led to a backlash from the alienist profession. In an eight-page article, 'The Newspaper Attack on Private Lunatic Asylums' in the *Journal of Mental Science*, its editor, Dr John Charles Bucknill, accused 'the mob of newspaper writers' of outrageous libels. Bucknill believed the Turner jury's verdict had flown in the face of all the available evidence. And rather than being pleased at how swiftly Metcalfe had been dealt with, the press claimed that the Turner case was typical of private care, rather than exceptional. From around 140 individuals in England and Wales who were licensed to receive insane people into their private institutions, just one 'unhappy person has been found unworthy of the trust reposed in him', Bucknill wrote. 'Ought they not rather to have dwelt upon the fact that the keepers of asylums are exposed to more intense provocation, to loss of self-control, than perhaps any other men, and yet that this has been the solitary instance in which foul language and harsh conduct has been brought home to any one of them.'

Bucknill conceded that far too many general medical practitioners were 'lamentably ignorant' of mental illness, and that consequently many of the certificates of insanity they signed had little diagnostic meaning and did nothing more than legally permit institutionalisation to take place. But it was not the fault of the asylum proprietor if the lunacy law was faulty and could be taken advantage of by malicious relatives or associates. 'It is a wonderful thing this newspaper press of ours,' Bucknill concluded, 'the fifth estate as it is called, the bulwark of right, the palladium of liberty, the great engine of education, the universal instructor of the people in all that is right, and, we must add, in all that is wrong, the fountain of the pure waters of truth but alas, sometimes also the sewer of calumnious falsehood.'

Mary Jane Turner died seventeen years later, in Isleworth in Middlesex, at the age of fifty-six; she does not appear to have been under any certificate of lunacy in her remaining years. The hope of those who had followed the case – that the Turners' passion could be rekindled – came to nothing. Charles remarried immediately upon her death, and when his second wife died, he married yet again, at the age of seventy-six. His standing had not been damaged by the lunacy inquisition, and he continued to work as the Bankruptcy Court official assignee until his retirement in 1871.

Mrs Turner had fascinated the nation as one of its favourite archetypes: a female victim of violence, imprisonment and humiliation, whose only fault was that she had loved her husband too powerfully (the assaults she had made upon him had had to be rewritten as 'passion' for this narrative to work). But the two further lunacy dramas of 1858 featured males whose behaviour had strained hard at the conventions of mid-century manliness.

Laurence Ruck was a gentleman farmer in Montgomeryshire, with an annual income of £1,500. He had married Mary Ann Matthews of Aberdovey in 1841, and by 1857 the couple had six children. Mr Ruck had always enjoyed a convivial drink, but in the spring of 1856 friends and locals noticed a swift deterioration in his behaviour. One night, after a dinner party at the home of his friend, Mr Thurston, the two men had retired from the other guests to smoke in the drawing room, where Mr Ruck downed a large brandy, yowled like a beast and kicked Mr Thurston hard in the stomach. He rushed out on to the lawn, where – with all the dining-room guests looking on – he committed 'an act of indecency', before disappearing into the night.

Thurston later stated that his friend had previously been of a shy and eccentric nature but that of late, he and others had noticed Mr Ruck walking in the country lanes with a strange pigeon-toed gait, looking wild, dishevelled and vacant. 'There is poor Ruck, gone mad,' Thurston remarked to his wife one day when, out driving in their carriage, they passed him in a lane. On another occasion, Ruck rode his horse straight at Thurston, who was on foot, shouting that he intended to kill him.

The Rucks' home, Pantlludw, was a cosy house set on a plateau on a thickly wooded hillside. Mr Ruck was busy remodelling it and creating intricate, rhododendron-lined paths, croquet grounds, a lily garden and a waterfall. It was 'a little fairy-story house in the middle of a wood', one family member later recalled. 'There was something wonderfully secret and peaceful about it.' Mrs Ruck and the children had removed themselves to her family home, eight miles away in Aberdovey, as the renovations got under way, though her husband would sometimes stay at Aberdovey, too. There would later be conflicting evidence about the state of the marriage, with Mary Ann and others saying that it was always close and affectionate, and that they never quarrelled; and Mr Ruck alleging that from two years after their marriage, Mary Ann had refused to have intercourse with him, and spent as much time as she could away from Pantlludw. With a number of Ruck children being conceived up until 1856, it is clear that they did still have sexual relations; affection – and consent – cannot be demonstrated, of course.

Pantlludw near Machynlleth in mid-Wales. The Rucks' home was on a hillside and was 'a little fairy-story house in the middle of a wood', one family member later recalled. But it was here that Laurence Ruck's behaviour became extremely odd.

Mr Ruck would often stay at the Wynnstay Arms in Machynlleth, where his 'excitability' was noted by staff and guests. He once took all his clothes off and told the staff he wished 'all the girls to see him so'. He also offered the landlady £500 if she would procure him a nursemaid he could have intercourse with, and offered £300 to the postman to be able to sleep with his wife. He would shout out in the public rooms, 'Mary Jones [his wife's cousin] has had two children by me. She has murdered them both. Here is a lock of their hair, and I shall be swung [hanged] for it.'

At Pantlludw one day, he locked himself into the drawing room and on the carpet constructed a bonfire of his clothing, and set it alight. He employed workmen to sink a shaft on his land to prospect for copper and iron ore. In a large trunk he kept a huge collection of corkscrews, string, candle stubs, chisels, bits of bread, stones, walnuts and pieces of old paper, and he would repeatedly unpack these, throw them at his wife, then repack them carefully. Servants were hard to keep. Mr Ruck would walk around the house at night with a candle, wandering in and out of everyone's rooms though not saying or doing anything; servants would often wake up screaming at the sight of him in his nightshirt. One day, when the rest of the staff were out of the house, he locked Mary Jones (who helped to look after the Ruck children) in her room and shouted through the door that he was going to shoot her (he owned at least four firearms). She wasn't rescued for a day and a half.

Mrs Ruck had the worst of it, though. Her husband would drive his carriage out into the countryside at three in the morning, and she would often go out into the woods and fields to coax him home. Much, much worse were his increasing accusations that she had been repeatedly unfaithful to him: he would accuse her of the 'grossest improprieties' in 'the most coarse and disgusting language'.

In October 1857, the couple embarked on a journey to Welshpool and then Manchester, before heading south to Berkshire, to visit friends in Reading. The excursion involved rail and horse-drawn vehicles, and Mr Ruck drank heavily throughout – and loudly accused Mary Ann of infidelity with any stranger who entered their carriage or coach. Their travelling companion was retired surgeon Richard Barnett, who had known the Rucks for years; Mr Ruck now accused Barnett of attempting to poison him so that he could make off with Mary Ann. When staying at hotels, Mr Ruck claimed that his wife and strange men made indecent signals to each other; he accused her of being a prostitute and said that the telegraph wires were 'speaking north, south, east and west' about her. The two alleged dead children of Mary Jones had been 'tormenting him and talking to him all night', he said, adding that Jones had murdered them.

By the time they reached Reading, Mr Barnett and Mary Ann had become convinced that Mr Ruck was a danger to other people, and possibly to himself. They called in Dr John Conolly.

Dr Conolly interviewed Mr Ruck on 3 November and was told all the stories about Mrs Ruck having connection with any man who had got into their carriage or compartment. 'My opinion is that Mr Ruck entertains insane delusions of a dangerous kind, and requires restraint,' the doctor wrote on the lunacy certificate, taking special note of Mr Ruck's ownership of firearms. The second certificate was signed by Richard Barnett, who also wrote out the lunacy order for Mary Ann to sign – including the phrases, 'partly hereditary', 'partly from intemperance' and 'profligate in his expenditure'. By law, this document was supposed to record only the signatory's words and beliefs. In fact, Mary Ann did not know whether there was any insanity in the Ruck line, and later admitted that she had not read the lunacy order. Barnett claimed that he had read it over to her and that he had once heard Mary Ann say that Ruck's late father and his brother were both 'eccentrics'.

Mr Ruck found himself in Moorcroft House, where Dr George Stillwell – the nephew of Louisa Nottidge's custodian, Dr Arthur Stillwell – had taken over as proprietor. Mr Ruck's keepers – two brothers, called Randall – could see little the matter with the patient, who was permitted huge amounts of freedom. He did not attempt to escape during fox and stag hunts arranged by the asylum, or the long rambles in the meadows close to Moorcroft.

On 14 November 1857 Lunacy Commissioners Campbell and Gaskell made their first of four visits. 'We have conversed with Mr Ruck and find that he is considerably improved and will shortly be discharged,' they recorded. 'It does not appear to us, however, that the delusions under which he labours are entirely removed.' Mr Ruck persisted in telling the Commissioners and a succession of doctors that his wife had been 'befouled' by other men; he also remarked that he would 'go two miles out of his way to avoid red petticoats'.

Dr Stillwell forbade anyone to visit Mr Ruck without the say-so of Mrs Ruck, as signatory of the lunacy order. All Mr Ruck's outgoing correspondence was sent straight to his wife and never reached its addressees. When Mary Ann came to see her husband, one of the Randall brothers was requested by Dr Stillwell to spy through the keyhole; he reported that the couple were very affectionate with each other. But on later visits, Mr Ruck reiterated his accusations of adultery; Stillwell advised Mary Ann that it was best if she did not visit again, as it seemed to 'excite' him. Mr Ruck did manage to persuade one of the Randalls to post a letter for him in a postbox in Hillingdon, and in this way he was able to make contact with a solicitor, George Wainewright.

Mr Ruck's brothers and sisters-in-law all believed in Ruck's sanity and were furious to learn that hereditary insanity had been alleged, when no Ruck had ever been lunatic. It was on their advice that Mr Wainewright travelled to Montgomeryshire to gather first-hand testimonies. Here, he discovered that Mary Ann Ruck was very highly thought of in the locality and many people were willing to testify in writing that her husband's allegations against her could only be explained by the increasing amount of alcohol he had been imbibing. This was the defence that solicitor Wainewright intended to use at the forthcoming inquisition; here was a plausible explanation for a basically sane man engaging in outrageous slanders. When, at last, on 14 June 1858, Mr Wainewright was able to inform his client of all these testimonials to his wife's virtue and his own out-of-character behaviour, Mr Ruck announced, 'What a fool I must have been!', as though the solution to his dilemma had suddenly been found. And it is with this narrative – that he had been drunk, and not delusional – that Mr Ruck, his counsel and supporters came to the lunacy inquisition, petitioned for by Mrs Ruck, at St Clement's Inn, Strand. It was a horrific ordeal for thirty-five-year-old Mary Ann; the awful testimony she had to relate and listen to 'showed only her patience and fortitude', in *The Times*'s view.

Mr Ruck's counsel admitted his odd behaviour between spring 1856 and November 1857: all he had to do now was to continue to abstain from alcohol and his delusions would remain at bay. However, several of the Welsh witnesses called by Mary Ann's counsel did not agree that drink had been at the heart of the problem. One of the Pantlludw servants, Mrs Williams, stated that Mr Ruck had appeared more 'wandering' than drunk when setting fires in the drawing room, or unpacking and repacking his rubbish-filled trunk; indeed, when he was 'tipsy' he tended, rather, to be 'quiet', she said. A local surgeon, Hugh Lloyd, told the inquisition that Mr Ruck's behaviour had not resembled any case of delirium tremens he had ever seen. Lloyd described Mrs Ruck as 'a model of a woman', but like each of the male witnesses testifying on behalf of Mrs Ruck, Lloyd was required to answer whether he had ever had 'connection' with her. Protests were voiced at this attempt to smear Mrs Ruck's reputation in trying to defend her husband's sanity, but the presiding Commissioner refused to intervene, although he knew that this was a 'painful' case and that 'no one could help feeling commiseration for the unhappy lady'.

The jury requested Mr Ruck to speak for himself and answer questions directly, and so Ruck – described in *The Times* as 'gentlemanly', close to forty years of age, of dark complexion and with a slight beard – stated calmly and quietly that the delusions had been 'the result of a disordered imagination', and had entirely left him. He no longer believed in his wife's infidelity, but he admitted that he had fathered two children upon his wife's cousin, Mary Jones, as part of an ongoing clandestine affair, while Mrs Ruck was away from Pantlludw during the renovations. Mr Ruck told the inquisition that the strain of trying to keep this long-standing sexual relationship secret from his wife had led him to drink heavily. But he also blamed his lover: Jones would never tell him the whereabouts of his illegitimate children, which increased his anxiety and led to his mental confusion.

As with females accused of 'moral insanity', a man's inability to fill his domestic role as a loving husband and respect-inspiring father could contribute heavily to an accusation of unsoundness of mind. A number of women in the nineteenth century were using the lunacy laws as a way of removing from their home a violent or extremely uncongenial paterfamilias – cheaper and less humiliating than a trip to the magistrate or (after 1857) the Divorce Court. The cases of Arthur Nowell (p. 432), John Gould (p. 398), Arthur Legent Pearce (p. 398) and Richard Hall (p. 437) appear to have had this subtext, with sympathetic doctors using the concept of moral insanity to help a wife to make the family home safe from a thuggish husband.

To excuse his illicit affair with Mary Jones, Mr Ruck laid the blame upon his wife. While Mrs Ruck's camp maintained that the marriage had been a happy one, Mr Ruck and his blood family stressed that it had failed by 1843, the year in which they alleged that Mrs Ruck made clear to her husband her aversion to intercourse with him. Mrs Ruck's failure to be a good wife had led Mr Ruck to be a bad husband, was their argument; and he had turned to heavy drinking to cope with the stress of the situation.

Mr Ruck told the jury he had been rushed into an asylum by a vengeful wife, when all he had needed was to be sent somewhere quiet so that he could stop drinking and recover his wits. Testifying on his behalf, alienist Dr Harrington Tuke told the jury that 'mania from drink' was the second most easily curable form of insanity (after puerperal, or post-natal, mania). Seven other high-profile doctors testified that Mr Ruck's was a case of 'drinking mania', that asylum incarceration was inappropriate and that the delusions would not recur so long as he did not drink.

Some specialists writing in these years estimated that perhaps as many of one-fifth of certified male lunatics had had their insanity brought on by drink, and while many delirium tremens cases got out of the asylum quickly, other men would spend years going in and out of asylum care, regaining a 'sound mind' but then returning to inebriation upon their release. Despite his boost from the eminent Harrington Tuke and his like-minded colleagues, the case for Mr Ruck's sanity did not look good. At Moorcroft House, the patient had had no access to alcohol, yet as late as May 1858, when he had been 'dry' for seven months, he was still rambling on about red petticoats, murdered children and his wife's gargantuan erotic appetite.

However, all of this was about to become mere background to a more elemental battle: the inquisition now turned into a trial of the workings of the certification system. George Stillwell was asked why he had written 'hereditary predisposition' next to Mr Ruck's name in the Moorcroft House casebook, even though it transpired that the Ruck family had never been affected by unsound minds. Stillwell replied that this was what he had been told by Drs Conolly and Barnett.

The casebooks furnished even more contentious data. Stillwell kept his books a little too diligently, because alongside Mr Ruck's notes was the information that John Conolly had been paid £15 by Stillwell for the admission of Mr Ruck to Moorcroft; it was also confirmed that Conolly was to receive a further £60 a year in connection with Ruck's detention at the asylum. That is, Mr Ruck would have to stay there if Conolly was to receive the £60. This looked very much like a conspiracy – and similar to one of John Perceval's blackest accusations: that money changed hands for the arrest and ongoing detention of doubtfully certificated English folk.

After a twenty-minute conference, the Clement's Inn jury returned a majority verdict of twelve to six in favour of Mr Ruck's sanity. It was greeted with loud cheering throughout the hall.

The newspaper storms created by the Lytton and Turner cases blew once again. The *Daily News* led the charge: comparing the English asylum to the 'bastille', its editorial stated, 'The question now becomes ventilated more and more every day. We thought it bad enough; but we were far from being prepared for the startling revelations brought to light by judicial investigations . . . Dr Conolly . . . breaks the spirit of the law, if not its express words, by consigning a rich patient – one for whom £400 a year is to be paid – to an asylum from which he receives an emolument.'

However, the *Journal of Mental Science* came out strongly in defence of Stillwell, stating:

> We do not entertain the shadow of a doubt that when Mr Ruck was admitted into Hillingdon House [*sic*] he was a dangerous lunatic . . . Granted that the certificate of insanity signed by Mr Barnett of Reading was a document most carelessly drawn up, and for scientific purposes worth as little as the certificates of medical men practically ignorant of mental disease usually are, what business was that of Dr Stillwell's, so long as the document was legally complete, and the patient when brought to his house was actually insane? If Dr Stillwell had not been able to satisfy himself of Mr Ruck's insanity after his admission into Hillingdon, we do not doubt that he would have effected that gentleman's speedy discharge.

The following year, Laurence Ruck sued Doctors Stillwell, Conolly and Barnett for assault and imprisonment. The case hinged upon Dr Conolly's relationship with Moorcroft House. It was illegal for a proprietor, partner or 'regular professional attendant' of an asylum to sign an alleged lunatic into that institution. Stillwell's casebooks strongly demonstrated formal links between himself and Conolly: there, in neat columns, it was written that Conolly received 15 per cent of the asylum's annual profits, in the form of regular payments in connection with eighteen of Moorcroft's forty patients. The judge found in Mr Ruck's favour and awarded damages of £500 against Conolly.

Dr John Conolly (1794–1866) was one of the country's most respected, and well-liked, alienists, but his involvement in the Ruck case damaged his standing.

In September 1859, Mrs Ruck felt she could no longer remain where her married life had so mortified her. On the day that she and her belongings were to set out from her parental home for a new life in London, the locals descended upon her to make a speech of appreciation and a presentation. To show their support during the 'unexampled trials of latter times', they had clubbed together to buy her a £50 clock, while the younger 'labouring-class' inhabitants ('these kindly Celts', as a newspaper called them) had paid for a morocco-leather-bound Welsh bible, so that she would not forget her native tongue. Mary Ann was unable to finish her thank-you speech for weeping in gratitude.

However, much against the odds, the couple appear eventually to have resumed an at least superficially cordial marriage. When Charles Darwin and his family came for a two-day visit to Pantlludw, ten years later, the Rucks seemed to be nothing other than a conventional couple. In 1874, Darwin's son Frank married the Rucks' daughter, Amy

Richenda; Amy died shortly after giving birth, two years later, but the two families remained close. Both Mary Ann and Laurence corresponded with Charles Darwin on such rustic curiosities as castrated lambs' horns, and whether sheep walk upwards or sideways when grazing on steep slopes. The 1891 Census records Laurence living in Aberdovey as a lodger with one Mary Morris, a fifty-six-year-old widow, and her daughter, Sarah. It is possible that Mr Ruck kept up a second ménage, and it is even possible the widow Morris was the Mary Jones of the 1850s. Rackety marital compromises of this kind were not so very unusual, the trick being to disguise the often polymorphous nature of Victorian bourgeois private lives – sexual selection having to go on furtively.

Mary Ann and Laurence Ruck in later years, top step, right hand side;
somehow they managed to patch up their marriage.

Mary Ann seemed to settle into a happy old age, living on until 1905. Her grandson, Bernard Darwin, recalled her in his autobiography as 'the noblest creature I have ever known' – proud, kind, unselfpitying. The Rucks were very unlike the 'predictable' Darwins, being 'exciting and adventurous, with a greater capacity for sudden plunges'. Darwin recalled Mary Ann and Laurence's life at Pantlludw as 'idyllic' – a rosy memory of childhood no doubt, but it seems that the relationship in old age may have been more than just a shabby compromise.

The Commissioners in Lunacy investigated the Conolly–Stillwell matter and found that their arrangement had been of 'a highly objectionable nature'; they stipulated that in future, Conolly should only be paid by Stillwell for individual medical visits to the asylum. Those Moorcroft patients whose certificates had been signed by Conolly had to be re-certified by another physician. Conolly, for his part, refused to alter his opinion of Mr Ruck, stating, a year later, 'I am perfectly satisfied that the patient was insane . . . his delusions were very serious, gross and dangerous.'

'God bless and reward him!' Dickens's *Household Words* had chirruped of Dr Conolly in November 1857 – the very month he had juggled Mr Ruck into Moorcroft. But despite Boz's warmth, Conolly's reputation was soiled. Six years later, Charles Reade would model his villainous alienist in *Hard Cash*, Dr Wycherley, largely upon Conolly. This horrified Dickens, who had begun serialising the work without having realised the attack that was to be mounted upon his hero in later chapters.

Around the same time, another celebrated alienist, Dr Forbes Benignus Winslow, was experiencing a similar loss of face, and the disapprobation of a jury. Winslow, like Conolly, was a big cheese; but the calamities of 1858 meant that he, too, was starting to smell past his best as another inquisition got under way.

Reverend William Leach had never striven to hide the three mental breakdowns he had suffered. In 1841, when he was aged thirty-seven, and again in 1852, he recovered fully after a short spell of erratic behaviour and mental confusion. Then in May 1853, he broke all the windows in the home that he shared with his mother in Southwick Street, Bayswater, West London, in order, he claimed, to allow the neighbours to be better able to hear his flute-playing; he was found attempting to get a tune out of an enema syringe. His family consulted Dr Winslow, who, hearing of his previous recoveries, advised that an attendant should come to live at the family home to keep a watch on William. Again, the reverend recovered.

Leach had been married but when his wife died, he had returned to live with his mother, Julia. The daughter of a baronet, Julia Leach was in her seventies, and her will bequeathed William £30,000. Her

only other child, Mrs Laura Sidden, was to receive £17,000. Mrs Leach
watched with annoyance as her son's study of Scripture took him
further and further from conventional Anglican beliefs. William told
his mother that the Day of Judgement was at hand and that all social
distinctions had therefore been abolished. Servants and poor people
were henceforth to be more kindly treated, and he insisted it was
God's wish that the staff at the Bayswater house eat at the dining
table with the family. Mrs Leach strongly objected, and when the rows
between them became more frequent and embittered, Reverend Leach
moved out of the house, leasing a cottage in Hammersmith.

Here, his servants took all their meals with him, he would kiss each
of the maids on the cheek in the morning and invited them to sit
upon his knee. He would play whist with the staff until 3 a. m. and
between deals would read to them from the Bible. When a succession
of armed burglaries was causing alarm among householders in West
London, and after an attempt had been made to break into his
Hammersmith home, Reverend Leach had purchased pistols and
undertaken target practice.

In June 1856, Leach agreed to a request by his brother-in-law, Dr
Henry Sidden, to undertake a financial transaction by which each of
the two men would receive £1,194. All concerned clearly considered
him of sound enough mind to complete this legal procedure. Sidden
retained almost all of the money in order to invest it for the reverend.

Then, six months later, the reverend told his family that he was planning to marry. He had been working very hard, he said, owing to the
illness of the rector of the church he was attached to, and when he
looked back at his career, he recognised that after the death of his wife,
the hard work he had undertaken for the church had 'placed him for a
great many years without any society, having no one about him but his
servants'; their company proved the perfect relaxation after long hours
of study. Leach abhorred the sort of man who would live with a woman
unmarried, or visit 'houses where men are in the habit of gratifying
their passions'. And so he had decided to marry one of his maids: Ann
Messenger, aged twenty-three, was a 'very well-conducted young
woman', he said, and he believed he 'should be very happy with her'.
He had already received the consent of her parents.

The Leaches immediately contacted Dr Winslow, who sent along
the medical superintendent of his asylum, Sussex House. Posing as a

deputation seeking advice about local parish schools, Superintendent Bartlett and two Sussex House keepers arrived unannounced at the reverend's home and as the bogus conversation got under way, the keepers pinioned him and then drove him off in the asylum carriage to the nearby institution.

Sussex House in Fulham Palace Road, Hammersmith, West London, was the Winslow family's asylum for males; across the road was Brandenburgh House, for females. Charing Cross Hospital now stands on the site of Sussex House.

During his detention at Sussex House, Reverend Leach would stand for hours with his arms stretched before him; he told Dr Winslow that he was praying for the return of the Church's 'miraculous gifts' – to bring the dead back to life, to heal the sick and to restore sight to the blind. When the doctor requested that the reverend trim his long beard, Leach informed him that the Bible stated that men who shaved were making themselves look like women. The Saviour demanded that he have a long beard.

None of Reverend Leach's friends, acquaintances and neighbours knew what had become of him. As he was popular in the locality, two tailors, a bootmaker and a builder set out to find him. When, after five months of searching, they established Leach's whereabouts, the tradesmen alerted the newspapers to his disappearance into an asylum, and in the spring of 1858 the publicity prompted the Lord Chancellor to order a lunacy inquisition. This resulted in a hung jury, and so Commissioner Barlow had to order a rerun.

At this second inquisition, Reverend Leach made a coherent defence of his religious vision, and the 'dictation' to him of the Holy Spirit, by which he tried to live his life. Dr Harrington Tuke – as in the Ruck case, testifying in favour of the sanity of the alleged lunatic – asserted that Leach's interpretations of the Bible were well within what could be considered 'normal'. Interviewing him at the asylum, Tuke had told Leach that not one clergyman in a hundred would think it acceptable to marry a servant. The reverend agreed, but – in one of several impressive displays of reasoning – told Tuke that although this was probably so, nevertheless, Ann Messenger was highly likely to make him a very good wife, and that these notional ninety-nine disapproving clergymen could not be aware of such a mitigating fact.

Dr Alexander Sutherland was present to put the opposing view. Reverend Leach's type of direct-connection religion was indicative of an unsound mind, Sutherland said, because it had no social dimension – he believed he was being addressed exclusively, not as part of a body of worshippers. What's more, Leach was delusional because he did not appear to have any awareness that his beliefs were in contravention of traditional Anglicanism: 'We are guided by the ordinary operations of the Holy Spirit; Mr Leach thinks that he is guided by the extraordinary operation. Our judgment is assisted; Mr Leach considers that his judgment is superseded by the Holy Spirit.' Like Winslow, Sutherland believed that Leach was exploited by his servants, who were using his credulity and generosity for their own ends – and that Ann Messenger had inveigled him into marriage simply for the £30,000 inheritance.

Dr Winslow had himself rejected traditional Anglicanism and in the early 1850s had become an Evangelical. It was his Evangelicalism that was behind his determination to save lunatics from the gallows – an ethical position that had caused him to be criticised by certain sections of English society, who accused him of thwarting the process of natural justice. But Reverend Leach's own private interpretation of Scripture – in particular, his world-turned-upside-down egalitarianism – was socially and morally unacceptable to Dr Winslow, who, as a Tory, believed in the rightness of a social hierarchy. One might be kind to the poor; one did not marry them. Winslow recognised that there was no intellectual confusion on Reverend Leach's part; but 'from all the circumstances connected with the case', and bearing in mind his history of breakdowns, Winslow concluded that the reverend was not fit to manage his own affairs. He had allowed his servants to manipulate him, and this was weak-mindedness born of a delusional misreading of Scripture.

Leach's counsel asked the reverend's brother-in-law, Dr Henry Sidden, whether it was true that Sidden's wife would inherit the full £47,000 inheritance if Leach were declared insane (and therefore unable to marry, or to make a will). Yes, it was, Sidden admitted. Did Sidden think it odd that Leach was of sound enough mind in the June of 1856 to execute the deed granting Sidden £1,194, but just six months later was too mad to know who he wanted to marry? No, said Sidden, this wasn't odd. Wasn't it also true that one of the two lunacy certificates had been signed by a Dr Gray, formerly of Guy's Hospital, subsequently assistant to Dr Sidden and now, at the time of the inquisition, the witness's business partner? Sidden confirmed that this was so. This raised serious doubts about the validity of Gray's certificate, and presented the jury with the scenario of a greedy family member conspiring to divert a harmless, ageing and lonely man's inheritance into his own hands. And it was Reverend Leach's very harmlessness that was emphasised by witness after witness, while the words 'cruel' and 'cruelty' were repeatedly used to describe his detention at Sussex House.

In summing up, Leach's counsel argued that while Reverend Leach had suffered from 'acute mania', there was 'no chronic disease of the brain'. He had previously recovered swiftly from his breakdowns, and further detention in an asylum would be the worst possible option for him. The jury agreed, and by a majority of nineteen to four found Leach to be of sound mind, a verdict that was welcomed by loud applause from the spectators.

Leach intended to sue his mother for false imprisonment, but called the action off at the last moment – perhaps at the urging of his new wife. For the reverend had married Ann Messenger as soon as the inquisition was over, and the couple went on to live to great old age, with four daughters and two sons. There is no indication of any serious relapse in Reverend Leach's mental health. The troublesome inheritance was delayed by the longevity of Julia Leach, who lived to be nearly ninety, dying just ten years before her son.

*   *   *

Dr Forbes Benignus Winslow (1810–1874) ran Sussex and Brandenburgh
Houses plus a lucrative single-patient practice and was most famous for his
work on the plea of diminished responsibility in criminal trials.

The inquisition severely damaged the reputation of Dr Forbes
Benignus Winslow. He had worked extraordinarily hard – with no
financial or family advantages – to build his career; as a child, he
had been so poor that he hawked cigarettes and newspapers in the
streets of Manhattan (his widowed mother had taken her children
with her to America in the 1810s). On his return to London he studied
at University College, then qualified as MD in Aberdeen, and his
career had flourished because of his work on the acceptance of the
plea of insanity as mitigation in murder cases. In 1847 he had been
able to purchase his Hammersmith asylums – Sussex House and
nearby Brandenburgh House, for women – and the following year
founded the influential *Journal of Psychological Medicine and Mental
Pathology*. He had been seen as the saviour of Mrs Cumming,
Chancery patient Ann Tottenham and many other wealthy alleged
lunatics. In terms of reputation, he had had a great deal to lose with
the Leach case. Dr Winslow wrote to the *Morning Chronicle*, claiming
that he had never tried to keep Reverend Leach's incarceration at
Sussex House a secret; that friends and acquaintances had been given
free access to him at the asylum. Leach's solicitor replied in the

letters pages, claiming that he himself had been turned away when he had wanted to consult his client, and many of the supportive locals had been kept away too.

Winslow's career hit a further low with the Windham Commission. During this inquisition into the mental soundness of immensely wealthy William Windham, in 1862, Winslow had found himself in a minority of two alienists arguing that Windham was morally insane. From early childhood, Windham, heir to Felbrigg Hall in Norfolk and its estates, had been wild – a succession of tutors and guardians, the masters of Eton, and a variety of concerned family friends had found him impossible to reason with. He was a compulsive masturbator (even in the presence of others), gorged food and then vomited before dinner guests, and insisted on donning servants' clothing and taking on their tasks around Felbrigg Hall. He had railway guard and Post Office uniforms made for him, and, wearing the latter, caused havoc by hijacking the mail cart and driving it around the Norfolk lanes. He nearly caused a fatal train crash at Cambridge railway station when, passing himself off as a guard, he blew the whistle and one train set off into the path of another. In London, he would dress as a Metropolitan Police officer and arrest women in the Haymarket, accusing them of soliciting. He fell into the clutches of notorious courtesan and gold-digger Agnes Willoughby, and despite her common-law marriage with her pimp plus her knowledge that Windham was by now infected with syphilis, the pair married. It was at this point that Windham's only living relative, his uncle, instituted a lunacy inquisition.

At the hearing, Dr Winslow, along with Dr Thomas Mayo (Mr Perceval's bête noire at Ticehurst Asylum), asserted that Windham could not possibly run the Felbrigg estate. Yet a contingent of high-profile alienists (which included Sutherland, Tuke, Conolly and Hood) argued the opposite; the jury, astonishingly, agreed, declaring Windham of sound mind. An Englishman had the right to marry a courtesan, calamitously impersonate petty officials, vomit at table, indulge in as much solitary vice as he pleased, and spend however much cash he liked. The Windham jury rejected any attempt to medicalise his outlandish behaviour. He died just two years later, aged twenty-five, after wrecking the entire Felbrigg estate by his spending – not least the colossal £20,000 cost of the lunacy inquisition. The complexity of the evidence and the length of the inquiry meant that legal fees were extremely high, despite the legislation that had been passed to lower such costs.

William Windham, heir to Felbrigg Hall in Norfolk, shortly before his death at the age of twenty-five. His lunacy inquisition was one of the most costly ever to take place.

Winslow was heavily criticised in some quarters of the press. Dickens's *All the Year Round* savaged him, in a piece entitled 'M.D. and M.A.D.'. Men have risen to be national heroes, the article stated, precisely because of that 'unhealthy restlessness that Dr Winslow's fingers would itch to put under lock and key . . . The jury of laymen of the world came to a decision contrary to Dr Winslow's. What confidence does this give us in a mad-doctor's accuracy of opinion concerning the sanity of any one of us?' It may also have come to Dickens's ears, via his very good friend, Lunacy Commissioner John Forster, that Winslow was becoming erratic as an asylum proprietor. A young official at the War Office had come to the Commissioners in January 1862 in great distress because his sister, a patient at Brandenburgh House, had been given immediate notice to leave by Winslow, who said he had been expecting a 'better' patient. The Commissioners told the young man to go to Winslow to tell him that this was against the lunacy law; but Winslow responded that if the young man would not remove her, he would be charged a new rate of seven guineas a week – double the cost of the most exclusive of English asylums. The Commissioners now intervened to organise a transfer of the woman to the less expensive Camberwell House in south-east London.

In the mid-1860s (not long after publication of *Hard Cash*) Forbes Benignus Winslow took to his bed for a year with a never-explained illness, or possibly a mental collapse of his own – one of the colossal Evangelical breakdowns of the century, as experienced by Gladstone, Nightingale and Ruskin. When he re-emerged, he found himself relentlessly inspected and criticised by Dr Charles Lockhart Robertson, one of the Lord Chancellor's Visitors of Chancery patients, who found that Winslow was regularly detaining wealthy patients who were either recovered or would do better back at home with their families, with a keeper. Even at the time of Winslow's death in 1874 Lockhart Robertson was still springing Chancery patients from his care.

The year after the 'lunacy panic', as the nation had come to think of it, John Stuart Mill published *On Liberty*. Mill was highly critical of a lay jury deciding on matters psychological:

> There is something both contemptible and frightful in the sort of evidence on which, of late years, any person can be judicially declared unfit for the management of his affairs . . . All of the minute details of his daily life are pried into, and whatever is found which, seen through the medium of the perceiving and describing faculties of the lowest of the low, bears an appearance unlike absolute commonplace, is laid before the jury as evidence of insanity, and often with success; the jurors being little, if at all, less vulgar and ignorant than the witnesses; while the judges, with that extraordinary want of knowledge of human nature and life which continually astonishes us in English lawyers, often help to mislead them. These trials speak volumes as to the state of feeling and opinion among the vulgar with regard to human liberty. So far from setting any value on individuality – so far from respecting the right of each individual to act, in things indifferent, as seems good to his own judgment and inclinations – judges and juries cannot even conceive that a person in a state of sanity can desire such freedom.

Mill appeared not to have noticed that the juries at the Turner, Ruck and Leach inquisitions had listened to all the tales of 'personal peculiarities' and decided that they were not indicative of lunacy. Indeed, his snobbish contempt for jurymen was even more strongly expressed elsewhere, when he wrote of 'the lying gossip of low servants [which is] poured into the credulous ears of twelve petty shopkeepers, ignorant of all ways of life except those of their own class, and regarding every trait of individuality in character or taste as eccentricity, and all eccentricity as either insanity or wickedness.'

The events of 1858 had rejuvenated the Alleged Lunatics' Friend Society. In January 1859, the campaign group hosted a well-attended public meeting at Exeter Hall in the Strand, to discuss the furore of the Lytton, Turner, Ruck and Leach cases. After speeches, a resolution was passed to petition once again for a government inquiry into the operation of the lunacy laws. And this time, the request was granted.

John Perceval's brother-in-law and cousin, Spencer Horatio Walpole, Home Secretary, was in the chair of the 1859 Select Committee on Lunatics, taking evidence over several months about all aspects of lunacy administration and patient care – the question of wrongful incarceration being just one of many matters under investigation. The Select Committee understandably focused most of its attention on the public asylum system, which was by now responsible for by far the greatest number of lunatics in England and Wales. That year there were believed to be 31,510 pauper insane, whereas private patients numbered 5,269. Of greatest concern, in England and Wales, the ratio of insane to sane appeared to be inexorably on the rise.* How many of these people really required institutionalisation? it was wondered. Were the English really getting madder, or were the county asylums filling up with 'naturals' and the confused elderly, who were a danger neither to themselves nor to others? The cure rates were far lower than had been anticipated when the great asylum-building regime had commenced in 1845, so what was the purpose of these vast institutions? Warehouses for a population who could not fend for themselves in the outside world? Or had they become a means of siphoning off those whose infirmities were holding back the economic energies of their families, and therefore, collectively, of the nation?

* See Appendix 2 on p. 392 for official statistics on lunacy.

An increase in numbers was, however, also in evidence among the very wealthy. Legislation was making lunacy inquisitions cheaper and faster and by 1859 almost twice as many inquisitions were being held as in the 1840s. The aim of various Acts had been to offer greater protection to the property of a larger number of alleged lunatics; but some wondered whether – notwithstanding the failures in the Turner, Ruck and Leach cases – the Acts had encouraged a greater number of unscrupulous people to attempt to declare unsound an eccentric wealthy relative.

Ann Tottenham, the Chancery lunatic who had been helped by Admiral Saumarez and the now-beleagured Forbes Winslow, was the only victim of mis-certification permitted to testify before the Select Committee, although Mr Perceval, Admiral Saumarez, Gilbert Bolden and campaigning magistrate Purnell B. Purnell were allowed to speak at length to the inquiry. Mr Perceval was something of an anachronism, sitting there before the committee with his Regency ringlets, urging that clergymen should be involved at every level of lunacy administration, badly bodging his survey of Continental lunacy systems, and provoking his questioner to ask him not to wander off into 'abstract and rather metaphysical questions' (he had been telling them that Galileo would have fallen foul of the English lunacy laws). He told his brother-in-law and the other committee members: 'I do not know and have never pretended, and I believe none of our committee has ever pretended, that cases of unjust confinement were general, as compared with the number of persons confined as insane. But I believe that cases of unjust confinement and still more of unjust detention are very frequent and numerous.' He claimed that in addition to Ann Tottenham, the Society could have brought to the Select Committee's attention twenty-six recent or current cases of false imprisonment, and 'I believe they are only a proportion.'

Lord Shaftesbury himself testified for three whole days. While denying that sane people were ever mis-certificated, he admitted that there was good reason to worry that the private asylums were detaining people who had recovered their sanity. Shaftesbury said:

Where a proprietor is unprincipled, see what advantages he has, and what power he has over his patient . . . It is therefore in their power to retard the cure of the patients indefinitely, and the temptation is inordinately great, and it is more than human nature can ordinarily stand . . . When there is temptation such as that, can the [Select] Committee not imagine all the self-delusions that a man would practise, and the disaffection with which he would look upon any returning symptom of health, how he would consider that the matter required further consideration, and so retard the period of a discharge, if it ever took place. I am certain that the temptation is so great that few people could resist it. I do not believe in fact that any person could resist it. I am certain that I could not resist it . . . This vicious principle of profit . . . vitiates the whole thing.

Clearly referring to the cosiness uncovered in the Ruck–Conolly–Stillwell case, Shaftesbury criticised a system in which 'a medical man signs a certificate for the purpose of getting an affluent patient into some friend's house, and the friend repays that by signing a certificate for another affluent patient to go into the other's house'.

John Conolly appeared as the alienists' representative, telling the Select Committee that his profession was extremely upset at 'the supposition that they are so peculiarly mercenary as to not be trusted at all'. Conolly stated that no one was ever committed to an asylum without just cause – even if the condition turned out to be easy to cure (such as delirium tremens). As to keeping recovered patients in asylums longer than was necessary, he claimed that this happened 'very seldom'. Passing lightly over his own law-breaking in the Ruck case, he stated he had only once 'accidentally' signed a faulty certificate.

A number of measures to stamp out wrongful incarceration were under consideration in 1859, including the admission of an independent doctor three weeks after certification to check on the progress of each patient; but Conolly argued that such intervention would so dishearten the profession that the best men would leave for other medical special-isms, condemning the nation to the care of men of inferior skills and morals. And until such a time as publicly or charitably funded institu-tions could care for middle-class and upper-class patients, it was crucial to maintain the existing private licensed houses. In fact, Conolly and Shaftesbury had attempted to raise subscriptions for a state-adminis-tered middle-class asylum, charging fees according to the patient's means, but had failed to attract sufficient funds from the public, and the idea had had to be shelved. John Perceval suggested that the government buy up one of the London private asylums and try running it as an experimental middle-class state asylum, but no notice was taken of this proposal.

Conolly denied that there was any significant difference in the rates of public and private patients that were 'discharged cured'. However, John Charles Bucknill had surveyed all the nation's county asylums and reported that the average cure rate was 39 per cent. Admiral Saumarez compared this figure with the estimated cure rate of 10–14 per cent for private patients, and the appalling rate of recovery among Chancery patients, with a total of just eleven out of 900 being released from certification in the ten years to 1859. Many observers attributed this to the unnecessary detention of high-fee payers; defenders of the private asylums, on the other hand, claimed that the less shameful nature of insanity among the lower classes meant that the poor entered the system more quickly when their symptoms became apparent, received curative treatment more promptly or at the very least enjoyed respite from the aggravating factors in their home lives. Admiral Saumarez agreed that the 'absurd principle of secrecy' was putting many middle- and landed-class lunatics at risk, and Shaftesbury, too, was surprisingly in tune with the Alleged Lunatics' Friends, stating that 'many persons whose families were afflicted with lunacy think that they are keeping the fact in entire privacy, but it is an error. If there is an insane relative of any family, it is invariably known; the world may not know where he is, but no family ever succeeded in suppressing a knowledge of the fact that there was a mad member connected with it.'

In July 1860, the Select Committee published its report. While it found that there was little reason to believe that there was any significant wrongful incarceration of the wholly sane, it nevertheless recommended extending the jury system to all lunacy cases, not restricting it to those where significant property was involved. It suggested that every lunacy certificate be signed by a magistrate – the very protection already afforded to paupers – and that its validity be reduced to just three months, at which point a re-certification should take place. Versions of these latter two safeguards were already in place in Scotland.

All these measures were rejected, thwarted by Shaftesbury's ongoing chronic anxiety that anything that complicated the asylum admission procedure would build in delay in treating, and curing, mental breakdowns. He remained convinced that the best cure rates related directly to the speed with which an individual's insanity had been identified and s/he had been placed under medical supervision. The slower rate of recovery among the wealthy was, he felt sure, largely the result of families and friends attempting to hide the problem, to deny – even to themselves – that a loved one was losing their wits.

Shaftesbury also believed that his Commissioners in Lunacy were making steady progress in eradicating the worst private asylums and the most corrupt medical men by stricter licensing and more thorough inspections.

The Alleged Lunatics' Friend Society was hit hard by the non-outcome of the Select Committee they had fought so long to establish. John Perceval described the report of the Committee as 'meagre', though he failed to appreciate the Society's rather poor performance at the inquiry. By 1862, the Friends were beginning to wind down operations. Mr Perceval wrote in that year that

> however insignificant we were, we had still been able to effect a great deal of good, and might still be further successful; which, indeed, has proved to be the case, for we have this year succeeded in releasing two patients . . . There can be no doubt of the necessity of the existence of such a Society, and it grieves me that no clergyman or other gentleman can be found to join us; and I am often perplexed to think whether this arises from apathy, timidity or from ignorance.

Little is known about the final years of the Society or indeed of Mr Perceval. It seems that in his late sixties he suffered a recurrence of his psychological problems. He died in 1876, aged seventy-three, just as he would not have wished to have ended his days: in one of London's large private madhouses, Munster House, in Fulham. It is highly unlikely that he ever met the woman who took up and pressed ahead with his life's work.

9

Dialoguing with the Unseen

Something awful happened to Louisa Crookenden on her wedding night. We don't know the precise nature of her allegations against her husband: they were regarded as so shocking that they were later recorded only as a flurry of euphemism, noted down by the astonished parties who heard them. Whatever occurred on the night of 1 September 1842 – sodomy, impotence, venereal infection, or just ordinary intercourse that a sheltered twenty-one-year-old had not been forewarned of – traumatised her. Neither Louisa nor her husband, Reverend George Lowe, eight years her senior, sought a judicial separation, and between 1843 and 1863, eight children were born (of whom four lived to adulthood). But Mrs Lowe decided to live for long spells apart from her husband, sometimes with her sister, Emily, sometimes with her mother, taking one or more of the children with her.

She could well afford to make her own semi-separate life for herself. Upon her father's death, shortly before her marriage, she had inherited £10,000 and her pre-marriage settlement permitted her to keep most of her inheritance and gave her an annual income of £1,000 for her sole use. But even the wealthiest wife could not escape the marriage disabilities, which made her a non-person in the eyes of the civil law, and so her money had to be disbursed to her by a trustee.

Her marital home was the vicarage of the Devon village of Upottery, four miles from Honiton, but she found her surroundings boring and stifling. Here, life was 'speeding away in the daily round of the common task,' she wrote, 'in rural affluence and bucolic repose . . . I require a bracing climate, and Devonshire is very relaxing, and I was altogether unable to ride and walk.' So while Reverend Lowe remained at Upottery, Mrs Lowe would be away for weeks at a time, visiting Exeter, London and Oxford and travelling abroad, to Paris and the spas of

Germany. Many of these trips, she later explained, had been taken because she was 'depressed in health, and weak'; she would also allude to suffering 'nervous' trouble.

There is no record of her feelings about the loss of four of her infants; childhood mortality was so high in those years (a quarter of all deaths were of children under one year old) that the grief and distress did not necessarily receive special mention. But it cannot have failed to have deepened the sense of desolation that had come upon Louisa at the time of her marriage. She later said of these years, 'I had a good deal of trial. I had a trying life; but there was nothing which affected me, on the whole, more than it would anybody else.' But that wasn't quite right: she attempted suicide, with opium, in 1854. She was thirty-three, and pregnant with her fourth child. However, she took such a large dose that she vomited instead, and would make no further attempt to end her life.

One afternoon, she noticed her husband staring at her. 'I do believe you are mad,' he said, out of the blue. She went to see a doctor and told him of this remark, saying, 'It is very queer, I do not half like it', and the doctor just shrugged and asked, 'Have you read "The Baronet's Bride" in *Warren's Tales*?' Master in Lunacy Samuel Warren had written a successful series of short stories, and 'The Baronet's Bride' featured an insane husband, whose actions scare his wife. Mrs Lowe did not know what to make of this reference.

She had spotted that George was writing a number of letters these days, the contents and recipients of which he would not reveal to her when she asked. When she silently approached him one day and looked over his shoulder, some of the words in the letter alarmed her. Later that day, when they were taking the air, she on a pony and he on foot alongside, Louisa asked her husband what the letter had meant but he would not tell her. So she tapped the pony with her whip and off it cantered across country, to the home of the vicar of the nearby village of Colebrook, who had known her since childhood. She explained to the clergyman that she suspected some plot was being set in motion and she authorised him to act on her behalf in the event of her disappearance. She then took herself to Exeter for a few days before returning to George and their uneasy marital stalemate.

In 1867, when she was forty-six, she found the remedy for her loneliness and anxiety. A spiritualist friend persuaded her to come

Louisa Lowe turned to spiritualism to help her with her
anxiety and unhappiness.

along to a table-tilting and -rapping session at an apartment above a
ham and beef shop in Red Lion Street, Holborn – the home of one
of Britain's best-known mediums, Mary Marshall. Mrs Lowe had found
it a grotesque notion that the departed should choose to communicate
with the living by assaults upon items of furniture. Mrs Lowe was
much more taken with Mrs Marshall's *planchette* board and its 'indicator', which spelt out spirit messages; and when two communications
from her own dead brother came through, she felt that she had found
'a stepping stone to God'. Mrs Lowe never ceased being a Church of
England Christian; and when later defending herself against accusations that she dabbled in the occult, she stated that her spiritualist
beliefs were 'in accordance with primitive Christianity'. It was always
the Christian Almighty who was communicating with her directly,
with no need for suspect characters such as Reverend Lowe interloping
between the Lord and his worshipper.

After the revelation in Holborn, Mrs Lowe began to sit alone with
a pen in her hand, and within a few weeks, unintelligible pen strokes
on paper gave way to characters and then words, and before long
'an unseen, impalpable agent' was guiding her hand to record 'the

names of all I loved best in Spirit-land'. These 'loving and holy guides' became her dearest companions and she was lonely no more. She spent days at a time in solitude with her pen and paper, 'dialoguing with the Unseen', using her 'brain ear'. Often it was quite mundane, suburban matters that came through. 'I leave my home at Thy bidding alone to travel to Norwood by the midday train, and find there is none,' she wrote to 'the Saviour', 'and Lord, my heart tells me here I sinned. At Thy bidding I drew on a banker I do not draw on usually, and withdrew my balance from another, without Thy giving me any reason till afterwards, when Thou saidst he would fail to-day.' However, as good friends will, the Saviour took it upon himself to tell her some unpleasant matters that he thought she really ought to be aware of: 'My child, it behoves thee to seek a divorce from thy husband.' The Saviour revealed that Reverend Lowe was a serial adulterer, and provided several names and addresses. As a result, Mrs Lowe went to Exeter, to the house of a stranger (a carpenter, as it turned out), banged on the door to gain admittance and accused the woman within of adultery with the vicar. The carpenter was at home, too, and saw Mrs Lowe off his premises very swiftly, using some choice language.

The moving fingers brought her a far more distressing communication regarding Reverend Lowe's sexual activities:

> [Question] 'Holiest Lord, vouchsafe of Thy mercy to write what Thou would'st I should tell Mary about Harriet.'
> [Answer] 'Tell her, my child, Harriet is not a good child and must go.'
>   'Saviour, Thou knowest my thoughts.'
>   'Write it, my child.'
>   'Holiest Lord, let it not seem distrust of Thee, but if she is, as I suspect, pregnant, and by G. L., is it not my duty to care for her?'
>   'My child, she is not pregnant, but she is his mistress.'

Harriet was George and Louisa's seven-year-old daughter.

The child was delicate and was described as suffering from 'water on the brain'; she lived at the vicarage in Upottery, as did Mary, the Lowes' twenty-one-year-old eldest surviving daughter. However, there was also in the household thirty-year-old servant Harriet Richards, and Mrs Lowe would later accuse her too of adultery with the reverend: as little Harriet was incapable of becoming pregnant, it is possible that the moving fingers had somehow conflated the two Harriets.

As Rosina Bulwer-Lytton's story suggests, talk of father–daughter incest was not unknown among the middling and upper social classes. But such allegations were outrageous, and if no corroborating evidence could be produced, the accuser could expect a backlash. And that is what Mrs Lowe and her troublesome fingers were about to experience.

In September 1870 Louisa was off by herself alone again in Exeter, staying in rooms she had rented at the house of one Miss Radford, at 23 East Southernhay. Reverend and Mary Lowe came to Miss Radford's to ask Mrs Lowe to come back to Upottery vicarage, but she refused. The discussion soon became heated, and Mrs Lowe locked herself in her suite of rooms. Her husband and daughter appeared to leave but the next morning, Mrs Lowe claimed that she could see the vicar outside her window. That evening, she demanded that Miss Radford give her more light so that she could search her bedroom, as she was convinced that George had secreted himself under the bed and would crawl out to attack her once she had retired for the night. Her landlady found this an extraordinary request, as the bedroom was small and the bed so low that no one would have been able to hide under it.

Two nights later, when Mrs Lowe complained that the key to her suite of rooms was missing, Miss Radford's servant lied and told her that there never had been a key. But when Mrs Lowe began to make a loud fuss, the servant reached under the mat and pretended to be surprised to find the key there. Later on, when Mrs Lowe rang for hot water, she discovered that the servant bell had been muffled. She now became very scared and would only open her door to receive refreshments; she felt that, somehow, her husband had infiltrated this haven she had created for herself. As a long-time sufferer from anxiety, she recognised the general aches, pains and indigestion that her mental state brought on and decided to consult Exeter's most prestigious physician, an old family acquaintance. She also hoped that he could recommend new lodgings.

Dr Thomas Shapter had been the hero of the city's 1832 and 1849 cholera outbreaks, writing an outstanding work on the epidemiology of the disease. Twice mayor of Exeter and once its sheriff, he was senior physician to the Devon and Exeter Hospital and to the Lying-In (Maternity) Hospital; and while no lunacy specialist, he was also physician to St Thomas's Hospital for Lunatics, near Exeter. His very high standing had, however, been damaged by a lunacy case of 1859: during an inquisition, it transpired that he had failed to dissuade an aged, wealthy, 'unsound' yet un-certificated woman from leaving her entire estate to him in the will that she made while in his private care. (Even his keenest supporters at the inquisition into the patient's soundness had had to admit that, at best, Shapter had acted 'imprudently' regarding her will.) When she consulted him, Mrs Lowe hadn't known this – or indeed that Shapter's own wife been confined as a lunatic in single-patient care since 1845.

Dr Shapter had treated the Lowe family off and on for a quarter of a century, and so it was natural that Louisa should seek his medical advice. However, 'I thought he seemed rather queer,' was Mrs Lowe's verdict on the consultation of Saturday evening, 24 September. She had begun by complaining about life at her lodgings and detailed her numerous minor ailments; but before long she spilled out all the reverend's iniquities and her fear of having to return to him. The consultation lasted two hours, and at seven o'clock in the evening, Dr Shapter insisted on walking her back to Miss Radford's. A little later he returned, and a little later still he was joined by Dr Kempe, another medical acquaintance who had occasionally treated her own family. She swallowed the story that Dr Kempe was visiting another lodger of Miss Radford's and then 'spoke pretty freely', as she later admitted, to both doctors. She did know, at the time, that she appeared to be agitated and 'excitable' and therefore avoided bringing up the subject of her 'passive writing', knowing how sceptics could react to such talk. She told the doctors that she realised her allegations about her husband sounded strange but claimed she had letters at her London address that could prove that they were true. When Dr Shapter made to leave, he said to her, 'Now, mind, I shall come in and see you tomorrow morning.' She would have preferred him not to do so, as she was gradually becoming aware of the possible significance of this odd scenario – of what two interviews with doctors could lead on to. 'I lived in a kind of chronic apprehension of this kind of thing,' she said later. 'It was a persistent delusion, a recurrent delusion . . . on the part of my husband, this idea of my insanity.'

She therefore left before dawn the next morning and went to stay with her sister-in-law, Anne Lowe, at Torquay. Returning a day later, she found that Miss Radford had emptied her rooms of her belongings and re-let the suite. Stunned and not knowing what to do next, she and Anne went to the Clarence Hotel to take tea, and on the way, Mrs Lowe sent a telegram – in Italian, to fox her pursuers – to Charles Roupell, a friend in London: 'I am in great danger. Come immediately.' After tea, as the two made to leave, a large woman blocked their way in the hotel lobby and requested that Mrs Lowe come with her. Outside, a carriage awaited. After a minor scuffle, Mrs Lowe knew that she had lost, and acquiesced in going into an asylum. 'I thought I should get in quietly and get out quietly,' she later said. She believed that the lunacy authorities would quickly see the mistake that had been made, and it could all be discreetly sorted out.

Mrs Lowe was taken to Brislington House, arriving at around ten o'clock on the night of Monday 26 September. Brislington was at that

The front view of Brislington House Asylum in the 1870s.

point housing over ninety patients and so was far from being the small private concern she had been expecting. Assisted by his brothers, Charles Henry Fox had taken over the running of the place in 1866, on the semi-retirement of his father, Francis Ker Fox (who, forty years earlier, had been so heartless to Mr Perceval). Upon admission, Mrs Lowe spoke at great length to Fox of her distressing intimate life. The asylum keeper wrote in his casebook:

> She labours under sub-acute mania, marked by restlessness, loquacity, voluble utterance without incoherence and a perversion of the moral sentiments. Though all here are perfect strangers to her, she has from the first betrayed an indelicacy in her conversation and a total absence of that womanly reserve and reticence upon her private affairs and sexual relations with her husband, which are usually observed. She describes with minutiae acts of alleged impotence on Mr Lowe's part, and at another time accuses him of adulteries; asserts that a fortnight since she found she was a spiritual medium, and by this means discovered who are her husband's mistresses, and where they live. She writes these revelations on leaves of trees, or any dirty scraps of paper she may casually find, and she liberally distributes them.

This was also when Mrs Lowe made her allegations about her wedding night, which Fox declined to detail in print.

Brislington failed to measure up to Mrs Lowe's exacting social and behavioural standards. The Lowes' joint estate was being charged at a rate of £300 per annum for her care, but the food, she noted, was no better than the fare served up at a London boarding house with a decent room for a mere £1 15s a week. Among the inmates, she recorded, language could be foul and quarrels frequent. One of the more violent patients repeatedly threatened her life, and the matron would burst into her room on occasion to insist that Mrs Lowe go and sit in the parlour with the maniacs, as she was being too solitary. Patients were locked into their rooms at 9 p.m., with a night keeper, who, in Mrs Lowe's case, turned out to be a loud and persistent snorer. And what little night-time sleep Mrs Lowe achieved in her top-storey room was shattered at dawn with 'blasphemous obscenities and maniacal cries'. Her room was also close to the dinner gong and a loud staff-bell, so her 'auditory nerves' were permanently on edge. The Reverend Francis Kilvert, who came to see his mad Aunt Emma at Brislington, at about the same time as Mrs Lowe's incarceration, described the eerie sounds of the asylum in his diary: 'As we walked up and down the lawn . . . I heard a strange uproar proceeding from the house. It sounded at first like a woman's voice in voluble expostulation and argument, then loud impassioned entreaty rising swiftly into wild, passionate, despairing cries, which rent the air for some time, and then all was still.'

If Mrs Lowe's allegations were true, then it seems that the ethos of grandfather Fox, Brislington's founder – strict segregation of the social classes and of the violent from the non-violent – had broken down. Indeed, Charles Henry Fox (going against the views of the Commissioners in Lunacy on this matter) believed that accurate categorisation on medical grounds was unworkable, because – he had observed – mania often lapsed into melancholia, while manic excitability could slump into stolid, unrousable immobility.

The Fox brothers were among those alienists (there was no consensus) who believed that masturbation caused insanity; or that the insane worsened their condition with its practice; or at least that there was some kind of cause and effect between masturbation and insanity; or something like that. So moving fingers of a different kind were fiercely policed at Brislington. Mrs Lowe was deemed to be one of the patients to be 'free from solitary propensity', as the Foxes put it, and so was told that her night-keeper would be withdrawn; but she realised that a keeper would be her only chance of exit from her room should a fire break out at night-time, and so she insisted on keeping the snorer with her after dark, for safety.

Mrs Lowe later claimed to have witnessed patients being exhibited in a strait-waistcoat to newly recruited servants as 'a raree show'. And she alleged that to pare the salary bill for attendants, the Foxes made unnecessary use of solitary confinement. She was shocked that female patients who were becoming fractious were rough-handled by male attendants. She was also astonished that the Foxes allowed lady patients to be addressed by servants as 'My dear', which, she believed, would do nothing to restore their self-respect or overcome their sense of lost position in life; although each would have denied it, Mrs Lowe and the Foxes were united by a shared sense of social hierarchy and decorum and highly alert to transgression of the appropriate gender and class behaviours.

Dr Fox acknowledged the economic basis of a great deal of mental ill health in England. In his view, his lady patients at Brislington tended not to have been exposed to one of the main causes of female psychological problems: the dreadful anxiety experienced by England's overworked needlewomen and other types of female 'artisan'. Poverty and its stresses, he stated, were responsible for the large number of female patients in the county asylums. By contrast, his wealthy patients tended to have been made mad by 'moral' (that is, emotional) stresses, including such factors as disappointment in love, jealousy and fright. And 'self-pollution', of course.

In fact, Brislington held more men than women in these years, and this imbalance was not unusual in private asylums. It was in the county asylums that women outnumbered men, by a ratio of around 55:45. This is not a huge differential and is explicable by the combination of such factors as the surplus of females over males in the general population and the greater longevity of women – male asylum patients tended to die significantly earlier than female, with elderly female dementia sufferers or other female 'incurables' living on within the public system, their numbers aggregating, and thereby helping to give rise to the myth that the threshold for insanity in Victorian women was set lower than for men. (See Appendix 2 on p. 392 for some official statistics.)

Upon her arrival, Mrs Lowe was refused permission to see a solicitor; and so she set about writing letters explaining her predicament, completing between fifty and eighty in four months. As the law stood, Dr Fox was obliged either to send these to the addressee, or, if he thought their contents were likely to be abusive or alarming, to set them aside for the Commissioners in Lunacy to read and decide their fate, which was either to forward them on to the intended recipients or to destroy them. In fact, Fox sent all the letters to Reverend Lowe, leaving it to him to make the choice. Mrs Lowe later claimed that only one of her letters ever reached its correct destination. Fox would never be prosecuted for this clear breach of the lunacy law; the fine of £20 would, in any case, have held little terror for the owner of Brislington House. Mrs Lowe later discovered that the Commissioners had never prosecuted anyone for 'misdealing' with a patient's correspondence.

After she had been at Brislington for three weeks, Mrs Lowe was paid her first visit by Commissioners James Wilkes and Robert Skeffington Lutwidge. Although this, too, contravened the rules, Wilkes and Lutwidge acceded to Dr Fox's request that he have a private conversation with them before they spoke to his patient. In addition, Dr Fox asked Mrs Lowe to declare to the Commissioners that she had been properly detained. During her interview, she later reported, Wilkes and Lutwidge kept popping in and out of the room, so she had in effect only a few minutes alone with them. She alleged that Commissioner Wilkes said to her, 'Oh, you believe the Bible and all that sort of thing', and had commented, 'All spiritualists are mad.' It is a mark of her naivety that she was astonished that Wilkes and Lutwidge left her behind when they departed Brislington: she had assumed the Lunacy Commission would have spotted immediately that her detention had been a mistake.

Two weeks later, on 1 November 1870, Dr Fox wrote in his casebook that Mrs Lowe was 'variable in mood', one day talking of nothing but Reverend Lowe's supposed adulteries and the next admitting that she had probably exaggerated the matter and ought to put it all behind her 'and not expose his conduct to the world'. Surprisingly, after that Dr Fox made no more casebook entries about Mrs Lowe for the next three months. During this time, as her conduct seemed unremarkable, she was moved to Heath House, one of several separate lodges in the grounds of Brislington. This may have been an acknowledgement that the main building, with its shrieks and cries, was likely to hold up her progress towards placidity. Dr Fox was, in fact, beginning to consider her to be fully recovered but was having difficulty in persuading the Commissioners that she was fit to be discharged. As a provincial asylum, Brislington was also subject to inspection by local magistrates. One of these, Dr William Budd (who, sadly, later himself became insane), had known Mrs Lowe and her children in earlier years and felt sure that she was of sound mind. 'I am in a great difficulty,' he told her, referring to the Commissioners' wish that she should stay in the asylum for the time being. Budd's dilemma highlights the ongoing battle for supremacy in the provinces between the Whitehall Commissioners and the local magistracy.

In the New Year, Emily Chamier, Mrs Lowe's widowed sister, arrived in London from her home in the South of France, alarmed at what the Lowe children had told her of their mother's sudden vanishing from Exeter. Emily did not think that Louisa was a lunatic; but nor did she believe any of the accusations made against George, and Emily and her brother-in-law would maintain a cordial relationship throughout. In fact, most of the Lowes and her own family, the Crookendens, were baffled by Louisa's behaviour, feeling that she was sane but that her allegations against her husband had no foundation. Emily went to see the Commissioners in Lunacy to plead for Mrs Lowe's release. In law, the patient him- or herself could only know the contents of the certificates upon their discharge, and even then, only if the Commissioners gave their assent. But Emily also contacted a London solicitor, John White, and White was eventually, at the discretion of the Commissioners, allowed to see the lunacy order and certificates upon which Mrs Lowe had been committed.

The certificates had been signed by Doctors Shapter and Kempe, the lunacy order by Reverend Lowe. Dr Kempe's certificate noted, 'Various delusions about her husband, &c, &c, &c.' – the three &cs giving the document an alarmingly insouciant air. Although Mrs Lowe had been careful not to bring up the subject of spiritualism in her talk with Dr Shapter, he had nevertheless written: 'I am told that she says she is in direct communication with the Saviour; that she writes much and often and says she can only write as God moves her fingers.' Mrs Lowe later contended that this was inadmissible hearsay; she had never used such an expression to anyone, and certainly not to Shapter. The certificates also included the erroneous statement that there had been madness among the Crookendens. Mrs Lowe had thought that she was protected by the Hippocratic oath when telling Kempe and Shapter of her concerns about her husband: 'I told them things in professional confidence, thinking them to be thoroughly trustworthy.' Instead, it had led to her incarceration.

She also queried the legitimacy of the interviews: each doctor examining an alleged lunatic was by law required to hold these interviews entirely separately – alone with the patient. Mrs Lowe had been subjected to a double act that complied with the letter of the lunacy law, but not with its spirit, in that Kempe and Shapter had each briefly left the room during the conversation at Miss Radford's and so could claim that each interview had been separate. Lord Coleridge, summing up in the (all-male) wrongful incarceration court case of *Nowell* v. *Williams*, would jokingly name this sleight of hand by physicians 'a Dutch barometer conversation': the ingenious mechanism on these fashionable household gadgets featured a little man coming out of his slot as another went back into his own slot when climatic conditions changed. This was similar, in Lord Coleridge's view, to the technique of the two lunacy doctors who had acted in collusion in *Nowell* v. *Williams*.

As for the lunacy order, George Lowe had answered the question of whether this was 'the first attack' of insanity with the statement: 'For the last twenty years [she] has been subject to what is termed hysteria.' And under the heading 'When and where under previous care and treatment' he had written, 'During this period of twenty years has been constantly under treatment'. Mrs Lowe would later argue that the latter was not an answer to the question, and that the term 'hysteria' had no true medical meaning.

By now Dr Fox was becoming keen to get her off his hands. He told the Commissioners he did not want her at Brislington beyond Lady Day (25 March). And finally the Commissioners began to budge. Wilkes and Lutwidge now informed their colleagues at the Lunacy Commission that further detention of Mrs Lowe was not desirable and on 19 January 1871 the Commissioners wrote to George Lowe, requesting that, 'The lady should be discharged.' Reverend Lowe informed Dr Fox: 'After the Commissioners' letter I suppose I must consent to Mrs Lowe's discharge and beg you will carry out the suggestion as soon as you may think advisable.' He enclosed a cheque for £10 to cover his wife's fare to London, where he assumed she would reside.

But just as Mrs Lowe was on the point of being released, Emily Chamier suddenly changed her mind about her sister's sanity. She informed the Commissioners that recent letters she had received from Mrs Lowe disclosed that shocking new revelations were once again coming from her fingers. Emily therefore concluded that Louisa was suffering an 'unyielding delusion' and that the seclusion of Brislington House had not eradicated what Emily had at first considered just a brief spell of confusion and excitement. Instead of release, Reverend Lowe and the Commissioners now decided, with Emily's support, that Mrs Lowe should be transferred to the care of Dr Henry Maudsley at the exclusive Lawn House in Hanwell, on the western edge of London, close to the Middlesex County Asylum. Maudsley had inherited this going concern upon marrying Anne, the daughter of John Conolly.

* * *

Lawn House Asylum in Hanwell, Middlesex – a tiny asylum for a maximum
of six wealthy women. The house was not far from the huge Middlesex
County Asylum, where Dr John Conolly made his name; Lawn House was
Conolly's private concern and he bequeathed it to his son-in-law Henry
Maudsley. The house was demolished in 1902 but the pond in front,
about which Louisa Lowe complained, remains in the recently renovated
Conolly Dell Park.

Henry Maudsley has a heroic reputation today, largely thanks to his
£40,000 grant for the building of what became the Maudsley Hospital,
in Denmark Hill, South London. He had been an outstanding young
medical student, who, with little family finance or connections, had
become one of the most respected British alienists by the mid-1860s.
But he was busy getting himself stuck in a Darwinian dead end – or
rather, in the bleaker rut of the T. H. Huxley strain of evolution theory.
He was to become unshiftable in his belief that 'mental disease' (as he
called it) was a purely physiological problem of poor 'organisation' and
defective structure; he thought that environment and personal history
had no bearing on an individual's psychological functioning. The nervous
system of someone from poor hereditary stock would inevitably function worse than that of someone whose lineage had experienced no
degeneration. Nature's purpose was fixed: all you could ever do was
function in the way your heredity permitted you to function. He
described this sad state of affairs as 'the tyranny of organisation'.

Maudsley was blunt, sardonic and unclubbable, and his increasingly hard line on the materiality of mental disease, and the pessimism of his inheritance theory, distanced him from many fellow workers in the field. Goings-on at Lawn House were an additional factor that would finally compel him to leave active public life and move further into his authorship and immensely lucrative, secretive, West End private consultancy for the very wealthy. However, Dr Maudsley was consistently inconsistent, and so it is hard to come up with definitive 'Maudsleyism'. Very late in life he wrote that, 'Consistency signifies prejudice and stagnation', and he changed his mind about many things over the course of his career, including masturbation (moving from viewing it as a significant cause of mental disease in adolescence and young adulthood to deciding that it was probably of little importance). In an unpublished note of 1912, he appeared to accept that even his evolutionism had flaws: 'To understand a man you must know not what he is, but what he has suffered.'

But Maudsley did remain pessimistic about women. Pioneering female doctor Elizabeth Garrett Anderson attacked Maudsley in print for his stance on gender, using late-Victorian racial theory to mock him as 'an Ashanti warrior', lobbing any antiquated projectile he could lay hands on as a weapon against the advance of civilisation and female equality. Because he believed energies to be finite, and that each creature was highly adapted to specific roles, Maudsley had concluded that women could not menstruate and engage in intellectual pursuits (at least, not without serious health consequences). Furthermore, as he detested all spiritualists as 'cranks', it is little surprise that Maudsley believed Louisa Lowe to be of unsound mind and that there was little hope of recovery. Here at last was the coldly mechanistic, atheistical scientist of Mrs Lowe's nightmares – the man who insisted that her messages from Beyond were indicative of ineradicable insanity. One day, when she asked Dr Maudsley, 'How can you keep me here? You know I am not insane!', he replied, Cheshire Cat-style, 'I never said you were not insane. Everybody is insane.' Later on, chewing it all over in the aftermath of the Lowe case, he would write, 'The line between sanity and insanity is like a line of demarcation between light and darkness – it is impossible to draw it.'

Dr Henry Maudsley (1835–1918) despaired of Louisa Lowe; he believed that
females, and especially those who believed in spiritualism, had inferior mental
'organisation' that was incapable of improvement.

Reading her passive writings, Maudsley noted that 'many of them
were of a very puerile character, some of them read very blasphem-
ously, and others rather tend to the obscene.' As an example of the
puerile and grandiose, Maudsley pointed to an exchange with the
'Almighty' that read: 'Mr [i.e. Dr] Kempe thinks me a beast and a
fool.' To which the Almighty had replied: 'My poor child, both he
and all men shall honour thee.' In another exchange, according to
Maudsley, Mrs Lowe had claimed to be the female Christ. Yet what
alarmed Maudsley most was that Mrs Lowe acted upon instructions
contained in these messages. She had attacked her husband's character
on the writing's say-so and had made an equally unfounded accusation
against a stranger (the carpenter's wife), which rendered Mrs Lowe a
'social nuisance', as Maudsley put it. Maudsley and Emily Chamier
were extremely concerned about the welfare of her young daughter,
Harriet, feeling certain that Mrs Lowe's passive writing and general
oddness had had a terribly disturbing effect on the physically debilitated
child. For her part, Mrs Lowe pointed out that right up until the time
of her seizure from Exeter, her husband had never tried to keep any
of the children away from her. Would he have allowed her such a

huge presence in their lives if he had truly believed her to be of unsound mind? she asked.

Maudsley quickly found Mrs Lowe to be a very 'disagreeable' patient. Lawn House had no locked doors within, and there were no gates or railings, as the five other ladies – although under certification – were resigned to the fact of having a better life with the Maudsleys than elsewhere, and so did not attempt to escape. (This perhaps suggests how terrible the home lives of these very wealthy women – aged between thirty-one and fifty-two – may have been.) They 'were there as friends and on intimate terms', declared Dr Maudsley, blurring, as many private proprietors did, the true nature of the transaction. But Mrs Lowe did try to flee, and this required Dr Maudsley to introduce locks and bolts into the house, which, he claimed, upset his other patients, no doubt reminding them that the country cottage aura of Lawn House was indeed illusory. Mrs Lowe made a run for it one day when out strolling with Mrs Anne Maudsley, but was swiftly re-taken. During another escape attempt, someone in the village of Hanwell spotted her, 'thinking she looked very insane and peculiar', and raised the alarm. After this, Mrs Lowe was not allowed out of the house, except on attended visits to Emily's rented home at Ealing; but Emily found Louisa's repeated accusations against Reverend Lowe highly distressing, and these visits stopped. The reverend, as signatory of the lunacy order, was the only person who could permit visitors to see Mrs Lowe, and he himself, Emily, daughter Mary, one son, and a Crookenden nephew all came to Lawn House, as did Charles Roupell, who was a very good friend of both Lowes and was perplexed and upset by their marital unhappiness. The reverend would not allow Mrs Lowe to see solicitor John White.

Dr Maudsley told Mrs Lowe quite openly that he would not be

allowing her written communication with the outside world, after he opened one of her letters that was filled with her usual accusations against her husband. Her letters to the Commissioners in Lunacy were delivered but were not responded to, and in the summer of 1871 Dr Maudsley asked her, 'Oh, do you think they would let out such a firebrand as yourself?' Lutwidge and Wilkes, who visited her four times at Lawn House, remained fixated on her passive writing. They asked her whether, if the power that moved her fingers so instructed her, she would seek a judicial separation from Reverend Lowe and would mount a criminal case for false imprisonment if she were to be liberated. To the first, she replied that she might, but not because the Saviour told her to; and to the second, she said she would give no promise not to go to law. She was angry that all the Commissioners sought to discuss with her were metaphysical or religious matters; she wanted to bring the discussion round to how monstrous it was that six entire months of rational behaviour in the asylums were not being taken into account, with a view to her liberation.

At close to £420 a year, the fees at Lawn House were extremely high, and Mrs Lowe delighted in detailing the squalor at the Maudsley establishment. She nicknamed it Pond Hall, and said that the entire place stank of sewage because the small lake at the front of the house received all the contents of the privies, and that these were in themselves disgusting beyond description – 'windowless and pestilential'. So bad was the smell from the pond, she claimed, it rendered the bedrooms at the front of the house unusable.

The food was very bad and there was not enough of it, and she claimed that the temperature in the dining room was a mere 42 degrees Fahrenheit because the Maudsleys were parsimonious with fuel. There were no attendants – just three maids and a companion kept by one of the ladies. All the staff were badly paid and had to sleep on the floors of the patients' rooms. Even worse, Mrs Lowe felt, these women were 'uncultivated' and could provide the ladies with 'no diversion from painful introspection' nor 'reawaken slumbering powers'. Lawn House, Mrs Lowe said, was a whited sepulchre: bright, fair and surrounded by flowers – and foul within.

Dr Maudsley, for his part, was thoroughly fed up with Louisa Lowe, and asked Reverend Lowe to take her away. The reverend, meanwhile, was setting in train a lawsuit which would ensure that any future asylum costs would have to be paid directly from Louisa's own money, and not from their joint finances; her trustee, in charge of disbursing her separate moneys to her, was refusing to settle the asylum bills, clearly unhappy about her incarceration, and demanding that the reverend pay up instead. The costs to April 1871, when George commenced his suit, were substantial: at Brislington House they had amounted to £140 5s 10d; and for Lawn House they had reached £61 19s 9d. If Mrs Lowe was to spend many more years in an asylum, the married couple's joint estate would be facing vast outlay. This lawsuit seems an extraordinarily cold act, and it is clear from the Chancery documents that the Lowe children had taken their mother's 'side', on this matter at least. Happily, the reverend's action backfired. He had repeatedly refused to petition for a lunacy inquisition, as his wife wished, but his lawsuit prompted the attention of the Lord Chancellor, who now decided to investigate how Mrs Lowe's considerable fortune was to be managed in future. As a result, Mrs Lowe was at last permitted access to a lawyer, and with solicitor John White she started compiling a list of witnesses who could vouch for her sanity.

She was entitled to choose whether the inquisition should take place in camera, before a Master in Lunacy, or in public, in front of a jury. She chose the latter because she wanted the world to know what had been done to her. And – contra John Stuart Mill – she wished to place her fate before the 'common sense' of the layman rather than the 'science' of the lunacy specialist, as she put it. She may also have been aware that juries were far more likely to return a 'sane' verdict than a Master in Lunacy; as we have seen, from the late 1850s, juries were rejecting cases where 'intellectual confusion' was not clearly evident and were not easily swayed by tales of 'moral insanity'. Commissioner Lutwidge was surprised at her choice, as a jury trial meant greater publicity, which – he believed – women would normally seek to avoid at all costs. He told her that a public hearing would be 'undesirable . . . We always advise ladies in these circumstances to keep quiet.'

This unexpected twist horrified Reverend Lowe. It also meant that the limelight of an inquisition would be shone upon Lawn House. As Maudsley's biographer has written, his asylum looked curiously old-fashioned for a man who so loudly embraced physiology and evolutionary biology. Maudsley believed that the large county asylums herded together too many diverse and poorly classified patients – a set-up that was highly unlikely to bring about any improvement in their condition. But Lawn House merely appeared to be performing the same action in miniature – as a holding pen for six unclassified ladies, offering only respite, not cure. Because he charged steep fees, he could easily be accused of exploiting the mentally troubled; and some might also question how it was that, with his many other famous professional commitments, Dr Maudsley could possibly be supplying top-quality personal care to these patients. Mrs Lowe was certain to make criticisms of Lawn House at her inquisition.

The reverend and the doctor decided to act and, with the Commissioners in Lunacy's approval, Mrs Lowe was shifted, to Otto House Asylum in Hammersmith. Here, visiting physician Dr George Fielding Blandford examined her and declared that she was fully recovered. Blandford agreed with the Lord Chancellor's suggestion that she should be allowed to live outside Otto House on probation, ahead of the inquisition. He asked her to sign a document, drafted by her husband's solicitor, which signalled her agreement to remain under certificate for three more months. She did so reluctantly, worried that it might look as though she was condoning her original incarceration.

Her solicitor John White found pleasant lodgings for her at 9 Bedford Place, Russell Square, where she moved in late December 1871. As part of the probation and inquisition process she was visited regularly by Dr Rhys Williams of Bethlehem, who found her to be sane and certificated her as such in April 1872. With that, no inquisition was needed: Mrs Lowe was a free woman after one year and three months of asylum detention and supervised probation.

Although Mrs Lowe was only fifty-one years old at the time of her release, one of her subsequent tracts about her experiences was subtitled *How an Old Woman Obtained Passive Writing, and The Outcome Thereof*. She selected as her persona the dignified middle-class matron – an unthreatening, unquestionably feminine creature. To have revealed her rage in its true colours would have turned her into a caricaturable figure à la Rosina Bulwer-Lytton – easy to mock, easy to ignore, easy to accuse of exaggeration and to condemn with the insult 'unfeminine'. 'I would much rather have had it [the incarceration] investigated quietly than before the public. I never had lived in public in my life before,' she wrote. For eighteen months she pursued justice without publicity, writing privately to the prime minister, the leader of the opposition, the current Lord Chancellor and the men who had filled that post in previous years. Many did not reply, and those who did refused to support her request for a government investigation into her case and those of other doubtful certifications. No woman relishes the spotlight, she announced (rather sweepingly), but because she had failed to achieve anything 'quietly', in July 1873 she founded the Lunacy Law Reform Association (LLRA), with offices in Berners Street, off Oxford Street.

Mrs Lowe made a long inaugural address from the stage of the Cavendish Rooms in Mortimer Street, nearby, on 17 July. Her audience was described as a very well dressed, 'select' crowd, with women far outnumbering men. As was the case at many a nineteenth-century public meeting loud agreement from the floor punctuated Mrs Lowe's speech; she frequently had to stop for bursts of applause and exclamations of sympathy. 'Shame!' individuals roared when she brought up the subject of male attendants handling a female patient. Her resolution, condemning the existing lunacy laws, was carried unanimously, funds were pledged, and the names and addresses of those wishing to join the campaign were collected. Emily Chamier had clearly been forgiven and reconciled with her sister and was bustling around at the meeting as an LLRA committee member and collector of subscriptions. Long after the meeting had officially broken up, groups of people remained in the Cavendish Rooms, discussing cases that they knew of, including those of individuals who were being confined within their own homes.

In her speech Mrs Lowe had addressed her inability to mount a civil case against her wrongdoers because she was a married woman. And she maintained that it was more common for women to be 'put away' without cause than men. Furthermore, not only did wives face legal disabilities in fighting their cases, women were more afraid of scandal and so were less likely to mount an action if they were released.

"THE NURSE CAME QUICKLY AROUND THE CORNER OF THE
WALL, HOLDING LADY GLYDE BY THE ARM."

Mrs Lowe and early members of her Lunacy Law Reform Association were
convinced that women endured higher levels of dubious certification – a
notion played upon, and heightened by, publication of *The Woman in White* in
1860, from which this illustration is taken. Marian Halcombe is waiting to
rescue Laura Fairlie from the small private asylum.

But in fact, the cases subsequently brought to the attention of Mrs
Lowe and the LLRA did not suggest a gender bias in the problem
of doubtful certification: the ratio in these is fourteen males to ten
females. (See Appendix 4.) But with the lurid real-life sagas of Lady
Lytton, Mary Jane Turner and now Mrs Lowe, plus the best-selling
fictional dilemmas of Laura Fairlie and Anne Catherick in *The Woman
in White*, lunacy law became, from the late 1850s, a focus of women's
rights campaigners. For them, the asylum – its deprivations and
entrapment, its insistence on a narrow range of acceptable behaviour,
its thwarting of autonomy – writ large the lack of freedom
that women, and wives in particular, experienced in everyday life.
'We always advise ladies to keep quiet,' Lewis Carroll's uncle had
told Mrs Lowe when she sought a jury hearing. But the insistence
that a woman be 'ladylike' was increasingly seen by many women

as a potential threat to the liberty of more than half of the English nation.

As her LLRA public appearances continued and her fame grew, Mrs Lowe was described in newspaper reports as having 'a commanding presence and good delivery'; she was tall, well-built and 'handsome'. When, in 1883, she published *The Bastilles of England; Or, the Lunacy Laws at Work*, it was a detailed and lucid condemnation of the entire system, and a plea for the 'civil rights' (an interesting early use of this phrase) of those accused of being insane. An alleged lunatic was in a far worse position than an alleged criminal on remand, she declared, who at least knew the nature of the accusation against him and who would face a public trial by jury. The lunacy laws were the only system in English public life that allowed an accuser preliminary and secret access to the very panel that was supposed to weigh up opposing arguments.

The alleged lunatic's only support were the Commissioners – yet they were 'an autocratic power in a free country', who had no check upon them but an oath of office and the workings of their own conscience. 'Who or what, then, are they?' Mrs Lowe asked. 'A triplet of briefless barristers, and another of patientless doctors, put round a big table . . . men who, hopeless of winning the great prizes of their respective professions, have renounced all chance of them, and accepted itinerating obscurity.' When a Lunacy Commissioner retired from his £1,500 a year (plus expenses) post, he became an honorary Commissioner, with a pension and full powers to make decisions, and in this way, she said, the Commission was silting up with the sick, the old and the purely 'ornamental'.

Of the seven visits paid to her by the Commissioners, Mrs Lowe alleged 'impatience, impertinence, ill-temper, and a firm, evident determination not to give me fair play'. While the law allowed the Commissioners to delve only into the past two years of a patient's life, Wilkes and Lutwidge had made her go back over her entire life, and focused on her suicide attempt of 1854. She also alleged that the Commissioners turned a blind eye to the abuse of the laws regarding patients' letters and did not scrutinise the copy certificates that they were sent following a patient's admission and so routinely failed to identify questionable certification.

The Commissioners' surviving minute books housed in The National

Archives reveal that dubious certificates and badly kept medical case-books did lead to the summonsing of certain doctors and proprietors to the Commission to explain themselves. Nevertheless, only verbal reprimands and threats of licence-removal tended to follow these often heated discussions. The modern researcher is left with the impression that Victorian overwork and diligence was combining fatally with complacency and naivety. The job was done thoroughly by the Commissioners; but the job itself appears to have been rubber-stamping, glossing over and hoping that everything would just right itself.

Only the Commissioners could initiate a prosecution for a breach of the lunacy laws – no private individual could do so, having instead to mount cases against individuals for assault, trespass and false impris-onment. But Mrs Lowe detailed the 'masterly inactivity' of the Commissioners in clear cases of cruelty, restraint, improper detention, defective certificates and casebooks, and poor physical conditions at asylums. Licences were occasionally revoked, she admitted, but this tended to happen only to proprietors without professional prestige or social connection to the Commissioners or the local JPs. Instead of a required 'distrustful watchfulness', the Commissioners habitually gave tacit approval to all manner of abuses – partly through identifying more with the doctors and proprietors than with the patient, and partly because they feared that if any substance were to be found in allegations of misconduct, the entire farcical nature of lunacy detec-tion and treatment would be exposed to the public. The entire function of the Commission, therefore, Mrs Lowe alleged, was a retrospective whitewashing of every asylum committal in England and Wales.

As the Alleged Lunatics' Friend Society had done thirty years earlier, the LLRA proposed a whole new national system of lunacy adminis-tration. Like the earlier campaign group, it demanded the abolition of private asylums. 'The physician who starts a madhouse,' Mrs Lowe argued, 'ipso facto exchanges his status as a scientific gentleman for that of a licensed victualler to the insane.' The certificate of lunacy was as readily obtainable as any other marketable commodity, she believed. Referring to her own experience, she now described her behaviour in Exeter shortly before her abduction as a bout of temporary 'confusion', which the medical men should have spotted; instead, it was pathologised. 'Unsoundness is not an evanescent phase but a protractedly morbid condition of the intellect,' she wrote. In fact, the phrase 'unsoundness of mind' should be replaced by 'incapacity for self-government', as the latter referred to an individual's actions, while the former suggested something intrinsic.

A locally elected inspectorate should replace the over-centralised Commissioners, who did not answer for their mistakes through the ballot box. The initial allegation that someone was a lunatic was to be made upon oath to the local magistrate, followed by a preliminary investigation that was to be strictly private. Every town in England and Wales should have a dedicated office attached to its civic buildings in which prima facie lunacy cases could next be swiftly determined by jury. The absurdly adversarial inquisition process should come to an end. 'Doctorcraft', as Mrs Lowe called it, would, 'like priestcraft, enslave us all', and must be replaced by the cool common sense of the ordinary man. Scientific obfuscation had replaced religious obfuscation, and 'the cloven foot of medical arrogance and greed peeps out', whenever straightforward solutions were suggested.

Only two types of lunacy should be recognised: 'incapacity for self-government'; and that same incapacity combined with actions that were dangerous to the self or to others. And only in cases of this latter 'dangerous mania' should the sufferer face deprivation of liberty, by placement on a 'probationary ward' that was not physically connected to an asylum. In such cases, a magistrate was to take sworn depositions from a medical man and from two eyewitnesses to the patient's dangerous behaviour; only when it was beyond doubt to the magistrate that this was a case of dangerous mania would the patient pass out of the control of any private person and into the hands of the state.

All the nation's asylums would be state run, and all correspondence would be correctly and honestly dealt with; a more generous and transparent system of visiting by friends and relatives should prevail; male handling of female patients must be banned; religious worship was to be provided in accordance with the patient's wishes; and all breaches of lunacy law were to be punished by a prison sentence – ranging from two days to two years – rather than by fines. Any member of the public should be entitled to prosecute breaches of the lunacy law, and a fast and inexpensive appeals system to a higher court should supersede the existing route via the Commissioners and Lord Chancellor.

Like many who had interested themselves in patient care, Mrs Lowe and her fellow campaigners had been impressed by the model settlement at Gheel in Belgium, where those with emotional and intellectual problems were cared for in a large community of foster carers who hosted them within their own houses in the town. She very much hoped that this kind of system could be devised in England. But there was one rather more iron-fisted LLRA proposal, foreshadowing some of the next century's less alluring state interventions in health matters. Writing in 1883 – an era of 'advanced humanitarianism', as she called it – Mrs Lowe argued that the supreme law must be the health of the nation. Both mental and physical disease should be eradicated for the common good, and it was 'profoundly immoral' that families attempted to hide a relative's insanity. The days of keeping madmen and madwomen at home, out of the glare of publicity and the shame of the asylum, had to come to an end, Mrs Lowe wrote, if the modern democratic state was radically to improve the health of its citizens. Therefore all 'hereditary diseases', including psychological malfunctions, must be made known to the authorities. She did not develop this proposal further, but it is an interesting example of how a traditional mid-Victorian mind was opening itself up to radical new ideas – some of them anticipating state socialism. She had hitherto been fastidious about appropriate class relations and inter-class decorum; but in the opening lines of *The Bastilles of England*, she addresses a notional working man – who she imagines may be wondering why her book will concern itself solely with private, and not public, asylums – describing herself as 'I, thy less industrious sister'. Her tone is distinctly apologetic as she explains to this labourer that she is part of the social class that consumes and disperses what another class manufactures.

As will be seen in the next chapter, many of the more mature adherents of spiritualism in the 1860s and 1870s experienced a profound change in their social and political outlooks. Mrs Lowe herself was 'now more than ever convinced a new and glorious day of progress is dawning for the human race'. She believed that modern spiritualism brought 'new thoughts' and 'some atmospheric change or modification of man's temperament'. Yet Mrs Lowe remained a Church of England Christian, believing that spiritualism invigorated – rather than replaced or dislodged – Anglican doctrine and practice. Victorian spiritualists have been portrayed by later commentators as under siege on two fronts: from atheistical materialists and from orthodox Christians. Twentieth-century observers have also liked to focus on female mediumship being attacked by male empiricists. However, a far greater jumble of allegiances is discernible among both the spiritualists and the non-believers, while various individuals simply changed their minds about the subject. Crucially, as we shall see, figures of great authority could not be relied upon to back the sceptics: judges, politicians, doctors and even certain alienists were either themselves part of the spiritualist movement or would defend spiritualists' rights to believe and practise without being accused of lunacy.

But was Mrs Lowe in fact practising spiritualism? Many who examined her felt that her passive writing had nothing to do with contacting the Other World. Dr Maudsley, although a despiser of 'cranks', wrote to fellow alienist Dr Charles Lockhart Robertson for his opinion. Robertson was the superintendent of the Sussex county lunatic asylum at Haywards Heath and also a Chancery Visitor in Lunacy. He was himself a spiritualist and in 1882 would become one of the first members of the Society for Psychical Research, the body that intended to probe the workings of the least understood phenomena of the human mind. (Against the odds, he and Henry Maudsley got on very well.) After interviewing Mrs Lowe on 7 October 1871, Robertson declared her to be of unsound mind, finding that the written messages conveyed her own bizarre and irrational thoughts. Dr Maudsley then asked leading spiritualist Benjamin Coleman for his views, and Coleman stated his belief that Mrs Lowe was not communing with a higher power. Dr Blandford of Otto House thought that Mrs Lowe's voices were simply a mode by which she could – without conscious knowledge – express obscene thoughts about her husband. In this, Blandford was in line with leading Edinburgh physician Dr Thomas Laycock, who himself had experimented with automatic writing and believed that it was in fact 'expressive of hidden mental states'.

As early as 1852 physiologist William B. Carpenter had identified what he called 'ideomotor activity and unconscious cerebration' as being behind spiritualism, mesmerism and a range of seemingly supernatural phenomena. Ideomotor activity was 'an involuntary response made by the muscles to ideas with which the mind may be possessed when the directing power of the will is in abeyance . . . Much of our mental work is done without consciousness,' Carpenter had written; this is an echo of Charlotte Brontë's thoughts about literary creation and was decades in advance of William James's, Carl

Jung's and Sigmund Freud's theories of the unconscious. (In fact, Dr Thomas Laycock would claim that he himself had developed this concept of the reflex action of the cerebrum even earlier – back in 1838.) In Carpenter's view, the conscious and unconscious parts of the brain did not always work in harmony, though he knew that science still lacked the technical means to discover anatomically why this might be the case. So a great deal of information was stored in the brain, he believed, without our knowing of its presence. Upon the sudden appearance of such information in the conscious part of the cerebrum, many were tempted to ascribe the phenomenon to supernatural forces.

For those doctors who accepted Carpenter's premise, Mrs Lowe had, without her conscious knowledge, found a mode of expressing the fears and suspicions which she felt unable to articulate in any other way than by her hand moving over paper without her volition. Today, we may see these fears as at least in part related to sexuality; but British mid- and late-Victorian theorists of the subconscious rarely made a link with the carnal – in print, at least. Indeed, James Crichton-Browne spoke for many at the end of the century when he stated that he found 'passages in Freud's writing capable of causing profound nausea'. But how anticipatory of the dreams of certain of Freud's patients is this passage of Mrs Lowe's dialogue with the Saviour, dating from 1869:

'Let me die.'

'My poor weary child, the spirits have not all lied, thy husband was on the roof in and out of the chimney half the night.'

'Father, thou saidst Satan helped him to slip in and out like an eel. Who, my friend and comforter, doubles him up like an opera hat; how can a great big six-feet man get in and out a chimney like this?'

'My child, no one doubled him up; he unbuilt the upper part of the chimney, and built it up again.'

By the time Mrs Lowe gave evidence to the 1877 Select Committee on Lunacy Law, she had long ceased mentioning her allegations of infidelity against her husband. When the panel put her in a tight spot about this, she reluctantly confessed that her passive writing had given her information about 'a third party' (i.e. Reverend Lowe) who had committed adultery. She was clearly by now very embarrassed about this aspect of her behaviour. Exonerating herself, she wrote on another occasion that she bitterly regretted 'the slanders' on her husband and stated that she had written an apology to him, which the reverend had accepted.

So how should posterity view Reverend Lowe? Had he used the lunacy laws to silence essentially truthful allegations fatal to his career and standing in society? Circumstantial evidence is all we have (since his daughter Harriet never wrote or spoke about these matters and nor did her siblings) and this does not back up Mrs Lowe's wildest claim. It was Reverend Lowe himself who came to Dr Maudsley to hand him his wife's written messages accusing him of sexually assaulting his young daughter – a candour that suggests his innocence rather than the opposite. Yet Reverend Lowe's incarceration of his wife and subsequent reluctance to have her released – despite Dr Fox's and Commissioners Wilkes's and Lutwidge's belief that she had recovered – reveal him to be extremely cold-hearted towards his confused and unhappy wife. And his attempt to make her pay for her asylum care from her own money adds to the impression of callousness. But despite seeming to enjoy initial support from her children during her time in the asylums and upon her release, by 1884 Mrs Lowe faced open hostility from her eldest child, Thomas, and her daughter Mary. Mary was appointed the reverend's 'guardian' when he became semi-paralysed following a stroke in 1881, living with him not far from the seafront in Bournemouth. She and Thomas refused Mrs Lowe access to Reverend Lowe, claiming that her presence would be 'dangerous to his life'.

Mrs Lowe's revenge on her immobilised husband was terrible: she launched an action for the 'restitution of conjugal rights'. In law, Mrs Lowe was entitled to reclaim her absent husband and to drag him back to the hearth and the marital bed – to protect her and to provide for her, as legally he was obliged. In the late eighteenth century, an estimated eight out of ten conjugal restitution cases in the London consistory courts had been initiated by wives; but in the new century, such instances had become rarer and rarer, and subsequently, for the most part it was the English wife who was compelled to return to beatings, rape, neglect and bullying in the marital home. In the mid-1880s, though, sauce for the goose once again became sauce for the gander, and this tactic was seen as cripplingly embarrassing for a husband. Which was exactly why Mrs Lowe did it. She did not want his company, protection or money; after all, she was the one with the cash and a high-profile vocation, as secretary of the LLRA, while he was confined to a chair in a house in Bournemouth – his occupation gone and his misdeeds paraded before the public.

Their daughter Mary swore an affidavit that the reverend had offered his wife her marital home upon her release from certification, but that Mrs Lowe had always preferred to live on her own, and that she was, in fact, as Mary put it, the 'deserter' of the marriage. However, the court ordered that seventy-two-year-old Reverend Lowe be medically inspected by two doctors, to test the truthfulness of his claim to be semi-paralysed. The examination took place on Valentine's Day, 1885.

Reverend Kennard's case was taken up by the campaigners when he was seized by madhouse keepers on the eve of his wedding. It made the front page of the *Illustrated Police News* in October 1881. See Appendix 4 on p. 401 for Reverend Kennard's story.

The Medium and Daybreak spiritualist magazine allowed Louisa Lowe to publicise her plight and that of other alleged lunatics. The masthead shows mysticism entering the bourgeois drawing room – the breaking dawn of a new way of thinking.

The court found in Mrs Lowe's favour and ordered Reverend Lowe to take her back into his home within fourteen days, on pain of a hefty fine, and to pay all the legal costs of the case. For only the third time in the century, an English husband was told by a judge that he had to live under the same roof as a wife he despised.

But Mrs Lowe had only been playing with him, and she never took up her conjugal rights. The reverend was dead within four months of the judgment.

Perhaps it was this kind of bloody-mindedness that alienated from Mrs Lowe many important associates within spiritualist circles and the lunacy reform movement. A split occurred in the LLRA in 1876, when a number of men broke away to form the Lunacy Law Amendment Society. It was said that Messrs Plumbridge, Atkins, Hurry, Morsely, Billington and Crutwell had not liked Mrs Lowe's devotion to spiritualism and found her approach to business matters erratic; it is possible, too, that her insistence that false incarceration was a feminist issue had angered male LLRA supporters – some of them the very men she had fought hard to free from certification and had helped to win justice against their conspirators.

She also fell out with James Burns, influential spiritualist and founder of the movement's journal, *The Medium and Daybreak*, which had been a useful vehicle for her cause. Desmond Fitzgerald, editor of the rival journal *Spiritual Notes*, libelled her in an open letter, describing her as a 'scolding lady' who had at one time been placed in an asylum when she became possessed by 'evil spirits, who led you into acts of folly and wickedness. I think it very likely that you are still in some degree under the influence of the same class of spirits.' Desmond wrote that he and fellow members of the British National Association of Spiritualists believed her actions had only helped to serve those who were endeavouring to crush the movement. Mrs Lowe took Fitzgerald to court for a criminal libel but after receiving a long apology in court, she called off the action.

Mrs Lowe failed first in court, then on appeal and finally in the House of Lords to make Dr Fox accountable for detaining her on deficient lunacy certificates. His defence was accepted that the certificates and lunacy order protected him from charges of assault and imprisonment, though the Lords took the opportunity to request the Commissioners in Lunacy to scrutinise more carefully in future the copy certificates sent to them by asylum proprietors; there ought to be no ambiguities in such crucial documentation, the Lords insisted.

Mrs Lowe, like John Perceval, crowned her career by prompting a Select Committee on Lunacy Law in 1877, which, as in 1859, took evidence on every aspect of the subject, not just wrongful incarceration. The Home Secretary felt the inquiry was needed 'because there were certain apprehensions abroad which it would be well to disprove', plainly certain that the committee's findings would uphold the status quo. She herself proved a very cogent witness, but James Billington, secretary to the rival Lunacy Law Amendment Society, was far from impressive, allowing the questioners to drive a coach and horses through his claims of widespread malicious incarceration and exposing his lack of a grasp of even the fundamentals of how lunacy administration worked.

In the intervening eighteen years, Lord Shaftesbury appears to have fossilised. There had been no incarceration that had not been at the very least 'plausible', he said; and there were no longer any cases of wrongful detention of a recovered patient. He was resistant to all suggestions of change, believing that since 1859 the Commissioners in Lunacy had brought about continual, significant improvement in the entire asylum system, and the private sector in particular. By non-renewal of private licences, a requirement to re-license every thirteen months, and an increasing refusal to allow new asylums to open that were not run by a qualified doctor, the private system had never functioned better, Shaftesbury claimed. And until such time as state-registered hospitals could provide accommodation suitable for middle- and upper-class lunatics, the wealthy should continue to have the option of private licensed houses.

His biggest worry was the rise in the 'scientific' specialists in lunacy, who

> surrender everything to science . . . [and] would almost take leave of common sense. There is no doubt that if you probe every human mind and every human heart, and test them by the severest formulas of science, you will find such moral curiosities, that anybody might very safely affirm, upon scientific grounds, that this or that person has a tendency to go out of his mind . . . You may depend upon this: if ever you have special doctors, they will shut up people by the score.

Yet, for the time being, no one was being shut up without good reason, argued His Lordship, exasperating Mrs Lowe, who felt that he had become out of touch in lunacy matters, and thus 'purely ornamental' within the Commissioners in Lunacy.

The *British Medical Journal* saw the Select Committee as a damp squib, believing that those who complained of wrongful incarceration had utterly failed to convince:

> Altogether, the mountain which had travailed has brought forth a mouse. The cases of grievance put before the Commissioners at great length turned out to be moonshine, and under such circumstances no really valuable result could be expected. A great deal of time has been wasted, for which the only compensation we can see is, that the public mind may possibly be reassured from the scare which first assumed important dimensions under the skilful manipulation of Mr Charles Reade, in his well-known *Hard Cash*.

The massive *Report* of the Select Committee, running to over 700 pages, had indeed found no case to answer on the part of the asylum proprietors and the Commissioners. It mooted several changes to the laws – none of them new and some of them quite in tune with the Lunacy Law Reform Association's agenda for change. Perhaps a magistrate, rather than the Commissioners in Lunacy, should examine all new certificates, and countersign or reject them; maybe an independent medical man could be appointed at each private asylum, together with increased visitation by the Commissioners, whose numbers in that case needed to increase. In the longer term, more public hospitals should be accessible to the wealthy; far more radically, the *Report* wondered whether the state should buy up all private asylums. Yet none of these proposals was acted upon, and no amending legislation followed. Mrs Lowe discovered – just as John Perceval had found – that obtaining a governmental hearing had merely ratified the status quo.

Mrs Lowe died in North London in 1901, at the age of eighty-one. By that time, she had been eclipsed by the formidable woman she had inspired, whose story at long last prompted legislative change.

'Be sure you don't fall, Georgie!'

She was up a ladder in the library, brushing down the music books on the upper shelves with a feather duster, wearing a dressing gown and an old, dirty apron. Her maid, Villiers, came into the room and announced that a Mr Shell and a Mr Stewart were downstairs and wished to see her. 'Send them up!' she said, believing them to be her friends, the music publishers Duff & Stewart, and that Villiers had mistaken Duff's name. It was an odd time to pay a call, ten o'clock on a Sunday morning, but never mind. She felt no need to change her attire; these visitors were well known to her, and in any case, she cared less and less for appearances. As she would later say, 'Being beautiful only helps men who are no good to fall in love with you.' She was still up the ladder when two men entered – not her Duff & Stewart at all, but strangers, announcing, 'Mrs Weldon, you do not know us, but we know you. We are spiritualists and we have read your letters to *The Spiritualist* newspaper on the education of children and we wish to place some infants with you in your school of music.'

Feather duster in hand, she descended, and asked them to please sit down; she would be happy to talk about this subject, to which she had dedicated the past eleven years of her life. Shell was lean and elderly; Stewart, younger, was, in her words, 'all blinks, winks and grins, and looked like a washed Christy [blackface] minstrel'. They asked her whether the children she educated were brought up to be spiritualists. She said no, spiritualism was an adult concern, and went on to explain her system of musical education for children, and the difficulties that some parents and relations had created, taking away a fully trained child and setting it to work in music halls or other disreputable venues; for that reason, she preferred to take in only orphans. Mrs Weldon was so confident in her system of training, she was sure that any child, no matter how young, who was taught by her could, after just three years, earn £1,000 a year from singing. If only she were to be put in charge of the Albert Hall, she continued, she could make it into a going concern (which it was failing to be in its earliest years). The conversation then moved on to other topics. The men asked whether an animal could be said to have a soul, and Mrs Weldon replied that she felt that her deceased pug dog, Dan Tucker, had 'an immortal spirit'; she could almost believe that he had had the soul of a man. She felt she was protected by her guiding spirits and they would warn her if she were ever to be threatened with any great danger. And she recounted a particular experience during which she had felt she had been enveloped in a shower of stars. Mrs Weldon was in full flow on her favourite subjects, and as a naturally loquacious and animated woman, she had much to say in reply to all the questions put to her by the two visitors. After half an hour Shell and Stewart left, and Villiers, along with the male servant, Bell, watched from behind as they went down the front steps, laughing.

At two o'clock that afternoon, a real old acquaintance was announced. Lieutenant-General Sir Henry de Bathe had known Mrs Weldon for sixteen years and had reason to be grateful to her. De Bathe was a magistrate, had been decorated for bravery at Sebastopol, and was a governor and the treasurer of St Luke's insane asylum at Old Street, central East London. But as a notorious old roué, running three separate ménages and with at least one illegitimate child, the general had been widely shunned when he attempted to present his new, adolescent, wife to Society; the couple had eloped when she was sixteen years old and had a child before marrying. Broad-minded and open-hearted, Mrs Weldon had taken no notice of the ostracism and had invited the new Lady de Bathe to visit her to show that she cared nothing for the snobbish, hypocritical scorn of others. However, since Mrs Weldon's separation from her husband three years earlier, in 1875, the general himself had been more aloof. She would once have considered him one of her most trusted advisers, but over the past three years they had seen each other, briefly, just once. She saw nothing odd, though, in him turning up on this Sunday afternoon, without notice; what was a little peculiar, she thought, was that he stayed for just ten minutes and didn't seem interested in hearing about her recent domestic problems, which were making her anxious and unhappy.

After the general left, Mrs Weldon carried on cleaning up the library. Rummaging around in the books, music scores and piles of disordered paperwork, she wondered whether she was likely to find any more letters like those she had come across when she had unlocked the library bureau; reading through them had deeply unsettled her.

Then at 8.30 p.m., while she was talking in the library with her elderly servant Tibby, Bell announced that Messrs Shell and Stewart had returned and wished to see her. She told Bell it was too late to receive anyone, but while Mrs Weldon and her servants had their backs to the library door, the two men entered and announced themselves. 'You are not Shell and Stewart,' said Mrs Weldon. The two men replied that they had come from her visitors of this morning and that they too were spiritualists wishing to hear her views on children, education and spiritualism. More flattered than annoyed by the intrusion, Mrs Weldon sat for an hour with the strangers, repeating for them her various psychic experiences and her child-rearing methodology. The younger man was in early middle age and he sat silent and immobile, with his arms folded across his body, staring at her so hard she wondered if he were trying to mesmerise her. The older man sat at the library table and wrote down everything she said.

She told them that she tried to channel her pupils' natural childish destructiveness by encouraging them to rip up rags into tiny pieces, which could then be used to stuff pillows and so on. The men asked her if any of the children were mediums, and she said no, only an adult could be a medium, but that one of the boys and one of the girls had told her they had seen Dan Tucker, the dead dog, walking near his grave in the garden; and Mrs Weldon said she had wished she'd seen him too. The older man said, 'I suppose you think he had a soul.' 'Oh I have no doubt of it!' she replied.

Mrs Weldon continued to talk passionately on these and similar themes but wondered if the older man was slightly deaf, as he would read back to her what he thought she had said and as often as not she had to correct him. Eventually, each man asked to leave the room for a moment, leaving her alone with the other. The older man walked to the large bay window and beckoned Mrs Weldon. Together they looked out at the beautiful moonlit garden, which stretched out southwards from Tavistock House, Tavistock Square, Bloomsbury. 'What a nice house you have,' he said, and then commented on how lovely the grounds were; and, she later remembered, 'as he turned around, he looked at me with a sort of glittering stare, which perfectly terrified me'.

When the younger man was alone with her, he asked if she sang at the piano all day, and she said, 'No, I only ever sing and play when I am teaching.' He told her she was young and had a very beautiful voice and she replied that he was extremely impertinent. 'I thought his questions silly and I thought him very rude,' Mrs Weldon later stated.

She mentioned to the pair her separation from her husband and informed them that he gave her an allowance to help with the running costs of her music school. But she couldn't help referring also to one of her current worries: pointing to the bureau she told them, 'I found in that drawer, letters proving that a most diabolical conspiracy exists against me, and I will read them to you. *That* is a providential cabinet, with providential drawers, and the key was left behind providentially.' But the men were not interested; in fact they rose immediately to leave.

What a lot of visitors in one day. It was unusual. A feeling of foreboding suddenly came upon her as she saw the pair out – was Dan Tucker trying to warn her of something? She confided to Tibby and Bell that she wondered if the visitors intended to do her harm and were in some way connected to those terrible letters. She told Bell to put the chain on the front door that night – a rare precaution.

Tibby wasn't resident at Tavistock House and left to go home; Villiers had not yet returned from her evening off. In order to feel safe, Mrs Weldon went down into the servants' quarters to be with Bell. At 9.45 p.m. they heard the iron gates that separated the driveway from Tavistock Square being opened and a carriage approach. When the doorbell rang Mrs Weldon told Bell not to admit anyone, 'as something I call my guardian angels had given me a sign, warning me I was in very immediate and grave danger. Death, I felt it meant . . .' Bell went upstairs and opened the door on the chain. On the steps stood a man and two women, all strangers; they had no card to present when asked, and so Bell would not allow them in. The knocking and ringing continued for some time. Mrs Weldon told Bell to extinguish all gaslight, so that it would appear the household had gone to bed. At last, the assault of the knocker and bell stopped and the carriage left – Villiers saw it leaving the square as she turned the corner from Euston Road, as she headed back to Tavistock House.

Tavistock House, on the far right of the terrace, was home to Charles Dickens between 1851 and 1860. In 1870, Mrs Weldon set up her music academy here.

The household slept badly and rose early on the Monday morning. Mrs Weldon was now certain what had been going on and sent out several messages. She sent a note to the police station at Hunter Street (a few streets to the east) to arrange for an officer to visit her; a telegram was sent to Sir Henry de Bathe, stating, 'Come at once, it is a matter of life and death' (he never responded); and she wrote to Mr Gladstone, who replied two weeks later that she ought to tell the Lunacy Commissioners about the matter. Finally, she sent a note to Louisa Lowe, knowing her to be the founder of the Lunacy Law Reform Association; she told Mrs Lowe that she felt 'these mysterious visits and visitors are something to do with the vile system you have denounced'. Mrs Weldon had never met the campaigner but had admired her writings in *The Spiritualist* and *The Medium and Daybreak*. She had hoped to deliver this message in person to Mrs Lowe's home in Keppel Street, just a quarter of a mile away, but when she emerged through the iron gateway into the north-east corner of Tavistock Square she became alarmed by the number of stationary cabs parked in the vicinity, and feared that one of them might be the equipage that had called so abruptly last night.

The Hunter Street police inspector turned up at 11.30 a.m. and agreed to have officers stationed in Tavistock House from six o'clock, in order to arrest anyone who attempted to trespass. But Mrs Weldon's husband's solicitor, James Neal, visited unexpectedly shortly afterwards, and on his way out instructed Bell to admit any man who came to call. When Bell refused, saying this was contrary to Mrs Weldon's wishes, Neal pointed out that it was an order from Mr Weldon himself, which overrode his mistress's demands. Bell silently resolved to do Mrs Weldon's wishes, not those of her husband.

Two hours later, one of the two women who had called the night before rang the bell. She was sent away and told to come back at 6.30 p.m. (when the police would be waiting). Then, five minutes later, Mrs Lowe arrived and sent up her card. 'I joyfully welcomed her,' Mrs Weldon later recalled. The women were conferring urgently in the library when Bell knocked; he was pale and shaking and said that the trio of the night before had forced their way into the hallway. Mrs Weldon dispatched Mrs Lowe to fetch the police and then locked herself in the library.

Her half-formed suspicions now came into horribly sharp focus. The man who had thrust himself into her hallway was Wallace A. Jones, keeper of Dr Lyttleton Stewart Forbes Winslow's two madhouses in Hammersmith, seven miles away in West London. The women with him were nurses Sarah Southey and Mary Anne Tomkins. Jones was brandishing what appeared to be a lunacy order for her apprehension, which had, he claimed, been signed by her husband. Mrs Weldon refused to believe this: their separation had been amicable, and although a coolness had subsequently arisen between husband and wife, she felt that Mr Weldon didn't have it in him to behave in this dastardly way. She pushed out from under the library door two messages – one to be delivered to her husband, asking him to come to her assistance; the other to one of her closest friends, Lise Gray, who arrived promptly at Tavistock House.

When the Hunter Street officers finally turned up, Mrs Weldon was persuaded by Police Sergeant James Banger to come out of the library so that the situation could be resolved. When she stepped out into the hall, Jones shouted, 'Grab her!' and the nurses lunged, but Mrs Lowe and Miss Gray tussled and struggled with them, extricating Mrs Weldon, who dashed back into the library and barricaded herself in, Mrs Lowe shouting after her, 'They are assaulting you! Have them arrested!' Mrs Lowe appealed to the police, who found themselves perplexed: should they be helping to apprehend a dangerous lunatic for whom an official order had been presented, or should they be arresting three trespassers on private property who appeared to be committing an assault? Banger and his colleagues later admitted that the Metropolitan Police rule book had failed to prepare them for such an occurrence. So another stand-off began, during which Mrs Lowe read the lunacy order for herself. She saw that it had indeed been signed not only by Harry Weldon but by Sir Henry de Bathe and informed Mrs Weldon through the library door that the treachery she had intuited was a lot more sinister than her wildest imaginings. 'You do not know how bad husbands are,' Mrs Lowe hissed through the keyhole.

Mrs Lowe then woman-handled the three burly madhouse staff out of Tavistock House. She was physically robust, but nevertheless this was quite a feat – particularly as she had done it in full view of Sergeant Banger and used as little force as necessary to avoid the risk of being charged with assault. The madhouse brigade, getting no help from the officers, drove off to obtain further instructions.

Mrs Weldon opened up the library door, and once inside, Mrs Lowe persuaded her that flight was now her only option. Villiers came in too, and stroked the hand of her stricken mistress, confirming that Harry's signature had indeed been on the lunacy order, as well as that of Sir Henry de Bathe. Mrs Weldon was distraught, but all present advised her to flee Tavistock House. 'I'd go, Ma'am,' said Bell, and the police could only echo this – 'Yes, do go, Ma'am.' In her slippers, with a cloak and bonnet pulled on, she rushed out into the square, Mrs Lowe puffing along behind her. A police officer hailed a hansom cab for them, and away they were trotted, to Keppel Street.

Close to midnight, another carriage rolled into the Tavistock House driveway. A policeman in the square, who had been briefed about the furore in the house that afternoon, watched as two of the three passengers went up the steps and rang the bell; there was no reply. The three were Dr Winslow, who had inherited the Hammersmith madhouses on his father's death in 1874; his brother-in-law, the lawyer, journalist and playwright Arthur à Beckett, and Harry Weldon himself. Dr Winslow approached the police officer and said he had been told at the station house that the constable would assist him; but the policeman told them he had received no such instructions. The men offered him money for his compliance, but the officer declined the bribe and watched as one of them went back to the house, pulled the bell again, clapped his hands together and declaimed, in stage melo-drama fashion: 'If it costs a thousand tonight, I must have Mrs Weldon!' But again there was no response, and the men returned to their vehicle and left the square.

On Tuesday morning news reached Mrs Lowe and Mrs Weldon that the carriage had travelled on to the LLRA offices in Berners Street, just half a mile west; it would surely, then, not be very long before it called at Keppel Street. Sympathetic friends offered their house as refuge to Mrs Weldon for the next seven days – at the end of which time the documentation permitting her seizure would expire. But with a coincidence found usually in the more tawdry literature of the day, their home overlooked Dr Winslow's asylums, Sussex House and Brandenburgh House, so another escape was required. Disguised as a Sister of Mercy Mrs Weldon made off, first to a lodging in Whitechapel and then to another in Bayswater, where we'll leave her for a while, no doubt contemplating how a life that had been so full of promise had taken such a vile turn.

Mrs Weldon was born Georgina Thomas in 1837, the eldest of five surviving children of fantastically snobbish parents, whose social ambitions were for the most part to be thwarted. Her father changed the family surname to the grander-sounding, ancestral 'Treherne' and this may have assisted him in winning a Tory seat in 1863 after twenty years of trying. The family had lived in Florence for twelve years, moving there when Georgina was three years old. There, she grew up highly cultured, and fluent in French and Italian. She was wild and wilful and got through seven governesses in one year. Papa opened all the family's letters and was a figure of terror to his wife and children. 'We never dared open our lips in his presence, scarcely daring to breathe without his snubbing us unmercifully,' wrote Georgina. The Trehernes' return to England did little to tame her: Mama burned Georgina's diaries for the years 1854 to 1859, in case they should compromise the family with their trenchant opinions and racy musings about the nature of love.

Georgina before her marriage, a watercolour copy of a
portrait by George Frederic Watts.

Georgina was very attractive; but there must have been something
more to her than her looks. Whatever it was, it fails, for the most
part, to come across when we survey the surviving images of her;
camera, brush and pencil have not captured the charisma that led to
so many conquests, if not carnal then at least emotional. Georgina
captivated many men, and at least one woman, when she entered
Society. Watts painted her and called her his 'wild little girl'; and she
told him that the key to her nature lay in the word 'excitable' –
although, as we shall see, 'excitable' had an altogether different
meaning for Victorian alienists.

Her beautiful voice would be remarked upon by many as one of
her most alluring qualities, whether she was speaking, singing or
haranguing. As professionalism would risk social ostracism, she sang
in an amateur capacity, in the drawing rooms of London, which gave
her access to the bourgeois-bohemian company of painters and writers
(she knew and was known by the Pre-Raphaelites and by Thackeray;
her relationship with Dickens was to prove more complicated).

All her life she was reckless – offending the genteel and thumbing her nose at decorum; but what she never appeared to learn about herself was that these rebellions brought her emotional and financial damage. She enjoyed flouting rules but became distressed when the easily predictable retribution for doing so arrived. It first occurred when she was in late adolescence: a promising match with a wealthy, well-connected young man was ended abruptly by his mother when Georgina was found unchaperoned in Watts's London studio with Lord Ward, a wealthy widower. She was afterwards unwelcome in the homes of certain families, since there could be no innocent explanation of the two being alone together where they did not expect to be discovered. This type of rejection did matter to Georgina, but she acted as though it did not.

Papa had virtually imprisoned her in the family home after this incident, but on a rare night out in 1858, at a ball, she met good-looking twenty-year-old Lieutenant William Henry Weldon of the 18th Hussars (he saw no active service). He was the son of a deceased Sheffield coal merchant, and in the brutal financial sizing-up that was the norm whenever middle- and upper-class love appeared to be kindling, Harry informed the Trehernes that he would shortly be coming into a trust fund of a couple of thousand pounds a year, that he would get another £2,000 per annum when his grandmother died, and yet another annual sum of £2,000 on the death of his mother. Papa and Mama were enraged that he had jumped the gun and written so vulgarly before being invited to present his credentials; and in any case, £10,000 a year was the lowest acceptable income for anyone hoping to marry their daughter. When Harry came into a lump sum inheritance of £7,500 on his twenty-first birthday he got through it in eighteen months – an uncharacteristically energetic act for a man who would be regarded by many as one of life's passengers. So by the time he and Georgina met again, and decided that they still had romantic feelings for each other, Harry ('My dear old Poomps', as she called him; she was his 'Tatkin') was deep in debt – and neither his grandmother nor his mother looked set to enter the next world in the near future.

The pair married in secret on 21 April 1860, Georgina having extracted a promise from Harry that he would allow her to go on the stage and earn her own living by singing. She was instantly disowned

Harry Weldon (above) and Georgina married in secret in 1860. 'The dirty old Guv cut me off within twenty-four hours,' she said of her father, who disinherited her as a result.

by the Trehernes: 'The dirty old Guv cut me off within 24 hours,' she wrote in her diary. She never saw Papa again; becoming increasingly deranged, he was confined, and died at Dr George Fielding Blandford's lunatic asylum at Long Ditton, Surrey, where four attendants had often been required to restrain him.

Georgina became pregnant on her honeymoon but lost the child at four months. For the first time her exuberance and lust for life faltered. She and Harry seemed very much in love in the first three years of their marriage, but although there were several false alarms, it appears that she did not become pregnant again. She remained upset by the coolness that had arisen between her family and herself, and she was devastated by the death of her favourite sister, Florence, in 1868. To add to her misery, she was living in humble conditions, in a small cottage in Beaumaris, Anglesey, next door to Harry's mother, with whom she did not get on. The only blessing is that she would not find out about a mistress of Harry's for many years to come. He kept Mrs Annie Lowe on a houseboat moored on the Thames at Windsor. Mrs Lowe was a dressmaker, and the mother of a son, Frank, whom Georgina would later conclude, probably mistakenly, was Harry's. Georgina would also later claim that her miscarriage was 'owing to his horrid ways . . . He was of disgustingly sensual habits', suggesting that he had communicated to her a venereal infection – presumably non-syphilitic, as neither went on to develop serious symptoms.

As the likelihood of becoming a mother lessened, and the love between husband and wife began to dwindle into friendly toleration, Georgina's musical ambitions crystallised. She had continued to be a drawing-room soprano, performing in Wales and in London during the Season, and in 1868 she decided that she also had a gift for teaching singing. Her best-informed biographer believed that her theory of music education was years ahead of its time, and Georgina persuaded Harry, who had by now come into his grandmother's money, to purchase the lease of Tavistock House, in 1871. She later claimed that the leasehold was paid for largely from her own savings and earnings from singing and teaching (which she was allowed to keep, following the passing of the 1870 Married Women's Property Act); but Harry believed it was his inheritance that had allowed them to rent such a prestigious property as Tavistock House.

As Mrs Weldon would write in her 1880 work, *The Ghastly Consequences of Living in Charles Dickens' House*, Tavistock House attracted huge amounts of unwanted attention. Dickens had lived there between 1851 and 1860, and although she never said so, Mrs Weldon may have intuited that the house was a curse on matrimony. For it was here that the Dickens marriage, already in trouble, fell to pieces, with the novelist ordering that his dressing room be converted into a separate bedroom for himself, and the door between this and Catherine Dickens's bedroom be sealed up. It was also where he wrote *Bleak House*, *Hard Times*, *A Tale of Two Cities* and *Little Dorrit*. People came from all over the world to look at the premises and sometimes, when they knocked on the door and asked to see the interior, Mrs Weldon would oblige. One day she was alarmed to see a man's head poking in through an open window; behind him was a heavily pregnant woman and some children. He introduced himself as Cadwalladwr Waddy, a barrister and direct descendant of Edward II. This should have been warning enough, but Mrs Weldon took the Welshman and his wife, Albertine Fanny Waddy, and the little

Waddys, on a tour of the grounds, and she chatted about her own Welsh ancestry.

Mr Waddy came back alone the following afternoon, but Mrs Weldon was busy; so he returned in the evening, with a red and a white rose intertwined and a letter addressing her as 'The Princess of Wales' and signed by 'The Prince of Wales'; and then every day, bearing gifts and love letters, calling her 'My Mountain Sylph'. He continued to write to her, insisting that they elope together to India and have a large family of Welsh royalty: 'Dye your hair bright red and your eyebrows pink,' he wrote, imploring her to come to Madras to 'sit by the sad sea waves of an evening'. Rather cruelly, Mrs Weldon packaged the letters up and sent them to Albertine Fanny, who replied that her husband was indeed a madman, that she had taken the children and returned to her parents, and that she expected him to be certified soon. This episode would later be used as ammunition by Harry Weldon and the mad-doctors, even though Mrs Weldon had merely been the unwitting target of a madman's ardour – which had all been caused by the fact that she had moved into Dickens's house.

But she couldn't blame it all on Boz. Where the novelist had prized domestic order and a well-organised household, Mrs Weldon made a Pandemonium of his former home. Her original plans for Tavistock House, to teach just fifteen resident girl pupils for two years, became hugely (her detractors would say grandiosely) distorted in scope, and Dear Old Poomps packed his bags after four years of it. His good-natured toleration of the goings-on at the house would be pointed up by his defenders in later years, but of course Harry did have Mrs Lowe-on-Thames and his beloved Clubland (he was a member of the Garrick) to escape to when things became too chaotic at Tavistock Square.

'Odious calumnies', as Mrs Weldon called them, had been bandied about in certain circles when celebrated French composer Charles Gounod came to live at Tavistock House in 1872. Novelist George Moore unkindly described Gounod as 'a base soul, who went about pouring a kind of bath water melody down the back of every woman he met'. The fifty-four-year-old creator of the operas *Faust* (1859), *Mireille* (1864) and *Roméo et Juliette* (1867) was, in part, fleeing an unhappy marriage, and he fell passionately for 'Mimi', as he called

Mrs Weldon. There is no evidence that this was ever a physical relationship, but the very fact of him living beneath the Weldons' roof for two and a half years led to scurrilous rumours. Once again, Mrs Weldon had shown lack of caution. Capturing Gounod for 'Mrs Weldon's National Training School of Music at Tavistock House' had been a coup, and the academy's profile was hugely enhanced, but then the scandal began to have an impact on pupil numbers. Despite his later complaints, Gounod found that his isolation from Parisian adulation allowed him to enter a prolific phase, with Mimi as his muse: at Tavistock House he cracked out two operas, a requiem mass, an oratorio, ten psalms and anthems, twelve choruses and sixty-three songs – all the more remarkable because in the rooms below his, tumult predominated. When Gounod told Mrs Weldon of L'Orphéon de la Ville de Paris – a government-funded singing and music school for destitute orphans – she turned her academy into 'Mrs Weldon's Orphanage'. She now took in abandoned or extremely poor children who found themselves renamed in commemoration either of past admirers of Georgina's ('Merthyr', 'Dagobert') or of Gounod's operatic creations ('Sapho-Katie', 'Sapho-Baucis', 'Mireille'). The children were allowed a quarter of an hour's 'yelling' every day, to let off steam and to loosen inhibitions as well as vocal cords. They ate no meat, and they wore no socks or shoes – to cut down the laundry bill and to avoid mess and noise. But mess and noise were sufficiently provided by Mrs Weldon's over-indulged and inadequately house-trained pugs, Dan Tucker, Whiddles, Mittie, Tity and Jarbey. The boisterousness of the household would later include the sound of the Rawlings – a family of street musicians comprising the sons and a daughter of a destitute blind accordion player from Lambeth. Mrs Weldon turned the Rawlings into a handbell-ringing act and would come to use some of the Rawlings brothers as spies and emissaries in her war against those whose calumny appeared to be holding back the school's success. This would backfire.

Mrs Weldon had been partly attracted to Tavistock House by the Dickenses' former schoolroom – a huge chamber that when converted into a performance space could accommodate an audience of ninety and a stage thirty feet deep. (It was here that Dickens used to write, direct and star in children's spectaculars, such as *Fortunio and His Seven Gifted Servants*, and, for adults, *The Frozen Deep*, co-written by and co-starring Wilkie Collins.) Now the Gounod Choir for adults would practise here, paying good money to be trained and conducted by the maestro himself; but the wild children, plus all the gossip, took a toll on attendance levels. One of the choristers claimed that Charles Rawlings's single thick eyebrow, running the entire width of his forehead, was perfectly disgusting and indicative of criminality. Mrs Weldon was angered by such unthinking, casual snobbishness. She was by now at the heart of social and political activism for all sorts of causes, including feminism, spiritualism, vegetarianism, anti-vivisectionism, anti-vaccinationism, land reform, the repeal of the blasphemy laws and support for the Rational Dress movement, whose aim was that no woman should have to wear more than 7lb of undergarments.

Regarding her musical enterprise, she urged intuition, amateurism and raw feeling as ways to break down the rigidity, hierarchy, conformity and closed-shop nature of the professional artistic circle. Mrs Weldon's assault on the music world chimed perfectly with the low-level unrest that was unsettling many sectors of the nation in the 1870s. There was a great deal of crossover between spiritualists such as Mrs Weldon and Mrs Lowe and all manner of political protest, and the leading paranormal publications of the day reveal the bundling together of religious, social and political restlessness. The world had been revealed to the adherents of spiritualism as less solid than they had supposed – it was in fact a universe of gases, emanations and electrical impulse. For many, this new sense of fluidity brought about a social and political, as well as religious, reawakening. One of the two leading English journals of spiritualism was called *The Medium and Daybreak*, the latter word reflecting the idea of an emergent new era (as did 'The Golden Dawn' movement, formed in the late 1880s) – a turning-away from convention, constriction, the cash nexus, and gender and class segregation.

Mrs Weldon's falling-out with the musical establishment would extend across two nations. When Charles Gounod stormed off back to his wife in Paris in June 1874, Mrs Weldon was distraught – she was not just hurt but left with a powerful sense of having been used, manipulated and then abandoned. Her pain quickly turned to anger. She sent the composer a bill for £9,791 13s 9d for his keep, although more than half of this she itemised as compensation for 'the injury done by infamous calumnies, lies and libels'. She refused to return two of his scores that he had accidentally left behind, which drew fierce criticism from the French press, who believed that a great man had been held captive in London by a talentless *rosbif* adventuress.

But Mrs Weldon carried on without the famous Frenchman. Each Monday evening, the children were transported to Langham Hall in the West End in an ancient omnibus that she had bought second-hand and painted brown. Here, they would perform their Sociable Evenings, with Mrs Weldon singing her own composition, 'Pussie's Christmas', the Rawlingses ringing their handbells and various children – some as young as two – singing solos or reciting verse.

Georgina's family found her singing and bell-ringing orphans an embarrassment.

Of all her alleged iniquities, it was the bus that mortified her family the most. Following Papa's death, Mrs Weldon was back in contact with them, but when Mama and eldest brother Dalrymple found out about the clapped-out vehicle – with huge writing on the sides and rear, announcing 'Mrs Weldon's Orphanage' and 'Mrs Weldon's Sociable Evenings. Langham Hall, 43 Great Portland Street. Every Monday 8 p.m.' – they became more sympathetic to Harry Weldon's predicament. Letters about Mrs Weldon's embarrassing behaviour began to be exchanged within her family. Dalrymple – 'the essence of a conceited prig', as she described him – wrote to his sister to implore her not to park or drive the bus anywhere near his London home.

The Duke of Bedford, ground landlord of Tavistock House, was no less perplexed and indignant when he learned that a self-navigating, self-steering hot-air balloon had been sitting for some time, inflated, at the front of the house, awaiting a patent and a commercial backer; to this eyesore was attached a sash bearing the legend MRS WELDON'S ORPHANAGE. The balloon had been the bastard brainchild of someone else Mrs Weldon had thoughtlessly, foolishly invited into her life – and the consequences were to be catastrophic for her.

She was in the habit of having the Rawlings brothers read out to her interesting snippets in the newspapers, and one day one of the brothers pointed out that a gentleman who had in the past come to see Monsieur Gounod with a libretto was now in the dock at Bow Street on a charge of child kidnap. She sent the Rawlingses off to the magistrates' court to find out more, and ended by inviting the accused, Anacharsis Ménier, and his wife, Angèle, to come and live at Tavistock House. She did not find out for some time that Anacharsis was a con artist of some standing in his native France, and that Angèle had been a Parisian street prostitute whom he had pimped before marrying her. The child they would be found not guilty of seizing was Angèle's niece, Bichette, who now joined Mrs Weldon's rescued orphans; and Angèle turned out to be very handy with the ouija board.

When Angèle moved in, Georgina cut her own hair short, and both began to wear severely tailored, heavy black clothing; when writing to Angèle, Mrs Weldon adopted a masculine persona. All of which powerfully suggests that this was a physical relationship, though the only person to have worked his way through Mrs Weldon's voluminous, but now lost, personal archive refused to accept that the friendship was 'suspect', to use his quaint term. Anacharsis Ménier later accused Mrs Weldon of having a sexual relationship with his wife; but he was a known liar and blackmailer, and would also accuse her of poisoning three of the orphans and burying them beneath Charles Dickens's mulberry tree (all that was down there were the bones of Dan Tucker, Tity and Jarbey). There is very little else in the surviving evidence that could approach the truth behind the rumours, apart from Georgina's own complaint about 'filthy allusions' that 'Madame Ménier lived with me *apart* from her husband'. What really matters is that the relationship between the women was deep and passionate – and it had placed in the hands of the unscrupulous Monsieur Ménier the wherewithal to blacken her name still further. Ménier would soon become the pivot of the plan to remove the inconvenient, expensive and mortifying Mrs Weldon from the sight of the world.

Things continued to fall apart in Tavistock House. Her enemies would allege that there were twelve untuned pianos, plaster was falling from the walls and ceiling and the gardens were becoming overgrown, although there is no evidence to substantiate such claims. Pupils now pretty much consisted only of orphans, and the Langham Place Sociable Evenings were costing more to stage and publicise than the ticket sales brought in. One night, Mrs Weldon had to call the police to eject one of the young Rawlings when he became aggressive, and when a purse went missing, a spiritualist told her that the culprit was a boy with a single brow – Charlie Rawlings. Daddy Rawlings had been accosted by three men who had offered to pay him for any information he could glean about Mrs Weldon's relationship with Charles Gounod; he had refused, but his sons were less honourable and began to sneak out tales to mysterious interrogators about the goings-on at Tavistock House.

Harry, meanwhile, was growing fidgety. His mother had died and had left him far less money than he had anticipated. So he now wanted to halve the annual allowance he paid to his wife and to sell the Tavistock House lease; but Georgina told him she would not agree to either request. To start divorce proceedings was expensive and potentially highly embarrassing as the existence of Harry's mistress and son might come to light. Though naturally indolent, he was in fact now in employment: Mrs Weldon had used her social contacts to obtain for him the post of Windsor Herald at the College of Arms – a position that probably would not withstand the ignominy of a divorce.

Mrs Weldon began to think bigger instead of smaller. Could she perhaps relaunch her teaching career in Paris? Should she and Angèle take the noticeably gifted Sapho-Katie on a world tour to earn some much-needed capital? In the autumn of 1877, the two women packed up the children and headed for the house of Angèle's sister in Normandy, where the orphans were left while Angèle and Mrs Weldon travelled to Paris to whip up interest in their plans. They left a trusted couple called Mr and Mrs Lowther in charge of Tavistock House, and maids to care for the remaining children, but almost immediately the ruthless Monsieur Ménier kicked the Lowthers out and took over.

Georgina with the woman she loved, Angèle Ménier.

The trip to France was a disaster, and it is not easy to excuse Mrs Weldon the self-absorption, lack of organisation and poor sense of priorities she displayed. In Paris nobody was interested in her project. Then measles broke out in the Normandy village where the children were staying and several of them became seriously ill; fourteen-month-old Mireille died. Mrs Weldon was distressed but failed to act quickly enough, though eventually she was able to find lodging and nursing care for the rest of the children with the nuns at the

convent in the town of Gisors. At this point she received a letter
from Harry announcing that he was in the process of selling the
Tavistock House lease – so where did she want her belongings to
be stored? On reading this news, Mrs Weldon fell to her knees and
asked of heaven what she must do. A celestial voice instructed her,
'Go home at once.'

Mrs Weldon arrived back at Tavistock House, unannounced, early
in the morning of 4 April. The house was even more disordered than
when she had left it six months earlier and she found boxes half packed
with her personal possessions. More shockingly, finding the key in the
lock of the library bureau, she sat down and read her way through
letters which revealed that her mother, her brother, her husband and
Ménier had been debating whether her eccentricity had tipped over
into insanity and whether, if she were to be detained in an asylum,
she might recover her wits. Mrs Weldon was horrified at the supine
attitude of her mother, who had written to Harry:

> Your letter coming like a clap of thunder, though not entirely unex-
> pected, has grievously surprised me. I've sent it to Dal[rymple], who
> will have it in four days more or less, perhaps three. Dr Blandford
> would be an excellent man to consult but it seems to me this would
> be premature. I hope very much you will not do anything precipitately.
> I feel really too unhappy. I had prayed to God to let me die before this
> terrible thing came to pass. You have precipitated this sad event by
> leaving your house at her behest.

In the bureau she also found a bundle of letters from poor mad
infatuated Cadwalladwr Waddy, who had continued to write to her.
These had been opened in her absence and carefully collated.

When Ménier and his heavily pregnant mistress Olive Nicholls
got out of bed at noon and came downstairs, Mrs Weldon noticed
that the Frenchman was wearing one of her watches. She recalled
him that day as 'fat as a pig, his blubber-like cheeks ashen pale, his
dirty, greasy hair longer than ever'. She demanded to know why her
belongings were being packed into trunks; Ménier replied that Harry
had told him that he was entitled to take goods to the value of £178
1s 1d in payment of wages owed to him, and that he was simply
packing up the items he liked best in the house. When Mrs Weldon

accused him of theft, since the items belonged to her, not to Harry, Ménier replied that the law would not support her in this: as a married woman, anything that was hers was Harry's, said Ménier. She had married before the passing of the 1870 and 1874 Married Women's Property Acts, and so these items were in law deemed to be Mr Weldon's, and not her own (although the laws did permit her to keep her own earnings). And if Mr Weldon would not sue, Ménier was confident Mrs Weldon would have no legal recourse to reclaim the objects.

Luckily, Mr Bell, who had just been appointed caretaker of Tavistock House by Harry, took an instant liking to Mrs Weldon, and seeing the rights and wrongs of the situation, suggested calling in Harry's solicitor, Mr Neal. While waiting for Neal to arrive, Bell helped Mrs Weldon to write an inventory of everything in the boxes that Ménier was intending to make off with. Ménier and his mistress now hurried from the house. 'Cheer up, Madam,' Bell told Mrs Weldon, 'I never saw a party run away from his debtor before.'

When Mr Neal turned up, he warned Mrs Weldon not to oppose Ménier, since any contretemps was likely to 'stir dirty water', as he put it. She later recounted the tales the Frenchman had told about her during her absence in France: 'I had put poison bottles around the house in various corners, which the babies found, died, and were buried in the garden. I got £1,000 for each baby, no questions asked [i.e. an illegal adoption]. Ménier had most compromising letters . . . proposing all sorts of dreadful things.' She found the last particularly amusing, knowing that what the foolish Frenchman intended to blackmail her with were the tragic outpourings of Cadwalladwr Waddy. She could hardly wait.

The letters in the bureau had furnished her with the address of Olive Nicholls, in Golden Square, Soho, and ignoring Neal's appeal for her to drop the matter, she took a carriage to Vine Street police station. Accompanied by detective Uriah Cooke, she surprised Ménier and Nicholls in their lodgings, which contained items of Mrs Weldon's clothing, silver plate, jewellery, paintings and small items of furniture. 'I give this man in charge for the theft of these items,' she said to Inspector Cooke. 'And I give this woman in charge for the murder of little children! She is mad!' shouted Ménier. The Frenchman was arrested and charged, the Treasury Solicitor (the nearest England had to a public prosecutor at that time) agreeing to bring the case for Mrs Weldon, even though Harry, in law the legal owner of her stolen belongings, would not come forward to prosecute. At his Old Bailey trial in the following September, Ménier would be found guilty and sentenced to six months' hard labour, despite the jury asking for clemency on the grounds that he was a foreigner and probably had not understood his written instructions from the Weldons or solicitor Neal.

Ménier's Bow Street committal proceedings took place on Saturday 13 April 1878 – nine days after Mrs Weldon had returned to Tavistock House. It was the next day, Sunday the 14th, that the mysterious visitors began to arrive, and on Monday the 15th the attempt was made to snatch Mrs Weldon and take her to the Hammersmith madhouse. Mrs Weldon's unexpected arrival from France had forced her ill-wishers to bring forward rapidly the plans they had hoped to have had more time to finesse. On 13 April Harry had gone to see Dr Lyttleton Stewart Forbes Winslow at his practice and home at 23 Cavendish Square. He told Winslow and the doctor's father-in law, alienist Dr James Michell Winn, that his wife had arrived back from France having abandoned a number of small children to their fate; meanwhile (he said), Mrs Treherne and Dalrymple had contacted him, concerned about the soundness of his wife's mind. Harry showed the doctors a number of letters from his mother- and brother-in-law, which included the phrases 'Things with G are coming to a dreadful pass and danger' and 'Her mental state resembles that of her poor father'. Harry also gave the following reasons for his concern about his wife's mental stability (the wife he had not seen for two years): the filth and dilapidation of Tavistock House; her neglect of her appearance and her wearing of tattered or outlandish clothing; allowing a chamber pot to stand beneath the sideboard in the dining room, in case any of the orphans should be caught short; allowing a white rabbit to run about and defecate on the dining-room table during mealtimes. Harry also mentioned 'the little gutter children, who had been picked up in the street and got the run of the whole house, so that he [Harry] was driven from room to room'. Would Winslow attempt an informal interview with his wife to give his professional opinion on her state of mind? Winslow and Weldon would later deny that at this time there had been any intention of committing Mrs Weldon to an asylum.

There is a whiff of Garrick Club intrigue here. Winslow may have been recommended to Harry by fellow Club member Arthur à Beckett, who was married to the doctor's sister; à Beckett's father and Winslow's father had been close friends, too. Perhaps word got round the Club that Harry was in search of an alienist, and à Beckett mentioned Winslow because he was an energetic opponent of spiritualism. In 1877, Winslow published *Spiritualistic Madness*, a slender book in which he blamed the table-rappers for a rise in female insanity (even though there had been no rise in female lunacy admissions over male). The case studies in the book comprised four males and two females but Winslow nevertheless concluded: 'The community of believers contains a large proportion of weak-minded hysterical women, in whom the seeds of mental disorder, though for a time latent, are only waiting for a new excitement to ripen into maturity.'

It was decided that father-in-law Dr Winn and Winslow would pose as Messrs Shell and Stewart respectively (adapting each man's middle name), pretending to be two spiritualists who were curious about the Weldon Orphanage, in order to gauge Mrs Weldon's sanity. Winslow told Harry that since he had not seen his wife for two years, a third party would need to co-sign the lunacy order. Could Harry suggest anyone to do so? Yes, he said, their old friend Sir Henry de Bathe, of whom Mrs Weldon was fond (overlooking the fact that the general had seen Mrs Weldon only once in the past three years). All Sir Henry would need to do in order to meet the requirements of the Lunacy Act, Winslow advised, would be to conduct a few minutes of conversation with her alone. And as De Bathe was a governor of St Luke's, he would be presumed to be able to spot a lunatic when he saw one.

So on Sunday the 14th, 'Shell and Stewart' paid their visit to Mrs Weldon. Winslow then walked home and wrote out the lunacy order for Sir Henry de Bathe and Harry to sign. The paperwork contravened the Act: the evidence on the document was supposed to have been the eyewitness testimony of its signatory, and although Harry had not seen his wife for two years, the statement he had signed claimed that her unsoundness had endured for the past twelve months. For good measure, and going on hearsay from Harry and the Trehernes, Winslow added 'hereditary insanity' to the lunacy order, attempting to bolster the case by dragging in poor raving Papa.

Those who would later damn Winslow for his role in this story have not, on the whole, understood that he almost certainly believed Mrs Weldon to be insane. All her talk of showers of stars, animals with souls, and voices issuing commands confirmed for him that spiritualism had devastating effects on the brain (particularly the female one). He believed that these effects were pathological and infectious: 'It is not unreasonable to conjecture that the morbid change in the nervous centres, which we see in individual cases producing such visionary results, may also become epidemic, and produce these aggregate delusions.' But in fact the Lunacy Commissioners had found not one case of spiritualism-related insanity in any asylum in the country.

Had he gone on to become a Jungian or Freudian, Winslow might have diagnosed within himself an unconscious desire to add to his family's revenues. While he may well have believed Mrs Weldon to be clinically batty, he was also in the professional habit of assisting people into his rather expensive custodial care. Perhaps there was something Oedipal too: his father had left a rather complicated will, in which Winslow Jnr was only allocated the role of manager, not sole owner, of the asylums – and so he was answerable to his mother and a family trust. His co-opting of his father's name ('Forbes') into his own birth name ('Lyttleton Stewart') is fodder for Freudians, though a more mundane explanation is that it helped the family firm by harking back to the famous Winslow *père* brand name.

Winslow Jnr was a classic over-diagnoser, considering to be mad almost everyone on whom he was asked to give a professional opinion. He would later claim that he had told Harry on the Sunday night that although Mrs Weldon's was an urgent case, she could be 'managed' at home with a lady companion. Winslow was adamant that it was Harry who had insisted on asylum care and had asked Winslow to recommend a good institution. At this point, said Winslow, he revealed to Harry that he ran Brandenburgh House. Mrs Weldon never believed this account, and nor would anyone else who heard it.

Dr Lyttleton Stewart Forbes Winslow (1844–1913) inherited his father's practice but was never popular in alienist circles.

Winslow had proposed charging Harry Weldon £10 10s a week for custody of Mrs Weldon, which puts his madhouses at the dearer end of private care. But the high fee nevertheless was lower than the £1,000 a year that Harry would have to pay to keep his wife at Tavistock House, so incarceration represented both a saving for Harry and the removal of an embarrassment.

Winslow composed the following report:

I have this day visited and examined Mrs Weldon with respect to her mental state. She informed me that a few days ago she received an invisible communication from the spirits demanding her immediate presence in London; this summons she forthwith obeyed, and started for England, leaving a number of children whom she had taken to Paris to educate. She told me that it was decreed by the powers and destiny that she was not returning to France. She gave me an account of a miraculous falling of stars which a short time ago came into her room and enveloped her in its brilliancy, and on which was inscribed the sufferings of Christ on the cross. She told me she had frequent revelations concerning the future. She also said that a dog belonging to her, but lately dead, contained the spirit of a man. She gave me an account of her children whom she received from a month old up to five years to educate, and informed me one of her little girls of the age of three could earn £1,000 by her voice. The conversation throughout my interview was inconsecutive and disconnected. Her present intention, she says, is to go from house to house and endeavour with the proceeds to purchase several more houses and found an institution for lying-in women and adopting the children to educate. Her manner, general conversation and demeanour were those of an insane person, and I am decidedly of the opinion that her condition is such as to require the immediate protection of her friends.

When, two weeks later, the plot was all going haywire, Harry wrote to Winslow that 'the business has been woefully mismanaged' and Winslow replied, 'I do not think you are prudent in giving up for the present the idea of putting your wife in a lunatic asylum.'

Winslow would later claim, 'I always prefer the patient's friends to select their own medical men . . . and the information he may obtain will be acquired from the patient or his relatives, not from me.' In fact, Winslow selected his own alienist investigators from a fairly narrow range. Over a twenty-two-year period, Dr Armand Semple had signed 45 of the 440 admissions into Brandenburgh and Sussex Houses; although he was not attached to the asylums in any formal way, Semple had a cosy professional relationship with Winslow. The two men, both thirty-three years old, had known each other since adolescence and dined together most Sundays at Cavendish Square. He certified patients for only two other asylums. Semple and Dr John Rudderforth (who seems to have been hired in a less pally way) were the second set of 'Shell and Stewart' – Semple the 'mesmeric' starer on the sofa, Rudderforth the uncertain taker of dictation at the library table. Each man received £5 5s from the 30 guineas Winslow had been paid by Harry; Winn received 8 guineas. These were generous payments: the usual fee for certification in these years was £2 2s.

When Harry had asked for his wife to be taken away to a madhouse, Winslow had telegraphed to his Hammersmith asylums from Cavendish Square, requesting a carriage, two nurses and keeper

Wallace A. Jones. When the first attempt at capture failed at Tavistock House, the carriage made its way to Cavendish Square and waited for Harry, Winslow and his brother-in-law à Beckett to make the second attempt. The next day, Mrs Weldon fled.

From what had Mrs Weldon escaped? An eyewitness account of the Winslow family's madhouses appeared in the *Pall Mall Gazette*. The reporter noted a 'not very brilliant performance on the piano by one of the patients' when he entered Brandenburgh House, where there were fifteen women at the time. Most were out in the garden and 'all wore a horrible air of settled depression', the reporter wrote. Looking vacant and never smiling, they marched around the lawn in twos and threes. The journalist believed that anyone of reasonably sound intellect would soon lose her wits if she had to keep such fiercely melancholic company. This was a view frequently expressed in nineteenth-century madhouse discourse – that the sane would become mad if they had to mix with the chronically ill.

Winslow claimed that of the average of nineteen patients admitted annually to both of his asylums, 80 per cent were discharged within a year. In the past fifteen years, there had been twelve escapes from Brandenburgh House but no suicides. There was also a high ratio of attendants to patients. Yet Dr Lockhart Robertson had told the 1877 Select Committee that he, for one, was very unhappy with the admission and detention procedures at Sussex House. As we saw in Chapter Eight, Robertson had become something of a bogeyman for Winslow Snr, who accused him of persecution, so diligent were his visits to the Sussex House Chancery inmates. Robertson continued his surveillance of the Winslow empire and would discover that two male Chancery patients were being detained by Winslow Jnr on faulty, hearsay-filled paperwork.

Winslow liked to tell the tale of how his sangfroid had once saved his life at Brandenburgh House. He had entered the room of a powerfully built woman of suspected homicidal tendencies and had closed the door behind him. During their conversation she pulled out a knife and, remarking how sharp it was, told him, 'I really must kill you, Doctor. I am very sorry, but it can't be helped.' 'Just one moment,' Winslow said, as she strode towards him. 'Don't you think it would be a shame to spill blood on this new carpet? Just let me go and call for a basin.' 'Perhaps it would, but be as quick as you can,' said his would-be assassin as he slipped from the room.

Winslow placed great emphasis on recreation in his asylums, and for this, he was viewed as rather advanced. A keen cricketer, tennis player and angler, he laid on frequent outings for these activities, taking a hearty part in them himself. There were also regular trips to concerts and plays in the West End, and a small stage at Sussex House allowed performances to be put on by the patients. The *Pall Mall Gazette* reporter noted with alarm the many artworks produced by the male inmates at Sussex House: 'The billiard room, which in other respects is a marvel of comfort and cosiness, has indeed an eerie aspect, with its walls adorned by the efforts of generations of artistic madmen who have once been inmates of Dr Winslow's asylum, who have covered them with pictures in oil, watercolours, black and white, landscapes in defiance of every principle of art, and distorted figures with hideous features.' (Sadly, these fantastical pieces appear to have been lost for good when Sussex House was pulled down in 1888; Brandenburgh House vanished four years later.)

Winslow's father had believed that an asylum's cure rate would be significantly higher if it had the feel of a large family home. The Winslows lived on site, with Winslow Jnr growing up at Sussex House; however, Winslow Snr's detractors claimed that before long, the head of the family was in fact living in his chambers in Albemarle Street, Mayfair, and later, the whole family did indeed depart for 23 Cavendish Square. In any case, some commentators were sceptical that recreating a family home had any therapeutic benefits at all for inmates. The family home was often, after all, the site of (if not the actual cause of) emotional collapse.

When her lunacy order expired, on Monday 22 April 1878, Mrs Weldon emerged from hiding and straight away had herself examined – separately – by two doctors. Both certified her sane. She then visited her mother and her brother, who appeared to be truly repentant, claiming that they had been inveigled into her husband's plot to have her declared of unsound mind. Dalrymple stated that he hadn't realised that Harry had wanted to put her in an asylum; he had assumed that some kind of home care, or a single-patient arrangement, would have been worked out. Mrs Weldon chose to believe him.

Mrs Treherne, meanwhile, explained that she had only sought a temporary term of respite care for her daughter, so that she would calm down a little. She was now willing to help in whatever way she could to restore Georgina's reputation. Next, Mrs Weldon visited Sir Henry de Bathe and his wife. At first they tried to deny any role in the events but, while trying to laugh it off, the general finally admitted that he had signed the order. 'You will repent this, both of you,' announced Mrs Weldon as she stalked out of their house.

One of her many geniuses was for publicity, and Mrs Weldon would spend the next ten years ensuring the most public of humiliations for her husband, the doctors and the so-called friends who had questioned her sanity. Their mistake had been to underestimate her, and they would pay for their complacency with damaged careers and shattered reputations. 'May God give me the means, give me the allies, to ruin them,' Mrs Weldon wrote in her diary. In fact, she needed no other people, not even the Almighty. Her retribution succeeded because of her intelligence, energy, theatrics, egotism, lack of self-doubt and huge charisma. Thousands rallied to her talks, concerts and platform appearances. She hitched a flight with one Captain Simmons and a 'cloud photographer', Mr Small, on their ascent from Hastings in a balloon called 'The Colonel', so that she could scatter leaflets about her case across the entire south coast. And when she was in court, the street outside would be filled with those who had failed to find a place in the public gallery, cheering her on her way in and out of the building. Her trials were the best shows in town; even Lord Tennyson had to battle his way to a seat. The court became her stage, now that her singing and teaching careers had collapsed. Here, she won the bemused approval of judges, barristers, newspaper editors and the medical press. She became the nation's 'second-favourite martyr' of the day – after the Tichborne Claimant (the obese Wapping butcher Arthur Orton, who was mounting his campaign to be recognised as the long-lost heir, Sir Roger Tichborne).

Like the Claimant, Mrs Weldon had huge appeal for those who feared the mysterious power of doctors and lawyers and believed that a supine parliament had failed to check the rise of the sinister professional classes. The wronged wife was still a highly attractive rallying point for a populace sickened by incidents in which wealth and power appeared to have silenced and crushed those they found inconvenient.

There were few rebellious causes to which Mrs Weldon would not lend her name and support. She joined the Magna Charta Association, with its narrow remit of supporting the claims of Arthur Orton to the Tichborne title, and its broader one of exposing the secret cabals that it was supposed ran the country. Mad-doctors fitted in perfectly with the Magna Chartists' gallery of criminal professionals who threatened English liberty: *The Englishman* newspaper reported that ardent Tichbornite Father Meyrick had been pronounced mad by 'Jesuit conspirators' and put in confinement in a Fulham asylum, whence he escaped over the wall, was recaptured, and sent to the Augustinian retreat of St George's, Burgess Hill in Sussex.

Mrs Weldon favoured a version of the French *conseil de famille* system, where substantial weight at a hearing was given to those in daily contact with the alleged lunatic. A writ against an alleged lunatic should be filed like any other writ at the High Court of Justice, she believed; and a lunacy order and certificates should be made upon oath, and compensation should be available for a wrongful detention, just as it was in the case of a miscarriage of criminal justice. A public register of lunatics and alleged lunatics should be kept, which would be consultable by any member of the public. To those who objected that 'we will all have our throats cut by raving lunatics' if asylum confinement became less common, Mrs Weldon responded: 'How many persons' throats are cut, women kicked to death, by raving, drunken, brutal husbands daily in this lovely country? Who cares? Of who are the community so afraid?'

She called for a complete overhaul of the Commissioners in Lunacy (an 'overpaid set of sinecurists') and the removal of Lord Shaftesbury as chairman. She asserted that former employees of the Ashley dynasty (Shaftesbury's family name) were benefiting from payments made to them to be keepers of Chancery single patients. Mrs Weldon deduced, from various conversations with escapees who turned up at Tavistock House, that Shaftesbury had pensioned off his poorer relations, former servants, governesses and so on by giving them Chancery lunatics to board, or by making them members of wealthy lunatics' committees. Mrs Weldon believed that she had made a breakthrough in discovering how this occult cabal functioned, and she used the word 'vampyres' to describe figures connected with Chancery. Given the opportunity, she would 'have stirred up so much mud that Chancery, high and mighty as it is, would have been properly besmirched, and have received thrusts far more deadly than Dickens ever levelled at the whole infernal structure'.

It is difficult to know what to make of Mrs Weldon's sinister conclusions about the plight of Chancery lunatics. While it chimes with Admiral Saumarez's criticisms of fifty years earlier, her allegations that Lord Shaftesbury took personal advantage of the single-patient system seem excessive. Mrs Weldon did not appear to appreciate that in an era when personal recommendation was the glue of public life, it might be a wise idea to lodge vulnerable people with those who were known to be trustworthy and kind: Shaftesbury would have been able to recommend his former servants with confidence. But for Mrs Weldon, Shaftesbury did 'not wish for any reform in laws which answer his and his colleagues' purpose so well. He does not want the light thrown on so much hideous wrong and cruelty. Not he! Charity is a very good cry, and it enables some pauper lords to live sumptuously, and to pay countless myrmidons.'

Charles Reade urged Mrs Weldon on, writing in her Tavistock House visitors' book: 'Justice is the daughter of Publicity.' Mrs Weldon got hold of a copy of Lady Lytton's *A Blighted Life*, reading it just one year after its author had died, and deduced from it that alienist perfidy must be hereditary, since Winslow Snr had been such an 'old intriguant' in the Lytton saga. Cometh the hour, cometh the woman, Mrs Weldon declared: 'I no longer hesitate, therefore, in making my own personality very prominent. It is necessary that I should do so, and I beg my readers will pardon the absence of false modesty they may observe in these pages. I cannot help being as the Creator made me, and I have no wish or desire to have been created differently.' An eyewitness gave his impression of one of her earliest lunacy-reform speeches, which lasted two and a half hours: 'She has a pleasing manner, smiles profusely, and speaks in a colloquial manner and with much fluency, delivering her remarks with telling emphasis . . . The audience of 200 laughed loudly at her jokes and cheered and hissed at all the appropriate places . . . "Don't laugh too loud," she told them, "or they will say you are 'excitable'."'

A passage that captures the more hilarious aspect of her indignation, and the hopping from subject to subject (the 'disconnectedness' the alienists had noted in her speech), is to be found in her 1882 pamphlet *Death Blow to Spiritualism – Is It*? With this publication, she intended to alert the public to the prosecution (and persecution) of Dr Henry Slade, a spiritualist of Upper Bedford Place, Bloomsbury, who took celestial dictation upon a slate:

> I know, although I am not a Pharisee, that I employ my time and my money better than most people do. I live to rescue forsaken children from starvation perhaps – from shame and crime certainly. I bring them up, I teach them myself. Surely I do no harm! I feel strong through the innocent claims of my little ducklings. So I walked down with my little brood one evening and I asked to see Dr Slade. A gentleman came down . . . and brought me word that if I could not come in the daytime, Dr Slade would, contrary to his habits, and gratis, appoint half-past seven the next evening. I went. I took my own slates, the slates upon which I teach my little children. I took a slate pencil. I made Dr Slade show me his nails, his feet, which had stockings on. I felt his ankles; yes, I did, ladies and gentlemen, I felt his ankles, so as to be able to feel certain he would not rap with instruments attached to his legs; and I did not let him touch my slates. I held them myself on the table and I myself got the writing inside them.

She will have had no idea why this is so funny but also potentially so dangerous to her – an internal monologue, self-involved and always off on a tangent, which could be twisted to demonstrate an unsoundness of mind. Trapped in her own misery, anger and self-righteousness, Mrs Weldon in her writings sometimes appears to have begun conversing with herself, rather than addressing the reader.

But that does not seem to have deterred her many followers. In the post she received declarations of erotic enchantment from men ('You are a perfect siren, yes, enchantress, Queen of Song. You have been with me in my dreams 'mid the loved faces of my children'), as well as warnings from asylum escapees about her safety ('Dear Madam, A lady warns you that if your house is not detached, people may listen to all you say. An instrument may be placed in any part of your house, they can receive all sounds to report all your words to your enemies . . .'). And the occasional abusive message that she should stop making a public spectacle of herself ('Go to a nunnery!').

Her friendship with Louisa Lowe foundered quickly, and it is likely that Mrs Weldon's fearsome egotism was to blame. She considered Mrs Lowe too timid in her approach to getting the law changed, and seems to have disliked sharing a platform with another woman. For her part, Mrs Lowe may have resented being usurped within the movement that she had founded; as we saw in the previous chapter, Mrs Lowe had already experienced a schism within her organisation. The break between the two women occurred as they struggled for the soul – and the publicity value – of one Mrs Walker. Tavistock House was now a place of safety for those who had escaped their asylums, as Mrs Walker had, after having been wrongfully incarcerated by her army major husband. But Mrs Walker began to miss her children and expressed the wish to return to her marital home in India. Mrs Weldon would not hear of this: it was a total betrayal of the cause and Mrs Walker was told that she should turn and fight every bit as hard as she herself had done. Mrs Weldon claimed that Mrs Lowe then inveigled Mrs Walker away from Tavistock House to Keppel Street, and encouraged her to patch things up with Major Walker.

Mrs Weldon – feeling betrayed and devastated, as usual – refused to return to Mrs Walker the boxes of her belongings that remained at Tavistock House, and so Mrs Lowe instituted proceedings against her at Bow Street magistrates' court. Mrs Weldon carried the day, though not without being thoroughly patronised by the magistrate, Sir James Ingham: 'No one who sees you, Mrs Weldon, will accuse you of acting corruptly. If anyone charges you with these base designs, send him a photograph of yourself, and he will be appeased.' The magistrate's comments were met with laughter from the court, the newspapers reported and Mrs Weldon happily reprinted; but 'the lady smiled, looked more fascinating than ever, and retired'. While she deplored a world that valued a woman mainly for her beauty and charm, Mrs Weldon loved to reprise and dwell on the acclaim her physical presence evoked.

Mrs Lowe now wrote to her, curtly requesting that she desist from making libellous statements about her, since this was not how a gentlewoman should behave; moreover, she was holding back the course of lunacy reform, to which Mrs Lowe had dedicated her life. From then on, Mrs Weldon would 'cut' Mrs Lowe socially. Mrs Weldon ran her own newspaper, *Social Salvation*, which went into libellous detail about her own battles and those of other wronged wives and harassed mediums. She used *Social Salvation* to ventilate her grievances against Mrs Lowe, and the spite in her comments reveals her at her very shabbiest. Remembering the day of her escape from Tavistock House, Mrs Weldon wrote:

> I had not been with her one hour before I felt I should prefer a lunatic asylum to her company . . . Mrs Lowe had herself been confined in a lunatic asylum and I cannot understand how it was she was ever allowed to be at large; for although I do not believe she will ever kill anyone or commit suicide, she is altogether unbearable and unliveable, and a most mischievous, dangerous person.

Mrs Weldon never liked to join any agitation unless she could become Queen Bee. (Poor Mrs Walker, by the way, did return to Major Walker, found him living with a mistress, and died of grief not long after.)

In early 1879, Mrs Weldon sketched out a brief autobiography and published it in the radical newspaper the *London Figaro*. It was a deliberately defamatory article, by which Mrs Weldon hoped to entice her husband, Sir Henry de Bathe and Dr Winslow to launch libel proceedings, so that she could use court privilege to reveal the plot to incarcerate her. Sure enough, on 14 February 1879 she wrote in her diary, 'No Valentine for me, but the very delightful news that Weldon and Sir Henry de Bathe have applied for a criminal information [for libel] against the *Figaro*.' But she was disappointed that the trial made hardly a splash in the newspapers; not as disappointed as *London Figaro*'s editor, though, who was found guilty and sentenced to three months in prison and a fine of £100. Dr Winslow did not break cover to sue. Never mind, there was more to come: Mrs Weldon paid sandwich-board men emblazoned with the words 'Body Snatcher' to parade outside Winslow's madhouses and 23 Cavendish Square. She gave a long lecture entitled 'How I Escaped the Mad Doctors' at her musical evenings (unlike most public speakers, she was able to break up her talks with songs) and later published it. Still Winslow did not sue. However, in the *British Medical Journal* he listed once more the reasons why he had believed her to be of unsound mind (spiritualism; listening to an inner voice; seeing a shower of stars; grandiosity – in having fantastical schemes that she believed only she could achieve) and stated that he had kept strictly within the letter of the lunacy law. 'I maintain that "auricular delirium" is one of the most unfavourable symptoms that exists in mental disorder,' Winslow wrote. But while the doctor would not take the bait, a musical impresario whom Mrs Weldon had denounced as a 'trigamist' successfully prosecuted her in a criminal libel trial, and in May 1880 at the Old Bailey she was sentenced to four months in Newgate Gaol. She served only thirty-seven days and when she emerged, a huge crowd shouted, 'Long live Mrs Weldon!' and threw flowers at her. She now added prison costume to her platform performances, and sang two songs about life behind bars and how she had been 'juggled into Newgate'.

But while she was inside, Harry had sold the lease of Tavistock House, which caused her huge distress – the music academy was now gone for good. Mrs Weldon hit back with a spectacular piece of bloody-minded litigation. 'I have made up my mind that nothing shall keep me from the protecting arm and the sacred roof of so generous and anxious a husband': she took a horrified Harry to court for restoration of conjugal rights (as we have seen, Louisa Lowe would swiftly copy Mrs Weldon's action). During *Weldon* v. *Weldon*, the state of their marriage was discussed in detail, and the judge found in Mrs Weldon's favour. It was a fantastic coup, underlining the sexual double standard and ensuring maximum embarrassment for dear old Poomps. While Harry's appeal was pending, the 1884 Matrimonial Causes Act was swiftly passed. Nicknamed the Weldon Relief Act, this law made sure that a spouse would not face indefinite imprisonment for failure to obey a conjugal restitution decree, but would instead be treated as a deserter of the marriage, and therefore liable to financial and child custody penalties, should the deserted party choose to pursue them.

'I wonder women can endure men,' Mrs Weldon wrote in her diary at about this time, angry that legislation to get males out of a tight spot seemed to speed through as laws to assist females appeared to face endless delay. But very slowly, inch by inch, the absolute power of male heads of families and the legal disabilities of married women were being chipped away at, with legislation that controversially allowed the state some role in family life (to protect wives and children from violence) and in sexual matters (to make men more answerable for a range of activities that were deemed to cause social harm). Parliament debated the private, personal and sexual life of the nation in the late 1870s and 1880s; this was partly the result of feminist-inspired pressure slowly making an impact, plus the piqued interest of the press in domestic and marital matters. The 1878 Matrimonial Causes Act gave magistrates and judges the power to grant a judicial separation to a wife whose husband had been convicted of an aggravated assault upon her; she could also be awarded custody of any children under ten years of age, and granted weekly maintenance. The Criminal Law Amendment Act of 1885 raised the age of consent for females from thirteen to sixteen and introduced a range of measures to assist the investigation and prosecution of sexual assaults and the trafficking of women. In 1886 the Contagious Diseases Acts, enforcing inspection and detention of prostitutes but not their clientele, were repealed, following years of feminist and libertarian opposition. In August 1889, an Act for the Prevention of Cruelty to Children assisted prosecutions for neglect and assault. Of even greater significance for Mrs Weldon, in 1882, the third Married Women's Property Act was passed, allowing wives their own separate legal identity. They could now enter into contracts in their own right – and bring civil lawsuits independently of their husbands. In her desire for justice, Mrs Weldon immediately took advantage of the new legislation.

Between 1884 and 1888 she mounted a total of seventeen legal actions (she called the lawsuits her 'children'), suing Harry, Winslow, Semple, Rudderforth, De Bathe, Gounod, Neal and the editor of the *Daily Chronicle*, among others. She turned herself into a legal expert, working at an office she had rented at Red Lion Court, Fleet Street, assisted by a former solicitor called Chaffers and a writ-server/ general agent called Harcourt. The Royal Courts of Justice opened in 1884 in the Strand, a two-minute stroll from Red Lion Court, bringing under one roof at long last the various civil courts and their personnel. The new building was the appropriately modern setting for a new kind of plaintiff – a married woman; and a new kind of lawyer – female. Nicknamed 'the Portia of the Law Courts', Mrs Weldon's insouciance, her sharp eye for the ludicrous posturings

MRS. WELDON.
BE SURE YOU DON'T FALL, GEORGIE!

of her enemies, and a killer sense of timing often had the counsel, jury and spectators in fits; most of the trial reports contain the bracketed words 'laughter', 'much laughter' and 'roars of laughter'. Some of the judges joined in with the knockabout aspect of the proceedings.

Showing up the arrogance and lack of consistency of the mad-doctors was fairly easy, and she did it with brio. Nevertheless, her first attempt against Winslow (for libel, trespass and assault) failed. The judge, Baron Huddleston, sympathised with Mrs Weldon, but stated that the doctor had acted within the letter of the lunacy law. Winslow had, said Huddleston, believed her to be mad – whether she actually was or not – and had found two independent doctors to interview her, separately, who also came to the same, if erroneous, conclusion.

All the paperwork had been in order, and there was no case for Winslow to answer.

In giving judgment, Baron Huddleston spoke at length of his amazement that an individual might be shut up in an asylum solely on the authority of a lunacy order that could have been signed by anyone. He was scandalised that even a 'crossing sweeper' could sign a lady or a gentleman into lunacy confinement. (Huddleston's 'crossing sweeper' instantly became one of the most famous and titter-inducing judicial dicta of the late nineteenth century.) Huddleston 'regretted to think that the plaintiff could have no redress for the serious inconveniences to which she had been put'.

Following this, Mrs Weldon's arch-enemy, Winslow's brother-in-law, William à Beckett, drew a surprisingly only semi-hostile cartoon of her for *Punch* (see p. 361), as she gingerly trod the tightrope of the law and found that it was not enough simply to have the moral high ground.

Mrs Weldon knew Huddleston to be a member of the Garrick and suspected another Club conspiracy. So on April Fool's Day 1884 she returned to court to ask for a new trial, which was granted by Justice Manisty, who declared that he could not think of a more important case, involving as it did the liberty of the person. 'It is revolting to one's sense of right that merely because the person has some strange or eccentric ideas, therefore she is to be shut up for life,' Manisty said.

Winslow had a much more hostile time of it the second time around, as well as during the later trial of Dr Semple. Justice Hawkins – the judge at the latter trial – even joined in the mockery of Winslow. In fact, this was a terrible time in the life of the doctor, and his natural ebullience had departed, no matter how blithe he appeared in court. Upon the death of his mother in March 1883, his brother-in-law à Beckett demanded that Winslow sign over to him an equal share in the profits from the Hammersmith madhouses. A Chancery suit followed, which Winslow would eventually lose, and the practice and business that his father had built up was slipping away from him by the time of his roasting at the law courts. He would very shortly have to abandon all connections with his asylums, keeping only one single patient – Cecil Wellesley, forty-nine, a former naval lieutenant, installed in Winslow's new family home on Hammersmith Mall.

At the trials it was established that Semple and Rudderforth's interviews had been technically 'separate', as the law required, with each man leaving the room for a few minutes; but this little piece of choreography (a 'Dutch barometer conversation' if ever there was one) had hardly achieved the independent medical assessments intended by the Lunacy Act. What's more, Winslow had drawn up his lunacy order ahead of Mrs Weldon's interviews; however, a lunacy order was not intended to 'capture' a patient but to receive one into an asylum, following the examinations. Justice Hawkins asked Winslow if it were normal for 'servants' (that is, the keeper and the nurses) to seize the lunatic, and when Winslow confirmed that it was how all asylums were run, the judge said this should be altered, no doubt abhorring, as Baron Huddleston had before him, the world-turned-upside-down nature of the lower orders laying hands upon their 'betters', with the full backing of the law.

Not one of the witnesses, from Sergeant Banger and Bell the caretaker to her choir members and neighbours, had ever entertained the notion that Mrs Weldon was insane. The judge had very much not wanted Mrs Weldon to summons her own mother, nor to read out portions of their correspondence, feeling that this would drag private, family life into the public arena. Nevertheless, she did so, and so heightened did the emotion become during the trial that one juror fainted when Mrs Weldon finished reading from a letter to Mama, dated 26 February 1878: 'I don't understand how anybody with blood in their veins would not fly from such persecution as I have suffered,' she had written. 'I am struggling against loss of money and reputation. Everybody for nine years seems to have been misinterpreting my object, &c. So it is always with those who have great ideas, &c.' When she turned to ask Winslow if these words had appeared to him to be those of a madwoman, the juryman swooned and the judge adjourned for the day. Now that mother and daughter were fully reconciled, Mrs Treherne gave evidence that she had never seriously considered her daughter anything more than eccentric, and strongly denied that insanity ran in her late husband's family. 'Mama, dear, you may now go,' said the plaintiff, dismissing her from the box with an informality that had probably never been seen before in a law court.

Yet again the Commissioners in Lunacy failed to cover themselves in glory. In the witness box, the Commission secretary Charles Spencer Perceval (nephew of John Perceval) was shambolic, unable to confirm whether it was normal for a proprietor to write out a lunacy order for an admission into his own asylum. When the judge asked if the Commissioners visited private asylums, Perceval replied that they visited each house six times a year, and more often if there were 'special circumstances' but that there could be two months between visits. This alarmed Justice Hawkins, who wondered whether someone could be snatched and kept for days or even weeks in an asylum without the Commissioners knowing of a complaint of wrongful incarceration; Perceval confirmed that this couldn't be ruled out.

Next on the stand was Lord Shaftesbury himself. While the rest of the nation had been thrilled by the Weldon shenanigans, Lord Shaftesbury told the court (and the House of Lords, when he was asked a question there about the case) that he had never even heard of it. He said he believed the asylum system had very much improved since 1859. When Mrs Weldon probed him on whether an asylum keeper had the legal right to arrest a person, he ducked the question, stating that her case had never come before the Lunacy Commissioners. But Hawkins would not let him get away with this, and repeated the question, 'Is it legal for a keeper to send out agents and servants to arrest someone as a lunatic?' Shaftesbury fumbled that it was a moot point, and it was an issue that had never been raised before. Hawkins would not let go: 'Surely it cannot be contended that a doctor has a right to arrest me, on an order for my reception into his lunatic asylum, just as though he were a policeman arresting me for some offence.' The defence barrister interjected that the Acts did so authorise, and that Baron Huddleston's judgment upon Winslow so held. Yet Mrs Weldon claimed that the Acts only allowed a proprietor to 'arrest' an escapee: he had no right to seize someone who was to be received into his establishment.

Shaftesbury confirmed that the certifying doctors must be entirely independent of the proprietor, and that if the latter filled out the order, and/or put a signature to it, he believed that rendered it invalid.

Mrs Weldon now called the two doctors she had consulted one week after the attempted capture. Dr James Edmunds said that he had spoken to Mrs Weldon for one hour and had formed the opinion that she was of sound mind, despite her 'peculiar notions as to the simplification of women's dress'. He told the court, 'All persons are, in a sense, of unsound mind,' causing riotous laughter.

'That was the very question I was going to ask!' chuckled Justice Hawkins.

'All persons except Your Lordship are, in a sense, or to some extent, unsound in mind.' More laughter.

Edmunds went on to explain that harmless unsoundness could turn into the dangerous kind and that it was the test of a physician's skill to discover if that change had taken place. Under cross-examination, Edmunds said that hearing voices could be a sign of insanity but that in his view it was not necessarily so, unless the voice compelled the hearer to obey. Mrs Weldon had spoken to him about spirits but that had not concerned him, as 'religious people often believe in strange things'. Indeed, Mrs Weldon brought up the fact that St Paul, John Wesley and Emanuel Swedenborg had all heard voices. More hilarity ensued when Edmunds declared he had always assumed that St Paul had been suffering either an epileptic fit or sunstroke on the road to Damascus.

Dr George Wylde was the second doctor who had declared Mrs Weldon sane, having known her for two years and being a spiritualist himself. 'Mrs Weldon is a very clever and humorous woman,' he told the court, 'with a little excitability, such as was very often observable in interesting women.' Spiritualist views needed to be seen in context, he said: there were 400 million Hindus and Buddhists who believed in the transmigration of souls, and no one would suggest they were all insane. And in any case, many accounts of the lives of the Christian saints reported that they were enveloped in light. Mrs Weldon had repeated in court the story of the shower of stars, explaining that it had happened as she lay in bed on the morning of 6 April 1878: 'It gave me great comfort as I believe spirits come in stars, and they seemed to come over me. I have experienced it since but have found out that it was the result of rubbing my eyes.' (Much laughter in court.) Mrs Weldon had written two years earlier, in 1882, that her spirit experiences mostly took place when 'alone in my own room, and not from courting spiritualistic seances'. She believed that spiritualism was a method of making closer contact with her God, the Christian Lord.

When Dr Winslow was in the witness box and blurted out that he believed all spiritualists belonged in an asylum, Justice Hawkins said, 'Then you have no right to the position you hold!' Mrs Weldon argued that Drs Winslow, Winn, Rudderforth and Semple had only heard what they had wanted to hear and had written down twisted versions of views that many spiritualists considered to be perfectly ordinary. Rudderforth had written 'three months' instead of 'three years' for the amount of time Mrs Weldon had said it would take for her to train a child. She recalled that when she had told Rudderforth of her pet white rabbit, describing it as 'a perfect daredevil', the doctor had replied, 'I dare say you thought it was the devil,' and he began to write something down. This had infuriated her, and she had cried out, 'Certainly not!' – and that she didn't believe in the Devil, 'only in human devils'. (The court chortled.) 'Yes, they rely very strongly on the rabbit,' she continued, noting how weak the mad-doctors' case was looking. For his part, Semple testified that he had been alone with her for fifteen minutes. 'She talked incessantly,' he said, with one subject running into another in a disconnected way. Yet he denied entertaining any malice towards her that night – 'It was rather the other way,' he told the court feelingly, clearly smitten. Semple, physician to the Royal College of Music, and author of *The Voice, Musically and Medically Considered*, admired her as a musician and as a woman.

Semple crumpled in the witness box and lost his case. 'He signed [the certificate] for a sinister motive,' declared Justice Hawkins. 'His negligence was gross and culpable.' The verdict was cheered outside in the street by a large crowd. Mrs Weldon was awarded £1,000 and Winslow was ordered to pay her £500 when he lost his case in the November. Neither man could find that sort of money with their ruined private practices. Nor could Gounod, who in 1885 was ordered to pay Mrs Weldon the colossal sum of £12,000 for a (non-lunacy-related) libel he had published about her. Henry de Bathe's treachery cost him £1,000.

Mrs Weldon, however, would never pursue her vanquished opponents for this money, even though her own circumstances were much reduced after Harry had disposed of Tavistock House. She and Angèle Ménier (and a menagerie that included a chimp, Titileehee) were living first in lodgings in Brixton and then at 58 Gower Street in Bloomsbury, and were making frequent visits to the orphans who were being brought up at the convent in Normandy, where they had remained following the disastrous trip of 1878. Mrs Weldon was still singing for her supper, earning £70 a week from the London Palladium for

One of Georgina's many stage personas was Sergeant Buzfuz,
the loquacious lawyer from *The Pickwick Papers*.

performing two songs each night, and appearing at various music
halls in an act based on Mr Sergeant Buzfuz (the loquacious lawyer
in *The Pickwick Papers*). She scarcely ever put a foot wrong in her
public life, but adapting and appearing in George Lander's play about
wrongful incarceration, *Not Alone*, was a rare mismanagement of her
persona. She played the rather unimaginatively named Hester
Stanhope (unless a reference to the great Regency female traveller
was intended), whose dastardly husband gets two medical men, Drs
Feese and Fubbs, to certify her insane and place her in an asylum
owned by Dr Pounceby, in order that he can marry a younger woman.
Mrs Stanhope escapes from the madhouse and mounts a campaign
to have the lunacy laws changed.

'Of the play, it is difficult to speak seriously,' the critic of the *Morning
Post* wrote, unimpressed by Mrs Weldon's venture on to the boards.
'A friendly reception was accorded to the play, but dissentient voices
were not unheard upon the appearance of the authors at its conclusion.' *The Era* was even less persuaded, stating, 'It would be idle to
say that there is not a feeling of relief felt when the piece is over.'
While demonstrating 'real histrionic ability', Mrs Weldon lacked the

Fame brought her a number of lucrative endorsement deals.

'finish' that only acting experience can bring. Mrs Weldon's increasing stoutness (despite her having taken up tricycling to keep trim) was noted as adding unintentional humour to the scene in which she was required to squeeze through the bars of Dr Pounceby's asylum. Her public simply preferred the non-fiction version of herself, and the dramas of her real life were deemed more powerful and moving than a fictional rendition. Then as now, it was noted that poor-quality imagined works failed to capture the weirdness, intensity and improbable plot twists of actuality.

And one of the biggest twists was that Winslow and Semple, a year after their defeat at her hands, formed the Mrs Weldon Release Committee, to protest at her gaoling for six months for her repeated libel against the trigamist music impresario Jules Rivière. When Mrs Weldon was released from Holloway, the doctors helped to organise a procession for her across London to Hyde Park, where she addressed a crowd that may have numbered as many as 17,000. Perhaps this is the tribute she demanded from them in lieu of the unpayable fines; their devotion to her cause was certainly more satisfying than dull old cash. Dr Semple remained as besotted with Mrs Weldon as the night he certified her, and in 1885 he moved in with her at Gower Street for a time – and brought with him his family, plus one of his own resident lunatics, kept within the Semple household for a fee. When his next child was born, he named her Georgina Angèle.

Dr Winslow, meanwhile, remained as egotistical a self-publicist as she, and the pair probably recognised each other as such. His reputation had taken a terrible blow, and his brother-in-law had grabbed the family asylums, but he could at least keep his name (and practice) prominent by joining her cause. In 1910 he was still chasing after the wrongful incarceration bandwagon by writing the introduction to Marcia Hamilcar's autobiographical account, *Legally Dead*, of her seventeen weeks' incarceration in an asylum, where she had been placed by her malevolent older sisters.

In later letters to Mrs Weldon, Winslow joshingly addresses her as 'Dear Loonie', which apparently she did not mind. In these, he admitted to being prematurely aged and thoroughly exhausted by all the battles; he also revealed that he was expecting more litigation from former patients, inspired by Mrs Weldon. (These cases don't appear to have materialised.) The only person to have seen the entire correspondence between Winslow and Mrs Weldon could detect no anger or resentment on either side.

Dr Winslow did a wicked thing in so casually attempting to carry out Harry Weldon's wishes. The doctor had indeed believed Georgina Weldon to be mad, but he hadn't troubled to look into her case carefully. He was not popular with fellow alienists, and the medical press actively disliked him. His vulgarity, ebullience, love of the limelight and failure to live up to his father's early and mid-career reputation made him unattractive to many. His biographer writes of his 'reckless kite-flying' of theories and notions, and, given the harsh lesson Mrs Weldon taught him, it is extraordinary that as late as March 1908, when he was in his mid-sixties, he became the first medical man to be charged with contravening the 1890 Lunacy Act. He had placed Ethel M. Davies with Mrs Edith Mary Lascelles at the latter's house in Burlington Gardens, Chiswick, West London;

but Mrs Lascelles was not licensed to board a certificated lunatic, and Winslow had known this. He had been seeking a safe, quiet, private place for Mrs Davies, with a discreet woman whom he trusted. The police had had to be called to the house when Ethel became loud and violent. Winslow pleaded guilty and was fined £50, Mrs Lascelles £10.

However, there is much in his later, post-Weldon career that redeems him. Because he saw insanity everywhere, he saved a number of people from the gallows. His father had been instrumental in winning the acceptance of the plea of insanity (and therefore diminished responsibility) in the criminal courts, and Winslow Jnr carried on this battle, involving himself in the investigations of such lesser-known late-Victorian/Edwardian studies in scarlet as the Old Kent Road Murder, the Devereux Trunk Mystery and the Girl in the Belfry. Chivalrous and patronising, he particularly could not bear it that a woman should swing for her villainy, women (in his view) being so less capable of controlling their emotions than men; but his pleading failed to save two particularly revolting murderesses of the day, Mrs Pearcey and Amelia Dyer. He was, however, a vocal member of the campaign to save the killers of Harriet Staunton (mentioned on pp. 206–7); and the reprieved Alice Rhodes came to his home upon her release to thank him for helping to save her life.

Winslow came up with an early definition of what we today call a psychopathic serial killer. He made a thorough nuisance of himself to the police during the Jack the Ripper investigation, and excitedly insisted on one G. Wentworth Bell Smith (or Bellsmith) as the culprit. But Winslow's schematisation of the outlook and behavioural traits of what was then called 'a homicidal maniac' did represent something of a breakthrough in the study of the criminal mind. His was an early instance of what is now called 'criminal profiling', and Winslow summarised what he believed were the likely habits and haunts of the Whitechapel Fiend. (But still, he couldn't resist falsifying a date in a document, in order to boost his case against Bell Smith.) Bell Smith, a Canadian commercial traveller in trusses, was a lodger at 27 Sun Street, Finsbury, and his behaviour there (noiseless rubber boots, bloodied clothing, habitual copying out of reams of the Old Testament) prompted his landlord to approach Winslow with his suspicions.

Two years later, he was involved in another pioneering project: he founded an outpatient centre where the poor who were suffering the early symptoms of nervous disorder could be treated as voluntary patients in a non-asylum setting. The Forbes Winslow Memorial Hospital (later the British Hospital for Functional Nervous Disorders) opened in February 1890 on the Euston Road, with opening hours that were convenient for working men and women. The hospital was viewed with suspicion and starved of cash by a legislature that had not yet digested the notions of mental outpatients, voluntary patients and preventive medicine in lunacy; and so it relied wholly on donations, and a considerable amount was raised from boxes placed in various pubs in London.

Winslow now believed that nine in ten mental health sufferers could avoid incarceration if diagnosed and treated early enough. He was one of the first English doctors fully to understand that mental health needed to lose the stigma of compulsory incarceration if the mind problems of the largest section of the population were to be successfully treated. While he blamed drink and hereditary mental weakness for much of the insanity of the poor, he also stressed that their living and working conditions caused great anxiety, which could lead to mental disturbance: 'These poor people worry about their children, their work, their earnings and their health – in fact, about almost all mortal things, and sooner or later their minds, deprived of diversion, give way.'

Winslow's transition from aggressively patriarchal Victorian bogeyman to twentieth-century humanitarian was further enhanced by his new-found approval of female doctors and by his attempts to drum up charitable payments for labouring folks who were out of work because of a nervous complaint. And his existential full circle was completed in 1910, when – thanks to an encounter with Italian medium Eusapia Palladino – he embraced spiritualism. Drawing-room seances hosted by the second Mrs Winslow helped to raise money for the Nervous Disorders Hospital.

We don't know what, if anything, Mrs Weldon made of this strange turn of events. For unknown reasons she had fallen out with Winslow again and she receives no mention in his entertaining, Holmesian memoirs, *Recollections of Forty Years*, published in 1910 (in which he complained that in the mid-1880s he had been made a 'cat's paw of the imperfections of lunacy law').

After an acrimonious split from Angèle in 1889, Mrs Weldon went to live at the Gisors convent in Normandy, to recuperate from eleven years of litigation and overwork. With an insatiable urge for righteousness, she wrote millions of words to ensure that posterity understood how wrong her adversaries had been. After Gounod's death in 1893 she wrote a devotional biography that attempted to analyse his genius. Now that he was dead, she got on with him better than she ever had since the early 1870s: a medium transmitted around 600 lines a month of communication from Gounod to Mrs Weldon, who allowed the composer to make the important decisions in her life at Gisors. For seven years she was deceived by the medium, who was revealed at last to have been duping her; but the communications did help her to come to terms with the pain of her losses – the pregnancies, the academy, the marriage, the deaths of all her various pets, the feeling that Angèle had used her, the friendships that had turned nasty, the Treherne family life that had been so frightening. The demolition of Tavistock House in 1901 (the British Medical Association's headquarters are on its site today) shook her badly, especially the fear that her dogs' remains might have been turfed up.

She returned to Britain in 1905 and, not content to be a living piece of recent history, she resumed litigation, including a Chancery suit against her brother Dalrymple's widow. 'So many old faces,' she wrote in her journal, of her return to the Royal Courts of Justice, 'so glad to see them. All of us looking so old.' When a woman in the crowd pointed her out as *the* Mrs Weldon, and said that she looked just like a judge, Mrs Weldon replied, 'Well, I must be an ugly old frump.'

Feeling the end was approaching, in 1913 she commissioned her deathbed photography in advance of her actual demise, which happened on 11 January 1914, six months after Dr Winslow's death. Such a noisy man, he lies forgotten in the brambles of the Old Cemetery in Barnes.

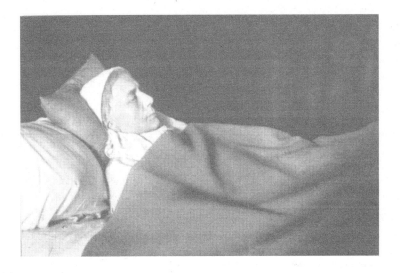

Her final pose: Georgina commissioned her deathbed photography in advance of her death.

The Savage New Century

The impact of Mrs Weldon's litigation frenzy was immense. The Portia of the Law Courts had fashioned an exemplary horror story that demonstrated precisely how the lunacy law might be used to send a sane person into confinement. While her lawsuits were under way, the House of Lords debated the slender threads by which individual liberty appeared to hang. Lord Salisbury, leader of the Conservative opposition (and soon to be prime minister), told the peers that it was now clear that something had to change in order to prevent the inconvenient being falsely imprisoned by their relatives or spouses. 'Motives of that kind were familiar in fiction,' he said, but he feared that 'they were not altogether strange in real life'. Literary and non-fiction melodramas – both played their parts in bringing home to the legislature the mechanics of a malicious incarceration.

In 1883, 1885, 1886, 1887 and 1888, lunacy law amendment bills failed to win parliamentary time in a hugely overcrowded agenda. In the meantime, the proprietors of private asylums became tightly organised to counter the threat to their trade. They argued, with some justification, that if wealthy people were to be compelled to use state-run asylums, they would simply lodge their troubled, or troublesome, family member in private care on the Continent – out of reach of inspection and regulation. Or there might occur an expansion of unlicensed, unregulated single-patient care in England – an underground network of private 'houses', with huge potential for patient abuse and malicious incarceration. However, the landscape of mental health was beginning to undergo small transitions that, taken together, would slowly change attitudes. As we have seen, Dr Winslow himself felt that the time was right for a voluntary, outpatient approach for the working classes. In the 1880s, the wealthy were also increasingly using private wards within the county asylums, and new wings or separate blocks for fee-paying mental patients were being constructed within many state institutions. Sanatoria and nursing homes began to emerge, taking in guests who felt the first symptoms of potential nervous collapse. While psychiatric problems continued to carry a social stigma, it seems that from the mid-1880s having a lunatic in the family was less likely to be viewed as a permanent blight on the standing of a public person, nor did it thwart inter-clan marriage alliances among wealthy families.

After seven years of parliamentary wrangles, the 1890 Lunacy Act at last placed the certification of all alleged lunatics under the auspices of a public figure – the magistrate. England appeared to have finally run out of patience with the private proprietor mad-doctors, whose cure rates failed to match those of county asylums and whose cavalier attitude to the nervously afflicted was out of step with the times. Laissez-faire was on the back foot in the late 1880s and early 1890s, and the Weldon case had powerfully demonstrated the pitfalls of permitting a free trade in lunacy. The Act therefore required that anyone wishing to have a private patient confined must petition a justice of the peace, supplying two separate doctors' certificates. The patient's regular physician was to be the signatory of one of the certificates (a proposal that John Perceval had made fifty years earlier), and if he was not, an explanation for this should be forthcoming. In sudden acute or violent cases an 'urgency order' could be obtained, bypassing the JP and requiring only one lunacy certificate; however, such an order was valid for just seven days, at the end of which the patient was to be discharged, or re-certified with the JP's approval and the completion of a second lunacy order. Chancery proceedings remained largely unchanged; but from 1890, the nation's 'Mrs Rochesters' – the uncertificated, home-confined family members – were subject to the visitation of the Commissioners in Lunacy, who could recommend to the Lord Chancellor that the confined person be freed entirely or sent to asylum care. The old problem remained, of course, of how the authorities found out about them.

Legislators had never believed John Perceval's, Louisa Lowe's or Georgina Weldon's assertions that wrongful incarceration was a common phenomenon; but they had been more persuaded regarding prolonged detention by private proprietors. And so from 1890, lunacy certificates were to be valid for one year only and had to be followed up with re-certification examinations. Moreover, no new licences were to be granted to private asylums.

The Lunacy Law Reform Association and the breakaway LLAS both welcomed the new Act, but wished that it had gone further, abolishing all private care and axing the 'hopelessly effete' Commissioners in Lunacy.

The first major test case for the new law came in 1895. Edith Lanchester was the epitome of the New Woman of the Nineties: educated to degree level, she was a white-collar worker, a Socialist, a feminist, and determined to spend the rest of her life with her lover, James Sullivan, a railway clerk, in their Clapham Junction lodgings, without marrying. Her father, a wealthy architect, was having none of this, and on the evening of Friday 25 October 1895, he and two of Edith's brothers dragged her to a carriage, tied her with rope, and deposited her at The Priory, Roehampton. It was all very old-fashioned.

An 'urgency order' had been written out by Dr George Fielding Blandford – the same doctor who had disagreed with Dr Maudsley and had declared Louisa Lowe sane. Blandford's rationale for author-ising Lanchester's detention sounded decidedly quaint in 1895, and indeed there was some sniggering when his diagnosis became public: 'She says she is going to live with a man below her in station because marriage is immoral. This she argued in a wholly irrational manner.' Blandford stated that certification would have been unquestioned if Miss Lanchester had threatened suicide; as it was, she was threatening 'social suicide', which had justified his saving her from 'utter ruin . . . She had a monomania on the subject of marriage, and I believed that her brain had been turned by Socialist meetings and writings, and that she was quite unfit to take care of herself.'

Coincidentally – and fortunately – just two days later the Commissioners in Lunacy turned up at The Priory for a statutory visit; and as her father had not yet had time to obtain a magistrate's order and a second lunacy certificate, they immediately freed Edith. She was brought back to Clapham in triumph by her comrades from the Social Democratic Federation, who helped to keep the tale of 'The Socialist Romance' in the newspapers for weeks. Fresh from his destruction of Oscar Wilde, the Marquess of Queensberry – atheist, divorcé – wrote James Sullivan a supportive letter, offering to pay any legal costs: 'I should like to shake you and your wife [*sic*] by the hand . . . You have a chance now of making a public protest, as everyone's attention is attracted. What is their idiotic [marriage] ceremony?' (Lanchester and Sullivan never married and lived together until James's death in 1945; their daughter, Elsa, went on to be the Hollywood star of *Bride of Frankenstein* – a different kind of horror story.)

The Lanchester case had shown that the new lunacy system seemed to be working, as the victim had been speedily freed. However, some things clearly hadn't changed. The Commissioners refused to take any action against Blandford or the Lanchester family. Her counsel also warned Edith not to go ahead with a private prosecution, as it would be an expensive failure to try to prove in court that malice – rather than a genuine mistake – lay behind the attempt to have her certified.

History is the study of change over time. But the stories in this book have demonstrated the stubborn unchangeability of many aspects of the lunacy issue. (Many, perhaps most, of the chapters also contain uncanny echoes for those who have experience of present-day mental health systems, whether as 'client', carer or health worker.) What, in essence, is so very different about the strategies and motivations of Edward Davies's mother in 1829, and Edith Lanchester's father in 1895? In terms of protest, the street 'mobbing' we saw in the Davies case died out shortly afterwards, but many thousands rallied to cheer Mrs Weldon. The spectators' galleries at lunacy inquisitions and post-liberation lawsuits were as crowded with well-wishers of the alleged lunatic in the 1890s as ever they had been in the 1820s. And in terms of patient advocacy, John Perceval's revolutionary late-Georgian ideas could have been written this very week.

As for the lunacy experts, until the misuses of Darwinist theory began to make their impact in the early twentieth century, little 'advance', or significant change, can be traced in psychological medicine. The range of explanations and classifications available in the 1820s was remarkably similar to those still in use at the start of the twentieth century; and even that great cause for self-celebration, the introduction of 'non-restraint', was more an aspiration than a reality, as many patients and inspectors testified down the years. No clear trajectory in the stories of lunacy and of wrongful incarceration is discernible between 1829 and 1890. Instances of greed, dishonesty and arrogance were evidently not unusual among the alienists in the stories in these pages, but trying to make monsters of such men as the Winslows, John Conolly, Henry Maudsley, George Man Burrows and the other celebrated mad-doctors would be as unwise as trying to demonise a barrister for the stances adopted while defending or prosecuting during a criminal trial: they would say whatever they needed to say in order to win a result. Lunacy decisions had an unfortunate adversarial quality to them, and so experts could become highly flexible if a wealthy alleged lunatic, or his/her family, employed them to give substance to a specific point of view. But in any case, as men at the coalface of perhaps the most uncertain science of all, their views on what constituted in/sanity were almost bound to be changeful – a Mad Hatter's tea party of shifting positions. It is immensely cheering to see the scientific attempt to define and promote 'normality' of behaviour failing spectacularly every time it was tested.

With regard to mental illness (but not mental disability, of which more shortly), the 1890 Lunacy Act remained in force until the passing of the Mental Health Act in 1959. Continental psychoanalysis had slowly gained acceptance in the initially unimpressed British Isles by the 1920s, while the understanding of psychological trauma was deepened by the study of 'shell-shocked' troops from the First World War. Greater knowledge and lessening embarrassment about mental ill health meant that by 1938 over one-third of all psychiatric admissions in England were voluntary. Five years before the passing of the 1959 Act, the asylum population of England and Wales reached its peak, at 148,000 patients. The new Act encouraged many of the large asylums to reassess their long-stay patients – a move that revealed the shocking extent of unnecessary incarceration. Between 1959 and the mid-1980s, a whole cohort was discovered – like the shaggy-haired and whiskered victims of the *ancien régime* found in the bowels of the Bastille in 1789, condemned for life by an arbitrary power and brought blinking into a world they scarcely recognised. There was the lad who had stolen a postal order in 1917 and was labelled first a 'moral defective' and then diagnosed 'of unsound mind'; the girl who was deemed 'subnormal' after her second illegitimate child; the teenage boy who had broken a window in Moss Side in 1948, and was discovered thirty-five years later in a top-security mental hospital. *The Times* described as 'barbaric' the imprisonment for life of three women discovered in a mental hospital near Doncaster in 1972, who between them had served 110 years for each having a child out of wedlock in the 1920s. The hospital was in the process of reviewing all 520 patients, and anticipated that around one-fifth would be released. Many elderly women were found who had passed their entire reproductive lives in a psychiatric hospital, having become helpless through decades of institutionalisation. It is perhaps one of the most common phenomena of the genealogical explosion of the past twenty years: the discovery of a great-grandmother, great-aunt or other female ancestor who was 'put away' for having an illegitimate baby. Time and again, these twentieth-century tragedies are brought to light by those researching their family history. The Victorian era has famously been dubbed 'the age of incarceration' by Michel Foucault; and yet to judge by the numbers of those detained in mental hospitals and homes for most of their lives, it is the middle decades of the twentieth century that deserve that unhappy title.

So how did this happen, when the whole drift from the 1880s had been towards policing the mad-doctors, placing emphasis on patients' rights to be heard, and ever-tighter scrutiny of psychiatric admissions? The answer lies in the uncertainty of where the boundary lay between 'lunacy' and all other types of 'unsoundness' of mind. Conditions in which the brain was in some way not deemed to be fully and correctly functioning were, throughout the nineteenth century, mixed together: 'idiocy', 'imbecility' and 'weak-mindedness' were terms that were never satisfactorily winnowed apart from 'lunacy' in legalistic and bureaucratic language. Each of these three conditions was understood to be a malfunction of the mind, which was present either from birth or from an early age and was untreatable. Idiots, imbeciles and the weak-minded could be confined under the 1845 Lunatics Act; and the loose wording of the 1890 Act did nothing to settle this unsatisfactory blending of very different diagnoses – which we today would divide into 'illness' and 'disability'. But in the late 1890s, a new category was devised that incorporated all those who were not delusional, manic or melancholic, but whose behaviour appeared to show either a level of intellect so low that they could not function in society, or a diseased psychology that rendered the sufferer unable to demonstrate any social or moral intelligence whatsoever. The terms 'mental deficiency', 'moral defective' and 'feeble-minded' were the late-Victorian/Edwardian reclassification of the earlier terms 'idiocy' and its fellow travellers 'moral idiocy' and 'moral insanity'. Alcoholics, sexual deviants, thieves, unmarried mothers, the habitually work-shy – all those with a record of persistent antisocial activities could be seen as victims of their own incurable, inherited mental structure and mental processes.

As we saw in Chapter Nine, Lord Shaftesbury – much maligned in these pages – had said: 'If ever you have special doctors, they will shut up people by the score.' And what happened between the turn of the century and the outbreak of the First World War with regard to the new 'feeble-minded' category suggests that he was right: the scientific expert was allowed into the driving seat of policy – 'proving' that the British race was in danger of degeneration and eventual extinction if its defectives were not taken out of circulation. The highly illiberal notion of 'detention for life' was being put forward as early as 1881, when it was firmly rejected by policymakers. But the eugenicist movement was able to make great capital out of a series of alarming events in late-nineteenth-century Britain. The arrival of compulsory education had incidentally provided the means by which to survey the 'fitness' of the nation's infants, and the discovery of high levels of shattered health and mental 'dullness' stunned even the most pessimistic; the difficulty in recruiting fit young males to fight the Boer Wars added to the panic. Looking south to Germany, and west to America, Britain deduced that its working/fighting population was falling behind in the competition for economic supremacy.

From 1904 to 1908 the Royal Commission on the Care and Control of the Feeble-Minded heard testimony from prison governors, schoolteachers, charity and local government workers who expressed their fears that the working classes were being swamped by the offspring of hideously fecund 'idiots', 'imbeciles', 'half-wits', or even the simply 'dull'. The girls – too retarded to give or withhold consent, and unaware of where babies came from – were taken advantage of by licentious males; the boys were hereditary petty criminals who grew up to be lifelong vicious recidivists. Even if these girls' and boys' intelligence quotients and reasoning skills appeared 'normal', persistent delinquency was an indicator of moral defectiveness – a condition that would be passed down to the defective's many offspring. The nation had to be protected from this internal threat; but it also had a duty to protect this blighted stock, by immuring them for their own good. 'Care and Control' went hand in hand in the Edwardian racial degeneracy debates.

Despite the frightening testimony of the hereditarian witnesses at the Royal Commission, the final report, published in 1908, threw out the notion of compulsory sterilisation for the feeble-minded, suggesting instead the building of gender-segregated 'colonies' where education and occupation would be provided for those deemed capable of improvement, and safe shelter for those who were not. A system of 'guardianship' within the young person's own community or home town was the best mode of proceeding; but local authorities should be given the right to impose detention for life – or at least until the defective was no longer able to reproduce. However, there were concerns about the state of 'public opinion': 'It would be very difficult in the present state of public feeling on the question of the liberty of the subject and so on, to enforce a wholesale detention of feeble-minded persons,' one medical officer told the Royal Commission. But eugenicists were extremely active at a local as well as national level, and most sizeable cities had a society 'For the Permanent Care of the Feeble Minded'. The panic engendered by eugenics supporters inspired Winston Churchill to write to Prime Minister Asquith in 1910, when the Royal Commission had still not resulted in any legislation: 'The unnatural and increasingly rapid growth of the feeble-minded classes, coupled with a steady restriction among all the thrifty, energetic and superior stocks, constitute a race danger which it is impossible to exaggerate. I feel that the sources from which the stream of madness is fed should be cut off and sealed up before another year has passed.'

That sense of a demographic emergency led to the formulation of the Mental Deficiency Bill two years later. The creation of a monster, the whipping up of public terror, is often the spur to liberty-curbing legislation, and during the parliamentary debates, few rose to their feet to defend English Liberty. Liberal MP for Newcastle-under-Lyme, Josiah Wedgwood, was one of the very few members who took an old-fashioned line on this. He told the House that attempts to prevent the 'feeble-minded' from breeding was

> about the most abominable thing ever suggested . . . There is an entire absence throughout the whole of the Bill of any suggestion that it would not be perfectly right and just on the part of the State to make what regulations they like for the lives of these people . . . The safeguards for the people themselves are remarkable by their absence . . . I think it is most important that the House should put its foot down firmly on the growing authority of specialists in the legislation of the country. You cannot argue the question. You are not on the same footing with them. Public opinion is absolutely valueless and unable to cope with the dictum of the specialist.

But Wedgwood was part of a tiny, albeit loud, minority, and after the third reading, only two other MPs joined him to vote against the Bill in August 1913; 180 voted in favour. Typical criticisms made of those who used the English liberty argument were that they were speaking 'nonsense' – that such talk was 'idle', 'specious', a mere 'play upon words', 'drivel'. Feeble-minded youngsters were 'at liberty' only to be neglected, abused and sexually exploited, and if libertarians had their way, all that would be guaranteed was 'the liberty to abuse liberty' and 'the liberty to breed lunatics'.

The Mental Deficiency Act of 1913 replaced the Commissioners in Lunacy with the Board of Control. Local authorities were obliged to identify feeble-minded children between seven and sixteen years of age, and if incarceration was felt to be required, the parents were to be enjoined to petition the local magistrate. If parents were deemed to be incorrigibly neglectful, or cruel, their permission was overridden. Young people coming before the juvenile courts were now liable to be labelled 'morally defective' and sent to permanent institutional care. Parents, too, could ask a JP to order their child into a colony, and many did decide to do so, unable to cope or, as in the notorious case of the Queen's cousins, Katherine and Nerissa Bowes-Lyon, simply unwilling to acknowledge handicap within the family.

The Act also contained a clause aimed at preventing any defective released on licence forming an attachment to a person of the opposite sex. When such relationships were discovered, a return to the custodial colony would follow.

The National Council for Civil Liberties estimated in 1947 that the number of confined 'mental deficiency' cases stood at 54,000, with a further 43,700 'under statutory supervision' in the community, and 5,700 under guardianship in their own homes or with foster carers. The Council believed that many had been confined on moral grounds alone, and had, in fact, a perfectly normal intelligence quotient.

Defectives were routinely transferred from the 'colony' institutions to lunatic asylums when accommodation became scarce in the former, or when the local authority decided not to spend its mental health budget on community-based care. In 1929 it was estimated that as many as a quarter of institutionalised 'defectives' were in lunatic asylums and not their own specialist institutions, or colonies. Some 'dull', 'feeble-minded' or otherwise tearaway youngsters confined under the Mental Deficiency Act did simply become insane as a result of inexplicable detention with no prospect of release, while having their babies forcibly taken from them will have psychologically damaged the young mothers in detention. We believe that the Victorians 'put away' in asylums the wayward young; but in fact it was the doctors and administrators of the twentieth century who were misusing the institutions of the former age.

George Dangerfield would identify 1913 as the date of the Strange Death of Liberal England, although he did not single out the Mental Deficiency Act as dealing the fatal blow. As war loomed, collectivism in all sorts of policy areas became the norm astoundingly swiftly. Perhaps liberty was the privilege of wealth; in an internationally competitive new century, and with conflict looming, it was a luxury the nation felt less able to afford. 'The convenience of society comes second,' Josiah Wedgwood had argued, in the debate on the Mental Deficiency Bill, 'the liberty of the British citizen first.' But not any longer, it seemed, if that citizen was in any way 'unfit'.

Industrial-scale wrong-headedness towards the mentally ill and the mentally disabled flourished throughout the twentieth century – though happily, Britain avoided the excesses of America, Canada, Scandinavia and, worst of all, Nazi Germany. However, this country did permit the use of insulin comas, lobotomy, chemical sedation and electro-convulsion to treat the mentally ill; and lifetime detention without appeal for those labelled mentally disabled. These would have been considered scandalous and outrageous intrusions in both Victorian public and government opinion; but they went largely uncondemned until the 1960s. Which is another book altogether.

Appendix 1

Lunacy legislation affecting wrongful confinement

Successive Acts of parliament included clauses addressing the prevention of the incarceration of the sane. The list below excludes minor amending Acts and legislation concerning other aspects of lunacy care.

1774 ACT FOR THE REGULATION OF PRIVATE MADHOUSES

This, the first legislation to regulate private lunacy care, laid down that madhouse keepers could accept a paying patient only upon the signed certificate of a medical man. No certificate was required if a patient was to be confined in his/her own home.

Every madhouse accommodating more than one lunatic required a licence. Five Lunacy Commissioners, elected by the College of Physicians, granted the licences within a seven-mile radius of London and inspected premises. Beyond, licensing and inspection were undertaken by local magistrates.

1828 MADHOUSE ACT

Two certificates of lunacy, each signed by a different doctor following a separate interview (the interviews to be undertaken within fourteen days of each other), were required for private patients; no physician could sign a certificate if he owned, co-owned or was a regular medical attendant at the receiving madhouse. A lunacy order, with an accompanying statement, was to be filled in by the individual alerting the doctors to an alleged lunatic. No certificate was required if a patient was to be confined in his/her own home or otherwise kept not for profit.

The Metropolitan Commissioners in Lunacy replaced the College of

Physicians inspectorate. Local magistrates retained their licensing and inspection powers in the provinces.

Notifications of admission and discharge of patients in all asylums/ licensed houses were to be sent to the Metropolitan Commissioners within seven days.

For pauper patients, only one doctor's certificate was required, with the second being signed by a magistrate, clergyman, schoolteacher, Poor Law officer or other civic figure.

Patients seeking to sue for false imprisonment had to commence any legal action within six months of liberation.

A Private Register of patients confined as single patients was created, but legislation of 1832 required that this was destroyed.

1845 LUNACY ACT

The Commissioners in Lunacy replaced the Metropolitan Commissioners and comprised three medical men, three lawyers and up to five unpaid laymen.

The two certifying doctors were not to be in partnership with each other, and must separately interview the alleged lunatic within seven days of each other The doctor must not be in any way related to, or in the pay of, the asylum proprietor.

Single patients were now required by law to be notified to the Commissioners, and the Private Register was reinstated.

Patients seeking to sue for false imprisonment had to commence any legal action within twelve months of liberation.

Only the Commissioners in Lunacy could prosecute asylum proprietors and doctors for contravening the Act.

1853 LUNACY AMENDMENT ACT

All hearsay evidence was now forbidden on a certificate of lunacy, with doctors required to state the observations they themselves had made of the alleged lunatic's behaviour.

1853 CHANCERY LUNATICS ACT

Chancery inquisitions were made less expensive, and a jury trial was no longer required, if a private hearing with a Master in Lunacy was preferred.

1862 LUNACY AMENDMENT ACT

No certificate was to be signed by any medical man receiving a percentage from an asylum's profits; or who had not seen the patient within the previous month.

Exact copies of the certificates and lunacy order/statement were to be sent to the Commissioners within one day of admission.

Chancery inquisitions were made even cheaper and faster.

1890 LUNACY ACT

In private cases, a magistrate was to examine all paperwork before an asylum admission, following the established procedure for a pauper alleged-lunatic. Two certificates from wholly disinterested doctors were required. The magistrate then either granted the admission order, dismissed it, or adjourned the decision for no longer than fourteen days. Paupers still required just one doctor's certificate, and a statement by a Poor Law official, plus the magistrate's order.

In an acute, homicidal or suicidal case, an Urgency Order admission required just one certificate, valid for seven days, pending full certification. Lunacy certificates were now finite, with re-examinations on a one-, two- or three-yearly basis.

Local authorities took over from the magistracy the inspection and licensing powers for provincial private asylums.

Only the Commissioners, the Attorney-General or Director of Public Prosecutions could prosecute misdemeanours under the 1890 Act.

Anyone could now request permission from the Commissioners to have a medical man examine an inmate, and if after two separate examinations the patient could be certified as not likely to cause injury to him/herself or to others, s/he could be discharged no less than ten days later.

Any proprietor could now, with the written permission of two Commissioners, receive an uncertified boarder for a specified finite period.

1913 MENTAL DEFICIENCY ACT

The concepts of 'moral defect' and 'feeble minded' were introduced. Youths appearing at juvenile courts could be sent to newly constructed 'colonies' for indefinite periods; parents could request their local authority to assess and confine 'defective' or 'mentally deficient' children; local authorities were, in addition, required to identify, classify and make provision for 'defectives'.

Any 'defective' allowed out of the colony on licence was forbidden from forming any attachment to a person of the opposite sex.

The Board of Control replaced the Commissioners in Lunacy.

1930 MENTAL TREATMENT ACT

Two new categories were introduced for patient admission: voluntary and temporary. By 1938, more than one-third of psychiatric admissions were voluntary.

1959 MENTAL HEALTH ACT

Regional mental health review tribunals were created to oversee individual cases and decide on discharge. The magistrate's role in lunacy admissions was ended.

Compulsory admissions were now either upon: an 'observation order', lasting twenty-eight days and requiring two certificates; a 'treatment order', valid for one year and also requiring two certificates, and extendable if required; or an 'emergency order', on the notification by a relative or welfare officer, lasting three days and requiring one certificate.

A relative could give the hospital seventy-two hours' notice of intention to remove a patient but had to have the permission of either the medical officer or the tribunal.

The category 'moral defective' was no longer recognised.

1983 MENTAL HEALTH ACT

The 'observation order' was now an 'assessment order', with provision for treatment as well. The validity of 'treatment orders' was halved to six months (from one year), to one year (from two) and so on. 'Emergency orders' permitted seventy-two hours' detention in genuine emergencies only. The right to a tribunal became automatic for all, rather than by application, as in 1959.

Appendix 2
Official lunacy statistics

Extreme caution should be exercised with these figures. They relate only to those people who were certificated, and therefore exclude the unknowable number of 'hidden' mentally ill; but they include many who were certificated while suffering no more than, for example, nervous exhaustion, melancholy or delirium tremens, as well as the eccentricities or character quirks of most of the subjects in this book.

The chief interest of these statistics is that they were used at the time to discuss the size and likely scale of the issue.

	Certified insane in England and Wales	Rate per 1,000 population	England and Wales population
1829	14,500–16,000 (estimate)	1.08–1.19	13.4 million
1844	20,893	1.26	16.5 million
1860	38,058	1.91	19.9 million
1875	63,743	2.67	23.9 million
1890	85,352	2.9	29.4 million

	In public institutions	In private asylums	Chancery lunatics
1844	16,821	4,072	515
1860	32,993	5,065	602
1875	56,403	7,340	945
1890	77,257	8,095	1,209

Sources: The Commissioners in Lunacy's annual tables; information adapted from Andrew Scull's *Museums of Madness* (1979), tables 8 and 10; the Lord Chancellor's Visitors in Lunacy file LCO 11/2 at The National Archives; while the 1829 figures are the estimates of physician Sir Andrew Halliday, whose personal survey found at least 14,500 certified insane in England and Wales but who calculated that the true figure was likely to be higher in his *A Letter to Lord Robert Seymour with a Report of the Number of Lunatics in England and Wales.*

MALE TO FEMALE RATIOS IN ASYLUM CARE

Regarding gender, there was a paucity of official returns in the earliest decades of the century. Few medical writers attempted to make any sex-related generalisations based upon statistical evidence. Dr George Man Burrows was an exception and his 1828 findings are included overleaf. John Thurnam, in his 1845 *Observations and Essays on the Statistics of Insanity*, attempted a sophisticated numerical model, using the 1841 census returns and asylum admission and discharge data, and found a slight preponderance of male lunacy over female.

Sociologist Joan Busfield, in 'The Female Malady? Men, Women and Madness in Nineteenth-Century Britain' (*Sociology*, February 1994), found that at the end of the century there was a 55:45 ratio of females to males in institutions, the result of females becoming long-stay patients and male inmates having a higher death rate in asylums. Female admission figures were no higher than male, and discharge rates differed little, Busfield found.

The following table has been compiled from various Lunacy Commission returns to the Lord Chancellor. It excludes lunatics in non-asylum care.

	Male total	Female total	Male private	Male pauper	Female private	Female pauper
1829*	949	1,099	469	480	399	700
1844	5,521	5,751	1,989	3,532	1,801	3,950
1859	10,797	12,084	2,565	8,232	2,616	9,468
1879	29,073	34,070	2,260	26,813	2,385	31,685
1896	41,360	48,752	1,852	39,508	2,484	46,268

* 1829 figures are for the London area only. A large proportion of pauper patients were in private asylums but paid for by the parish, as there was comparatively little public accommodation for them. Source: *Report from the Metropolitan Commissioners in Lunacy*, 1830.

Average number of lunatics in private asylums in England and Wales, 1812–24:

Females: 3,443

Males: 4,461

Source: George Man Burrows's *Commentaries* (1828), p. 241.

Inmates of the Middlesex County Asylum at Hanwell, 1827:

Females: 546

Males: 307

Source: ibid.

Appendix 3

*Brief outlines of cases highlighted by
the Alleged Lunatics' Friend Society*

In addition to the individuals mentioned in Chapter Three, the following instances of apparently wrongful asylum incarceration came to the attention of members of the Society, before its demise in 1863. It is possible that the Society knew of more cases, but few annual reports were published by John Perceval and his colleagues.

Captain Joseph Digby was violently seized from his home at 12 Beaumont Street, Marylebone, London, on 5 May 1844, and taken to Moorcroft House Asylum, in Hillingdon, Middlesex. This was on the say-so of Digby's wife, although she persuaded an aged brother of the captain to sign the lunacy order, so that she would not be responsible if there were to be recriminations. His brother had not seen the captain for fifteen years, and this was very much against the spirit of the 1828 Madhouse Act, which sought the provision of up-to-date information on alleged lunatics. Captain Digby was in the asylum for thirteen weeks, but – assisted by his wife's sister and her husband – he threatened to mount a lawsuit for conspiracy if he were not released. Fearing such a move, Mrs Digby agreed to his discharge. Neither alienist John Conolly nor the Metropolitan Commissioners in Lunacy had considered Digby to be mad but they were reluctant to release him without his wife's consent. Captain Digby abandoned his proposed lawsuit because of its expense. When his story became known, he was inundated with letters from people who claimed that the same thing had happened to them, signing themselves with such pseudonyms as 'A Victim' and 'One of the Miserables'. The captain became an active and founder member of the Alleged Lunatics' Friend Society.

William White, a seventy-two-year-old pensioner resident at the Charterhouse in London, quarrelled with the institution's doctor who then had him certified, on 1 August 1844. Luke James Hansard intervened and a long list of petitioners to White's sanity was compiled. The Charterhouse had imposed a three-month ban on any contact between White and the outside world, but Hansard's agitation compelled the Metropolitan Commissioners to look at the case closely and they agreed that White was sane, and freed him. White became an active member of the Society.

Edward Fletcher, an epileptic aged twenty-eight, was confined to Kensington House Asylum in London by his Uncles Charles and James. Edward's father had died in 1848, and his bequests to his son had been interfered with by the uncles. If Edward were to make a will, they would lose out financially, and so they cooked up a madhouse plot to ensure that he was unable to draw up a will. In July 1858, after three months' confinement, Edward escaped through a small gate in the garden wall and into Kensington Road, wearing two suits, the outer of which he pawned for cash. When cornered by the keeper and a policeman several days later, he made a dash across the rooftops of Covent Garden, ending up in a woman's lodgings. She listened to his tale and offered him her clothing. Wearing her crinoline, but failing to cover up his thick black moustache, Edward walked downstairs and out into the street, and evaded his pursuers. He was given refuge by novelist Charles Reade, who later made heavy use of the Fletcher case in his 1863 novel, *Hard Cash*. The Society assisted in the prosecution of the uncles for unlawful confinement, during which the judge reiterated Baron Pollock's 1849 legal opinion that only those 'dangerous to themselves or to others' were eligible to be placed in an asylum. Reade was critical of the quality of assistance the Society provided to Edward.

James Hill, a bankrupt merchant from Huntingdonshire, with ten children and Radical political sympathies, became violent and delusional in May 1850 and his wife had him committed to Kensington House. However, he swiftly recovered but found that all access to him was forbidden and that his letters to the Commissioners in Lunacy were suppressed. He was released in May 1851 and in January 1852, backed by the Society, he sought compensation for wrongful confinement from the proprietor, but lost the lawsuit.

Charles Verity was transferred from Northampton Gaol to Northampton Hospital's Refractory Lunatics Ward in September 1856 after attempting to hang himself during a two-year sentence for receiving stolen goods. He wrote to John Perceval in April 1857, outlining the extreme violence of the attendants, which included a killing. Mr Perceval succeeded in getting an inquiry into the abuse, which substantiated Verity's reports. Verity was now deemed to be sane and was transferred back to gaol to serve the rest of his sentence.

Ellen Finn was committed to Warburton's Asylum in Bethnal Green, East London, in 1844 by her husband, Police Sergeant James Finn, after eighteen years of marriage. Following a violent row, Sergeant Finn found two doctors to certify his wife. However, Ellen's sister paid for two independent doctors to examine her at Warburton's: they found her sane and she was discharged. The couple eventually agreed to a judicial separation.

'T. C. H.', aged forty-seven, was described as being of 'weak mind' and suffering 'nervous excitement' but with no signs of insanity. He had inherited £6,200 on the death of his father in 1831, and then £3,800 from an uncle, for both of whom he acted as executor. In 1843, he announced his intention to marry a Mrs B——, a widow, and his two brothers had him seized and incarcerated in Fiddington Asylum (aka Willett's) near Market Lavington in Wiltshire. If T. C. H. were to marry, certain inheritable moneys would no longer be available to his brothers. He managed to alert a lawyer, and an eminent doctor came to the asylum, examined him and pronounced him sane. This episode cost him £1,200 and seven months' loss of liberty. He suffered low spirits subsequently, and in 1848 his brothers again managed to get him certified, this time into Ridgeway House, near Bristol, where the proprietor claimed that T. C. H. would be certain to commit suicide if freed. This time around, T. C. H. had just announced his intention to marry a Miss H——. He stayed at Ridgeway House until February 1849 when Gloucestershire magistrate Purnell B. Purnell came to inspect the premises. Upon liberation, T. C. H. married Miss H——, in March 1849, and regained most of his property. Purnell notified the Society of this case, plus 150 other dubious certifications in West Country madhouses.

James Drury was fifty-nine when his case came to the attention of Purnell B. Purnell and the Society in the late 1840s. He had been living as a 'nervous patient' in lodgings not far from Fishponds Asylum near Bristol when he was inveigled into the asylum proper on faulty certificates. He spent twenty years at Fishponds. His income of £200 a year was administered by a trustee, who paid himself a total of £400 over the two decades. The Commissioners in Lunacy would not accept that Drury was sane, or that his funds were being embezzled. Purnell got him released and into lodgings pending a lunacy inquisition and an investigation into the missing funds.

Edward Vicars, in his mid-forties, a wine and spirit merchant of Liverpool, was a heavy drinker who, during an attack of delirium tremens, was put into Walton Lodge Asylum in February 1847 by his sister, Hannah, and brother, Matthew. Among other delusions Vicars expressed during the tremens was the notion that he had no stomach and that food went directly into his legs; and that the local magistrates had been using electricity to trigger insanity in the patients at Walton Lodge, feeding it into the asylum through telegraph wires. Vicars escaped in March 1848, to find that his property had been sold off by his brother and a business partner. The Society represented Vicars at his subsequent lunacy inquisition, in August 1849, at which the jury declared him sane.

John Gould of Bath was placed in the asylum of Charles Cunningham Langworthy at Box in Wiltshire in 1840. He admitted that he had been a heavy drinker and that his relationship with his wife had become very strained, but said that they had agreed amicably to a separation. His wife and son had him certified when he was suffering delirium tremens, and assumed control of his property. When Gould was released, thirteen years later, he intended to mount a legal case to regain his business and some leasehold property, but decided not to proceed when he found out the enormous likely cost of the case.

Arthur Legent Pearce was discovered in Bethlehem Hospital by John Perceval in 1850. The former doctor had been confined ten years earlier following a violent assault upon his wife. Mr Perceval did not argue that Pearce was sane but was horrified at the conditions Pearce was kept in and at the erosion of his capital in patient fees. To help him, Mr Perceval published a volume of Pearce's poetry, *Poems by a Prisoner in Bethlehem* (1851).

George Hubback was in his sixties when he was consigned to Kensington House. His supporters claimed that Hubback, who had once been a boon companion of the Prince Regent, was simply suffering from diabetes and that his wife did not wish to care for him any more. He died in September 1839.

Richard Hennah of Blackheath, south-east London, was a heavy drinker whose father had him certified into Blacklands House Asylum, Chelsea, West London, in an attempt to dry him out.

Reverend Wing of Thornhaugh, in Cambridgeshire – described as harmless, nervous and irritable – was put into Kensington House by his son, a Gray's Inn attorney, and died there.

Robert Orme Smith, aged about fifty, spent thirty years in Warburton's Asylum, on the lunacy order of bank director John Bowden. Fifteen years into his captivity he escaped, and made it to Bowden's home to ask what he had done with his money and property, but was recaptured.

Miss Mackray, first name unknown, was incarcerated in Elm House Asylum in Chelsea, which the Society believed was entirely inappropriate for her nervous but not 'unsound' condition. In 1857, they persuaded the Commissioners in Lunacy to have her removed to a private house in Whittington Villas, Upper Holloway, North London, run by a Mrs Pope. However, Miss Mackray escaped from here and was able to make contact with her own solicitor to fight her certification.

Mr Evans, first name unknown, eventually won £30 from a relation after he had been able to prove that there had been a conspiracy to place him, sane, in Bethlehem Hospital.

Mr S—— was confined by order of his relations, who then seized his lease-hold farmhouse. The Society helped to liberate him, and solicitor Gilbert Bolden obtained an annuity from his relations in compensation for the seized farm.

No name: a young man was found confined in an asylum upon a lunacy order from his father, which, the Society reported, 'contained statements of his having been insane when at college, which was without foundation'. The boy drank too much and his father stated that he had 'an utter want of self-control [which] produced, on each indulgence, attacks of excitement amounting to positive insanity'. He was under certificate from 1846 to 1849 and although the Commissioners in Lunacy recommended his discharge, the proprietor and the father refused.

No name: a man was placed in Wyke House Asylum in Brentford, Middlesex, because of his addiction to Holloway's Pills, a quack medicine. He escaped, was recaptured and placed in Sussex House Asylum, escaped again and remained at liberty.

No name: a mother and stepfather confined their daughter, who was of slightly weak intellect, in a West Country asylum. Her friends were not allowed to visit her. The stepfather's lunacy order was found to be 'informal' in nature and contained falsified documents put forward as evidence of her insanity.

No name: a woman was put away by her father – firstly in Moorcroft House and subsequently at Lawn House, Hanwell – in order to control her money. The Society failed to persuade the Commissioners in Lunacy and a judge to intervene, but when a local magistrate became involved, the woman was released immediately.

SOURCES

Captain Digby and Ellen Finn: *Hansard*, Parliamentary Debates, 3rd series, 82, cols 410–13, 11 July 1845.

William White and John Gould: Luke James Hansard's *What Are To Be the Tendencies of the Community of the British Nation? To Sanity? or To Insanity? A Question*, 1845.

Edward Fletcher: *Daily News*, 8 July 1859; and Wayne Burns, *Charles Reade: A Study in Victorian Authorship*, 1962.

James Hill: *The Times*, 30 January and 18 February 1852.

Charles Verity: PP 1860, LVIII.959, *Accounts and Papers: Return of Charges of Ill-usage and Cruelty towards Patients in Northampton Hospital, 1857, Evidence by Commissioners in Lunacy on Inquiry*.

'T.C.H.' and James Drury: *Report of the County Chairman* [Purnell B. Purnell] *to the Gloucestershire Epiphany Court of Quarter Sessions*, 2 January 1849.

Edward Vicars: *Liverpool Mercury*, 7 and 28 August 1849.

Arthur Legent Pearce: *Poems by a Prisoner in Bethlehem*, ed. John Perceval, 1851.

George Hubback, Richard Hennah, Reverend Wing, Robert Orme Smith: Richard Paternoster, *The Madhouse System*, 1841.

Miss Mackray: Nicholas Hervey, 'Advocacy or Folly', and The National Archives, MH 50/9, Minute Book of the Commissioners in Lunacy, February 1858–December 1858.

Young man with 'utter want of self-control': *First Report of the Alleged Lunatics' Friend Society*, 1846.

Mr Evans, Mr S——, the daughter of slightly weak intellect, and the Holloway's Pills addict: *Report of the Alleged Lunatics' Friend Society*, 1851.

Woman put away by her father: *Report from the Select Committee on Lunatics*, 1859.

Appendix 4

Brief outlines of alleged wrongful incarceration cases that received the support of the Lunacy Law Reform Association (LLRA) or of its breakaway group, the Lunacy Law Amendment Society (LLAS)

These are the cases that appear in the surviving documentation, and there may well have been more.

Julia Wood was a Shaker certified insane in 1875 after pledging £2,000 to build the Girlingite religious community's new lodge in the New Forest. Wood's nephew wrote out a lunacy order and went with two doctors and police officers to the Shaker encampment. When Wood resisted seizure, other Shakers tried to prevent her being taken, but the doctors and officers grabbed her and carried her to a waiting carriage, 'her grey hair streaming in the wind', as *The Times* had it. She spent seven years in Laverstock House Asylum, near Salisbury, Wiltshire, before the Home Secretary discharged her because of a technical error on the certificates; as she walked to the end of the asylum's drive, she was apprehended by doctors with fresh, correctly filled out certificates. The LLRA applied repeatedly to the Commissioners in Lunacy to be allowed to send an eminent London alienist and a lawyer to interview Wood, but were each time refused. She died in 1903 in Ashwood House Asylum, Kingswinford, in the West Midlands.

Alice Petschler, a widow with three children, had set herself up as a photographer in order to support herself upon the death of her husband. Her wealthy and well-connected sister, Harriet Cuffley, objected to her being in 'trade', and in November 1871 had Mrs Petschler consigned to the Macclesfield County Asylum as a pauper – even though Mrs Petschler had an income and assets worth £200. Mrs Cuffley achieved this illegal use of the public asylum system by seeking out not a local magistrate to sign the lunacy order, but a sympathetic vicar friend and the Altrincham Poor Law Officer, whom she knew socially. To certify a non-pauper lunatic as a pauper was a misdemeanour; and neither man had ever met Mrs Petschler. During her detention, which lasted ten months, Mrs Petschler was warned not to alert the visiting JPs or the Commissioners in Lunacy to her plight, as this would convince them that she was mad. While she was confined, Mrs Petschler's photography business was sold off. In Manchester, a committee comprising the mayor, town clerk, JPs, barristers and bankers pressed for an investigation of the case by Whitehall's Local Government Board. Subsequently, the Commissioners in Lunacy received mild censure for failing to have spotted the illegality of the paperwork. Public funds were collected so that Mrs Petschler could bring a legal case, but this failed, and she could afford no further action. Even the powerful Manchester support committee baulked at pursuing the case further.

J. L. Plumbridge, a wealthy fruit merchant of Thames Street in the City of London, began to suffer bouts of diarrhoea in 1873. It occurred to him that his illness might be the result of his food being tampered with, and he uttered this thought; on hearing this, one of his business associates decided the notion was delusional, wrote out a lunacy order and found two doctors to certify him. Plumbridge's family had gone along with the associate's actions, as he had persuaded them that certification would mean a swift cure to a temporary bout of insanity. But the associate went on to install his own son in Plumbridge's business, and ran it so badly that it came close to collapse. He refused to tell the family which asylum Plumbridge had been taken to and they lost all sight of him. He was first at Northumberland House, Stoke Newington, North London, where he was badly treated and tried to escape, assaulting two keepers in the process. He was next placed in Sussex House Asylum, Hammersmith, West London. He later wrote: 'The asylum has a river on one side and I escaped and swam across it but was recaptured. I was confined every night in what was called a seclusion room, the windows of which were blocked up with wood in which small holes were bored to admit the light, the door was fastened outside with three enormous iron bolts, my clothes were every night taken away, and the only furniture consisted of a hard mattress on the floor. Worse than all, however, separated from this den by only a thin wooden partition, was another of these seclusion rooms, in which raving madmen and the most noisy and violent patients were every night immured, so that, as I could hear them as plainly as though they were in the room with me, I could scarcely get any rest from the groans and cries that were often kept up through the livelong night.' Plumbridge escaped again by going over the wall and fleeing to Boulogne. Upon his return to England, he decided not to mount a legal action because he felt he could not prove malicious intent. He had himself certified sane by two doctors, despite influential alienist Dr Charles Lockhart Robertson saying that Plumbridge was still 'convalescent'. He received a great deal of help from Louisa Lowe, founder of the LLRA, then fell out with her, and became treasurer of the LLAS. In 1876 he wrote an anonymous account of his and other patients' experiences, *Slavery in England: An Account of the Manner in Which Persons without Trial are Condemned to Imprisonment for Life.*

William Thomas Preston, a barrister and once a member of the Athenaeum, was confined in Barnwood Asylum, near Gloucester, in the mid-1850s, having been found lunatic by inquisition. His younger brother gained control of all his assets. Louisa Lowe said that Preston had recovered his wits, but that the Commissioners, the Lord Chancellor and the local magistrates wavered because they had listened to slanderous stories put about by the very people who benefited from Preston's ongoing incarceration. Dr Lockhart Robertson told Lowe that Preston was 'a most dangerous lunatic . . . He cannot be trusted in the road with a woman'; but Mrs Lowe countered that he had spent much of his time before confinement at the Athenaeum, where all the servants were young women, and he had always been 'proper' towards them. However, so concerned were Barnwood Asylum staff, they ensured that Preston had a very discreet male attendant who shadowed Preston, but kept himself out of sight, whenever he went out for walks around Gloucester. The doctors claimed that it was very odd that Preston liked to darn his own clothes with string – and that he heard voices. Lowe argued that although the latter could be of concern, all sorts of religious experiences featured the hearing of voices, and so in itself, it was not evidence of insanity. Preston had hoped to be a witness at the 1877 Select Committee on Lunacy Law, but was not called. He died shortly afterwards.

Sir Samuel Fluyder, baronet, was certified into Ticehurst Asylum in Sussex on 30 September 1839 by Drs Sutherland and Monro and the lunacy order of Fluyder's brother-in-law, Cobbett Derby Jnr of Brighton. Fluyder had been his father's heir, and had never been thought insane – until he came into his inheritance. A solicitor who believed that Fluyder had always been sane contacted the LLRA in 1873, but Fluyder never won his freedom, dying in the asylum in March 1876.

Miss M——, the joint heir, with her two brothers, to a wealthy aunt, was a 'nervous patient' who boarded with a Miss P—— at 42 Harley Street. On Saturday 20 March 1880, her elder brother, Colonel Le Champion, sent two female keepers from Northumberland House, who barged past the servants and up to Miss M——'s room, where she had retired for the evening. They handed her a letter saying that she must accompany them to the asylum. The servant dashed back down to the sitting room where there were a number of other ladies, who all came up to defend Miss M——. During the melee, two policemen were called in, who thought that the letter was 'all right', and after an hour and a half of 'terrible scenes', Miss M—— was dragged into the carriage. She was kept at Northumberland House for eight weeks, held on lunacy certificates procured at Bath and signed by medical men who had chatted with her there a few days before her capture. The colonel drafted a letter for her to sign, stating that she accepted that she was now under certificate but could come out on 'parole' and would do all that she was told. The colonel's plan was to encourage the aunt to change her will to exclude this now 'lunatic' niece. Miss M—— alleged that the colonel kept her on the move, changing lodgings every three days, and tried to agitate her into a state of mania, but that he never managed it. Miss M—— said that she had written to the Commissioners in Lunacy about this, but that they had replied that she must continue to be self-controlled during her probation, and that the colonel would no doubt before long release her from certification.

Peter Chance, a printer from Stourbridge, Worcestershire, was a man of some means and had local political ambitions; but in May 1874 he was confined by his wife as a pauper in the local county asylum, on the certificate of one medical man and one magistrate. Mrs Chance's action had been triggered by her husband's decision to sell his freehold properties and to convert the money into an annuity for himself; this would have lessened the amount of her inheritance upon his death. Later, when the true extent of his wealth was revealed to the authorities, along with the illegality of his having been declared a pauper, Chance underwent a lunacy inquisition and was declared sane. He wished to sue for perjury the business associate who had conspired with Mrs Chance but found that he was unable to afford to do so, the £600 cost of the inquisition having almost bankrupted him.

Elizabeth Donney, seventy-seven, of Marylebone, was seized from her almshouse and placed in the lunatic ward of the local workhouse after telling the almshouse physician that money had gone missing from her bureau. The physician wrote out an informal (and, as such, illegal) certificate for her admission to the lunatic ward, stating she was 'old and silly'. Her daughter quickly removed her, but Mrs Donney died shortly afterwards. A subsequent coroner's court hearing heard of the illegal removal and detention.

James George Lamb, of Curtain Road, Shoreditch, East London, was confined to Northumberland House by his wife and sons, who did not like the way he was managing the family business. Other family members requested an inquisition, and Drs Harrington Tuke and J. Russell Reynolds swore affidavits that Lamb was insane. Mrs Lamb, however, changed her mind, and just before the inquisition was to start, went to the asylum and discharged her husband. He died of lung disease the next year, and Louisa Lowe claimed that this was a result of ill-treatment at the asylum.

In his letter to Lowe, Lamb had alleged that Lunacy Commissioner John Cleaton had a very cosy relationship with the owner of Northumberland House, and that Cleaton's 'inspection' of the asylum consisted of a good lunch and a guided tour, and that whenever a patient would begin to say something not to the owner's liking, s/he would be silenced.

Reverend Robert Bruce Kennard of Marnhull, Dorsetshire, a wealthy clergyman in his sixties, was to be married to Miss Bade, a former governess to his family, at Woodford in Essex. But on the day of the wedding, he was abducted to a room at 41 Hunter Street, St Pancras, central London, and detained there pending the arrival of doctors to certify him. Reverend Kennard bribed one of his abductors, escaped and married Miss Bade two days later. The culprit was a relative who had hoped to benefit from the vicar remaining unmarried.

Mr P——, in his youth, had taken a common-law wife in colonial Africa and had a child with her; they later separated. Much later, in England, he married a wealthy widow, but an Act of parliament retrospectively made legal all the questionable colonial common-law marriages that had been contracted. Upon this, the new Mrs P—— had the now elderly man certified into Grove House Asylum, Bow, East London. Mr P—— was described as rational, genial and kindly; he suffered slight paralysis and was confined to a bed in a shared ward. Mrs S—— was his first wife's daughter and she wished to remove her father and care for him at home. When she confronted Mrs P——, the latter admitted that she had acted for financial reasons: she also said she would not have him released until she had sent to Africa to find out the truth about his earlier marriage, and whether it would affect her standing in his will. Before she received her answer, Mr P—— had a seizure and died at Grove House.

Reverend J. W. Thomas sustained a head injury in 1860, which caused him mental difficulties, and he was confined for fourteen years. He recovered in 1863, but was unable to obtain his freedom because, the doctors claimed, he was very pernickety about his food, tied his shirt in an odd way, and preferred to sleep with his pillow at the foot of the bed. The LLRA believed that the true reason to delay the reverend's release was the family's belief that he would take revenge on them for his incarceration.

Catherine Linnett, one-time servant to the Lord Chancellor's Masters in Lunacy, at 45 Lincoln's Inn Fields, fell ill in 1877 and was prescribed morphia by Dr John Charles Bucknill – who had been appointed one of the Lord Chancellor's visitors. She became incoherent and delirious, and her husband called in two obscure local doctors, who initially refused to certify her insane. However, Mr Linnett wore them down, and she was taken to Bethlehem Hospital. Seven months later, she was allowed home, having shown no signs of insanity.

Henry John Field of Cheltenham, a silk mercer and draper, was incarcerated by his wife and spent eleven years in Gloucester County Asylum, escaped and was later found to be sane. An 1871 inquiry into his case by the local magistrates found several sane people detained in the asylum.

Mr Elliott escaped from Barming Heath Asylum in Kent, and many of his friends and some previous employers went to the magistrates to testify to his soundness of mind, one man even saying that he was keeping a job vacant until Elliott could take up the position. While the Commissioners were pondering his case, Elliott's certificates became invalid since he had managed to stay at liberty for long enough.

Isaac Hall, an open-air preacher in Southport, and 'well-known character' (according to the local newspaper), spent sixteen months in Lancaster Asylum.

Mrs Traiman, matron of Heath House at Brislington Asylum, had formerly been an inmate at Brislington during Mrs Lowe's incarceration. Mrs Traiman's husband had had her put away, but when he died, her relatives petitioned the Commissioners to have her case reviewed. Pending her hearing, she was allowed to become a carer of female Brislington patients.

Mrs Cureton was kept as a single patient, though sane, for three and a half years by her uncle and cousin.

Barnard Grant was consigned to Colney Hatch Asylum, Middlesex, after his wife plied him with drink and called in a doctor and magistrate, telling them that his paralytic behaviour was in fact recurring insanity.

Alexander Kay, an artisan, escaped from an asylum in 1882, went back to his family and his trade in Clapham, South London, and seven months later was arrested as an escapee and held by the police for twenty hours while two doctors examined him. However, he was freed by a magistrate who declared him sane.

Beatrice Keating was a single patient whose plight worried the mayor and the townsfolk of Margate in Essex. She was being pursued by Dr Henry Gristock Trend of Highbury New Park, North London, who wanted to take her into his small asylum.

No name: a fast-living West End doctor put away his amiable, accomplished but 'feeble-minded' daughter who had got wind of some seedy escapade of his. With the help of two unnamed compliant colleagues, he placed her in an unlicensed house with unsuitable people, where her mental condition swiftly deteriorated. Her own mother came to the LLRA when her appeal to the Commissioners had proved fruitless.

No name: the wife of a Tunbridge Wells general was on her way with him to a wedding when they stopped off at a hotel in Brighton, where two doctors came over to talk to her. This was, in fact, a lunacy consultation, arranged by the general, and they certified her. She was placed in various single houses until her family found out and threatened her husband with exposure, whereupon she was liberated. The general later agreed to a judicial separation, gave her full custody of the children and a maintenance allowance. He said he had just wanted to 'shelve' her for a while.

No name: an Exminster spiritualist confined for his mediumship.

SOURCES

Julia Wood: *The Times*, 2 March 1875.

Alice Petschler, Peter Chance, William Thomas Preston, Reverend W. F. Thomas and Barnard Grant: *Report from the 1877 Select Committee on Lunacy Law*.

J. L. Plumbridge: *Slavery in England*, circa 1876.

Samuel Fluyder, Miss M——, James George Lamb, Reverend Robert Bruce Kennard, Mr P——, Catherine Linnett, Henry John Field, Mr Elliott, Mrs Traiman, Mrs Cureton, Alexander Kay, Beatrice Keating, the daughter of the West End doctor and the wife of the Tunbridge Wells general: Louisa Lowe, *The Bastilles of England*, 1883.

Elizabeth Donney: *The Times*, 27 January 1876.

Isaac Hall: *Medium and Daybreak*, 25 July 1873.

The Exminster spiritualist: *The Spiritualist*, 13 November 1874

Notes

Inconvenient People: Andrew Scull's 1980 essay, 'A Convenient Place to Get Rid of Inconvenient People: The Victorian Lunatic Asylum' inspired my title. Scull quotes Victorian alienist Andrew Wynter's 1870 *Edinburgh Review* article, 'Non-Restraint in the Treatment of the Insane', in which Wynter writes of lunatic asylums: 'If we make a convenient lumber room, we all know how speedily it becomes filled up with lumber.'

Preface

Page xvii 'The fear that the English were sleepwalking . . . curb individual freedom': *Inconvenient People* does not explore the Scottish or Irish lunacy systems – the former often referred to by campaigners as far superior to the English. For further reading on Scotland: *'They're in the Trade of Lunacy': The Scottish Lunacy Commissioners and Lunacy Reform in Nineteenth-Century Scotland* by Jonathan Andrews, 1998. For the liberty issue in Ireland: *Fools and Mad: A History of the Insane in Ireland* by Joseph Robins, Dublin, 1986, pp. 80–87; and *Insanity and the Insane in Post-Famine Ireland* by Mark Finnane, 1981, pp. 113–22. • **Page xviii** 'For the poor . . . their retention': Purnell B. Purnell, *Report of the County Chairman to the Gloucestershire Epiphany Court of Quarter Sessions*, 1849, p. 4. • Gender not an obvious factor: Elaine Showalter's *The Female Malady: Women, Madness and English Culture, 1830–1980* (1985) was part of the wave of academic work that rightly refocused historical studies on to the female experience. *Inconvenient People* is not a backlash, but an attempt to reposition the discussion. • **Page xix** 'A Case Humbly Offered': published in the *Gentleman's Magazine*. Peter McCandless, 'Insanity and Society: A Study of the English Lunacy Reform Movement, 1815–1870', University of Wisconsin PhD, 1974, p. 37, alerted me to the 1763 article as a watershed in concerns about the unregulated madhouse trade and to the eleven-year wait for the first Act. • **Page xx** 'H Broadway A Potcarey . . . to be Don at Home': *Report from the Select Committee on the Provisions for Better Regulation of Madhouses in England, 1814–15*, p. 51.

1: Being 'Burrowsed'

Page 1 'Triumph over oppression and cruelty': the *Carmarthen Journal* and the *Chester Courant*, quoted in *The Times*, 30 January 1830. • **Page 2** 'I cannot help being witty . . . a cannon': *Morning Chronicle*, 18 December 1829; no image of Edward Davies appears to have survived. • **Page 5** Oakfield Court, off Haslemere Road, marks the site of Oakfield House. • 'I'll make you repent this before the end of the year!': *Quarterly Review*, March 1830. • **Page 8** James Brookbank laughed 'until his sides shook': *Morning Post*, 28 December 1829. • **Page 9** Dr Blundell 'a dirty filthy fellow': *Morning Chronicle*, 28 December 1829. • **Page 10** 'Sir, it is beneath the dignity . . . do you see this?': ibid., 16 December 1829. • **Page 11** 'Well calculated to inspire respect in the class of patients under his care': 'Memoir of the Late Dr George Man Burrows', *London Medical Gazette*, 11 December 1846. • **Page 16** The figure of 373 inquisitions between 1820 and 1830: Akihito Suzuki, *Madness at Home: The Psychiatrist, the Patient and the Family in England, 1820–1860*, 2006, Table 1. • **Page 18** Portland Terrace was at the southern end of today's St John's Wood High Street. • 'Oh God! . . . confined rooms': *Morning Chronicle*, 15 December 1829. • The Clapham Retreat was close to Union Road. • **Page 19** 'Addicted to unnatural offences' and 'The British public . . . success of my cause': *The Times*, 22 December 1829. • **Page 20** The *Anderdon* v. *Burrows and Others* case was reported in full in *The Times*, 27 April 1830. • **Page 21** 'Private arrangement . . . delicacy of the investigation' and 'to emancipate himself from the thraldom of his mother': *Morning Chronicle*, 26 October 1829. • **Page 22** 'Unsoundness of mind . . . declaration of lunacy': ibid., 15 December 1829. • **Page 23** 'Extremely excited . . . manner': ibid., 26 October 1829. • 'Don't be excited, Ma'am . . , you see the consequences': *The Times*, 17 December 1829. • **Page 25** 'A delusion of manner about him . . . Nonsense!': the *Standard*, 18 December 1829. • 'Was difficult to suppress' and 'Mr Davies had not only thought himself a Pitt in finance . . . for His Majesty's subjects': *Morning Chronicle*, 28 December 1829. • **Page 26** 'Dr Burrows is cautioned . . . by BLOOD only': *A Letter to Sir Henry Halford, Bt, KCH, President of the Royal College of Physicians &c, Touching Some Points of the Evidence, and Observations of Counsel, on a Commission of Lunacy on Mr Edward Davies* by George Man Burrows, MD, 1830, p. 3. • 'The effervescence . . . animadversions on my character': ibid. • 'Persecution . . . unsettle the steadiest intellect': *The Times*, 28 December 1829. • 'The extraordinary case of

Mr Davies . . . to be prosecuted at the public expense': *Quarterly Review*, March 1830. • **Page 27** 'This perverse concealment . . . baneful effect': *Commentaries on the Causes, Forms, Symptoms and Treatment, Moral and Medical of Insanity* by George Man Burrows MD, 1828, p. 103. Available online. • 'Malady appeared to be progressive': Burrows, *A Letter to Sir Henry Halford*, p. 12. Akihito Suzuki's illuminating study, *Madness at Home*, explores in depth the role that family testimony played in lunacy diagnosis in nineteenth-century England. I am indebted to *Madness at Home* for leads to further reading on the Edward Davies story. • 'Eccentricity itself is a link in the catenation . . . ripen into perfect insanity': Burrows, *Commentaries*, p. 130. • **Page 28** 'I consider the maniacal odour . . . no other proof of it': ibid., p. 297. Dr Forbes Benignus Winslow claimed some eighteen years later that he, too, could smell insanity: 'The skin [of a lunatic] gives evidence of disease. It has an appearance of having been rubbed over by some greasy substance; this is accompanied by a peculiar fetid or cutaneous exhalation, which symptom is very perceptible when the disease is in its advanced stage, and is generally indicative of organic and hopeless disease of the brain': *On the Incubation of Insanity*, 1846, p. 19. • **Page 29** *The Lancet*'s Witchfinder-General comparison is referred to in Suzuki, *Madness at Home*, p. 70. Alienist Dr John Conolly claimed that the alleged smell of a lunatic was nothing more than the stink of the asylum. • 'The infancy of our knowledge': Burrows, *Commentaries*, p. 159. • 'As to the evidence of the medical witnesses . . . pompous, vulgar and absurd': 'Law Versus Physic', *London Medical Gazette*, 2 January 1830. 'There is nothing of which the public . . . they should be so': ibid., 3 December 1829. • 'Suffering from functional disorder . . . bordering upon delirium': *London Medical Gazette*, 9 January 1830. • 'The physician's own mind . . . any other person': Haslam quoted in *Quarterly Review*, March 1830. • **Page 30** 'The majority of the insane are men': Burrows, *Commentaries*, pp. 240–1. • **Page 31** 'It frequently happens . . . the production of it [the note]': Burrows, *A Letter to Sir Henry Halford*, pp. 9–10. • 'What a revolution! . . . encouraging them': ibid., p. 22. • The dissolution of Hodgson & Davies, *London Gazette*, 1 September 1843.

2: The Attorney–General of all Her Majesty's Madmen

Unless otherwise stated below, all descriptions and direct quotations regarding John Perceval's illness and recovery, and his time at Brislington House and Ticehurst, are taken from *A Narrative of the Treatment Experienced by a Gentleman during a State of Mental Derangement*, 1838, published anonymously, and his enlarged reprise of the subject, with the same title, printed in 1840 under his own name, as Volume 2. This second volume is available to read online. • **Page 36** Trophimus Fulljames's allegations of cruelty at Brislington are in The National Archives, HO 44/12, ff.124, 198, 214, 403, 420, 431 and 432 (the illustrations); and HO 44/13, ff.2, 7, 23, 46. HO 44/12 f.31 is an amazing little dossier compiled by Fulljames of many cases of alleged wrongful incarceration and asylum cruelty, 1820–23 – one of the earliest of such endeavours. In HO 44/13, f.7 Dr Edward Long Fox writes that Fulljames, who had a 'cunning, specious manner', was a bankrupt London stockbroker who had fired a pistol at the Prince Regent in St James's Park, and had once come into the House of Lords with a basket of medicinal herbs to distribute, Ophelia-style. Trophimus's brother, Thomas, a well-known land surveyor, had taken him into his home, along with Trophimus's wife and nine children, but his behaviour became increasingly erratic, following the death of his wife in 1820. He lived to the age of eighty-four, dying in Wells, Somerset, in 1864. He appears to have taken no further part in lunacy care campaigning, though he suffered periodic breakdowns, and was in Kensington House Asylum in London for a spell in 1855. • **Page 40** John Bellingham had been imprisoned for debt while in Russia on business and his appeals for British government assistance and compensation for this had been ignored. He festered, and plotted murderous revenge. He was executed seven days after the killing – his long and coherent testimony in court undermining any attempt to have the sentence commuted by reason of criminal lunacy. However, Andro Linklater, in his 2012 book *Why Spencer Perceval Had to Die*, alleges that Bellingham, far from being a deranged grudge-holder, was part of an elaborate plot to punish Perceval for his assaults upon the slave trade. Legend has it that when the dying prime minister was moved from the lobby into the Speaker's drawing room, one of his sons, 'a fine boy of about thirteen years of age happened accidentally to come down [from Downing Street, where the family lived] a few moments after the assassination took place . . . The unhappy child's distress is beyond description.' (Reported in *The Globe*, 12 May 1812 and *Freeman's Journal*, 16 May 1812.) John's brothers Henry and Dudley Montague were nearest to the age of thirteen in 1812, but both were away at Harrow; John was nine years old and was in London, and it may be that it was he who saw his newly dead father. He never, though, in his writings, alluded to this. When John's sister Frederica died in 1900, aged eighty-eight, among her belongings was the Speaker's bloodstained rug on to which the dying prime minister had been moved. (*The Assassination of the Prime Minister: John Bellingham and the Murder of Spencer Perceval* by David C. Hanrahan, Stroud, 2008, p. 173.) • **Page 45** Andrew Roberts's website www.studymore.org.uk alerted me to Spencer Perceval Jnr's role as a Metropolitan Commissioner. • **Page 46** Sadly, despite Dr Fox's precautions, one of his sons, aged five, died in a bedroom fire on the premises. A maid managed to rescue two other Fox children. (Annie Fox, *Brislington House*

Quarterly News, Centenary Number, Bristol, 1904.) Annie Fox's commemorative pamphlet also reveals that Mrs Edward Long Fox was once chased by a patient with a meat knife and had to lock herself in a kitchen cupboard pending rescue. • 'A hospital for the curable . . . incurable': Francis Ker and Charles Fox, *The History and Present State of Brislington House near Bristol*, Bristol, 1836. • **Page 47** One more glimpse from the archives that confirms Mr Perceval's portrait of Dr Fox Snr as a smug, religiose hypocrite is the latter's Uriah Heep-ish replies to Whitehall's queries, following Trophimus Fulljames's allegations, found in The National Archives, HO 44/13, f.7. • **Page 50** Half of Chancery lunatics related to government officials: *The Laws of Lunacy and Their Crimes, as They Affect all Classes of Society* by Richard Saumarez, 1859, p. 36. • 'Vulgar error': letter dated 10 June 1839 to Baron Lyndhurst, published in *Letters to the Rt Hon Sir James Graham, Bt, and to Other Gentlemen upon the Reform of the Law affecting the Treatment of Persons Alleged to be of Unsound Mind*, 1846. • Lady Carr hadn't always been so lacking in spirit. In 1790, she eloped and married Spencer Perceval in East Grinstead in so much haste that she was still wearing her riding gear. • **Page 52** The Bristol Riots: twelve rioters died and many more corpses were found in the burnt-out buildings; four alleged ringleaders were executed and the head of the local militia committed suicide during his court martial for failure to disperse the rioters. • Pay and staffing levels at Brislington: Leonard Smith, 'A Gentleman's Mad-Doctor in Georgian England: Edward Long Fox and Brislington House', *History of Psychiatry*, 19, no. 2, June 2008, p. 173. • **Page 54** Delay of at least four months: Nicholas Hervey, 'Advocacy or Folly: The Alleged Lunatics' Friend Society, 1845–1863', *Medical History*, no. 30, 1986, p. 250. • Metropolitan Commissioners' dissatisfaction with provincial asylum visitation: letter dated 7 December 1841, The National Archives, HO 45/74. • Much of Ticehurst's landscaped grounds has survived, together with the main building and Charles Newington's own family home, Heathlands, close by the asylum building. • **Page 57** 'The glory of the old system . . . cudgelled him': letter to the Home Office, dated 1 August 1845, printed in *Letters to the Rt Hon Sir James Graham, Bt*, p. 47. This is Foucault in a nutshell, 120 years before the French philosopher spotted the moral treatment fallacy. • **Page 58** 'The attorney-general of all Her Majesty's madmen': *Report from the 1859 Select Committee on Lunatics*, Session 2, p. 23. • Goldsmid's family's malpractice at the Exchequer Bill Office had contributed to one of the most embarrassing fiscal crises of Mr Perceval's father's government, though Mr Perceval never alluded to this in his writings. Goldsmid would be discharged from Ticehurst in 1842 as 'not-cured' and died the following year. Charlotte MacKenzie, 'A Family Asylum: A History of the Private Madhouse at Ticehurst in Sussex, 1792–1917', PhD thesis, University of London, 1986, pp. 103 and 156. • **Page 61** 'Lady Carr thought proper . . . his station in life': letter from Dr Robert Stedman to the Home Office, dated 20 June 1838, The National Archives, HO 40/40. I am grateful to Nicholas Hervey's 'Advocacy or Folly' for alerting me to Stedman's letter; and to MacKenzie's 'A Family Asylum', p. 154, for confirmation of the date of Mr Perceval leaving Ticehurst. • **Page 62** 'Calculated to inflame the lower orders . . . I have written this': The National Archives, HO 40/40. • 'The infidel spirit of modern "liberality"': Introduction to Perceval's *Narrative*, vol. 2, 1840, p. xxii. • **Page 63** 'The chief branch of his complaint . . . well-informed person': *The Examiner*, 9 August 1840. The review was anonymous, but the *Examiner's* chief literary critic was John Forster, who in fifteen years' time would become secretary to the Commissioners in Lunacy, and later, a Commissioner himself. He was a Liberal barrister and friend of Commissioner in Lunacy Bryan Waller Procter. Politically, Forster was very far removed from Mr Perceval, and, as later chapters will show, Forster continued in his certainty that 'exaggeration' was behind many lunatics' complaints, particularly regarding wrongful incarceration. • 'Details such as he has given . . . to the public': 'The Late Dr Cheyne's Life and Essays', *Dublin University Magazine*, October 1843. • Notting Hill Square is today's Campden Hill Square. • 'By a singular and providential occurrence': quoted in Peter McCandless, 'Insanity and Society', p. 212.

3: The Alleged Lunatics' Friend Society

Page 65 'Very gentlemanly' appearance and 'The answers to the questions . . . possessed by the querist': *The Times*, 25 August 1838. • **Page 66** 'To the blessings of a free press': Richard Paternoster, *The Madhouse System*, 1841, p. 16. • 'You have behaved like a mother to me': *The Times*, 6 September 1838. • The alleged murder of John Milroy: Paternoster, *The Madhouse System*, p. 55. • **Page 67** 'A more heartless ruffian . . . speech and gesture': diary entry dated 9 September 1838, quoted in *The Life and Work of the Seventh Earl of Shaftesbury* by Edwin Hodder, 3 vols, 1887, vol. 1, p. 105. Available online. • **Page 68** The William Bailey story is told in *A Letter to the Secretary of State for the Home Department Upon the Unjust and Pettifogging Conduct of the Metropolitan Commissioners in Lunacy, in the Case of a Gentleman Lately under their Surveillance* by John Perceval, 1844. Mrs Bailey had used Dr John Haslam to find her husband insane – one of the men who swore to Edward Davies's insanity, in Chapter One. The first certification of Mr Bailey, in 1835, cited the following as evidence of his insanity: that during a long business trip to France he showed no interest in his children (in fact, he asked Mrs Bailey to come to Boulogne with them, so they could spend family time together);

that he spent too much money on sending presents to his children, while in France; that he once used a ladder to get back into a house he had rented, when he had lost his key; that one night, finding he had no lucifers in his house, he walked to the nearest turnpike to obtain a light. The second certification, in 1839, stated that Mr Bailey had written an angry letter to an auctioneer with whom he was in dispute, in which Mr Bailey threatened to 'horsewhip' him. • **Page 69** 'A cold, forbidding reply . . . the imputation of lunacy': Perceval, *A Letter*, p. 38. • **Page 71** The fullest account of the Lewis Phillips case is found in Hansard Parliamentary Debates, 3rd series, 82, cols 410–413, 11 July 1845. Available online. • **Page 72** Gilbert Bolden: Bolden was also involved in the growing law-amendment movement, which sought to modernise, streamline and make less expensive the English legal system, not least the infamously cumbrous court of Chancery. What's more, Perceval, Bailey and Saumarez also had roles in their local communities as Poor Law officers, attempting to permeate a system that they did not agree with, in order to mitigate its harshest operations. • 'The privilege which belongs to every Englishman . . . or by attorney': *Report of the Alleged Lunatics' Friend Society*, 1851, p. 25. • 'By such a provision . . . from its social peace': *First Report of the Alleged Lunatics' Friend Society*, 1846, p. 31. • **Page 73** 'It is known how much weakness and futility . . . generosity': *A Letter*, p. 5. • 'Void of the honest manliness . . . sham benevolence': Thomas Mulock, *British Lunatic Asylums, Public and Private*, 1858, p. 33. Mulock had himself been confined in Stafford Asylum in 1830, on the word of a local bigwig who had taken against him. He is more famous for his campaigning against the Highland Clearances and for being the father of novelist Dinah Craik (1826–1887). • 'Jesuitical old humbug': Georgina Weldon in *Social Salvation*, April/May 1884 issue, p. 4. • **Page 74** '[I] Did not wish . . . harmony to the heart': diary entries for 24 September and 13 November 1828 (when he was a Metropolitan Commissioner), quoted in Hodder, *Life and Work*, vol. 1, pp. 104–6. • **Page 75** 'Scarcely believe that he is the man . . . public-spirited school': letter from Perceval to the Home Secretary dated 9 May 1861, The National Archives, HO 45/7102, f.6. • **Page 76** 'Transmission of ideas': Nicholas Hervey is the author of the first and most authoritative work on the Alleged Lunatics' Friend Society, 'Advocacy or Folly: The Alleged Lunatics' Friend Society, 1845–1863', *Medical History*, no. 30, 1986. Available online. My account of the Society in this chapter has been built upon the work done by Hervey and by Peter McCandless in his 1974 PhD, 'Insanity and Society'. I am grateful to both for leads to original source material. Hervey spots that many of the Society's concepts and suggestions exerted influence upon policymakers and lawmakers, but that this was never openly acknowledged at the time. • 'Persons who are termed morally insane . . . in a decidedly sane state': *Supplemental Report of the Metropolitan Commissioners in Lunacy to* *the Lord Chancellor, Relative to the General Condition of the Insane in Wales*, 1844, pp. 165 and 176. Available online. • Ferry told the court: 'Sorry I am that I did it, and I never will forget it as long as I live, but I had not my senses about me at the time. I loved her too well. Sorry I am that I did it.' *Morning Post*, 3 August 1843. • **Page 77** 'They follow and persecute me . . . to murder me': *The Times*, 4 March 1843. • **Page 78** 'Friend' in the Alleged Lunatics' Friend Society. This worked on several levels: the confined patient was often unable to raise the alarm with an outsider in order to contest their incarceration; in such isolation, they became 'friendless'. What's more, the legal disabilities suffered by married women, who could not bring civil cases, could be surmounted if they were able to enjoin what the law called 'a next friend' to take the action on their behalf, so 'Friend' conveys the sense of a body that would fight a lawsuit for someone. Finally, the Society was offering companionship for those who had been emotionally shattered by being accused of insanity by relatives or associates. • 'The railway speed and confusing commotion . . . steaming hot-headedly on their course': Luke James Hansard, *What Are To Be the Tendencies of the Community of the British Nation? To Sanity? or To Insanity? A Question*, 1845, p. 9. Available online. • The make-up and likely number of members of the Society: Hervey's 'Advocacy or Folly', p. 254. • **Page 80** Procter and Lutwidge as drafters of the lunacy legislation: Nicholas Hervey, 'A Slavish Bowing Down: The Lunacy Commission and the Psychiatric Profession, 1845–1860', in W. F. Bynum, Roy Porter and Michael Shepherd (eds), *The Anatomy of Madness*, vol. 2, 1985, p. 103. • 'Uncle Skeffington': Judy Miller and E. Fuller Torrey, in the interesting essay 'The Capture of the Snark' (*Richmond Review*, 2001, available online), identify the Lunacy Commissioners as the characters in *The Hunting of the Snark*. Lewis Carroll appears to have been in error when he stated that his beloved uncle had been universally popular, as surviving letters show the irritation and dislike he aroused in a number of his Commission colleagues. Commissioner Bryan Waller Procter wrote in 1867, 'Poor Wilkes is going to travel with Lutwidge. He does not like it, and I quite feel his distaste for his colleague.' (Letter from Procter to John Forster, dated 22 April 1867, quoted in *Barry Cornwall: A Biography of Bryan Waller Procter* by Richard Willard Armour, 1935, p. 317.) • **Page 82** Statistics on the rate of county asylum-building: Scull, *Museums of Madness*, p. 136. Scull notes that Cambridge, Sussex, London and Norfolk remained the most stubborn administrations regarding the statutory requirement. • 'Odious defects': *Report of the Alleged Lunatics' Friend Society*, 1851, p. 5. • 'A blot upon our legislature': *First Report of the Alleged Lunatics' Friend Society*, p. 25. Full details of the Society's successes and failures regarding the 1845 legislation are found in this report. • **Page 83** 949 institutions to be inspected nationwide: D. J. Mellett, 'Bureaucracy and Mental Illness: The Commissioners in Lunacy 1845–90', *Medical History*, no. 25, 1981, p. 230.

• **Page 84** 'The alter ego to the Lunacy Commission': Hervey, 'Advocacy or Folly', p. 246. • The Anne Tottenham story is found in *Report from the 1859 Select Committee on Lunatics*, Session 1, pp. 13–15, and Richard Saumarez, *The Laws of Lunacy, Especially as they Affect the Lunatic Wards of Chancery*, 1858, p. 25. • 'I would rather see the Devil in my asylum than you': quoted in McCandless, 'Insanity and Society,' p. 210. • **Page 86** The Purnell table is displayed prominently on the Museum's first floor and a picture of it is to be found on the V&A website. • Messrs Pulverstoft and Dixon: Hervey, 'Advocacy or Folly', p. 263. • 'The members of this Society . . . domestic calamity': *Medical Times*, 4 January 1851. • **Page 87** 'His sympathies with the insane . . . feeble and weak': letter to the *Northampton Herald*, dated 4 September 1858, quoted in Hervey, 'Advocacy or Folly', p. 270. • 'I have heard from two or three quarters . . . the late Mr Drummond': letter dated 14 July 1854, The National Archives, HO 45/5542. • Mr Perceval thought Royal Bethlehem Hospital should be abolished and the buildings bought by the state to refashion into a gallery; today, the building's surviving sections house the Imperial War Museum. • **Page 88** 'Uncouth . . . propensities': Peithman's casebook, Bethlem Art and History Collections Trust. • **Page 89** 'My heart bled . . . so elegant a mind': John Perceval, *The Case of Dr Peithman LLD*, 1855, p. 25. • 'A certain eccentricity . . . proverbially eccentric': ibid., p. 26. • **Page 90** 'No answer, he is half crazy himself': letter dated 5 July 1854, The National Archives, HO 45/5542. • 'What on Earth Has He Done?': *Punch*, 23 September 1854. • **Page 91** 'His simplicity of character . . . the glory of England to maintain': letter dated 21 August 1854, quoted in Perceval, *Case of Dr Peithman*, pp. 8–9. • **Page 92** 'Hideous "Holy Office" . . .': *Letters to the Rt Hon Sir James Graham, Bt . . .*, p. 7. 'Restoring us to the cruelty of the Inquisition': letter to the Home Office, dated 5 April 1861, The National Archives, HO 45/7102. 'That monstrous tribunal': letter to George Grey, Home Secretary, dated 16 December 1848, The National Archives, HO 44/52. 'The general servility of mind . . . admitted of': letter to the Home Office, dated 27 May 1861, The National Archives, HO 45/7102. • 'The sobriety and severity . . . to give females every protection': letter to the Home Secretary, dated 5 April 1840, The National Archives, HO 44/36 f.229. • **Page 93** 'A perfect illustration . . . abuses of our present laws': letter to the *Morning Post*, 12 July 1849.

4: 'Oh Hail, Holy Love!'

Page 95 'I sent for them from Brighton . . . "the will of God"': *Bridgwater Times*, 28 June 1849. Except where stated otherwise below, all direct quotations are taken from *The Times*'s extensive coverage of the ensuing court case, on 25, 26 and 27 June 1849, or from the *Bridgwater Times*'s coverage of the same on 28 June 1849. • **Page 96** Howard and Grey correspondence cited in Joshua John Schweiso, 'Deluded Inmates, Frantic Ravers and Communists: A Sociological Study of the Agapemone, a Sect of Victorian Apocalyptic Millenarians,' PhD thesis, University of Reading, 1994, p. 117. • **Page 97** 'An estimated one in ten marriages . . . property settlements': Lee Holcombe, *Wives and Property: Reform of the Married Women's Property Law in Nineteenth-Century England*, Oxford, 1983, p. 46, quoting Hansard, 3rd series, 142, col. 410, 20 May 1856. • William Cobbe was the brother of Victorian feminist Frances Power Cobbe. Sally Mitchell, in *Frances Power Cobbe: Victorian Feminist, Journalist, Reformer*, 2004, p. 215, notes that references to Prince 'appeared not infrequently, and always pejoratively,' in Frances's journalism. So complete was William's separation from his family that he was the only Cobbe family member not to return home for his parents' funerals. • **Page 102** Moorcroft House: 'Moorcroft: The History of a House and Its Inhabitants' by Ian C. Davis (unpublished), *c.*1993, Hillingdon Local Studies Library. Moorcroft House usually accommo-dated thirty to fifty patients in these years; by 1861, all of Moorcroft's patients were male, the females having been moved to another nearby asylum. Davis's pamphlet provides a glimpse of some of the patients at Moorcroft in the Edwardian years: the Indian prince who regularly ordered a gold pipe from Dunhill's, only to throw it in the fire upon its arrival. The quiet barrister who would occasionally, after reading the *Daily Telegraph*, shout a torrent of abuse out of the window. The American who would yell, 'Get in the train, Maud!' during billiard games (p. 24). The asylum buildings are still standing, in Harlington Road, Hillingdon. • **Page 104** Frederick Ripley's interactions with the Commissioners in Lunacy: entries dated 3 December and 10 December 1846, in the Minute Book of the Commissioners in Lunacy, The National Archives, MH 50/2. • Thomas Cobbe's activities: discussed in Joshua John Schweiso, 'Religious Fanaticism and Wrongful Confinement in Victorian England', *Social History of Medicine*, vol. 9, no. 2, August 1996, p. 173. • **Page 105** Monomania: Margaret Homberger's PhD thesis, 'Wrongful Confinement and Victorian Psychiatry, 1840–1880', University of London, 2001, contains the fullest account of the monomaniac-theory dilemma, with particular reference to literary representations of the diagnosis. • John Perceval's defence of Louisa's religious beliefs: *Morning Post*, 12 July 1849. • **Pages 107–8** Emily and Edmund's conversation with the Commissioners in Lunacy: The National Archives, MH 50/3, Minute Book of the Commissioners in Lunacy, entry dated 11 May 1848. • **Page 109** 'We have no business with the world . . . the devil's kingdom': *Spiritual Wives* by William Hepworth Dixon, 2 vols, 1868, p. 244. Available online. • Schweiso, 'Deluded Inmates', p. 130, reveals that there were five children under the age of twelve at the Agapemone itself in 1851, four more at one of the farms owned by the sect, and a further eight registered at the school in Four Forks. • **Page 111** Pollock (1783–1870) was a Tory member of parliament and former Attorney-General. His hands-off, laisser-aller approach to the issue of lunacy contrasts with Conolly's Benthamite Radicalism, advocating state-backed measures to bring about social 'progress'. • **Page 115** '. . . suggestions made by voices in the air . . . all sense of modesty': *A Remonstrance with The Lord Chief Baron Touching the Case Nottidge versus Ripley* by John Conolly MD, 1849. • **Page 118** 'Conolly's changing views . . . enlightenment to error': Andrew Scull, 'A Brilliant Career? John Conolly and Victorian Psychiatry', *Victorian Studies*, vol. 27, Winter 1984. • 'The public mind seems drunk . . . receptacles of their victims': 'The Lord Chief Baron and the Nottidge Case' by Dr Forbes Benignus Winslow, *Journal of Psychological Medicine and Mental Pathology*, vol. 2, October 1849. • **Pages 119–20** 'One is driven with shame . . . camp of gypsies': Knight Bruce's damning judgement on Brother Thomas, *The Times*, 23 May 1850. • **Page 120** George Thomas Nottidge custody case: Maeve E. Doggett, in *Marriage, Wife-Beating and the Law in Victorian England*, 1992, points out that Agnes's victory happened in a court of equity, not of common law. Equity considered the child's interest to be paramount; common law recognised no rights in the mother. • 'I do not believe the reports . . . out of his bedroom': The National Archives, MH 50/3, Minute Book of the Commissioners in Lunacy, entry dated 11 May 1848. • **Page 122** 'This is the day of judgement . . . relieved me': the coroner's hearing on the Mary Maber case is reported in the *Morning Chronicle*, 17 June 1856. • **Page 123** 'Prima facie grounds . . . something wrong in the establishment': Coroner Munckton's verdict and further allegations about life in the Agapemone, *The Times*, 9 June 1856. • **Page 124** 'I have never felt so strange a joy . . . in that hour': Dixon, *Spiritual Wives*, p. 319, from which all details of The Great Manifestation are taken. • **Page 126** 'Intends to leave him . . . return to her husband': quoted in Doggett, *Marriage, Wife-Beating*, p. 29. • **Page 127** 'Have erred . . . done His will upon them': Dixon, *Spiritual Wives*, p. 251. • 'The traces of much pain . . . hush about them': ibid., pp. 233–4 and p. 241. • **Page 128** On Sunday 7 September 1902, Smyth-Pigott preached in north-east London, 'I am the Son of Man', claiming that he was the Second Coming. A riot ensued, and 5,000–6,000 people demonstrated against him in Clapton, shouting 'Humbug!', 'Nonsense!' and 'Liar!' • **Page 129** In *The Abode of Love: A Memoir*, Edinburgh, 2006, Kate Barlow writes a vivid account of growing up in the vast shadow of the Agapemonites. Barlow attempted as a child to piece together the mystery of the odd complex that had been run by her 'dangerously charismatic' grandfather, Prince's successor.

5: 'If I had been poor, they would have left me alone'

Except where stated otherwise below, all direct quotations are taken from 'The Important Lunacy Case of Catherine Cumming', printed as an appendix to vol. 5 of the *Journal of Psychological Medicine and Mental Pathology*, April

1852, and available online; or from *The Times* reports of her second lunacy commission, printed between 8 and 26 January 1852 inclusive. • **Page 133** 'I have hitherto done my duty to him and I will still continue to do so': the *Standard*, 22 September 1846. • **Page 138** Dr Millingen's failings: entries dated 26 February and 2 April 1846 in the Minute Book of the Commissioners in Lunacy, The National Archives, MH 50/1. John Gideon Millingen is not to be confused with the Dr (Julius) Millingen, in whose arms Lord Byron had expired in 1824. • Millingen's relationships with Thackeray and Dickens: E. Gaskell, 'More About Spontaneous Combustion', *The Dickensian*, January 1973. • The Society for the Protection of the Insane: Nicholas Hervey, 'A Slavish Bowing Down', p. 115. • 'Full of delusions . . . certainly of unsound mind': entries dated 21 and 24 May 1846 in the Minute Book of the Commissioners in Lunacy, The National Archives, MH 50/1. • York House had been built for the Bishop of York, but its fine Tudor rooms were destroyed in the eighteenth century (including a richly ornamented domed roof and painted wood panelling) and the house later became firstly the site of Battersea's renowned enamelling trade and then a distillery. (*Historic Battersea* by Sherwood Ramsey, 1913.) It next became an asylum, then the Price's Candles factory, demolished and rebuilt in the 1870s. The site was excavated in 2002. • **Page 146** 'A morbid perversion of the natural feelings . . . the business of life': Prichard quoted in 'The Meaning of Moral Insanity' by Eric T. Carlson and Norman Dain, *Bulletin of the History of Medicine*, vol. 36, 1962, p. 131. • **Page 147** 'Gay and smiling and evidently in high spirits': *The Era*, 27 September 1846. • **Pages 147–8** 'If Mrs Cumming . . . disgrace our statute book': the *Sun* editorial quoted in the *Liverpool Mercury*, 2 October 1846. • **Page 148** 'A compromise with a lunatic!' *The Lancet*, 14 February 1852. • **Page 149** Sutherland's 185 private patients: *The Care of the Insane and Their Legal Control* by John Charles Bucknill, 1880, p. 112. • *The Woman in White*: Paul Lewis, in his 2010 pamphlet, 'Walter's Walk', traces the route precisely. • **Page 154** William Vesalius Pettigrew: Pettigrew would be admonished by the Commissioners in later years for signing patients into Munster House Asylum in Fulham, which was also owned by Elliott – the suspicion being that Pettigrew was proving a little too reliable in drumming up business for the Elliott madhouse empire in South and West London. Pettigrew wrote a letter to the Commissioners, complaining that they had even dared to question him, and sure enough, the Commissioners did not pursue the matter further. Minute Book of the Commissioners in Lunacy, The National Archives, MH 50/9, p. 40. • **Page 157** The Eyre Arms inquest: Dr Millingen had not been called to give evidence, because the Commissioners in Lunacy mistakenly believed that he had died. John Gideon Millingen would live on until 1862 but no one appeared to notice the mistake, not even the newspapers or the medical press. • **Page 158** 'Insanity does not admit of being defined . . .

derangement of the mind': Forbes Benignus Winslow, *The Plea of Insanity in Criminal Cases*, 1843, p. 74; available online. • **Pages 159–60** The jurymen's visit to Gothic Villa: Mrs Cumming's terse self-justification and mocking of a world that she felt had misused her calls Miss Havisham irresistibly to mind, particularly Chapter XI, when the ghastly Pocket relatives visit. • **Page 172** *A Practical Treatise on the Law Concerning Lunatics, Idiots and Persons of Unsound Mind* by Leonard Shelford, 1833; 2nd edn 1847: Leonard Shelford, 1795–1864, was a Nemo-style law-writing recluse who, in his Temple chambers, compiled treatises condensing and clarifying complex legal issues, including summaries of recent cases and precedents. • **Pages 173–4** 'With the exception of the cats . . . connected with the inquiry': *The Lancet*, 17 January 1852. • **Page 174** 'From my judicial recollection of the facts . . . the proceedings in lunacy were proper': *The Times*, 11 February 1854. • '. . . as rational and composed . . . to proceed': reported in *The Lancet*, 14 February 1852. The Lord Chancellorship had just changed hands, Lord St Leonard's taking over from Lord Truro. His verdict on her sanity is quoted at the very end of 'The Important Lunacy Case of Catherine Cumming', *Journal of Psychological Medicine and Mental Pathology*. • **Page 175** 'The merciful hand . . . certain easy formalities': *The Lancet*, 9 July 1853. • **Page 176** 'There was a decorous expression of applause in the body of the court': *Trewman's Exeter Flying Post*, 8 April 1852. • **Pages 176–7** English Reports, a digitised database of law cases, 1220 to 1867, provided details of the Inces' and Hoopers' later legal entanglements. Their later lives were pieced together from Census and birth and death indexes.

6: 'Gaskell is Single-Patient Hunting'

Page 179 'A dangerous lunatic': The National Archives, MH 50/1, Minute Book of the Commissioners in Lunacy, entry dated 22 October 1845. • **Page 180** 'This is my protector . . . do me harm': *The Times*, 30 January 1847. • 'A person of weak and unsound mind . . . very comfortable': MH 50/1, entries dated 19 November and 4 September 1846 respectively. • **Page 181** 'Obscene and blasphemous . . . security and comfort': *The Times*, 18 November, 1846. • **Page 184** 'I engaged Dr Quail . . . in my power to do so': *Morning Post*, 24 February 1848. • Estimated 5,000 single patients in 1828: physician Sir Andrew Halliday, quoted in McCandless, 'Insanity and Society', p. 26. • **Page 185** 'The three Commissioners . . . secrets within secrets': *Report from the 1859 Select Committee on Lunatics*, Session 1, p. 30. • **Page 186** 'We have spent years and years . . . no knowledge whatever': ibid. The only documentation relating to the Private Register to survive is the Minute Book of the Commissioners in Lunacy's Private Committee, in The National Archives, MH 50/41. Frustratingly, it runs for only fourteen months, c.1845–46. The Private Committee comprised Shaftesbury and

Commissioners Turner and Mylne. • **Page 187** 'He was always weak in the head . . . into some mischief': the Charles Luxmore case is told in The National Archives, HO 45/3813. • **Page 188** 'Remarkably amiable, quiet and inoffensive . . . a more unfortunate mode of showing it, he had never heard of': *Examiner*, 2 August 1851. • 'to render the parties implicated liable to punishment . . . might exercise their discretion': The National Archives, HO 45/3813. • **Page 190** 'A general prejudice . . . screen patients': entry dated 14 January 1846 in the Minute Book of the Commissioners in Lunacy, The National Archives, MH 50/1. • **Page 192** 'His mental condition was that of chronic mania . . . a prisoner by nature': The Lancey case is told in the *Asylum Journal of Mental Science*, vol. 2, 1855, pp. 114–20. Bucknill was the founding editor of the *Journal*. • **Page 193** The local vicar: *Supplemental Report of the Metropolitan Commissioners in Lunacy to the Lord Chancellor, Relative to the General Condition of the Insane in Wales*, 1844, reveals that local vicars brought to light several family-confined people. The report was clearly commissioned to provide proof of the need to build county asylums in North Wales, to encourage the poorer population to come forward with their insane. At that time, North Wales had no asylum at all, either public or private. • **Page 194** 'Epileptic fits are treated . . . people as vermin': quoted in Charlotte MacKenzie, *Psychiatry for the Rich: A History of Ticehurst Private Asylum, 1792–1917*, 1992, pp. 98–9. • 'We have endeavoured year by year . . . very sorry for it': *Report from the Select Committee on Lunatics*, Session 1, p. 34. • **Pages 195–6** 'Private List': letter in the Forster Collection of the National Art Library at the Victoria & Albert Museum, Forster MS 48 f. 43. • **Page 196** 'Makes me quite sick . . . shook his head about other places': letter dated 25–30 September 1842, in G. N. Ray, *The Letters and Private Papers of William Makepeace Thackeray*, 1945, 4 vols, vol. 2, p. 81. • John Sutherland suggests, in *Victorian Fiction: Writers, Publishers, Readers*, 1995, that Isabella's care was low cost, and D. J. Taylor, in *Thackeray*, 1999, pp. 231–2, points out that in paying £2 a week to her carer, Mrs Bakewell, the novelist was not being parsimonious. • 'Straighten out their wayward children': Nicholas Hervey's 'A Slavish Bowing Down' cites Morison's diaries for such incidents, p. 116. • Dr James Crichton-Browne on cruelty to Chancery single patients: *Report from the 1877 Select Committee on Lunacy Law*, p. 66. • 'Gaskell is single-patient hunting': National Art Library, Forster MS 48, letter dated 13 October 1863. • **Page 197** 'Oh you devils, let me go . . . kill me': the Winn case is detailed in The National Archives, MH 51/778, from which all details are taken. • **Page 198** 'Masturbation was the cause of all this': Blandford's letter, dated 6 March 1882, ibid. • **Page 199** 'The victim to be interesting . . . be a villain': 'Mr Wilkie Collins at Home', *John Bull*, 29 December 1877. • 'Newspaper novelists': H. L. Mansel, *Quarterly Review*, April 1863; 'the novelist with a purpose': A. W. à Beckett, *The à Becketts of 'Punch': Memories of Fathers and*

Sons, 1903, p. 146. The novel's serialisation was under the title *Very Hard Cash*. For further reading on Sensation Fiction, *The Maniac in the Cellar: The Sensation Novels of the 1860s* by Winifred Hughes, 1980; Barbara Fass Leavy, 'Wilkie Collins's Cinderella: The History of Psychology and *The Woman in White*', in *Dickens Studies Annual*, vol. 10, 1982; D. A. Miller, '*Cage Aux Folles*: Sensation and Gender in Wilkie Collins's *Woman in White*,' in Jeremy Hawthorn (ed.), *The Nineteenth-Century British Novel*, 1986; Helen Small, *Love's Madness: Medicine, the Novel and Female Insanity, 1800–1865*, Oxford, 1996; Lynne Marie DeCicco, *Women and Lawyers in the Mid-Nineteenth-Century English Novel: Uneasy Alliances and Narrative Misrepresentation*, Lampeter, 1996; Matthew Sweet's introduction to the 1999 Penguin edition of *The Woman in White*; Maria K. Bachman and Don Richard Cox's introduction to the 2006 Broadview Press edition of *The Woman in White*; Elaine Showalter, 'Family Secrets and Domestic Subversion: Rebellion in the Novels of the 1860s', in Anthony S. Wohl (ed.), *The Victorian Family: Structure and Stresses*, 1978; Tamara Silvia Wagner, 'Sensationalizing Women's Writing' in Annette R. Federico (ed.), *Gilbert and Gubar's Madwoman in the Attic after Thirty Years*, University of Missouri Press, 2009. • **Pages 199–200** The lack of success and swift denouement of *Very Hard Cash*: Sutherland, *Victorian Fiction*, pp. 157–8. • **Page 200** 'Perchance half-forgotten': à Beckett, *The à Becketts of 'Punch'*, p. 146. However, George Orwell – strangely, in my view – believed that, ultimately, Reade would prove more significant than George Eliot. 'Of all the nineteenth-century novelists who have remained readable, he is perhaps the only one who is completely in tune with his own age.' 'Charles Reade', essay in the *New Statesman and Nation*, 17 August 1940, available online. • **Pages 200–1** 'Fatal Fortune': this Collins story fictionalises the case of thirty-seven-year-old James Tovey-Tennent, old Etonian and Oxford graduate, who was placed in High Beach Asylum in Essex by his father in 1853. On the beach at Deal in Kent he had met a German woman, and swiftly decided he wished to marry her. His father was very angry and had him committed. After his father's death, James was allowed (though still under certification) to live with his sister at Goring in Oxfordshire. Here, he would row on the Thames with a statue of the Virgin in his boat; but this eccentricity apart, all the locals, including a senior police constable, testified that he was entirely sane. In 1866 he inherited a huge, £60,000 fortune from his uncle, which led to an inquisition to determine his fitness to manage his estate. He was found insane. However, on single-care probation from his latest asylum, Tovey-Tennent met a Miss Hancock at the Scarborough seaside, and married her in secret. The marriage was legally void, as lunatics were not able to contract a marriage, and Tovey-Tennent was sent back to the asylum. He escaped, and with his wife fled to America. (*The Times*, 27 April, 8 and 9 May 1867.) 'Fatal Fortune' is available online. • **Page 201** 'It snatched and growled . . . strange wild animal . . . three generations': Jane comes face to face with Bertha in Chapter 26; in Chapter 27, Mr Rochester tells Jane the story of his courtship and marriage. • **Page 202** 'This I know . . . as little deserve blame': Charlotte Brontë's introduction (available online) to Emily Brontë's *Wuthering Heights*. • 'My perverse brains set to work without consulting me': *Ladies' Home Treasury*, 1 November 1888. • 'I agree with them . . . compassionate it as such': letter dated 4 January 1848 to W. S. Williams, reprinted Wise, Thomas J. and Symington, J. A. (eds), in *The Brontës: Their Lives, Friendships and Correspondence*, Oxford, 1932, 4 vols, vol. 2, pp. 173–4. • **Page 204** In 1979 . . . published their famous theory: Sandra Gilbert and Susan Gubar, *The Madwoman in the Attic*, 1979. • **Page 205** 'no law to prevent a Mr Rochester . . . in *Jane Eyre*': *British Medical Journal*, 15 February 1879. • **Page 206** 'A woman of station . . . the foundation of his tale': *The Times*, 14 January 1865, which carried coverage of the Hammond case. The Penge Mystery is told at length in the *Manchester Times*, 19 May 1877. A rather moving, fictionalised version, *Harriet*, was published in 1934 by Elizabeth Jenkins and has recently been reissued.

7: The Woman in Yellow

Page 208 The Bulwer Lytton Fiction Contest was launched in 1982 by Professor Scott Rice of the San José State University in California, to find the worst opening line of a novel. Personally, I can see little wrong (except for the parenthesis) with the start of *Paul Clifford*, the tale of a highwayman, published in 1830, which begins: 'It was a dark and stormy night; the rain fell in torrents – except at occasional intervals, when it was checked by a violent gust of wind which swept up the streets (for it is in London that our scene lies), rattling along the housetops, and fiercely agitating the scanty flame of the lamps that struggled against the darkness.' The novel goes downhill from there, though. • Bulwer-Lytton was christened Edward George Earle Lytton Bulwer, his mother being a Lytton, his father a Bulwer. Upon his mother's death and his inheritance of Knebworth in 1843, he rearranged his name as Bulwer-Lytton (the hyphen is often not used, especially by his wife). • **Pages 208–9** '"Edward!" . . . galvanised rag bag': T. H. S. Escott, *Edward Bulwer, First Baron Lytton of Knebworth, A Social, Personal and Political Monograph*, 1910, pp. 65–7. • **Page 209** 'White shoulders . . . safe and secure distance': Samuel Carter Hall, *Retrospect of a Long Life*, 2 vols, 1883, vol. 1, p. 264. • 'Hate *you*? . . . turn into hatred?' and 'It is a dim, heavy, desolate evening . . . the church just beyond': quoted in Victor Alexander Lytton, *Life of Edward Bulwer, First Lord Lytton*, 2 vols, 1913, vol. 1, pp. 168 and 181. • 'I married my wife against all my interests . . . bound to her': ibid., vol. 1,

p. 184. • **Page 210** 'If you marry this woman . . . most miserable man in England': Escott, *Edward Bulwer*, p. 135. • **Page 213** 'Why didn't you answer me? . . . like a tiger': Louisa Devey, *Life of Rosina, Lady Lytton, with Extracts from her MS Autobiography*, 1887, pp. 83–4. • 'You have been to me perfection as a wife . . . leave you all the rest': *A Blighted Life: A True Story* by Rosina Bulwer Lytton, 1880, p. 33. • **Page 214** 'Other little incidents . . . legally a right to do so': quoted in Leslie Mitchell, *Bulwer Lytton: The Rise and Fall of a Victorian Man of Letters*, 2003, p. 38. • 'Marriage is Saturnalia for men, and tyranny for women': *Very Successful!!*, 3 vols, 1856, vol. 3, p. 36. Available online, as are a number of Lady Lytton's novels. • **Page 215** 'Infernal machine of occult power': *A Blighted Life*, p. 4. • 'Consecrated palladium of puffery and party': *The Budget of the Bubble Family* by Rosina Bulwer Lytton, 1840, preface. Available online. The 'Bubbles' are the Bulwers. • **Pages 216–7** 'The next day, Dr Roberts . . . the pea lurks under': *A Blighted Life*, p. 43. • **Page 217** 'Oh! when you find in her who bears your name / . . . Being too stingy to pay, his fare o'er the Styx': both poems quoted in Marie Mulvey-Roberts's introduction to the 1995 reprint of Lady Lytton's *Shells from the Sands of Time*, 1876, p. xii. • **Page 218** 'It will be a rather tragical fate . . . pinchbeck': letter from Thomas Carlyle to his brother John, dated 1 August 1840. The Carlyles' letters are available to read online at http://carlyleletters.duke-journals.org/ • **Page 219** 'The actual cause of her death . . . her murderer': Devey, *Life of Rosina*, p. 250. In fact, Marshall Hall had been a brilliant pioneer in the discovery of the structure of the spinal cord and the working of human reflexes. But he was widely disliked in England for what was perceived as haughtiness and arrogance. • **Page 220** 'To be forwarded . . . Hotel St James's London': *The Collected Letters of Rosina Bulwer Lytton*, 3 vols, ed. Marie Mulvey-Roberts, 2008, vol. 3, p. 202. • 'Opening a drawer full of dead wasps . . . disgust': Victor Alexander Lytton, *Life*, vol. 2, p. 267. • 'To that white-livered little reptile Robert Lytton': ibid., vol. 2, p. 275. • 'Dunghill divinity': *Collected Letters*, vol. 2, p. 136. 'Pothouse Plutarch': ibid., vol. 2, p. 256. 'That patent humbug': *A Blighted Life*, p. 4. 'After twenty-five years' bitter experience . . . sure to follow': ibid., p. 4. • **Page 221** 'One has only to look . . . their fiendish lineaments': ibid., p. 9. • 'Vulgar parvenu extravagance . . . penny-a-liner': *Collected Letters*, vol. 1, p. 285. 'Sir, As it is my intention . . . sensual, selfish Pigheaded Queen': ibid., vol. 1, p. 285. • Inspector Field 'used in all sorts of delicate matters, and is quite devoted to me': the Pilgrim edition of *The Letters of Charles Dickens*, ed. Madeline House et al., Oxford, 12 vols, vol. 6 (1850–1852), p. 380. • **Page 222** 'For it would have been highly indiscreet . . . even of Landor': R. H. Super, *Walter Savage Landor: A Biography*, 1957, pp. 307–8. • **Page 223** 'It may be both wise and merciful to place her under personal restraint': Mitchell, *Bulwer Lytton* p. 46. • 'Her general behaviour . . . her face with paint': letter from

Trenchard dated 19 November 1853, Letter Catalogue, Knebworth House Archives. • **Page 223** 'The month of June 1858 . . . publicly expose the ruffian': *A Blighted Life*, p. 26. • **Page 224** 'A dirty little mean town . . . cold shivers': ibid., p. 27. • 'A few open carriages full of enthusiasm and crinoline': leader column, *Daily Telegraph*, 10 June 1858. • **Page 225** The three competing versions of the hustings furore are found in Escott, *Edward Bulwer*, p. 297; Jane Carlyle's letter to Thomas Carlyle, dated 12 July 1858; Lord Lytton's account, Knebworth House Archives, Box 42/75. • 'The moment the cowardly brute . . . when I went': *A Blighted Life*, pp. 29–30. Her precise words at the hustings and their reception cannot be verified by any other source. • **Page 227** 'Well, I don't know . . . at Hertford on Wednesday': Lady Lytton's account of the interview at the hotel in Taunton, *A Blighted Life*, pp. 30–32. • **Page 228** 'Impudent-looking, snub-nosed man . . . determined manner': ibid., p. 31. The account of her seizure and incarceration are found on pp. 32–55 of *A Blighted Life*. • **Page 230** Wyke House, off Syon Lane, had Robert Adam additions and alterations, undertaken in the late 1770s. It became Dr Jamieson's Boarding School for Young Gentlemen from 1826, and then from 1846 a lunatic asylum. Until 1970, it remained in use as a mental health rehabilitation unit. Despite Grade II listing, a vigorous local campaign to save it and a public inquiry, Wyke House was demolished in the 1970s. • 'Mr Hill, I sent for you . . . my children': Lady Lytton's account of her reception at Wyke House, *A Blighted Life*, pp. 35–6. Dr Hill's memories of her first day at Wyke House are found in his 1858 journal, Knebworth House Archives, Box 42/94, entry dated 23 June. • **Page 231** 'In this highly moral country (very!) . . . elles appellent un chat un chat': document at Knebworth House Archives in Box 42/96. • Inverness Lodge: although Lady Lytton would later refer to her place of incarceration as having had a 50-foot banqueting room with a groined roof – which Wyke House, and not Inverness Lodge, is more likely to have had – it is probable that she spent the bulk of her time at the Hill family home, Inverness Lodge, which is today a social club. A number of locals remember being told creepy tales about the building by older relatives – of a hidden attic chamber, secret tunnels leading to Kew and a cat disappearing in the cavity walls (www.bhsproject.co.uk/prop_invernesslodge.shtml). It retains a finely decorated ceiling, which, according to one local legend, was raised so that the 'Swedish Nightingale' Jenny Lind (1820–87) would have better acoustics when she came to sing there. It is possible this is the ceiling that Lady Lytton was referring to in *A Blighted Life*, p. 42. • **Page 232** 'Feelings are quite perverted . . . extremely dangerous': The Diary of Robert Gardiner Hill, 1 January to 29 April 1859, entry 11 March, Knebworth House Archives. • Drunk every day of his life': Hill's journal, entry 26 June 1858. • **Pages 232–3** 'A man had a right . . .

if she was pretty enough': ibid., entry 5 July 1858. • **Page 233** Procter 'by far the best and most gentlemanlike' of the Commissioners; and 'Those letters, I confess, startled me': *A Blighted Life*, p. 40. • Women dressed as men at Knebworth: Hill's journal, entry 2 July 1858. • 'I must really say . . . promissory notes': *A Blighted Life*, p. 31. • **Page 234** Dr John Conolly 'would sell his mother for money': ibid., p. 39. • 'Examine as carefully and pathologically . . . evidence of diseased intellect': Lytton's letter to Hood, undated but from the summer of 1858, Hertfordshire Archives and Local Studies, DE/K C28/22. • **Page 235** 'If Liberty generates such trifles . . . among the insane?': Robert Gardiner Hill, *Lunacy: Its Past and Its Present*, 1870, p. 84, quoted in 'Non-Restraint and Robert Gardiner Hill' by Justin A. Frank, *Bulletin of the History of Medicine*, vol. 41, no. 2, 1967. • 'I feel my health is giving way': letter dated 7 July 1858, *Collected Letters*, vol. 3, p. 101. 'From one of those terrible dreams . . . walls and house-tops.' ibid., p. 106. • **Page 236** Locked up in Buckingham House or the Palais des Tuileries: *A Blighted Life*, p. 49. • Account of the defence committee meeting in Taunton: *Somerset County Gazette and West of England Advertiser*, 13 July 1858. • 'Her undoubted peculiarities of temper . . . the sole invention of such a genius': ibid., 9 July 1858. • **Page 240** 'The right honourable novelist . . . crinoline': *Daily Telegraph*, 10 June 1858. • 'The case looked very bad against Bulwer': Jane Carlyle to Thomas Carlyle, 12 July 1858; 'No more mad than I am . . . that abstruse matter': Thomas to Jane, 13 July 1858. • **Page 241** 'Insolent, rude and feckless . . . quite hors de combat': Mitchell, pp. 208 and 209. • 'If we give up these places . . . primitive barbarianism': Escott, *Edward Bulwer*, p. 317. • 'Began tapping that bay window of a paunch of his': *A Blighted Life*, p. 50. 'The dulcifluous Dr Forbes Winslow': ibid., p. 54. • **Page 242** 'I think it but an act of justice . . . unjustifiable': all three letters appeared in the *Daily Telegraph*, 19 July 1858, and were syndicated to other national newspapers. • Winslow's worries were expressed in a speech reported in the *York Herald*, 17 August 1858. • **Page 244** '. . . suitable abode . . . sold by Sir Edward BL': the Burkitt row, and subsequent dispute about Lady Lytton's incarceration, is reported in Hill's diary, 11–31 March 1859. • 'I have not at present . . . determined not to be defeated': letter from Hood to Lytton, 19 March 1859, Hertfordshire Archives and Local Studies, DE/K O25/199. • **Page 245** 'Most violent and excited way . . . to know this': copied into Hill's diary, on 18 March 1859. • 'I am quite convinced . . . care and treatment': letter, Knebworth House Archives in Box 42/79. • 'Pray, pray be careful . . . to get medical men to certify': Mitchell, *Bulwer Lytton*, p. 63. • 'More bad than mad': Victor Alexander Lytton, *Life*, vol. 2, p. 326n. • '. . . in cases where there is method . . . the opportunity': undated letter ('Saturday afternoon') from John Forster to Lytton; and 'until success is absolutely obtained', dated 11 October 1857, both Hertfordshire Archives and Local Studies, DE/K C23/72. • **Page 247** 'I was not your "adviser"': Mitchell, *Bulwer Lytton*, p. 3. • 'It would be a momentous scandal . . . views I held and suppressed': Hertfordshire Archives and Local Studies, DE/K C23/72. • 'It seems impossible . . . so formally': Pilgrim edition of *The Letters of Charles Dickens*, vol. 8 (1856–1858), p. 583. • **Pages 247–8** I read the allegation that Dickens wrote to Dr Harrington Tuke about having his wife committed in 'The Tukes' Asylum in Chiswick' by Pamela Bater in *Brentford and Chiswick Local History Journal*, no. 14, 2005, pp. 7–10. Harrington's great-grandson, David Tuke, told me in a phone conversation of 2 September 2011 that his late second-cousin, Yolande, had read the relevant correspondence and told him of its contents. • *Not So Bad As We Seem* had also 'starred' Robert Bell, co-proprietor of nearby Manor House Asylum, and Rosina claimed that Bell had been trying to get her declared mad for years. • **Page 248** 'Her mind has, at times, been certainly confused': Pilgrim Dickens *Letters*, vol. 8, p. 559. • 'As if the very birds in the air . . . Downing Street': *A Blighted Life*, pp. 56–7. • 'Smuggled abroad in such electric telegraph haste': letter from Lady Lytton to Lord Shaftesbury, 25 October 1858, Hertfordshire Archives and Local Studies, DE/K C29/5. • **Page 249** 'The great failure of your book . . . my own husband': Escott, *Edward Bulwer*, pp. 331–2. • 'Great trash': Kenneth Robinson, *Wilkie Collins, A Biography*, 1951, p. 137. • 'Had whispered . . . inconvenient wife': letter quoted in 'Rosina Bulwer-Lytton and the Rage of the Unheard' by Virginia Blain, *Huntington Library Quarterly*, Summer 1990. • **Page 250** 'From a happy wife who pities a persecuted one': manuscript original held at Hertfordshire Archives and Local Studies, DE/K C29/23. • **Pages 250–1** 'In this country . . . domestic wrongs': *Hertford Mercury*, 24 July 1858. • **Page 251** Figures on pre and post-1857 initiation of divorce: *Family Ties: English Families, 1540–1920* by Mary Abbott, 1993.

8: Juries in Revolt

Page 252 'Ministers sometimes wept . . . more easily shocked': G. M. Young, *Victorian England: Portrait of an Age*, 1936, p. 14. • **Page 253** 'A woman of some accomplishments': *York Herald*, 24 July 1858. • 'A strumpet . . . he would leave her back there': ibid. • **Page 254** 'My dearest Mary . . . live apart': ibid., 31 July 1858. • **Page 257** 'A want of collectedness about her.': *York Times*, 24 July 1858. • 'I find Mrs Turner . . . ignorant and beastly': *Standard*, 26 July 1858. • 'You have stripped before many men . . . the tricks of a whore': *York Times*, 24 July 1858. • **Pages 257–8** 'Dear Sir . . . I shall break my heart': *York Herald*, 31 July 1858. • **Page 258** 'Oh she is mad . . . no more mad than I am': ibid. • **Page 259** 'A lady rather above the middle stature . . . connected and unvarying': *Standard*, 26 July 1858. • **Page 261** 'It is perhaps best . . . a woman of a decided character, in many ways': letter dated 29 August 1857, in the Forster Collection of the National Art Library, Forster MS 48 f. 65. • 'You would be sorry . . . anything at all': *York Times*, 24 July 1858. • **Page 262** 'Convey my gratitude to Mr Turner': *Liverpool Mercury*, 27 July 1858. • **Pages 262–3** 'all of our minds when we have felt unwell . . . Fathers, husbands and brothers . . . recovered her intellect . . . considerable caution': *Standard*, 26 July 1858 • **Page 264** 'Could Metcalfe break into English homes and steal away our English wives': ibid., 9 August. • **Page 265** 'Show that everything is *couleur de rose* . . . gratifying averages': *Morning Chronicle*, 27 July 1858. • 'An ambulatory sham': *Hampshire Advertiser & Salisbury Guardian*, 31 July 1858. • 'Madwomen to lie nude upon straw!': *Lloyd's Weekly Newspaper*, 1 August 1858. • 'No act could be more indifferent to . . . social importance': *York Herald*, 31 July 1858. • **Page 266** Census of 1881: Metcalfe and his wife were living in Amitie Cottage, Grouville, Jersey, with their grown-up daughter, Eleonore, and three servants. • 'The mob of newspaper writers . . . calumnious falsehood': 'The Newspaper Attack on Private Lunatic Asylums', *Journal of Mental Science*, vol. 5, October 1858, pp. 146–52. • **Page 267** 'There is poor Ruck, gone mad': 'The Commission of Lunacy on Mr Ruck', *Journal of Mental Science*, vol. 5, October 1858, p. 123. All direct quotations from the Ruck case are taken from this article, unless otherwise stated below. • **Page 268** 'A little fairy-story house . . . peaceful about it': Bernard Darwin, *The World That Fred Made, An Autobiography*, 1955, pp. 90 and 94. He recalled his grandfather, Laurence's, 'demoniac passion for beautifying and altering and improving . . .' • **Page 270** Dr George Stillwell: the Stillwell family were proving themselves to be short-lived: Arthur Stillwell had died in 1853 at the age of thirty-nine. His nephew, George, would also die young, in 1867, aged just thirty-four. • **Page 271** 'Showed only her patience and fortitude': *The Times*, 25 August 1858. • **Page 274** 'The question now becomes ventilated . . . receives an emolument': *Daily News*, 27 August 1858. • 'We do not entertain the shadow . . . speedy discharge': *Journal of Mental Science*, October 1858, pp. 150–151. • **Page 275** 'Unexampled trials . . . kindly Celts': *Daily News*, 17 September 1859. • **Page 276** Letters between the Rucks and the Darwins: www.darwinproject.ac.uk • 'The noblest creature I have ever known . . . sudden plunges': Darwin, *The World That Fred Made*, p. 84. • **Page 277** John Conolly's reputation: the only lengthy in-depth critical study of John Conolly's career and personal life is Elizabeth Mary Burrows's PhD thesis 'Enigmatic Icon: A Biographical Reappraisal of a Victorian Alienist', Oxford Brookes University, 1999. Diligent archival research by Burrows has thrown an important new light on the non-restraint movement in Victorian England, and suggests the means by which Conolly's reputation came to be so bloated. • 'A highly objectionable nature': *The Fourteenth Report of* *the Commissioners in Lunacy*, 1860, p. 51. • 'I am perfectly satisfied . . . and dangerous': Conolly's evidence to the 1859 *Select Committee on Lunatics*, Session 1, p. 180. • 'God bless and reward him!': 'Things Within Dr Conolly's Remembrance', *Household Words*, 28 November 1857. 'Juggled': I have borrowed Georgina Weldon's irresistible phrase for how she was got into Newgate Prison: see p. 359. • *Hard Cash*: it is generally believed that 'Dr Wycherly' was based on Conolly, but the character is more likely to be a composite, as Reade is known to have been fixated on the Leach case, and 'Wycherly' features some of Dr Winslow's idiosyncrasies. 'Wycherly' combines syllables from both men's surnames. Dickens published a disclaimer in *All the Year Round*, 26 December 1863, in order to distance Conolly from 'Wycherly'. • **Page 278** 'Placed him for a great many years without any society . . . but his servants': 'The Commission of Lunacy on Reverend Mr Leach', *Journal of Mental Science*, vol. 4, 1857–58, p. 620. All direct quotations from the Leach case are taken from this article, unless otherwise stated below. • **Page 280** 'We are guided by the ordinary operations . . . superseded by the Holy Spirit': 'Case of the Rev. W. J. J. Leach', *Journal of Psychological Medicine and Mental Pathology*, vol. 17, 1 October 1858, p. 675. • **Page 282** Winslow's letter to the *Morning Chronicle*, 19 August 1858. • **Page 283** The sorry tale of William Windham is found in *An Inquiry into the State of Mind of W. F. Windham Esquire of Felbrigg Hall, Norfolk*, 1862, available online. • **Page 284** 'Unhealthy restlessness . . . any one of us?': 'M.D. and M.A.D.', *All the Year Round*, 22 February 1862. • Young official from the War Office: letter from Bryan Waller Procter to Forster, dated 20 January 1862, National Art Library, Forster MS 48. • **Page 285** Dr Lockhart Robertson's bad opinion of the Winslow asylums: *Report from the 1877 Select Committee on Lunacy Law*, pp. 200–2. • 'There is something both contemptible . . . such freedom': John Stuart Mill, *On Liberty*, p. 83. • **Page 286** 'The lying gossip . . . insanity or wickedness': *The Principles of Political Economy, With Some of Their Applications to Social Philosophy*, vol. 2, Book 5, chapter 11, 'Limits of the Province of Government', p. 458 of the Great World Classics edition, published in 1900. • Statistics on pauper and private patients, and the lunacy/idiocy rate: *Evidence from the 1859 Select Committee on Lunatics*, Session 2, pp. 31, 94 and 186. (Hereafter, *Select Committee, 1859*.) These statistics obviously cannot include the unknown single patients who had not been brought to the Commissioners' attention, as mentioned in Chapter Six. • The county asylums filling up: on the county asylum system see Andrew Scull's *Museums of Madness*, and Peter Bartlett's *The Poor Law of Lunacy: The Administration of Pauper Lunatics in Mid-Nineteenth-Century England*, 1993; Janet Saunders has queried the notion that the 'feeble-minded' and other categories of the mentally 'handicapped' were incarcerated wholesale in the mid-1840s to 1880s, in 'Quarantining the

Weak-Minded: Psychiatric Definitions of Degeneracy and the Late-Victorian Asylum', in *The Anatomy of Madness*, vol. 3, 1988. • **Page 287** 'Abstract and rather metaphysical questions': *Select Committee, 1859*, Session 2, p. 16. 'I do not know . . . frequent and numerous': ibid., p. 15. 'I believe they are only a proportion': ibid., p. 46. • **Pages 287–8** 'Where a proprietor is unprincipled . . . I could not resist it': ibid., p. 56; 'This vicious principle of profit . . . vitiates the whole thing': Session 1, pp. 54 and 57; '. . . prevails in some circumstances . . . the other's house': ibid., p. 97; 'The supposition that they are so peculiarly mercenary as to not be trusted at all': ibid., p. 179; 'very seldom': ibid., p. 176; 'accidentally': ibid., p. 168. • **Page 289** Average cure rates in county asylums and for Chancery patients: ibid., Session 2, pp. 94 and 31. • 'Absurd principle of secrecy': ibid., p. 17. • 'Many persons whose families . . . mad member connected with it': ibid., Session 1, p. 62. • **Page 290** 'Meagre': John Perceval's complaints about the 1859 Select Committee are found in his letter to the Home Office of 17 February 1861, The National Archives, HO 45/7102. • 'However insignificant we were . . . from ignorance': letter to *John Bull*, 25 January 1862.

9: Dialoguing with the Unseen

Page 291 'Speeding away in the daily round . . . bucolic repose': *The Bastilles of England; Or, the Lunacy Laws at Work*, 1883, p. 105. • 'I require a bracing climate . . . anybody else.' *Report from the 1877 Select Committee on Lunacy Law*, p. 236. (Hereafter, Select Committee, 1877.) • **Page 292** 'I do believe you are mad . . . *Warren's Tales?*': ibid., p. 241. • **Page 293** Mary Marshall: the medium's critics pointed out the extreme and unusual muscularity of both Mrs Marshall and her niece, who assisted her, and the fact that both women wore vast crinolines and thus carried about their persons an expanse of storage space, by means of which, the sceptics believed, the women achieved their furniture-moving phenomena. • 'A stepping stone to God': *Quis Custodiet Ipsos Custodes?* no. 3: *How an Old Woman Obtained Passive Writing and The Outcome Thereof*, 1873, p. 5. This series of pamphlets, critical of the lack of safeguards in lunacy law, asks Who Will Guard the Guards? • 'In accordance with primitive Christianity': *Quis Custodiet Ipsos Custodes?* no. 1: *Report of a Case Heard in Queen's Bench, November 22, 1872*, 1873, p. 3. • **Pages 293–4** 'Unseen, impalpable agent . . . brain ear': *Quis Custodiet*, no. 3, p. 5. • **Page 294** The trip to Norwood, to the bank, infidelity with 'Harriet' and wish for divorce: Select Committee, 1877, p. 323. • **Page 296** Thomas Shapter and the will of wealthy Phoebe Ewings: *Trewman's Exeter Flying Post*, 18 August 1859; and Mrs Lowe's account of it, *Bastilles of England*, p. 106. • 'I thought he seemed rather queer': Select Committee, 1877, p. 241. 'Now, mind, I shall come in . . . idea of my insanity': ibid. • **Page 297** 'I thought I should get in quietly and get out quietly': ibid., p. 244. • **Page 298** 'She labours . . . distributes them': ibid., p. 343. • **Pages 298–9** Mrs Lowe's account of conditions at Brislington House: Supplement to the spiritualist magazine *The Medium and Daybreak*, 25 July 1873. • **Page 299** 'As we walked up . . . then all was still': Kilvert's *Diary*, quoted in 'Psychiatry in the 1870s: Kilvert's Mad Folk', by Edward Hare and Alexander Walk, *Psychiatric Bulletin*, no. 3, 1979, p. 153. • **Page 300** The Foxes' account of their patients' illnesses is found in the *Report Respecting the Past and Present State of Brislington House*, 1865. The appendix to this brochure (disguised as a report) shows that the average age of a patient at admission was thirty-seven years and four months, the illness having endured for an average of one year and four months before admission. Between 1845 and 1864, the following categories of illness were noted by the Foxes: cases of mania, 181; melancholia, 146; dementia, 48; idiocy, 4; delusional insanity, 14. Total 393. The causes were stated as: anxiety (the most common cause in the table, just ahead of 'cause unknown'), and then a variety of physical illnesses and emotional states – hysteria, suppressed lactation, concussion, gastric fever, puerperal fever, flu, smallpox, epilepsy, senility, sunstroke, masturbation, overwork, jealousy, hereditary mental weakness and congenital imbecility, political excitement, religious excitement, disappointed affections, fright, scrofula and battle wounds. • **Page 301** 'Oh, you believe the Bible . . . are mad': *Quis Custodiet*, no. 1, p. 11. • 'Variable in mood . . . conduct to the world': Select Committee, 1877, p. 343. • 'I am in a great difficulty': ibid., p. 237. • **Page 302** 'I am told . . . God moves her fingers': ibid., p. 242. • 'I told them things in professional confidence . . . trustworthy.': ibid., p. 245. • **Pages 302–3** Account of *Nowell* v. *Williams*, *Pall Mall Gazette*, 14 November 1879. Dr Nowell had been confined to Northumberland House Asylum in Stoke Newington, North London, in 1877 by his brother, who alleged that the doctor had become insanely jealous that Mrs Nowell was unfaithful to him, and had used violence against her and their daughter repeatedly. Nowell won his case for false imprisonment, in large part because one of the certifying doctors had received £700 in 'consultant' fees from the asylum's proprietor. • **Page 303** 'The lady should be discharged . . . think advisable': reported (much later) in *The Times*, 6 August 1885. • 'Unyielding delusion': Select Committee, 1877, p. 321. • **Page 305** 'Consistency signifies prejudice and stagnation': quoted in 'Henry Maudsley, Philosopher and Entrepreneur' by Trevor Turner in *The Anatomy of Madness*, vol. 3, 1988, p. 159. • 'To understand a man . . . what he has suffered': quoted in *Henry Maudsley: Victorian Psychiatrist, A Bibliographical Study* by Michael Collie, 1988, p. 55. To Collie's biography (the first lengthy study of Henry Maudsley) I am indebted for my information about Maudsley, supplemented by Trevor Turner's essay, which appeared in the same year as Collie's book. • 'Ashanti warrior': ibid., p. 51. • 'How can you keep me here? . . . everybody is insane': Select Committee, 1877, p. 242. 'The line between sanity and insanity . . . impossible to draw it': ibid., p. 79. • **Page 306** 'Mr Kempe thinks me a beast . . . all men shall honour thee': ibid., p. 323; • **Page 307** '. . . as friends and on intimate terms . . . peculiar': ibid., p. 324. • **Page 308** 'Oh, do you think . . . yourself?': *Quis Custodiet*, no. 1, p. 13. • 'Windowless and pestilential': ibid., p. 15. • 'Uncultivated . . . slumbering powers': Mrs Lowe's lengthier criticisms of Lawn House are in *The Bastilles of England*, p. 84. • The site of Lawn House is to the west of today's Conolly Road and Lawn Gardens. • **Page 309** Details of the lawsuit: The National Archives, C 16/729/L70, *Lowe* v. *Lowe*, Bill of Complaint in Chancery, April 1871. • '. . . undesirable . . . to keep quiet': Select Committee, 1877, p. 238. • **Page 310** Professional commitments: among his other positions, Maudsley had consultancy roles at the West London Hospital and St Mary's Hospital, Paddington, held the Chair of the Medical Faculty at University College London and was editor of, and contributor to, the *Journal of Mental Science* for many years. Collie, *Henry Maudsley*, pp. 36–7. • **Page 311** 'I would much rather . . . in my life before': Select Committee, 1877, p. 239. • Report of the inaugural LLRA meeting: *The Medium and Daybreak*, 25 July 1873. • **Page 313** 'Commanding presence . . . handsome': *Morning Post*, 26 May 1874. • Mrs Lowe's and the LLRA's detailed criticisms of the lunacy laws and recommendations for their improvement were published as the appendix to *The Bastilles of England*, while other suggestions appeared in the supplement to *The Medium and Daybreak*, 25 July 1873. Unless otherwise stated, all quotes on the LLRA recommendations for change come from these two sources. • **Pages 314–5** 'Unsoundness . . . protractedly morbid condition of the intellect': *Quis Custodiet*, no. 3, p. 4. • **Page 315** 'Doctorcraft . . . enslave us all': *The Spiritualist*, 13 November 1874. • 'The cloven foot of medical arrogance and greed peeps out': *The Bastilles of England*, p. 153. • **Page 316** 'New thoughts . . . man's temperament': *Quis Custodiet*, no. 3, p. 4. • Alex Owen's *The Darkened Room: Women, Power and Spiritualism in Late Nineteenth-Century England*, 1989, and Janet Oppenheim's *The Other World: Spiritualism and Psychical Research in England, 1850–1914*, 1985, present the full social context within which British spiritualism thrived. • **Page 317** 'Expressive of hidden mental states': Dr Laycock's experiments with passive writing are revealed in *What the Doctor Thought* by James Crichton-Browne, 1930, p. 31. • Carpenter's ideomotor activity and unconscious cerebration: Oppenheim, *The Other World*, pp. 242–3. • **Page 318** 'Passages in Freud's writing capable of causing profound nausea':

Crichton-Browne, *What the Doctor Thought*, p. 240. • 'Let me die . . . built it up again': Select Committee, 1877, p. 324. Owen, *The Darkened Room*, points out the probable sexual source of this episode. • **Page 319** 'Slanders': *Quis Custodiet*, no. 1, p. 16. • 'Dangerous to his life': Mrs Lowe's petition for restitution of conjugal rights, 6 October 1884, The National Archives, J 77/326. • Late-eighteenth-century conjugal restitution cases in the London consistory courts initiated by wives: 'At the Limits of Liberty: Married Women and Confinement in Eighteenth-Century England' by Elizabeth Foyster, *Continuity and Change*, no. 17, 2002, p. 51. • **Page 320** 'Deserter' of the marriage: Mary Lowe's affidavit, The National Archives, J 77/326. • **Page 321** The LLRA–LLAS schism was revealed by Mr James Billington at the 1877 Select Committee (p. 308). He said that the breakaway group hadn't been 'satisfied with the manner in which business was conducted; they thought they could work in a better direction', and felt that Mrs Lowe's spiritualism would cause extra prejudice against them. (Later, Mrs Weldon's spiritualism didn't seem to bother them.) • **Page 322** 'Scolding lady . . . same class of spirits': details of the Desmond Fitzgerald trial, *Morning Post*, 1 December 1880. • 'Because there were certain apprehensions . . . well to disprove': quoted in *The Bastilles of England*, p. 95. • **Page 323** State-registered hospitals and the wealthy: experiments in housing large numbers of private patients in special quarters at Stafford, Nottingham and Gloucester county asylums had failed, as subscriptions had been hard to come by, and the wealthy still disliked the stigma of being housed in an essentially pauper institution. • 'Surrender everything to science . . . they will shut up people by the score': Select Committee, 1877, p. 545. • 'Altogether, the mountain . . . his well-known *Hard Cash*': *British Medical Journal*, 13 April 1878.

10: 'Be sure you don't fall, Georgie!'

Page 325 'Being beautiful . . . looked like a washed Christy minstrel': *Storm Bird: The Strange Life of Georgina Weldon* by Edward Grierson, 1959, pp. 52 and 163. All quotations from *Storm Bird* are reproduced courtesy of Mr Grierson's daughter, Anne Monroe. • **Page 327** 'I suppose you think he had a soul!': *The Times*, 17 July 1884. Quotations from this interview and subsequent events are from reports in *The Times*, 10, 17 and 29 July. • **Page 332** 'We never dared open our lips . . . snubbing us unmercifully': Brian Thompson, *A Monkey among Crocodiles: The Life, Loves and Lawsuits of Mrs Georgina Weldon*, 2000, p. 65. • **Page 335** 'The dirty old Guv cut me off within 24 hours': Grierson, *Storm Bird*, p. 29. • Papa's death at Blandford's Asylum: Thompson, *Monkey among Crocodiles*, p. 11.

• **Page 336** 'Owing to his horrid ways . . . sensual habits': *Social Salvation*, February 1884. These comments may have been prompted by the widely publicised action for divorce by Lady Campbell in 1884, who charged her husband with 'cruelty' as a result of his communicating venereal disease to her. Allegations of venereal infection feature in around 10 to 15 per cent of divorce or separation actions taken by wives in the final thirty years of the nineteenth century. (Gail Savage, '"The Wilful Communication of a Loathsome Disease": Marital Conflict and Venereal Disease in Victorian England', *Victorian Studies*, vol. 34, 1990.) In 1872, American physician Emil Noeggerath had attributed 90 per cent of sterility in wives to venereal infection by their husbands. This notion of the male body as the site of physical danger to mothers and children (rather than prostitutes infecting men) slowly began to gain momentum in Britain in the late 1880s. (*Feminizing Venereal Disease: The Body of the Prostitute in Nineteenth-Century Medical Discourse* by Mary Spongberg, New York, 1997, p. 148.) • 'Theory of music education was years ahead of its time': Grierson, *Storm Bird*, p. 52. • **Page 337** 'Dye your hair bright red . . . sad sea waves of an evening': *The Ghastly Consequences of Living in Charles Dickens' House*, 1880, reprinted in *Women, Madness and Spiritualism*, edited by Roy Porter, Helen Nicholson and Bridget Bennett, vol. 1: *Georgina Weldon and Louisa Lowe*, 2003, pp. 11–12. This volume also reprints *The History of My Orphanage; or, The Outpourings of an Alleged Lunatic*, 1878; *How I Escaped the Mad Doctors*, 1879; and *Death Blow to Spiritualism – Is It? Dr Slade, Messrs Maskelyne & Cooke and Mr W. Morton*, 1882, all by Georgina Weldon. • 'Odious calumnies': Georgina Weldon, *Musical Reform*, 1875, preface. • 'A base soul . . . every woman he met': George Moore quoted in Thompson, *Monkey among Crocodiles*, p. 104. • **Page 341** Dalrymple 'the essence of a conceited prig': *Social Salvation*, July–October 1884 combined issue, p. 4. • The friendship not 'suspect': Grierson, *Storm Bird*, p. 149. Molly Whittington-Egan, in her biography, *Doctor Forbes Winslow: Defender of the Insane*, 2000, reports that the sixty-five packing cases of Mrs Weldon's papers have gone missing; however, Dr Joanna Martin has in fact managed to reassemble a great deal of the Weldon archive material. • **Page 342** 'Filthy allusions': *Social Salvation*, February 1884, p. 3; '*apart* from her husband.' ibid., April–May 1885 combined issue, p. 4. • **Page 344** 'Your letter coming like a clap of thunder . . . leaving your house at her behest': Thompson, *Monkey among Crocodiles*, p. 170. • 'Fat as a pig . . . greasy hair longer than ever': Grierson, *Storm Bird*, p. 159. All quotations from this episode are taken from Grierson. • **Pages 346–7** 'The little gutter children . . . he was driven from room to room': *Morning Post*, 28 November 1884. • **Page 347** 'The community of believers . . . to ripen into maturity': Lyttleton Stewart Forbes Winslow,

Spiritualistic Madness, 1877, p. 20. • **Page 348** 'It is not unreasonable to conjecture . . . aggregate delusions': ibid., p. 36. • **Pages 349–50** 'I have this day . . . putting your wife in a lunatic asylum': *The Times*, 17 March 1884. • **Page 350** 'I always prefer the patient's friends . . . not from me': Winslow interviewed in the *Pall Mall Gazette*, 24 September 1884, 'Topics of the Day, The Lunacy Laws: A Visit to Dr Forbes Winslow's Asylum'. I am grateful to Molly Whittington-Egan's biography of Winslow for alerting me to this report, which is likely to have been a public relations exercise, in response to the Weldon trials and the problems being caused by Winslow's brother-in-law. • **Page 351** Dr Lockhart Robertson's criticisms of Sussex House: Select Committee, 1877, pp. 50 and 71; Winslow Jnr's rebuttal of these charges, pp. 200–202. • **Pages 351–2** 'I really must kill you, Doctor . . . as quick as you can': *Pall Mall Gazette*, 24 September 1884. • **Page 353** 'You will repent this, both of you': Grierson, *Storm Bird*, p. 172. 'May God . . . to ruin them': ibid. • Even Lord Tennyson had to battle his way to a seat: over forty years earlier, Alfred Tennyson had stayed at Dr Matthew Allen's High Beach Asylum, during a bout of what we call depression. • Bemused approval: Roy Porter, in his introduction to *Women, Madness and Spiritualism*, p. 20, suggests that Mrs Weldon was indulged to some extent by senior legal figures because she represented more of a curio than a serious threat to male exclusivity in the legal profession; by comparison, the rising number of female doctors faced genuine hostility, as they were a perceived danger to the gender status quo in medicine. • 'Second-favourite martyr': Grierson, *Storm Bird*, p. 174. • **Page 354** The Magna Chartists and Father Meyrick: *The Englishman*, 25 March 1876 and 12 June 1880. I am grateful for these references to Rowan McWilliam, whose 2006 book *The Tichborne Claimant: A Victorian Sensation* examines in depth the various cross-currents of popular radicalism in the 1870s and 1880s. • 'We will all have our throats cut . . . so afraid?': *Social Salvation*, July–October 1884 combined issue, p. 5. • 'Overpaid set of sinecurists': *Social Salvation*, September 1883. • **Page 355** Shaftesbury did 'not wish . . . countless myrmidons': ibid., April–May combined issue, p.4. • 'Justice is the daughter of publicity': visitors' book for Tavistock House, 1871–1913, National Art Library, MSL/1952/1618. Reade here has adapted Jeremy Bentham's 'Publicity is the soul of justice'. • 'Old intriguant': *Social Salvation*, September 1883. • 'I no longer hesitate . . . to have been created differently': Preface to *The History of My Orphanage*. • 'She has a pleasing manner . . . "they will say you are 'excitable'"': *Illustrated Police News*, 16 November 1878. • **Page 356** 'I know, although I am not a Pharisee . . . I myself got the writing inside them': *Death Blow to Spiritualism – Is It?* pp. 9–10. • **Pages 356–7** Extracts from letters sent to Mrs Weldon: Grierson, *Storm Bird*, pp. 174 and 133 . • **Page 357** 'The lady smiled . . . and retired':

Weekly Dispatch, 7 July 1878. • **Page 358** 'I had not been with her one hour ... dangerous person': *Social Salvation*, July–October 1884 combined issue, p. 6. • 'No Valentine for me . . . against the *Figaro*': Philip Treherne, *A Plaintiff in Person: The Life of Mrs Weldon*, 1923, p. 78. • **Page 359** 'I maintain that "auricular delirium" . . . mental disorder': *British Medical Journal*, 25 January 1879. • 'Juggled into Newgate': *Social Salvation*, February 1884. • 'I have made up my mind . . . anxious a husband': *Ghastly Consequences*, p. 5. • 'I wonder women can endure men': Grierson, *Storm Bird*, p. 192. • **Page 362** Huddleston 'regretted to think . . . to which she had been put': *The Times*, 19 March 1884. • 'It is revolting to one's sense of right . . . shut up for life': *The Times*, 9 April 1884. • **Page 363** 'I don't understand how anybody with blood in their veins . . . those who have great ideas, &c.': *The Times*, 14 July 1884. • **Page 365** 'All persons are . . . rubbing my eyes': the testimony of Drs Edmunds and Wylde was reported in *The Times*, 11 July 1884. • 'Alone in my own room, and not from courting spiritualistic seances': *Death Blow to Spiritualism – Is It?*, p. 9. • 'No right to the position you hold!': *The Times*, 12 July 1884. • **Page 366** The Semple trial: Mrs Weldon brought up in court Dr Semple's own father's disastrous career. In 1862, Semple Snr, also an alienist, had been prosecuted and fined £150 for mis-certifying Richard Hall, a wealthy china dealer of Tottenham Court Road. Hall's wife had told Dr Semple Snr that her husband of fifty years was a violent madman, and the doctor wrote this straight on to the certificate, using 'sham scientific balderdash', according to the *Political Examiner* newspaper. Hall, sane, was swiftly freed from Munster House in Fulham, and mounted his successful suit for false imprisonment. Hall's case had been extraordinary in that it had been the Commissioners in Lunacy who, for once, had acted without reference to the order signer (Mrs Hall) and had liberated the patient. Their statutory visit to Munster House had occurred, coincidentally, two days after Hall's admission, and on interviewing him, they were convinced of his sanity. • **Page 367** 'Of the play, it is difficult to speak seriously . . . its conclusion': *Morning Post*, 15 October 1885. • 'It would be idle to say . . . real histrionic ability': *The Era*, 17 October 1885. • **Page 369** 'Dear Loonie' and the other correspondence between Winslow and Mrs Weldon: Whittington-Egan, *Doctor Forbes Winslow*, pp. 143–5. Edward Grierson read the correspondence before it was lost. • 'Reckless kite-flying': ibid., p. 117. Whittington-Egan's is a generous and fair-minded account of the man. • **Pages 369–70** Mrs Lascelles case: *The Times*, 9 March 1908. • **Page 371** The Forbes Winslow Memorial Hospital: 'Avoiding the Asylum: Pioneering Work in Mental Health Care, 1890–1939' by Louise Westwood, PhD thesis, University of Sussex, 1999, p. 42. 'These poor people . . . deprived of diversion, give way': ibid., p. 47. Donations in boxes in various pubs in London: Whittington-Egan, p. 246.

• 'Cat's paw': Winslow, *Recollections of Forty Years* . . . , 1910, p. 23. Available online. • **Page 372** 'Well I must be an ugly old frump': Grierson, *Storm Bird*, p. 278.

Epilogue: The Savage New Century

Page 375 'Motives of that kind . . . in real life': *Morning Post*, 5 May 1884. • **Page 377** 'Hopelessly effete': *The Times*, 8 May 1890. • 'She says she is going to live . . . unfit to take care of herself': *British Medical Journal*, 2 November 1895. • **Page 378** 'I should like . . . ceremony?': the *Standard*, 9 January 1896. • **Page 380** Elderly women at a Doncaster mental hospital: *The Times* 22 and 25 May 1972. • **Page 382** 'It would be very difficult . . . wholesale detention of feeble-minded persons': *Report of the Royal Commission on the Care and Control of the Feeble-Minded*, 1908, testimony of Dr Arthur Downes, senior medical officer of the Local Government Board, p. 102. • 'The unnatural and increasingly rapid . . . another year has passed': quoted on Andrew Roberts's studymore website. • **Page 383** 'About the most abominable thing . . . dictum of the specialist': Hansard, 5th Series, 41, cols 710 and 714, 19 July 1912. • 'Defective released on licence': in *Outside the Walls of the Asylum: Community Care and Mental Deficiency, 1913 to 1945*, Dorothy Atkinson, Sheena Rolph and Jan Walmsley reveal that reasons why Somerset 'defectives' out on licence were returned to the institution from community life included 'homosexual practices', 'associating with the opposite sex', 'seen talking to a schoolgirl', 'an incestuous relationship with her father', 'associating with undesirable men' and 'interfering with little girls' (pp. 195–6). • **Page 384** 'The convenience of society . . . the British citizen first': quoted in *The Borderland of Imbecility: Medicine, Society and the Fabrication of the Feeble Mind in Late-Victorian and Edwardian England* by Mark Jackson, Manchester, 2000, p. 215. Jackson's book alerted me to the Strange Death link.

Bibliography

All items were published in London, unless otherwise stated. Many are available online, and it is worth typing the title into a search engine to check for recent digital uploads.

NEWSPAPERS AND PERIODICALS

All the Year Round
Bridgwater Times
British Medical Journal
Daily News
Daily Telegraph
Dickensian
Dublin University Magazine
Edinburgh Review
Englishman
Era
Examiner
Freeman's Journal
Gentleman's Magazine
Globe
Hampshire Advertiser & Salisbury Guardian
Hertford Mercury
Household Words
Illustrated Police News
John Bull
Journal of Mental Science (formerly the *Asylum Journal of Mental Science*)
Journal of Psychological Medicine and Mental Pathology
Ladies' Home Treasury
Lancet
Liverpool Mercury

Lloyd's Weekly Newspaper
London Gazette
London Medical Gazette
Manchester Times
Medical Times
Medium and Daybreak
Morning Chronicle
Morning Post
New Statesman and Nation
Pall Mall Gazette
Political Examiner
Punch
Quarterly Review
Social Salvation
Somerset County Gazette and West of England Advertiser
Spiritualist
Standard
Sun
The Times
Trewman's Exeter Flying Post
Weekly Dispatch
York Herald
York Times

UNPUBLISHED PAPERS

THE NATIONAL ARCHIVES

MH 50/1 Minute Book of the Commissioners in Lunacy, August 1845–December 1846

MH 50/2 Minute Book of the Commissioners in Lunacy, December 1846–March 1848

MH 50/3 Minute Book of the Commissioners in Lunacy, March 1848–June 1849

MH 50/9 Minute Book of the Commissioners in Lunacy, February 1858–December 1858

MH 50/41 Minute Book of the Commissioners in Lunacy's Private Committee, 1845–46

MH 51/778 Lunacy Commission and Board of Control, correspondence and papers on the illegal detention of an alleged lunatic

C 16/729/L70, *Lowe* v. *Lowe*, bill of complaint in Chancery, April 1871

J 77/326, Mrs Lowe's petition for restitution of conjugal rights, 6 October 1884
HO 40/40 Home Office disturbances correspondence, 1838
HO 44/12 Home Office domestic correspondence, 1773–1861
HO 44/13 Home Office domestic correspondence, 1773–1861
HO 44/36 Home Office domestic correspondence, 1773–1861
HO 44/52 Home Office domestic correspondence, 1773–1861
HO 45/74 Reports of provincial asylums to Metropolitan Lunacy Commission
HO 45/3813 Home Office registered papers on lunacy and lunatics
HO 45/5542 Home Office registered papers on lunacy matters, 25 January–17 September 1854
HO 45/7102 Home Office registered papers on c.1841–71 lunacy bills

NATIONAL ART LIBRARY (VICTORIA & ALBERT MUSEUM)

MSL/1952/1618 Visitors' book for Tavistock House, 1871–1913
Forster Collection MSS 48, correspondence between Bryan Waller Procter and John Forster

KNEBWORTH HOUSE ARCHIVES

Diary of Dr Robert Gardiner Hill, 1 January–29 April 1859
Box 42/94 Dr Gardiner Hill's journal
Box 42/96 MS by Rosina Bulwer-Lytton
Box 42/75 MS report of Lord Lytton on the hustings
Letter from Henry Trenchard to Lord Lytton, 19 November 1853, Letter Catalogue
Box 42/79 Letter from Lord Shaftesbury to Lord Lytton, 29 July 1858

HERTFORDSHIRE ARCHIVES AND LOCAL STUDIES

The Bulwer-Lytton archive, shelfmarks DE/K C23/72, DE/K C28/22, DE/K C29/5, DE/K C29/23, DE/K O25/199

HILLINGDON LOCAL STUDIES LIBRARY & ARCHIVES

Davis, Ian C., *Moorcroft: The History of a House and its Inhabitants*, c.1993

BETHLEM ART AND HISTORY COLLECTIONS

Casebook for Dr Peithman, 1840–54

PARLIAMENTARY PAPERS

Hansard Parliamentary Debates: 3rd series, 82, cols 410–13, 11 July 1845; 3rd series, 142, col 410, 20 May 1856; 5th series, 41, cols 710 and 714, 19 July 1912

PP 1814–15, IV.80, *Report from the Select Committee on the Provisions for Better Regulation of Madhouses in England*

PP 1844, XXVI.299, *Supplemental Report of the Metropolitan Commissioners in Lunacy to the Lord Chancellor, Relative to General Conditions of the Insane in Wales*

PP 1859, Session 1, III.75, *Report from the Select Committee on Lunatics*

PP 1859, Session 2, VII.501, *Report from the Select Committee on Lunatics*

PP 1860, XXII.349, *Report from the Select Committee on Lunatics*

PP 1860, LVIII.959, *Accounts and Papers: Return of Charges of Ill-usage and Cruelty towards Patients in Northampton Hospital, 1857, Evidence by Commissioners in Lunacy on Inquiry*

PP 1860, XXXIV.231 (338), *The Fourteenth Report of the Commissioners in Lunacy to the Lord Chancellor*

PP 1877, XXX.I, *Report from the Select Committee on Lunacy Law*

PP 1908, XXXV.83 [Cd. 4215], *Report of the Royal Commission on the Care and Control of the Feeble-Minded*

BOOKS, ARTICLES, THESES, PAMPHLETS AND DATABASES

Abbott, Mary, *Family Ties: English Families 1540–1920*, 1993

À Beckett, A. W., *The à Becketts of 'Punch': Memories of Fathers and Sons*, 1903

Alleged Lunatics' Friend Society, reports, 1846 and 1851

Andrews, Jonathan, *'They're in the Trade of Lunacy': The Scottish Lunacy Commissioners and Lunacy Reform in Nineteenth-Century Scotland*, 1998

Armour, Richard Willard, *Barry Cornwall: A Biography of Bryan Waller Procter*, 1935

Atkinson, Dorothy, Rolph, Sheena and Walmsley, Jan, 'Community Care and Mental Deficiency, 1913 to 1945', in *Outside the Walls of the Asylum: Community Care and Mental Deficiency, 1913 to 1945*, ed. Peter Bartlett and David Wright, 1999

Barlow, Kate, *The Abode of Love: A Memoir*, Edinburgh, 2006

Bartlett, Peter, *The Poor Law of Lunacy: The Administration of Pauper Lunatics in Mid-Nineteenth-Century England*, 1993

Bater, Pamela, 'The Tukes' Asylum in Chiswick', *Brentford and Chiswick Local History Journal*, no. 14, 2005

Bennett, Bridget, Nicholson, Helen and Porter, Roy (eds), *Women, Madness and Spiritualism*, 2 vols, 2003

Blain, Virginia, 'Rosina Bulwer-Lytton and the Rage of the Unheard', *Huntington Library Quarterly*, Summer 1990

Brontë, Charlotte, *Jane Eyre*, 1847; and introduction to Emily Brontë's *Wuthering Heights*, 1847

Bucknill, John Charles, *The Care of the Insane and their Legal Control*, 1880; and 'The Newspaper Attack on Private Lunatic Asylums', *Journal of Mental Science*, vol. 5, 1859

Bulwer-Lytton, Edward, *Pelham*, 1828; *Richelieu*, 1839; and *Paul Clifford*, 1830

Bulwer-Lytton, Rosina, *A Blighted Life: A True Story*, 1880, reprinted Bristol, 1994, ed. and introduction by Marie Mulvey-Roberts; *The Budget of the Bubble Family*, 1840; *Very Successful!*, 1856; and *Shells From the Sands of Time*, 1876, reprinted Bristol, 1995, ed. and introduction by Marie Mulvey-Roberts; *The Collected Letters of Rosina Bulwer Lytton*, 3 vols, ed. Marie Mulvey-Roberts with Steve Carpenter, 2008

Burrows, Elizabeth Mary, 'Enigmatic Icon: A Biographical Reappraisal of a Victorian Alienist, John Conolly MD, 1794–1866', PhD thesis, Oxford Brookes University, 1999

Burrows, George Man, *A Letter to Sir Henry Halford, Bt, KCH, President of the Royal College of Physicians &c, Touching Some Points of the Evidence, and Observations of Counsel, on a Commission of Lunacy on Mr Edward Davies*, 1830; and *Commentaries on the Causes, Forms, Symptoms and Treatment, Moral and Medical, of Insanity*, 1828

Busfield, Joan, '"The Female Malady?" Men, Women and Madness in Nineteenth-Century Britain', *Sociology*, February 1994

Carlson, Eric T. and Dain, Norman, 'The Meaning of Moral Insanity', *Bulletin of the History of Medicine*, vol. 36, 1962

Collie, Michael, *Henry Maudsley: Victorian Psychiatrist, A Bibliographical Study*, 1988

Collins, Wilkie, *The Woman in White*, 1860; and *Fatal Fortune*, 1874

Conolly, John, *A Remonstrance with The Lord Chief Baron Touching the Case Nottidge versus Ripley*, 1849

Crichton-Browne, James, *What the Doctor Thought*, 1930

Darwin, Bernard, *The World That Fred Made, An Autobiography*, 1955

Devey, Louisa, *Life of Rosina, Lady Lytton, with Extracts from her MS Autobiography*, 1887

Dickens, Charles, *The Letters of Charles Dickens*, 12 vols, vol. 6, 1850–52, and vol. 8, 1856–58, the Pilgrim edition, ed. Madeline House, Graham Storey and Nina Burgis, Oxford, 1988 and 1995 respectively

Dixon, William Hepworth, *Spiritual Wives*, 2 vols, 1868

Doggett, Maeve E., *Marriage, Wife-Beating and the Law in Victorian England*, 1992

English Reports, 1220–1867, an electronic database of legal cases

Escott, T. H. S., *Edward Bulwer, First Baron Lytton of Knebworth, A Social, Personal and Political Monograph*, 1910

Finnane, Mark, *Insanity and the Insane in Post-Famine Ireland*, 1981

Fox, Annie, *Brislington House Quarterly News, Centenary Number*, Bristol, 1904

Fox, Francis Ker, and Fox, Charles, *The History and Present State of Brislington House near Bristol*, Bristol, 1836; and *Report Respecting the Past and Present State of Brislington House*, Bristol, 1865

Foyster, Elizabeth, 'At the Limits of Liberty: Married Women and Confinement in Eighteenth-Century England', *Continuity and Change*, no. 17, 2002

Frank, Justin A., 'Non-Restraint and Robert Gardiner Hill', *Bulletin of the History of Medicine*, vol. 41, no. 2, 1967

Gaskell, E., 'More About Spontaneous Combustion', *The Dickensian*, January 1973

Gilbert, Sandra and Gubar, Susan, *The Madwoman in the Attic*, Yale, 1979

Grierson, Edward, *Storm Bird: The Strange Life of Georgina Weldon*, 1959

Hall, Samuel Carter, *Retrospect of a Long Life*, 2 vols, vol. 1, 1883

Hamilcar, Marcia, *Legally Dead: Experiences during 17 Weeks' Detention in a Private Asylum*, 1910

Hanrahan, David C., *The Assassination of the Prime Minister: John Bellingham and the Murder of Spencer Perceval*, Stroud, 2008

Hansard, Luke James, *What Are To Be the Tendencies of the Community of the British Nation? To Sanity? or To Insanity? A Question*, 1845

Hare, Edward and Walk, Alexander, 'Psychiatry in the 1870s: Kilvert's Mad Folk', *Psychiatric Bulletin*, no. 3, 1979

Haslam, John, *Observations on Madness and Melancholy*, 1809

Hervey, Nicholas, 'A Slavish Bowing Down: The Lunacy Commission and the Psychiatric Profession, 1845–1860', in W. F. Bynum, Roy Porter and Michael Shepherd (eds), *The Anatomy of Madness*, vol. 2, 1985; and 'Advocacy or Folly: The Alleged Lunatics' Friend Society, 1845–1863', *Medical History*, no. 30, 1986

Hodder, Edwin, *The Life and Work of the Seventh Earl of Shaftesbury*, 3 vols, 1887

Holcombe, Lee, *Wives and Property: Reform of the Married Women's Property Law in Nineteenth-Century England*, Oxford, 1983

Homberger, Margaret, 'Wrongful Confinement and Victorian Psychiatry, 1840–1880', PhD thesis, University of London, 2001

'The Important Lunacy Case of Catherine Cumming', *Journal of Psychological Medicine and Mental Pathology*, vol. 5, April 1852

An Inquiry into the State of Mind of W. F. Windham Esquire of Felbrigg Hall, Norfolk, 1862

Jackson, Mark, *The Borderland of Imbecility: Medicine, Society and the Fabrication of the Feeble Mind in Late-Victorian and Edwardian England*, Manchester, 2000

Jenkins, Elizabeth, *Harriet*, 1934

Lewis, Paul, 'Walter's Walk: Walter Hartright meets the Woman in White', 2010

Linklater, Andro, *Why Spencer Perceval Had to Die*, 2012

Lowe, Louisa, *The Bastilles of England; Or, the Lunacy Laws at Work*, 1883; and *Quis Custodiet Ipsos Custodes?*, no. 1, 'Report of a Case Heard in Queen's Bench, November 22 1872', 1873; and no. 3, *How an Old Woman Obtained Passive Writing and The Outcome Thereof*, 1873

Lytton, Victor Alexander, *Life of Edward Bulwer, First Lord Lytton*, 2 vols, 1913

MacKenzie, Charlotte, 'A Family Asylum: A History of the Private Madhouse at Ticehurst in Sussex, 1792–1917', PhD thesis, University of London, 1986; and *Psychiatry for the Rich: A History of Ticehurst Private Asylum, 1792–1917*, 1992

McCandless, Peter, 'Insanity and Society: A Study of the English Lunacy Reform Movement, 1815–1870', PhD thesis, University of Wisconsin, 1974

McWilliam, Rowan, *The Tichborne Claimant: A Victorian Sensation*, 2006

Mellett, D. J., 'Bureaucracy and Mental Illness: The Commissioners in Lunacy 1845–90', in *Medical History*, no. 25, 1981

Mill, John Stuart, *On Liberty*, 1859; and *The Principles of Political Economy, With Some of Their Applications to Social Philosophy*, Book 5, 1862 (reissued in 1900 by Great World Classics)

Miller, Judy and Torrey, E. Fuller, 'The Capture of the Snark', *Richmond Review*, 2001

Mitchell, Leslie, *Bulwer Lytton: The Rise and Fall of a Victorian Man of Letters*, 2003

Mitchell, Sally, *Frances Power Cobbe: Victorian Feminist, Journalist, Reformer*, 2004

Mitford, John, *Description of the Crimes and Horrors of Warburton's Madhouse*, 1823

Mulock, Thomas, *British Lunatic Asylums, Public and Private*, 1858

Oppenheim, Janet, *The Other World: Spiritualism and Psychical Research in England, 1850–1914*, 1985

Owen, Alex, *The Darkened Room: Women, Power and Spiritualism in Late Nineteenth-Century England*, 1989

Paternoster, Richard, *The Madhouse System*, 1841

Perceval, John, *A Narrative of the Treatment Experienced by a Gentleman during a State of Mental Derangement; Designed to Explain the Causes and the Nature of Insanity and to Expose the Injudicious Conduct Pursued towards many Unfortunate Sufferers under that Calamity*, vol. 1, 1838, and vol. 2, 1840. The second volume is available online, as is an abridged version of both volumes, *Perceval's Narrative: A Patient's Account of His Psychosis, 1830–1832*, edited by Gregory Bateson, 1962; *A Letter to the Secretary of State for the Home Department Upon the Unjust and Pettifogging Conduct of the Metropolitan Commissioners in Lunacy, in the Case of a Gentleman Lately under their Surveillance*, 1844; *Letters to the Rt Hon Sir James Graham, Bt, and to Other Gentlemen upon the Reform of the Law affecting the Treatment of Persons Alleged to be of Unsound Mind*, 1846; and *The Case of Dr Peithman LLD*, 1855

Plumbridge, J. L., *Slavery in England: An Account of the Manner in Which Persons Without Trial are Condemned to Imprisonment for Life*, circa 1876

Prichard, James Cowles, *Treatise on Insanity and Other Disorders Affecting the Mind*, 1835

Purnell, Purnell B., *Report of the County Chairman to the Gloucestershire Epiphany Court of Quarter Sessions*, 1849

Ramsey, Sherwood, *Historic Battersea*, 1913

Ray, G. N., *The Letters and Private Papers of William Makepeace Thackeray*, 4 vols, 1945

Reade, Charles, *Hard Cash*, 1863

Robins, Joseph, *Fools and Mad: A History of the Insane in Ireland*, Dublin, 1986

Robinson, Kenneth, *Wilkie Collins, A Biography*, 1951

Saumarez, Richard, *The Laws of Lunacy, Especially as they Affect the Lunatic Wards of Chancery*, 1858; and *The Laws of Lunacy and Their Crimes, as They Affect all Classes of Society*, 1859

Saunders, Janet, 'Quarantining the Weak-Minded: Psychiatric Definitions of Degeneracy and the Late Victorian Asylum', in *The Anatomy of Madness*, vol. 3, 1988

Savage, Gail, '"The Wilful Communication of a Loathsome Disease": Marital Conflict and Venereal Disease in Victorian England', *Victorian Studies*, vol. 34, 1990

Schweiso, Joshua John, 'Deluded Inmates, Frantic Ravers and Communists: A Sociological Study of the Agapemone, a Sect of Victorian Apocalyptic Millennarians', PhD thesis, University of Reading, 1994; and 'Religious Fanaticism and Wrongful Confinement in Victorian England', *Social History of Medicine*, vol. 9, no. 2, August 1996

Scull, Andrew, *Museums of Madness: The Social Organization of Insanity in Nineteenth-Century England*, 1979; 'A Convenient Place to Get Rid of Inconvenient People: the Victorian Lunatic Asylum' in King, A. D. (ed.), *Buildings and Society*, 1980; and 'A Brilliant Career? John Conolly and Victorian Psychiatry', *Victorian Studies*, vol. 27, Winter 1984

Shelford, Leonard, *A Practical Treatise on the Law Concerning Lunatics, Idiots and Persons of Unsound Mind*, 1833; 2nd edn 1847

Showalter, Elaine, *The Female Malady: Women, Madness and English Culture, 1830–1980*, 1985

Smith, Leonard, 'A Gentleman's Mad-Doctor in Georgian England: Edward Long Fox and Brislington House', *History of Psychiatry*, 19, no. 2, June 2008

Spongberg, Mary, *Feminizing Venereal Disease: The Body of the Prostitute in Nineteenth-Century Medical Discourse*, New York, 1997

Super, R. H., *Walter Savage Landor: A Biography*, 1957

Sutherland, John, *Victorian Fiction: Writers, Publishers, Readers*, 1995

Suzuki, Akihito, *Madness at Home: The Psychiatrist, the Patient and the Family in England, 1820–1860*, 2006

Taylor, D. J., *Thackeray*, 1999

Thompson, Brian, *A Monkey among Crocodiles: The Life, Loves and Lawsuits of Mrs Georgina Weldon*, 2000

Treherne, Philip, *A Plaintiff in Person: The Life of Mrs Weldon*, 1923

Turner, Trevor, 'Henry Maudsley, Philosopher and Entrepreneur', in Andrew Scull (ed.), *The Anatomy of Madness*, vol. 3, 1988

Weldon, Georgina, *The Ghastly Consequences of Living in Charles Dickens' House*, 1880; *The History of My Orphanage*, 1878; *Death Blow to Spiritualism – Is It? Dr Slade, Messrs Maskelyne & Cooke and Mr W. Morton*, 1882; *How I Escaped The Mad Doctors*, 1879, all reprinted in a single volume, *Women, Madness and Spiritualism*, edited by Roy Porter, Helen Nicholson and Bridget Bennett, vol. 1, *Georgina Weldon and Louisa Lowe*, 2003; and *Musical Reform*, 1875

Westwood, Louise, 'Avoiding the Asylum: Pioneering Work in Mental Health Care, 1890–1939', PhD thesis, University of Sussex, 1999

Whittington-Egan, Molly, *Doctor Forbes Winslow: Defender of the Insane*, 2000

Winslow, Forbes Benignus, 'The Lord Chief Baron and the Nottidge Case', *Journal of Psychological Medicine and Mental Pathology*, vol. 2, October 1849; *On the Incubation of Insanity*, 1846; and *The Plea of Insanity in Criminal Cases*, 1843

Winslow, Lyttleton Stewart Forbes, *Recollections of Forty Years, Being an Account at First Hand of some Famous Criminal Lunacy Cases, English and American*, 1910; and *Spiritualistic Madness*, 1877

Wise, Thomas J. and Symington, J. A. (eds), *The Brontës: Their Lives, Friendships and Correspondence*, Oxford, 4 vols, 1932

Wynter, Andrew, 'Non-Restraint in the Treatment of the Insane', in *Edinburgh Review*, vol. 131, 1870

Young, G. M., *Victorian England: Portrait of an Age*, 1936

WEBSITES

Roberts, A., 1997, Social Science History, Middlesex University, London, www.studymore.org.uk

The Economic History Services website provides a translation between nineteenth-century pounds, shillings and pence and today's sums, www.eh.net

The Letters of Thomas Carlyle and family, carlyleletters.dukejournals.org

Charles Darwin's correspondence, www.darwinproject.ac.uk

Inverness Lodge local memories, www.bhsproject.co.uk/prop_invernesslodge.shtml

Picture Credits

Oakfield House (p. 6) Bruce Castle Museum (Haringey Culture, Libraries and Learning); Furnival's Inn Coffee House (p. 12) Look and Learn Ltd; Clapham Retreat (p. 20) reproduced from the 1870 Ordnance Survey map; Trophimus Fulljames at Brislington (p. 38–9) The National Archives; the assassination of Spencer Perceval (p. 40) Mary Evans Picture Library; Brislington House Asylum from the back (p. 46), Edward Long Fox (p. 48) and the Brislington gatepost (p. 53) all reproduced by kind permission of the Syndics of Cambridge University Library; Kensington House Asylum (p. 67) Royal Borough of Kensington & Chelsea, Family & Children's Service; Commissioner Bryan Waller Procter (p. 81) Cambridge University Library; Effra Hall Asylum (p. 85) London Borough of Lambeth Archives; Purnell B. Purnell (p. 85) Gloucestershire Archives; Moorcroft House (p. 102) English Heritage; Prince rides out from the Agapemone (p. 110) *Illustrated London News*; the Agapemone chapel (p. 124) and lawns (p. 126) both Rod and Celia Fitzhugh/from the Rod Fitzhugh Collection; York House Asylum (p. 136) Getty Pictures; Dr Millingen (p. 139) courtesy of *The Dickensian* magazine; Walter Hartright and Anne Catherick in *The Woman in White* (Harper's Weekly edition) (p. 149) courtesy of Paul Lewis/www.wilkiecollins.com; Edward Lancey (p. 191) Cambridge University Library; Rosina Bulwer-Lytton (p. 210), Lord Lytton (p. 212), Emily (p. 214), 'Extraordinary Narrative' pamphlet (p. 239) and Robert Lytton (p. 243), all Knebworth Estates/www.knebworthhouse.com; Wyke House (p. 229) © The Georgian Group Pardoe Collection; Inverness Lodge (p. 231) Local Studies Collection, Chiswick Public Library; John Forster portrait (p. 246) © Victoria & Albert Museum, London; Acomb House (p. 256) Imagine York/City of York Libraries, Archives & Local History Department; Sussex House Asylum (p. 279) © London Borough of Hammersmith and Fulham Local Studies Library/London Metropolitan

Archives; Brislington House Asylum (p. 297) Cambridge University Library; Lawn House Asylum (p. 304) London Borough of Ealing Local Studies Centre; *Punch* planchette cartoon (p. 307); Marian waiting by the asylum wall from *The Woman in White* (Harper's Weekly edition) (p. 312) courtesy of Paul Lewis/www.wilkiecollins.com; Tavistock House (p. 329) London Borough of Camden Local Studies and Archives Centre; Georgina Weldon painted by Watts (p. 333), Harry Weldon (p. 335), sketch of the orphans (p. 340), Georgina with Angèle (p. 343), 'Be Sure You Don't Fall, Georgie!' cartoon (p. 361), Georgina as Sergeant Buzfuz (p. 367) and on her deathbed (p. 373), all courtesy of Anne Monroe/estate of Edward Grierson.

Index

www.vintage-books.co.uk